UNITED NATIONS CONFERENCE ON TRADE AND DEVELOPMENT

UNCTAD

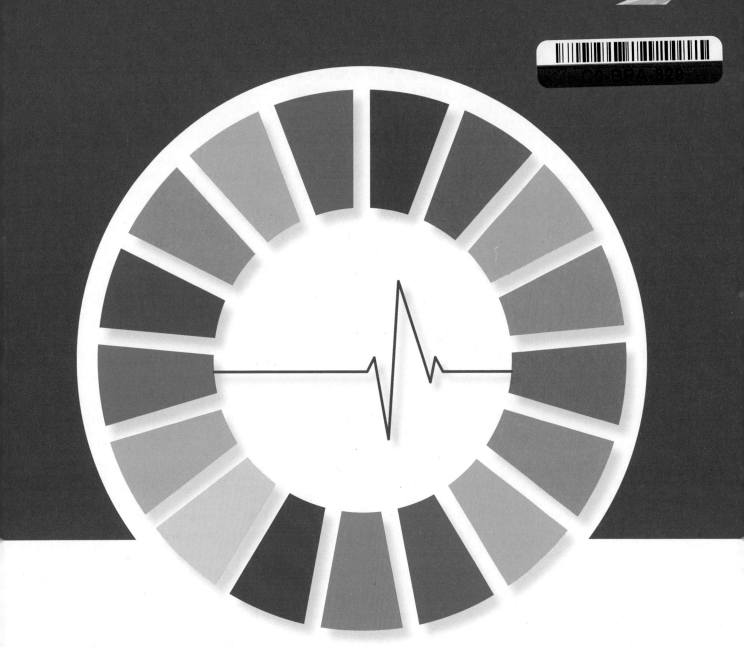

SDG Pulse 2021

UNCTAD TAKES THE PULSE OF THE SDGS

UNITED NATIONS
Geneva, 2022

Foreword

In 2015, the United Nations launched the 2030 Agenda for sustainable development and corresponding SDGs. To support this programme a Global Indicator Framework was adopted by the United Nations Statistical Commission (2017) and subsequently by the United Nations (2017). That framework comprises 232 statistical indicators designed to measure the 17 goals and their respective 169 targets.

This third edition of the SDG Pulse illustrates in a very concrete way how UNCTAD is contributing to the 2030 Agenda. The report not only presents statistical updates and data-driven analysis for the indicators for which UNCTAD is a custodian or co-custodian, but it also presents a range of other complementary indicators that provide a wider context and more nuance to these complex topics.

This report also presents some case studies from UNCTAD's capacity development programme from a statistical perspective – presenting our activities and successes in hard numbers. These case studies are important as they illustrate the Results Based Management approach adopted by UNCTAD – helping us to improve our responsiveness and accountability to member states.

Finally, this report will every year, highlight a thematic issue of immediate relevance. This year's theme addresses remoteness as a challenge for sustainable development and how to mitigate geographic distance, especially from the perspective of SIDS. Dedicated analysis on SIDS' economic, social and environmental vulnerabilities and strengths is provided in Development and globalization: Facts and figures 2021. We propose a composite index of remoteness (see Cantu-Bazaldua, 2021) to consider more comprehensively the implications of remoteness. The index will help guide policy measures to enhance connectivity through digital, socio-cultural and political means.

Steve MacFeely
Head of Statistics and Information
UNCTAD

References

- Cantu-Bazaldua F (2021). Remote but well connected? Neighboring but isolated? The measurement of remoteness in the context of SIDS. Available at https://unctad.org/publications.
- United Nations (2017). Resolution adopted by the General Assembly on 6 July 2017 on the Work of the Statistical Commission pertaining to the 2030 Agenda for Sustainable Development. A/RES/71/313. New York. (accessed 17 May 2021).
- United Nations Statistical Commission (2017). Report on the forty-eighth session of the Statistical Commission (7-10 March 2017). E/2017/24-E/CN.3/2017/35. New York. (accessed 1 June 2021).

Introduction

Welcome to the third edition of UNCTAD's SDG Pulse – UNCTAD's annual statistical publication reporting on developments relating to the 2030 Agenda for Sustainable Development (United Nations, 2015) and the Sustainable Development Goals (SDGs). The purpose of this report is to: provide an update on the evolution of a selection of official SDG indicators and complementary data and statistics; provide progress reports on the development of new concepts and methodologies for UNCTAD custodian indicators; and to also showcase, beyond the perspective of the formal SDG indicators, how UNCTAD is contributing to the implementation of 2030 Agenda. The report will also investigate thematic issues of relevance to 2030 Agenda – this year, the report discusses remoteness as a challenge for achieving the 2030 Agenda.

The report is organized by four broad categories:

 Theme

The report can be read by theme. Here the indicators are sub-divided across the three themes to which UNCTADs work contributes: multilateralism for trade & development; productive growth; and structural transformation. Through this thematic lens, a wide range of indicators are presented and issues discussed, including: recent trends in trade, including barriers to trade, and policies to promote trade; investment, transport infrastructure, ICT for sustainable development, and debt sustainability; and industry, high value-added and sustainability.

 Goals and indicators

The SDG indicators presented in this report are also categorised by goal. The goals and indicators selected reflect UNCTAD's broad mandate of economic and sustainable development. These indicators are supplemented with other complementary indicators. The SDG indicators presented in this report are:

GOAL 2

Goal 2: Zero hunger

- Indicator 2.a.2: Total official international support to agricultural sector
- Indicator 2.b.1: Agricultural export subsidies
- Indicator 2.c.1: Indicator of food price anomalies

GOAL 8

Goal 8: Decent work and economic growth

- Indicator 8.9.1: Tourism direct GDP
- Indicator 8.a.1: Aid for Trade commitments and disbursements

GOAL 9

Goal 9: Industry, innovation and infrastructure

- Indicator 9.1.2: Passenger and freight volumes, by mode of transport
- Indicator 9.2.1: Manufacturing value added
- Indicator 9.2.2: Manufacturing employment
- Indicator 9.4.1: CO_2 emission per unit of value added
- Indicator 9.5.1: Research and development expenditure
- Indicator 9.5.2: Researchers relative to population
- Indicator 9.a.1: Total official international support to infrastructure
- Indicator 9.b.1: Proportion of medium and high-tech industry value added
- Indicator 9.c.1: Proportion of population covered by a mobile network

GOAL 10

Goal 10: Reduce inequality

- Indicator 10.a.1: Proportion of tariff lines with zero-tariff*
- Indicator 10.b.1: Total resource flows for development

GOAL 12

Goal 12: Responsible consumption & production

- Indicator 12.6.1: Number of companies publishing sustainability reports*

GOAL 16

Goal 16: Peace, justice and strong institutions

- Indicator 16.4.1: Total value of inward and outward illicit financial flows*

GOAL 17

Goal 17: Partnership for the goals

- Indicator 17.2.1: Net official development assistance, total and to LDCs
- Indicator 17.3.1: FDI, ODA and South-South Cooperation*
- Indicator 17.4.1: Debt service as a share of exports of goods and services
- Indicator 17.5.1: Implement investment promotion regimes for LDCs*
- Indicator 17.6.2: Fixed Internet broadband subscriptions
- Indicator 17.8.1: Proportion of individuals using the Internet
- Indicator 17.10.1: Worldwide weighted tariff-average*
- Indicator 17.11.1 Developing countries and LDCs' share of global exports*
- Indicator 17.12.1: Tariffs faced by developing countries, LDCs and SIDS*

Custodian agencies are responsible for developing international standards and recommending methodologies for monitoring SDG indicators. They are also tasked with compiling and verifying country data and metadata, and for submitting the data, along with regional and global aggregates, to the global SDG report and database by the United Nations Statistics Division. SDG Pulse covers the following UNCTAD custodian indicators, but also many other SDG indicators to describe sustainable development comprehensively.

UNCTAD is the custodian or co-custodian agency for several SDG indicator falling under goals 10, 12, 16 and 17. To see UNCTAD custodian indicators and find related SDG Pulse sections.

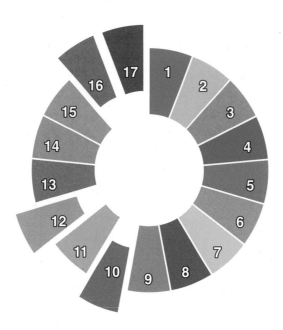

 UNCTAD in Action

UNCTAD runs a wide-ranging capacity development programme to support progress towards the 2030 Agenda. This report presents some case studies from UNCTAD's development programme from a statistical perspective – presenting UNCTAD's activities and successes in hard numbers. These case studies are important as they also illustrate the Results Based Management approach adopted by UNCTAD – helping us to improve our responsiveness and accountability to member states.

 In Focus

Every year, the SDG Pulse will highlight a specific aspect of the 2030 Agenda and discuss this issue from the slant or perspective of statistics. This edition discusses remoteness as a challenge for sustainable development and how to mitigate geographic distance, especially from the perspective of SIDS. Dedicated analysis on SIDS' economic, social and environmental vulnerabilities and strengths is provided in Development and globalization: Facts and figures 2021. We propose a composite index of remoteness (see Cantu-Bazaldua, 2021) to consider more comprehensively the implications of remoteness. The index will help guide policy measures to enhance connectivity through digital, socio-cultural and political means.

Disclaimer

The designations employed and the presentation of material on this web site do not imply the expression of any opinion whatsoever on the part of the Secretariat of the United Nations concerning the legal status of any country, territory, city or area or of its authorities, or concerning the delimitation of its frontiers or boundaries. A dispute exists between the Governments of Argentina and the United Kingdom of Great Britain and Northern Ireland concerning sovereignty over the Falkland Islands (Malvinas). The final boundary between the Republic of Sudan and the Republic of South Sudan has not yet been determined. The final status of the following territories has not yet been agreed or determined: Abyei area, Aksai Chin, Arunachal Pradesh, Bi'r Tawil, Hala'ib Triangle, Ilemi Triangle, Jammu and Kashmir, Kuril Islands, Paracel Islands, Scarborough Shoal, Senkaku Islands, Spratly Islands.

The designations "developing" and "developed" are intended for statistical convenience and do not necessarily express a judgement about the stage reached by a particular country or area in the development process.

Notes

* Indicators for which UNCTAD is a custodian or co-custodian agency.

References

- AidFlows (2019). Glossary of AidFlows terms. Available at http://www.aidflows.org/about/ (accessed 17 June 2019).
- Cantu-Bazaldua F (2021). Remote but well connected? Neighboring but isolated? The measurement of remoteness in the context of SIDS. Available at https://unctad.org/publications.
- IMF (2014). *External Debt Statistics: Guide for Compilers and Users*. IMF. Washington, D.C.
- ITU (2014). *Manual for Measuring ICT Access and Use by Households and Individuals*. International Telecommunication Union. Geneva.
- OECD (2015). *Frascati Manual 2015: Guidelines for Collecting and Reporting Data on Research and Experimental Development*. OECD Publishing. Paris.
- OECD (2021a). DAC glossary of key terms and concepts. Available at http://www.oecd.org/dac/dac-glossary.htm (accessed 20 April 2021).
- OECD (2021b). Glossary of statistical terms. Available at https://stats.oecd.org/glossary/index.htm (accessed 11 May 2021).
- UNCTAD (2016). *World Investment Report 2016: Investor Nationality: Policy Challenges*. United Nations publication. Sales No. E.16.II.D.4. Geneva.
- UNESCO Institute for Statistics (2020). Glossary. Available at http://uis.unesco.org/en/glossary (accessed 15 March 2021).
- UNIDO (2017). *Industrial Development Report 2018, Demand for Manufacturing: Driving Inclusive and Sustainable Industrial Development*. United Nations publication. Sales No. E.18.II.B.48. Vienna.
- United Nations (2008). *International Standard Industrial Classification of All Economic Activities (ISIC) Revision 4*. United Nations publication. Sales No. E.08.XVII.25. New York, NY.
- United Nations (2015). Transforming our world: the 2030 Agenda for Sustainable Development. A/RES/70/1. New York. 21 October.
- United Nations (2021). SDG indicators: Metadata repository. Available at https://unstats.un.org/sdgs/metadata/ (accessed 20 April 2021).
- United Nations, European Commission, IMF, OECD and World Bank (2009). *System of National Accounts 2008*. United Nations publication. Sales No. E.08.XVII.29. New York.
- UNOSSC (2020). About South-South and Triangular Cooperation. Available at https://www.unsouthsouth.org/about/about-sstc/ (accessed 29 April 2020).

Contents

Glossary

A-C

3G	Third generation of cellular network technology
4G	Fourth generation of cellular network technology
Ad-valorem equivalent	A tariff that is not a percentage of the price of the product (e.g. dollars per ton) can be estimated as a percentage of the price – the ad valorem equivalent. (WTO, 2021a)
Advanced reporting requirement	Advanced reporting requirement represents a set of reporting elements, beyond the minimum reporting requirement, which demand additional information from companies in their sustainability reports for the purpose of measuring SDG indicator 12.6.1 (UNCTAD, 2019a).
AfCFTA	African Continental Free Trade Area (AfCTA)
AGOA	African Growth and Opportunity Act
Aid for Trade	Measures aimed at assisting developing countries to increase exports of goods and services, to integrate into the multilateral trading system, and to benefit from liberalized trade and increased market access. It is considered as part of ODA. Effective Aid for Trade will enhance growth prospects and reduce poverty in developing countries, as well as complement multilateral trade reforms and distribute the global benefits more equitably across and within developing countries (WTO, 2006). It is measured as gross disbursements and commitments of total ODA from all donors for Aid for Trade (United Nations, 2021).
Aid for Trade commitments	Aid for Trade commitment is a firm obligation, expressed in writing and backed by the necessary funds, undertaken by an official donor to provide specified assistance to a recipient country or a multilateral organisation (OECD, 2021a; AidFlows, 2019).
Aid for Trade disbursements	Aid for Trade disbursements refer to the release of funds to or the purchase of goods or services for a recipient; by extension, the amount thus spent. Disbursements record the actual international transfer of financial resources, or of goods or services valued at the cost to the donor (OECD, 2021a; AidFlows, 2019).
AIS	Automatic identification system (AIS)
ALDC	Division for Africa, Least Developed Countries and Special Programmes
ASYCUDA	Automated System for Customs Data
Asymptomatic	When a condition produces no symptoms, or a person shows no symptoms.
AU	African Union
B2B	Business to Business
B2C	Business to Consumer
BEPS	Base erosion and profit shifting
BIT	Bilateral Investment Treaty (BIT) is a type of international investment agreement (IIA) made between two countries regarding promotion and protection of investments made by investors from one country in the other country's territory, which commits the host country government to grant certain standards of treatment and protection to foreign investors (nationals and companies of the other country) and their investments (UNCTAD, 2021a).
Blended finance	Blended finance combines concessional financing—loans that are extended on more generous terms than market loans— and commercial funding.
BoP	Balance of payments

Broadband	A general term meaning a telecommunications signal or device of greater bandwidth, in some sense, than another standard or usual signal or device. In data communications, this refers to a data transmission rate of at least 256 kbit/s. In the context of Internet, this can be delivered via fixed (wired) or mobile networks (ITU, 2014).
CAPI	Computer assisted personal interview
Carbon intensity	Carbon intensity is the amount of emissions of carbon dioxide (CO_2) released per unit of another variable such as gross domestic product (GDP), output energy use or transport (IPCC, 2014).
Carbon price	Carbon price is the price per unit of avoided or released carbon dioxide (CO_2) emission, or its CO_2 equivalent (IPCC, 2014).
Carbon tax	Carbon tax is a levy on the carbon content of fossil fuels (IPCC, 2014).
CATI	Computer assisted telephone interview
CBERA	The Caribbean Basin Economic Recovery Act
CCCT	Commonwealth Caribbean Countries Tariff (CCCT) is a Preferential Trade Arrangements (PTAs) categorized as other type of PTAs. The provider of CCCT is Canada. CCCT entered into force on the 15th of June 1986 (WTO, 2021b).
CCSA	Committee for the Coordination of Statistical Activities
CH_4	Methane
CO_2	Carbon dioxide (CO_2) is a colourless, odourless and non-poisonous gas formed by combustion of carbon and in the respiration of living organisms (OECD, 2021b).
CO_2e	Carbon dioxide equivalent (CO_2e) is a measure used to compare the emissions from various greenhouse gases based upon their global warming potential. It represents the quantity of carbon dioxide that has equal global warming potential as the given quantity of a greenhouse gas (OECD, 2021b).
Comply-or-explain approach	Comply-or-explain approach is a reporting practice under which companies are invited to explain the reasons for not providing all requested information in their sustainability reports or for not publishing a sustainability report at all (UNCTAD, 2013).
Concessional loans	Loans that are extended on terms substantially more generous than market loans. The concessionality is achieved either through interest rates below those available on the market or by grace periods, or a combination of these (OECD, 2021b).
Containerised transport	Freight transport using intermodal containers of standard dimensions, i.e. containers that can be moved seamlessly between ships, trucks, trains and other modes of transport as well as storage. The two most used are the 20-foot and the 40-foot containers. They form the basis of the main units of measure currently applied in transport: the twenty-foot equivalent Unit (TEU) and the forty-foot equivalent unit (FEU). (World Shipping Council, 2020)
CoP	Communication on Progress (CoP) is a voluntary, public report through which a company informs stakeholders about its efforts to implement the principles of the United Nations Global Compact (2013).
COVID-19	Infectious disease caused by the strain of coronavirus SARS-CoV-2 discovered in December 2019. Coronaviruses are a large family of viruses which may cause illness in animals or humans. In humans, several coronaviruses are known to cause respiratory infections ranging from the common cold to more severe diseases such as Middle East Respiratory Syndrome (MERS) and Severe Acute Respiratory Syndrome (SARS). The most recently discovered coronavirus causes coronavirus disease COVID-19 (WHO, 2020b).
COVID-19 death	Defined for surveillance purposes as a death resulting from a clinically compatible illness in a probable or confirmed COVID-19 case, unless there is a clear alternative cause of death that cannot be related to COVID-19 disease (e.g. trauma). There should be no period of complete recovery between the illness and death. Further guidance for certification and classification (coding) of COVID-19 as cause of death is available in WHO (2020a).
CSTD	United Nations Commission on Science and Technology for Development

CTS	Consolidated Tariff Schedules

D-F

DAC	Development Assistance Committee
Data revolution	Data revolution refers to the transformative actions needed to respond to the demands of a complex development agenda, improvements in how data is produced and used; closing data gaps to prevent discrimination; building capacity and data literacy in "small data" and big data analytics; modernizing systems of data collection; liberating data to promote transparency and accountability; and developing new targets and indicators (see http://www.undatarevolution.org/data-revolution/).
DDA	Doha Development Agenda (DDA) refers to the latest Doha Round of world trade negotiations among the WTO memberships. The round is also known semi-officially as the Doha Development Agenda and was launched in November 2001. Its aim is to achieve major reform of the international trading system through the introduction of lower trade barriers and revised trade rules. The fundamental objective of DDA is to further liberalising trade in order to improve the trading prospects of developing countries. The main issues at stake are: Reforming agricultural subsidies; Ensuring that new liberalisation in the global economy respects the need for sustainable economic growth in developing countries; Improving developing countries' access to global markets for their exports (WTO, 2020b).
Debt service	Payments made to satisfy a debt obligation, including principal, interest and any late payment fees (IMF, 2014).
Debt sustainability	A country's capacity to finance its policy objectives through debt instruments and service the ensuing debt (IMF, 2014).
DFQF	Duty-free and quota free
DGDS	Division on Globalization and Development Strategies
DIAE	Division on Investment and Enterprise
DITC	Division on International Trade and Commodities, UNCTAD
DMFAS	Debt Management and Financial Analysis System Programme
DTAs	Deep trade agreements (DTAs) cover not just trade but additional policy areas, such as the international flows of investment and labor, and the protection of intellectual property rights and the environment. Their goal is integration beyond trade, or deep integration.
DTL	Division on Technology, Innovation and Trade Logistics
Duty-free	Not subject to import tariffs.
E-commerce	Sale or purchase of goods or services, conducted over computer networks by methods specifically designed for the purpose of receiving or placing of orders; it can involve business-to-business (B2B) or a business-to-consumer (B2C) transactions (OECD, 2021b).
EBA	Everything But Arms (EBA) is a European Commission's 'zero' tariff initiative for LDCs covering all products except the arms trade.
ECLAC	United Nations Economic Commission for Latin America and the Caribbean
ECOWAS	Economic Community of West African States
Emission	Emission is the discharge of pollutants into the atmosphere from stationary sources such as smokestacks, other vents, surface areas of commercial or industrial facilities and mobile sources, for example, motor vehicles, locomotives and aircraft (OECD, 2021b).
Employed in R&D in FTE	Employed in R&D in FTE is the ratio of working hours spent on R&D during a specific reference period (usually a calendar year) divided by the total number of hours conventionally worked in the same period by an individual or by a group (OECD, 2015).

Energy intensity	Energy intensity is the ratio between gross inland energy consumption and GDP. It measures how much energy is required to generate one unit of GDP.
ESCAP	Economic and Social Commission for Asia and the Pacific
EU	European Union
EVI	Economic Vulnerability Index
Excess mortality	Term used in epidemiology and public health to define the number of deaths which occurred in a given crisis above and beyond what we would have expected to see under 'normal' conditions. The WHO define 'excess mortality' as "mortality above what would be expected based on the non-crisis mortality rate in the population of interest. Excess mortality is thus mortality that is attributable to the crisis conditions. It can be expressed as a rate (the difference between observed and non-crisis mortality rates), or as a total number of excess deaths." To calculate 'excess mortality' in a given period, the number of people who had died over this period is compared with the number expected to have died (WHO, 2008).
Export concentration index	This index measures, for each product, the degree of export market concentration by country of origin. It tells us if a large share of commodity exports is accounted for by a small number of countries or, on the contrary, if exports are well distributed among many countries. The index ranges from 0 to 1 with higher values indicating more market concentration (UNCTAD, 2018b).
Export restrictiveness	The average level of tariff restrictions imposed on a country's exports as measured by the MA-TTRI.
Export subsidies	Export subsidies refer to the granting of support by governments to some beneficiary entity or entities to achieve export objectives. Export subsidies may involve direct payments to a firm, industry, producers of a certain agricultural product etc. to achieve some type of export performance. In addition, export subsidies may include low cost export loans, rebates on imported raw materials and tax benefits such as duty-free imports of raw material. They can also take the form of government financed marketing. Most subsidies have existed in agriculture (United Nations, 2021).
External debt	External debt is understood as outstanding amount of those actual current, and not contingent, liabilities that require payment(s) of principal and/or interest by the debtor at some point(s) in the future and that are owed to nonresidents by residents of an economy (IMF, 2014).
F-gases	Fluorinated gases
FACTI	International Financial Accountability, Transparency and Integrity for Achieving the 2030 Agenda
FAO	Food and Agriculture Organization of the United Nations
FDI	Foreign Direct Investment (FDI) is an investment involving a long-term relationship and reflecting a lasting interest and control by a resident entity in one economy (foreign direct investor or parent enterprise) in an enterprise resident in an economy other than that of the foreign direct investor (FDI enterprise or affiliate enterprise or foreign affiliate) (UNCTAD, 2016).
Food price anomalies	Food price anomalies refer to abnormally high or low market prices for food commodities. The indicator relies on a weighted compound growth rate that accounts for both within-year and across-year price growth. The indicator directly evaluates growth in prices over a particular month over many years, taking into account seasonality in agricultural markets and inflation, allowing to answer the question of whether or not a change in price is abnormal for any particular period. It is measured by SDG indicator 2.c.1 (United Nations, 2021).
FTE	Full Time Equivalent (FTE) unit of labour is the hours worked by one employee on a full-time basis. The concept is used to convert the hours worked by several part-time employees into the hours worked by an equivalent full-time employee (ideally the comparison is standardized for gender and industry sector).

G-J

GATS	General Agreement on Trade in Services
GATT	The General Agreement on Tariffs and Trade (GATT) is a multilateral agreement, originally negotiated in 1947 in Geneva among 23 countries, to reduce tariffs and other trade barriers. It provides a framework for periodic multilateral negotiations on trade liberalisation (WTO, 2021c).
GATT-94	The GATT 1994 is contained in Annex 1A of the WTO Agreement. It incorporates by reference the provisions of the GATT 1947, a legally distinct international treaty applied provisionally from 1948 to 1995 (WTO, 2021c).
GDP	Gross domestic product
GERD	Gross domestic expenditure on research and development
GHG	Greenhouse gas (GHG)
GHS	Global Health Security
GII	Gender Inequality Index (GII) measures gender inequalities in three aspects of human development: reproductive health, measured by maternal mortality ratio and adolescent birth rates; empowerment, measured by proportion of parliamentary seats occupied by females and proportion of adult females and males aged 25 years and older with at least some secondary education; and economic status, expressed as labor market participation and measured by labor force participation rate of female and male populations aged 15 years and older (UNDP, 2020).
Gini	Gini index or coefficient, named after Italian statistician Corrado Gini, is a measure of statistical dispersion used to determine inequality among values of a frequency distribution. It can be used to measure the inequality of any distribution. Here a Gini index of 100 indicates perfect inequality, and 0 (zero) indicates perfect equality. It is a widely used indicator of income inequality or wealth concentration within an economy or society. It indicates how far the distribution of income among individuals (or households) deviates from a perfectly egalitarian distribution.
GLI	Grubel-Lloyd Index (GLI) is calculated on products categorized as manufacturing intermediate inputs (e.g. parts and components), computed at the industry level (as defined by the 4 digit Harmonized System classification) and then aggregated at the sectoral level using bilateral trade shares. (UNCTAD, 2021b)
Global Diplomacy Index	Global Diplomacy Index includes a full listing of all diplomatic representations abroad from 61 countries, for a total of 7320 missions (Lowy Institute, 2019).
Global Presence Index	Global Presence Index is a composite index that assesses 130 countries along three pillars: economic (investments and exports of goods, services and energy), military (troops and military equipment) and soft power (development cooperation, education, science, technology, culture, sports, tourism and migration) (Elcano Royal Institute, 2020).
Global Soft Power Index	Global Soft Power Index is a composite index calculated from extensive public opinion surveys and expert assessments, evaluating the soft power of 60 countries, mostly high- and middle-income economies, along seven pillars: business and trade, governance, international relations, cultural and heritage, media and communication, education and science, and people and values. The data collection of the 2020 index took place in autumn 2019.
GNI	Gross national income
GNP	Gross national product
Goods loaded	Merchandise destined for export, also referred to as "outbound trade volumes". (UNCTAD, 2019b)
Goods unloaded	Merchandise destined for import, also referred to as "inbound trade volumes". (UNCTAD, 2019b)
GPT	Generalized preferential tariff

Greenhouse gases	Greenhouse gases are gases that cause the 'greenhouse effect' by letting solar radiation reach the Earth's surface and absorbing infrared energy emitted by the Earth. The concentration of some greenhouse gases in the atmosphere is rising as a result of human activities, leading to an increase of the Earth's average temperature. The most important of these gases comprise: carbon dioxide (CO_2), methane (CH_4), nitrous oxide (N_2O) and fluorinated gases (F-gases), such as hydrochlorofluorocarbons (HCFCs) and hydrofluorocarbons (HFCs) (WMO, 2019).
GRI	Global Reporting Initiative
GSP	Generalized System of Preferences
Gt	Gigaton
GTA	Global Trade Alert
GVC	Global value chain
GWP	Global Warming Potential (GWP) is an index measuring the radiative forcing following an emission of a unit mass of a given substance, accumulated over a chosen time horizon, relative to that of the reference substance, CO_2. The GWPthus represents the combined effect of the differing times these substances remain in the atmosphere and their effectiveness in causing radiative forcing (IPCC, 2014).
HDI	Human development index
HS	The Harmonized System (HS) is an international nomenclature developed by the World Customs Organization, which is arranged in six-digit codes allowing all participating countries to classify traded goods on a common basis. Beyond the six-digit level, countries are free to introduce national distinctions for tariffs and many other purposes.
IAEG-SDG	Inter-Agency and Expert Group on Sustainable Development Goals indicators
ICCS	International Classification of Crime for Statistical Purposes
ICD	International Classification of Diseases
ICT	Information and communications technology (ICT) is a diverse set of technological tools and resources used to transmit, store, create, share or exchange information. These resources include computers, the Internet, live broadcasting technologies, recorded broadcasting technologies and telephony (UNESCO Institute for Statistics, 2020).
IDA	International Development Association
IDB	Integrated Data Base
IEA	International Energy Agency
IFF	Illicit financial flow
IIA	International Investment Agreement (IIA) are treaties with investment provisions (e.g. a free trade agreement with an investment chapter) between two or more countries include commitments regarding cross-border investments (foreign investment or FDI), typically for the purpose of protection and promotion of such investments. They include two types of agreements: (1) bilateral investment treaties and (2) treaties with investment provisions (UNCTAD, 2021a).
IIP	Index of Industrial Production (IIP) is a measure of the change in the volume of goods or services produced over time. Its main purpose is to provide a measure of the short-term changes in value added over a given reference period, usually a month or a quarter. The index covers the industrial sector, including mining, manufacturing, electricity and gas, and water and waste (United Nations, 2010).
IIRC	International Integrated Reporting Council

Illegal economic activity	Illegal production comprises (1) the production of goods or services whose sale, distribution or possession is forbidden by law; (2) production activities which are usually legal but which become illegal when carried out by unauthorised producers, e.g., unlicensed medical practitioners; (3) production which does not comply with certain safety, health or other standards could be defined as illegal; and (4) the scope of illegal production in individual countries depends upon the laws in place, e.g. prostitution (United Nations et al., 2009).
ILO	International Labour Organization
IMF	International Monetary Fund
IMO	International Maritime Organization (IMO)
Import restrictiveness	The average level of tariff restrictions on imports as measured by the TTRI.
IMTS	International Merchandise Trade Statistics
INDICO	Integrated Digital Conferencing (INDICO) is a web-based conference and management system used in more than 90 instances all over the world. In this publication, Indico refers to the web-based conference storage and management system managed by the United Nations Office at Geneva instance (Indico-unog) (UNOG-Indico, 2020).
Informal economy	The informal economy comprises (i) the production of goods and market services of households; and (ii) the activities of corporations (illegal, underground) that may not be covered in the regular data collection framework for compiling macroeconomic statistics. This scope of the informal economy considers not only the domestic activities, but also the cross-border transactions of resident units (IMF, 2019).
Investment guarantee	An insurance, offered by governments or other institutions, to investors to protect against certain political risks in host countries, such as the risk of discrimination, expropriation, transfer restrictions or breach of contract (UNCTAD, 2015). (UNCTAD, 2015)
IPA	Investment Promotion Agency
IPCC	Intergovernmental Panel on Climate Change
ISAR	International Standards of Accounting and Reporting
ITC	International Trade Centre
ITU	International Telecommunications Union

K-M

km	kilometre
Laboratory-confirmed cases	Cases where there has been detection of SARS-CoV-2 nucleic acid in a clinical specimen.
Land-use change	Land-use change refers to a change in the use or management of land by humans, which may lead to a change in land cover (IPCC, 2014).
Latency rate	Latency rate is a network performance metric, measured as the round-trip time that it takes for a packet of data to travel from a sending node to the nearest receiving server in each country and back. It is collected by Measurement Lab from a high number of tests performed across networks every day. A higher latency indicates a worse connection quality, therefore affecting network performance and opportunities to use ICTs for business or private connections.
LDC	Least developed country
LHS	Left Hand Side
Living wage	Living wage is defined by the Global Living Wage Coalition to mean the remuneration received for a standard workweek by a worker in a particular place sufficient to afford a decent standard of living for the worker and her or his family. Elements of a decent standard of living include food, water, housing, education, health care, transportation, clothing, and other essential needs including provision for unexpected events.
LLDC	Landlocked developing country
MA-TTRI	An index measuring the average level of tariff restrictions imposed on exports.
Main bulks	This category includes iron ore, grain, coal, bauxite/alumina and phosphate. Starting on 2006, the category was restricted to iron ore, grain and coal only, while bauxite/alumina and phosphate were moved to the category "other dry cargo". (UNCTAD, 2019b)
Medium and high-tech industry	Medium and high-tech industry is an industry in which producers of goods incur relatively high expenditure on research and development (R&D) per unit of output. The distinction between low, medium, and high-tech industries is based on R&D intensity, i.e. the ratio of R&D expenditure to an output measure, usually gross value added. For a list of the particular economic activities, considered to be medium and high-tech (UNIDO, 2017).
MFN	Most-favoured-nation
MFN tariffs	Most Favoured Nation (MFN) tariffs are a tariff level that a member of the General Agreement on Tariffs and Trade of the WTO charges on a good to other members, i.e. a country with a most favoured nation status (see UNCTAD, 2018a) It applies to imports from trading partners-members of the World Trade Organization (WTO), unless the country has a preferential trade agreement. It is the lowest possible tariff a country can assess on another country.
Minimum reporting requirement	Minimum reporting requirement refers to a core set of economic, environmental, social and governance elements of sustainability information requested from companies in their sustainability reports for the purpose of measuring SDG indicator 12.6.1. Only reports including this information are counted towards the indicator (UNCTAD, 2019a).
MNC	Multinational corporation
MNE	Multinational enterprise
Mobile money	A service in which the mobile phone is used to access financial products and services (GSMA, 2010).
MOPAN	Multilateral Organization Performance Assessment Network (MOPAN)

MVA	Manufacturing value added (MVA) is the net-output of all resident manufacturing activity units. It is obtained by adding up their outputs and subtracting intermediate inputs (United Nations, 2021). Manufacturing can broadly be understood as "the physical or chemical transformation of materials, substances, or components into new products" (United Nations, 2008), consisting of sector C in the International Standard Industrial Classification of all Economic Activities (ISIC) revision 4 (United Nations, 2021).

N-P

N_2O	Nitrous oxide
NAFTA	North American Free Trade Agreement
Nairobi Package	The Nairobi Package is a series of Ministerial Decisions adopted at the WTO's Ministerial Conference in Nairobi, 2015. The issues covered relate to agriculture, cotton and LDCs (WTO, 2021d).
Net-exporter of CO2	Net-exporter of CO_2 is a country in which more emissions are generated by the production of goods it exports to other countries than by the production goods it imports from other countries.
NO_2	Nitrogen dioxide (NO_2) is a product of combustion, for instance emitted by road transport, and is generally found in the atmosphere in close association with other primary pollutants. Nitrogen dioxide is toxic, and its concentrations are also often strongly correlated with those of other toxic pollutants. As it is easier to measure, it is often used as a proxy for them. There is growing concern about rising levels of NO_2 in fast-growing cities with large numbers of vehicles (WHO, 2006).
Non-observed economy	According to the OECD, the groups of activities most likely to be non-observed are those that are underground, illegal, informal sector, or undertaken by households for their own final use. Activities may also be missed because of deficiencies in the basic statistical data collection programme (OECD, 2012).
NSO	National statistical office
NTBs	Non-tariff Barriers
NTFC	National Trade Facilitation Committee
NTMs	Non-tariff measures (NTMs) are policy measures other than ordinary customs tariffs that can potentially have an economic effect on international trade in goods, changing quantities traded, or prices or both such as technical barriers to trade, price-control measures, etc. (UNCTAD, 2021c)
ODA	Official Development Assistance (ODA) are resource flows to countries and territories which are: (a) undertaken by the official sector; (b) with promotion of economic development and welfare as the main objective; (c) at concessional financial terms (implying a minimum grant element depending on the recipient country and the type of loan). In addition to financial flows, technical co-operation is also included (OECD, 2021a).
OECD	Organization for Economic Cooperation and Development
Official international support	For the purpose of the SDGs, official international support refers to assistance in the form of official development assistance and other official flows (United Nations, 2021).
OIE	World Organisation for Animal Health
ONS	Office for National Statistics of the United Kingdom
OOF	Other official flows (OOF) are transactions by the official sector with countries and territories which do not meet the conditions for eligibility as ODA, either because they are not primarily aimed at development or because they do not meet the minimum grant element requirement (OECD, 2021a).
P&C	Principles and Criteria

Pandemic	Commonly described by the WHO as 'the worldwide spread of a new disease', no strict definition is provided. In 2009, they set out the basic requirements for a pandemic: 1. New virus emerges in humans 2. Minimal or no population immunity 3. Causes serious illness; high morbidity/mortality 4. Spreads easily from person to person 5. Global outbreak of disease. The US Centre for Disease Control uses a similar approach, but with a reduced set of criteria. It is very difficult to gauge whether the spread of a disease should be termed an outbreak, epidemic or pandemic. In other words, when to declare a pandemic isn't a black and white decision (Doshi, 2011).
Paris Climate Agreement	The Paris Agreement is an agreement within the UNFCCC aiming is to strengthen the global response to the threat of climate change by keeping a global temperature rise this century well below 2°C above pre-industrial levels and to pursue efforts to limit the temperature increase even further, to 1.5°C. It aims to strengthen countries' ability to deal with the impacts of climate change. To reach these ambitious goals, appropriate financial flows, a new technology framework and an enhanced capacity building framework are intended to support developing countries, in line with their national objectives (UNFCCC, 2016).
PBL	Planbureau voor de Leefomgeving
PCI	Productive Capacities Index (PCI) is a multidimensional composite index that measures productive capacities of economies by using eight categories: natural and human capital, energy, institutions, private sector, structural change, transport and information, and communication technologies, which together yield the multidimensional productive capacity index. The choice of indicators to measure productive capacity is based on the UNCTAD (2006) definition and the availability of comparable data.
PHEIC	Public health emergency of international concern (PHEIC): Serious public health events that endanger international public health. This term is defined in as "an extraordinary event which is determined [...]: • to constitute a public health risk to other States through the international spread of disease; and • to potentially require a coordinated international response". This definition implies a situation that: is serious, unusual or unexpected; carries implications for public health beyond the affected State's national border; and may require immediate international action. The responsibility of determining whether an event is within this category lies with the WHO Director-General and requires the convening of a committee of experts, the IHR Emergency Committee. This committee advises the Director-General on the recommended measures to be promulgated on an emergency basis, known as temporary recommendations. Temporary recommendations include health measures to be implemented by the State Party experiencing the PHEIC, or by other States Parties, to prevent or reduce the international spread of disease and avoid unnecessary interference with international traffic (WHO, 2005).
PIANC	The World Association for Waterborne Transport Infrastructure (PIANC)
PMI	Purchasing Managers' Index (PMI) is a monthly indicator of expected economic activity, collected by surveying senior executives at private sector companies. The PMI is a weighted average of five sub-indices measuring new orders, output, employment, suppliers' delivery times and stocks of purchases. It is calculated for the total economy as well as for specific sectors, such as manufacturing, construction, services, etc. A figure of 50 indicates that no change in economic production is expected; a value above 50 means that the economy is expected to grow, a value below 50 that it is expected to contract (Refinitiv, 2021).
PNG	Publicly Non-Guaranteed debt (PNG) is an external debt of the private sector that is not contractually guaranteed by a public sector unit resident in the same economy (IMF, 2014). Unless otherwise indicated, only long-term debt (maturity of more than one year) is included.
PPG	Publicly guaranteed debt (PPG) is an external debt liabilities of the private sector, the servicing of which is contractually guaranteed by a public unit resident in the same economy as the debtor (IMF, 2014). Unless otherwise indicated, only long-term debt (maturity of more than one year) is included.
PPI	Private Participation in Infrastructure

PPP	Purchasing power parity
Private flows	Private flows consist of flows at market terms financed out of private sector resources and private grants. They include FDI, private export credits, securities of multilateral agencies and bilateral portfolio investment. Private flows other than FDI are restricted to credits with a maturity of greater than one year (OECD, 2021a).
Productive capacity building	Strengthening economic sectors – from improved testing laboratories to better supply chains – to increase competitiveness in export markets (Negin, 2014).
PTAs	Preferential Trade Arrangements (PTAs) can be established under paragraphs 4 to 10 of Article XXIV of GATT (WTO, 2020a) between parties through which one party can grant more favourable trade conditions to other parties of the arrangement and not to other WTO members.
Public bond debt	Public debt in the form of sovereign international bonds traded in international capital markets (UNCTAD, 2017).
Public sector debt	All debt liabilities of resident public sector units to other residents and nonresidents (IMF, 2014).

Q-S

QUAD	QUAD countries refers to Canada, EU, Japan and the United States.
R&D	Research and development (R&D) comprise creative and systematic work undertaken in order to increase the stock of knowledge – including knowledge of humankind, culture and society – and to devise new applications of available knowledge (OECD, 2015) (see also United Nations et al., 2009, para 10.103).
R&D intensity	R&D intensity is defined as the ratio of gross domestic expenditure on research and development (GERD) to GDP (OECD, 2015).
R&D services	Research and experimental development (R&D) comprise creative and systematic work undertaken in order to increase the stock of knowledge – including knowledge of humankind, culture and society – and to devise new applications of available knowledge. (The OECD Frascati Manual) The definition used for international trade (MSITS 2010) includes testing and product development that may give rise to patents, as an addition.
Remittances	The term remittances can refer to three concepts, each encompassing the previous one. "Personal remittances" are defined as current and capital transfers in cash or in kind between resident households and non-resident households, plus net compensation of employees working abroad. "Total remittances" include personal remittances plus social benefits from abroad, such as benefits payable under social security or pension funds. "Total remittances and transfers to non-profit institutions serving households (NPISHs)" includes all cross-borders transfers benefiting household directly (total remittances) or indirectly (through NPISHs) (IMF, 2009).
Revealed comparative advantage in exports	Revealed comparative advantage in exports is the proportion of a country group's exports by service category divided by the proportion of world exports in the corresponding category.
RHS	Right Hand Side
RTA	Regional trade agreement
Sanitary and phytosanitary measures	Any measure applied: (a) to protect animal or plant life or health within the territory of the trade partner from risks arising from the entry, establishment or spread of pests, diseases, disease-carrying organisms or disease-causing organisms; (b) to protect human or animal life or health within the territory of the trade partner from risks arising from additives, contaminants, toxins or diseases causing organisms in foods, beverages or feedstuffs; (c) to protect human life or health within the territory of the trade partner from risks arising from diseases carried by animals, plants or products thereof, or from the entry, establishment or spread of pests; or (d) to prevent or limit other damage within the territory of the trade partner from the entry, establishment or spread of pests (UNCTAD, 2003).
SASB	Sustainability Accounting Standards Board
SDG	Sustainable Development Goal
Serological tests	Tests that do not detect the virus itself but instead detect antibodies produced in response to an infection.
Seroprevalence	Level of a pathogen in a population, as measured in blood serum.
SG	Secretary General
Shadow economy	The shadow economy includes all economic activities which are hidden from official authorities for monetary, regulatory, and institutional reasons (Medina and Schneider, 2018).
Short-term debt	Debt liabilities having a maturity of one year or less; maturity can be defined on an original or reminaing basis (IMF, 2014). Interests in arrears on long-term debt are included within short-term debt.
SIDS	small island developing States
SITC	Standard International Trade Classification
SITS	Statistics of International Trade in Services
SME	Small- and medium-sized enterprise

SNA	System of national accounts
Soft infrastructure	Ideas and conceptual frameworks that give shape and direction to what is eventually physically manifest (*FutureStructure*, 2013).
South-South Cooperation	Broad framework of collaboration among countries of the Global South in the political, economic, social, cultural, environmental and technical domains. It includes trade, FDI, regional integration efforts, technology transfers, sharing of solutions and experts, and other forms. Involving two or more developing countries, it can take place on a bilateral, regional, intraregional or interregional basis (UNOSSC, 2020).
SPS	Sanitary and phytosanitary measures
Stocks-to-use ratio	Stocks-to-use ratio for a given commodity in an economy is the ratio of market-year ending stock over domestic consumption (Bobenrieth et al., 2013). For the world it is as world stocks divided by world use.
Sustainability report	Sustainability report is a document published by an entity describing the economic, social, environmental impacts caused by its activities; it is composed of a certain number of disclosures along the main pillars of sustainable development (GRI, 2019).

Tanker trade	This category includes trade in crude oil, refined petroleum products, gas and chemicals. (UNCTAD, 2019b)
Tariff line	A single item in a country's tariff schedule. A single item in a country's tariff schedule (United Nations, 2021).
Tariff peak	A single tariff or a small group of tariffs that is/are particularly high.
Tariffs	Tariffs "are customs duties on merchandise imports, levied either on an ad valorem basis (percentage of value) or on a specific basis (e.g. $7 per 100 kg). Tariffs can be used to create a price advantage for similar locally produced goods and for raising government revenues. Trade remedy measures and taxes are not considered to be tariffs." (United Nations, 2021)
TBT	Technical barriers to trade (TBT) are measures referring to technical regulations, and procedures for assessment of conformity with technical regulations and standards.
TDB	UNCTAD Trade and Development Board
TEU	Twenty-foot Equivalent Unit
TFA	The WTO Agreement on Trade Facilitation came into force on 22 February 2017 following its ratification by two-thirds of the WTO membership. The TFA contains provisions for expediting the movement, release and clearance of goods, including goods in transit. It also sets out measures for effective cooperation between customs and other appropriate authorities on trade facilitation and customs compliance issues. It further contains provisions for technical assistance and capacity building in this area.
Tier 1	Tier 1 means that a SDG indicator has been classified by the IAEG-SDG as being conceptually clear, has an internationally established methodology and standards are available, and data are regularly produced by countries for at least 50 per cent of countries and of the population in every region where the indicator is relevant.
Tier II indicator	SDG indicator that is conceptually clear, has an internationally established methodology and standards are available, but data are not regularly produced by countries (United Nations Statistics Division, 2020).
Tier III indicator	SDG indicator for which there is no internationally established methodology or standards yet available, but methodology or standards are being (or will be) developed or tested (United Nations Statistics Division, 2020).
TORs	Terms Of References
Total resource flows	In the context of the IAEG-SDG, these flows quantify the overall expenditures that donors provide to developing countries, including official and private flows, both concessional and non-concessional. Specifically, they include ODA, OOFs and private flows (United Nations, 2021).
Tourism direct GDP	Tourism direct GDP measures direct contributions of tourism to the national economy, since tourism does not exist as a separate industry in the standard industrial classification. Instead, it is embedded in various other industries. (no SDG metadata)
Tourism sector	Tourism sector is the cluster of production units in different industries that provide consumption goods and services demanded by visitors. Such industries are called tourism industries because visitor acquisition represents such a significant share of their supply that in the absence of visitors, the production of these would cease to exist in meaningful quantities (UNWTO and ILO, 2014).
TRAINS	Trade Analysis and Information System
TTRI	Tariff trade restrictiveness index (TTRI) is an index measuring the average level of tariff restrictions imposed on imports.

Underground economy	Underground production consists of activities that are productive in an economic sense and quite legal (provided certain standards or regulations are complied with), but which are deliberately concealed from public authorities for the following reasons: (i) to avoid the payment of income, value added or other taxes; (ii) to avoid payment of social security contributions; (iii) to avoid meeting certain legal standards such as minimum wages, maximum hours, safety or health standards, etc; or (iv) to avoid complying with certain administrative procedures, such as completing statistical questionnaires or other administrative forms (United Nations et al., 2009).
UNDESA	United Nations Department of Economic and Social Affairs
UNECA	United Nations Economic Commission for Africa
Unemployment	The unemployed comprise all persons of working age who were: (a) without work during the reference period, i.e. were not in paid employment or self-employment; (b) currently available for work, i.e. were available for paid employment or self-employment during the reference period; and (c) seeking work, i.e. had taken specific steps in a specified recent period to seek paid employment or self-employment. Future starters, that is, persons who did not look for work but have a future labour market stake (made arrangements for a future job start) are also counted as unemployed, as well as participants in skills training or retraining schemes within employment promotion programmes, and persons "not in employment" who carried out activities to migrate abroad in order to work for pay or profit but who were still waiting for the opportunity to leave (ILO, 2020).
UNEP	United Nations Environment Programme
UNESCO	United Nations Educational, Scientific and Cultural Organization
UNESCO UIS	United Nations Educational, Scientific and Cultural Organization Institute of Statistics
UNFCCC	United Nations Framework Convention on Climate Change
UNFPA	United Nations Population Fund
UNGC	United Nations Global Compact (UNGC) is a voluntary initiative based on company-level commitments to adopt sustainability and socially responsible principles and to take steps to support UN goals (United Nations Global Compact, 2020).
UNODC	United Nations Office on Drugs and Crime
UNSD	United Nations Statistics Division
VAR	Vector autoregression

W-Z

Weighted mean applied tariff	The average of effectively applied rates weighted by the product import shares corresponding to each partner country (World Bank, 2021).
Weighted tariff-average	Weighted average of tariffs applied to imports of goods in HS chapter 01-97. The tariffs are weighted by the value of the imported goods to which they are applied. It is expressed as percentage of the value of goods imported. The average level of customs tariff rates applied worldwide can be used as an indicator of the degree of success achieved by multilateral negotiations and regional trade agreements. See metadata for indicator 17.10.1 (United Nations, 2021).
WHO	World Health Organization
WMO	World Meteorological Organization
WRI	World Resources Institute
WTO	World Trade Organization
WTO TFA	World Trade Organization Agreement on Trade Facilitation

References

- AidFlows (2019). Glossary of AidFlows terms. Available at http://www.aidflows.org/about/ (accessed 17 June 2019).

- Bobenrieth E, Wright B and Zeng D (2013). Stocks-to-use ratios and prices as indicators of vulnerability to spikes in global cereal markets. *Agricultural Economics*. 44(s1):43–52.

- Doshi P (2011). The elusive definition of pandemic influenza. Bulletin of the World Health Organisation. *WHO Bulletin*. 89(7):532–538.

- Elcano Royal Institute (2020). Elcano Global Presence Index. Available at https://www.globalpresence.realinstitutoelcano.org/en/home (accessed 5 June 2021).

- *FutureStructure* (2013). What is soft infrastructure? November.

- GRI (2019). Available at https://www.globalreporting.org/information/sustainability-reporting/Pages/default.aspx (accessed 19 April 2019).

- GSMA (2010). Mobile money definitions July. Available at https://www.gsma.com/mobilefordevelopment/resources/mobile-money-definitions (accessed 28 May 2020).

- ILO (2020). Unemployment rate. Available at https://www.ilo.org/ilostat-files/Documents/description_UR_EN.pdf (accessed 15 June 2020).

- IMF (2009). *International Transactions in Remittances: Guide for Compilers and Users (RCG)*. IMF. Washington, D.C.

- IMF (2014). *External Debt Statistics: Guide for Compilers and Users*. IMF. Washington, D.C.

- IMF (2019). Final report of the task force on informal economy. Available at https://www.imf.org/external/pubs/ft/bop/2019/pdf/19-03.pdf (accessed 10 February 2020).

- IPCC (2014). *Climate Change 2014, Synthesis Report, Contribution of Working Groups I, II and III to the Fifth Assessment Report (5AR) of the Intergovernmental Panel on Climate Change*. IPCC.

- ITU (2014). *Manual for Measuring ICT Access and Use by Households and Individuals*. International Telecommunication Union. Geneva.

- Lowy Institute (2019). The 2019 Lowy Institute Global Diplomacy Index. Available at https://www.lowyinstitute.org/publications/2019-lowy-institute-global-diplomacy-index (accessed 5 June 2021).

- Medina L and Schneider F (2018). Shadow economies around the world: What did we learn over the last 20 years? IMF Working Papers No. WP/18/17. (accessed 9 June 2020).

- Negin J (2014). Devpolicyblog. Available at http://www.devpolicy.org/understanding-aid-for-trade-part-one-a-dummys-guide-20140228/ (accessed 19 June 2019).

- OECD (2012). Measuring the non-observed economy: A handbook. Available at https://www.oecd.org/sdd/na/measuringthenon-observedeconomy-ahandbook.htm (accessed 17 May 2021).

- OECD (2015). *Frascati Manual 2015: Guidelines for Collecting and Reporting Data on Research and Experimental Development*. OECD Publishing. Paris.

- OECD (2021a). DAC glossary of key terms and concepts. Available at http://www.oecd.org/dac/dac-glossary.htm (accessed 20 April 2021).

- OECD (2021b). Glossary of statistical terms. Available at https://stats.oecd.org/glossary/index.htm (accessed 11 May 2021).

- Refinitiv (2021). Eikon. (accessed 1 June 2021).

- UNCTAD (2003). Course on Dispute Settlement - Module 3.9. WTO: SPS Measures. UNCTAD/EDM/Misc.232/Add.13. Available at https://unctad.org/en/Pages/DITC/TNCD/Dispute-Settlement-in-International-Trade.aspx (accessed 29 June 2020).

- UNCTAD, ed. (2006). *The Least Developed Countries Report 2006: Developing Productive Capacities*. United Nations. New York and Geneva.

- UNCTAD (2013). Best practice guidance for policymakers and stock exchanges on sustainability reporting initiatives. TD/B/C.II/ISAR/67. Geneva. 28 August. (accessed 6 March 2019).

- UNCTAD (2015). *Investment Policy Framework for Sustainable Development*. UNCTAD/DIAE/PCB/2015/5. Geneva.

- UNCTAD (2016). *World Investment Report 2016: Investor Nationality: Policy Challenges*. United Nations publication. Sales No. E.16.II.D.4. Geneva.

- UNCTAD (2017). Debt Vulnerabilities in Developing Countries: A New Debt Trap? (Volume I: Regional and Thematic Analyses). Available at https://unctad.org/webflyer/debt-vulnerabilities-developing-countries-new-debt-trap-volume-i-regional-and-thematic (accessed 1 July 2021).

- UNCTAD (2018a). *Trade and Development Report 2018: Power, Platforms and the Free Trade Delusion*. United Nations publication. Sales No. E.18.II.D.7. New York and Geneva.

- UNCTAD (2018b). Indicators explained #1: Export Market Concentration Index. UNCTAD/STAT/IE/2018/1 June. Available at https://unctadstat.unctad.org/EN/IndicatorsExplained.html (accessed 18 June 2020).

- UNCTAD (2019a). Enhancing the comparability of sustainability reporting. Available at https://www.un-ilibrary.org/content/books/9789213632710c004 (accessed 1 July 2021).

- UNCTAD (2019b). *Review of Maritime Transport 2019*. United Nations publication. Sales No. E.19.II.D.20. New York and Geneva.

- UNCTAD (2021a). International Investment Agreements Navigator. Available at https://investmentpolicy.unctad.org/international-investment-agreements (accessed 20 April 2021).

- UNCTAD (2021b). UNCTADStat. Available at https://unctadstat.unctad.org/EN/Index.html (accessed 21 April 2021).

- UNCTAD (2021c). Classification of Non-Tariff Measures. Available at https://unctad.org/en/Pages/DITC/Trade-Analysis/Non-Tariff-Measures/NTMs-Classification.aspx (accessed 15 May 2021).

- UNDP (2020). Human Development Report 2020. The next frontier. Human development and the Anthropocene. Human Development Reports. New York. (accessed 9 February 2021).

- UNESCO Institute for Statistics (2020). Glossary. Available at http://uis.unesco.org/en/glossary (accessed 15 March 2021).

- UNFCCC (2016). Paris Agreement. FCCC/CP/2015/10/Add.1. Paris. 29 January. (accessed 31 May 2019).

- UNIDO (2017). *Industrial Development Report 2018, Demand for Manufacturing: Driving Inclusive and Sustainable Industrial Development*. United Nations publication. Sales No. E.18.II.B.48. Vienna.

- United Nations (2008). *International Standard Industrial Classification of All Economic Activities (ISIC) Revision 4*. United Nations publication. Sales No. E.08.XVII.25. New York, NY.

- United Nations (2010). International Recommendations for the Index of Industrial Production 2010. Available at https://unstats.un.org/unsd/industry/Docs/F107_edited.pdf (accessed 26 May 2020).

- United Nations (2021). SDG indicators: Metadata repository. Available at https://unstats.un.org/sdgs/metadata/ (accessed 20 April 2021).

- United Nations, European Commission, IMF, OECD and World Bank (2009). *System of National Accounts 2008*. United Nations publication. Sales No. E.08.XVII.29. New York.

- United Nations Global Compact (2013). UN Global Compact policy on communicating progress. Available at https://www.unglobalcompact.org/library/1851 (accessed 6 March 2019).

- United Nations Global Compact (2020). United Nations Global Compact Database. Available at https://www.unglobalcompact.org (accessed 6 February 2021).

- United Nations Statistics Division (2020). Tier classification for global SDG indicators. Available at https://unstats.un.org/sdgs/iaeg-sdgs/tier-classification/ (accessed 15 May 2020).

- UNOG-Indico I (2020). Available at indico.un.org (accessed 21 May 2020).

- UNOSSC (2020). About South-South and Triangular Cooperation. Available at https://www.unsouthsouth.org/about/about-sstc/ (accessed 29 April 2020).

- UNWTO and ILO (2014). *Measuring Employment in the Tourism Industries: Guide with Best Practices*. Madrid and Geneva.

- WHO (2005). *International Health Regulations*. WHO. Geneva.

- WHO (2006). Air Quality Guidelines, Global Update 2005. Available at http://www.euro.who.int/__data/assets/pdf_file/0005/78638/E90038.pdf?ua=1 (accessed 11 May 2020).

- WHO (2008). Glossary of humanitarian terms. Definitions: Emergencies. Available at https://www.who.int/hac/about/definitions/en/ (accessed 5 May 2020).

- WHO (2020a). Emergency use ICD codes for COVID-19 disease outbreak. Available at https://www.who.int/classifications/icd/covid19/en/ (accessed 15 June 2020).

- WHO (2020b). Q&A on coronaviruses (COVID-19). Available at https://www.who.int/emergencies/diseases/novel-coronavirus-2019/question-and-answers-hub/q-a-detail/q-a-coronaviruses (accessed 11 May 2020).

- WMO (2019). Available at https://public.wmo.int/en/our-mandate/focus-areas/environment/greenhouse%20gases (accessed 11 June 2019).

- World Bank (2021). Tariff rate, applied, weighted mean, all products (%). Available at https://data.worldbank.org/indicator/tm.tax.mrch.wm.ar.zs (accessed 12 May 2020).

- World Shipping Council (2020). Containers. Available at http://www.worldshipping.org/about-the-industry/containers (accessed 13 May 2021).

- WTO (2006). Aid for Trade Task Force - Recommendations of the Task Force on Aid for Trade. WT/AFT/1.

- WTO (2020a). The basic rules for goods. Available at https://www.wto.org/english/tratop_e/region_e/regatt_e.htm (accessed 15 May 2020).

- WTO (2020b). WTO report finds growing number of export restrictions in response to COVID-19 crisis. Available at https://www.wto.org/english/news_e/news20_e/rese_23apr20_e.htm (accessed 20 June 2021).

- WTO (2021a). Glossary - a guide to 'WTO speak.' Available at https://www.wto.org/english/thewto_e/glossary_e/glossary_e.htm (accessed 1 July 2021).

- WTO (2021b). General Agreement on Tariffs and Trade 1994. Available at https://www.wto.org/english/docs_e/legal_e/06-gatt_e.htm (accessed 18 April 2021).

- WTO (2021c). The General Agreement on Tariffs and Trade (GATT 1947). Available at https://www.wto.org/english/docs_e/legal_e/gatt47_01_e.htm (accessed 18 April 2021).

- WTO (2021d). Nairobi Package. Available at https://www.wto.org/english/thewto_e/minist_e/mc10_e/nairobipackage_e.htm (accessed 10 June 2021).

Multilateralism for trade and development

"In a free trade, an effectual combination cannot be established but by the unanimous consent of every single trader, and it cannot last longer than every single trader continues of the same mind.".

— Adam Smith, The Wealth Of Nations

Multilateralism for trade and development

Protectionism was already on the rise before the world economy was struck in 2020 by the global outbreak of the COVID-19, which affected global trade through both supply and demand shocks. Merchandise trade declined in 2020, and many governments imposed barriers to exports of medical products and lowered the tariffs on imports of agricultural products to maximize the supplies of critical goods on domestic markets. The COVID-19 health crisis has introduced a new agenda for multilateralism, focused on areas including economic recovery, climate, global health, and trade. Resilient world trade is seen as an engine to build back better post-COVID world, and as an important means to achieving the 2030 Agenda for Sustainable Development. This theme on multilateralism for trade and development of SDG Pulse:

1. Provides analysis and statistics on International trade in developing economies, including merchandise and services trade, such as tourism.
2. Assesses progress in the special and differential treatment for developing countries and studies new developments in Towards inclusive trade in a post-COVID world.
3. Analyses trade restrictions and distortions in world agricultural markets and presents statistics on the links between Trade, food security and sustainable agriculture.
4. Examines the role of Policies to promote trade (International cooperation and multilateral mechanisms), including Aid for Trade, in support of developing countries, particularly LDCs.

> *In a free trade, an effectual combination cannot be established but by the unanimous consent of every single trader, and it cannot last longer than every single trader continues of the same mind. The majority of a corporation can enact a bye-law, with proper penalties, which will limit the competition more effectually and more durably than any voluntary combination whatever.*
>
> — Adam Smith, The Wealth Of Nations

Developing countries' share of global exports of goods and services has increased over the last two decades, but **plateaued for goods at around 45** per cent since 2012, and for services exports dropped to 28 per cent in 2020.

UNCTAD, ITC & WTO SDG indicator 17.11.1

The target of doubling the share of LDCs' exports in global exports by 2020 has now been missed

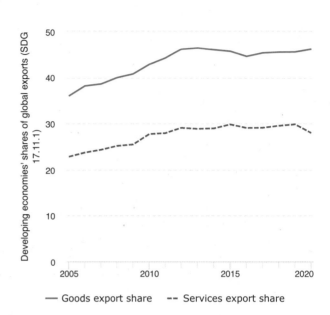

Developing economies' shares of global exports (SDG 17.11.1)

— Goods export share   -- Services export share

Import tariffs applied by developed countries to products from LDCs registered **almost no decline** since 2015 and amounted to about **1.13%** in 2019.

UNCTAD, ITC & WTO SDG indicator 17.12.1

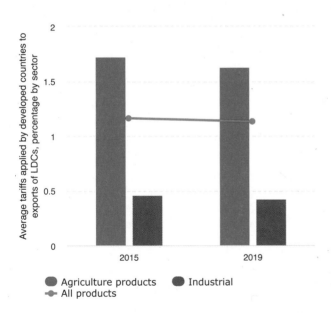

Average tariffs applied by developed countries to exports of LDCs, percentage by sector

● Agriculture products   ● Industrial
-●- All products

Share of zero tariffs applied to LDCs' exports up from **54%** in 2010 to **66%** in 2019.

UNCTAD, ITC & WTO SDG indicator 10.a.1

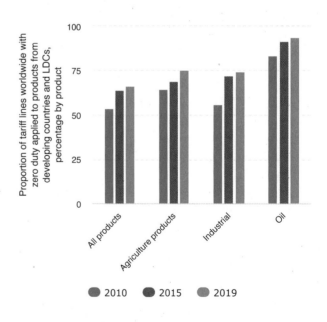

Proportion of tariff lines worldwide with zero duty applied to products from developing countries and LDCs, percentage by product

● 2010   ● 2015   ● 2019

Great progress in abolishing trade-distorting subsidies, with agricultural export subsidies reaching their **lowest levels ever in 2018**.

SDG indicator 2.b.1

Unprecedented **73% decline** in commercial flights from January to April 2020 due to COVID-19. Recovery in ensuing months, but still **30% below pre-pandemic levels**.

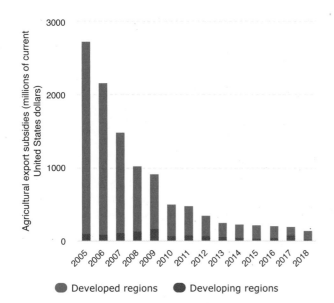

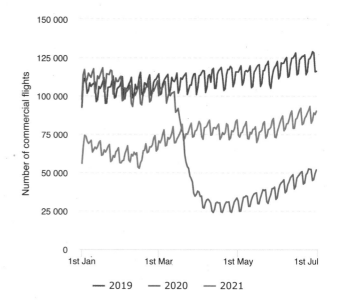

I. International trade in developing economies

SDG indicators

Target 17.11: Significantly increase the exports of developing countries, in particular with a view to doubling the least developed countries' share of global exports by 2020.
Indicator 17.11.1: Developing countries' and least developed countries' share of global exports (Tier I)

Target 8.9: By 2030, devise and implement policies to promote sustainable tourism that creates jobs and promotes local culture and products.
Indicator 8.9.1: Tourism direct GDP as a proportion of total GDP and in growth rate (Tier II)

The target of doubling the share of LDCs' exports in global exports by 2020 has now been missed

Trade is recognized as a key factor for the 2030 Agenda, including poverty reduction and economic growth (Tipping and Wolfe, 2016). SDG target 17.11 aims to significantly increase the exports of developing countries, and in particular with a view to doubling the LDCs' share in global exports by 2020. This target has now been missed. Even before the COVID-19 pandemic, the prospects of this target being met were implausible. As will be seen below, there has not been a substantial increase in the share of exports for LDCs or for developing economies in general since 2012. LDCs' exports have been hit hard after the outbreak of the pandemic, with the volume of exports declining by 16.9 per cent during the second quarter of 2020, year-on-year basis, the worst performance since the drop recorded in the second quarter of 2009 (16.3 per cent). Although LDCs' exports volume index decreased only by 2.9 per cent in the first quarter of 2021, recovery from the economic impact of the COVID-19 pandemic is not in sight yet.

The COVID-19 pandemic has disrupted global trade and poses additional challenges for developing economies and other vulnerable economies in fulfilling SDGs.

COVID-19 pandemic poses a significant challenge to the world trade

The pandemic could lead to a *"lost decade"* for sustainable development, states the most recent Financing for Sustainable Development Report (United Nations, 2021a). The crisis has temporarily slowed down the contribution of trade to the achievement of SDGs, such as poverty alleviation, food security, and decent jobs. Yet, reinforcing global trade is essential for a recovery for many developing countries and in particular for LDCs.

World merchandise exports rose by just over 50 per cent over ten years, from 2009 to 2019, reaching US$19 trillion in 2019. 2020 got off to a rocky start due to the COVID-19 pandemic. The value of global merchandise exports dropped to US$17.6 trillion in 2020, falling by 7.5 per cent compared to 2019. Many COVID-related confinement measures affected global trade especially during the second quarter of 2020, when the export volume index declined of 16.9 per cent, year-on-year (UNCTAD, 2021a).

In 2019, global services trade was valued at US$6.1 trillion, recording an increase of almost 70 per cent from ten years earlier (UNCTAD, 2021a), and in 2020, it fell down to almost US$5 trillion, a drop of almost 20 per cent from 2019.

Trade in goods and services is particularly important for SIDS and LDCs, for which its share in GDP accounts, on average, around 45 per cent and up to 30 per cent of GDP, respectively (UNCTAD, 2021a).

Small and vulnerable economies have been hit hard because of their dependence on trade as a driver of economic growth, their small domestic markets and low levels of diversification all of which increase their vulnerability to external shocks – as the global financial crisis demonstrated.

Loss of US$1.3 trillion in exports revenues from tourism in 2020

It is likely that resource-rich developing countries will also be affected by the strong reduction in commodity prices (see figure8 below), caused by reduced international demand for such goods and a drop in the production of transformed manufactured goods (see Towards sustainable industrialization and higher technologies) (UNIDO, 2021).

Global exports are still dominated by goods, with a 78 per cent share in 2020. Exports of goods accounted for 82 per cent of total exports in developing economies in 2019 and have become more diversified with manufactured goods representing the largest item of merchandise exports (70 per cent of total goods exports in 2019). LDCs, on the contrary, are highly dependent on exports of commodities, which represent more than 70 per cent of their merchandise exports. High dependence on commodity exports increases the vulnerability of LDCs to global shocks, such as the COVID-19 crisis.

However, similarly in non-commodity dependent LDCs, such as in Bangladesh, Cambodia and Haiti, that rely mostly on low-skilled and labor-intensive manufacturing exports, the economies are at risk of contracting sharply if global demand for manufacturing exports remains depressed in 2020 and beyond. In 2020, the spread of COVID-19 shadowed the world's economy: FDI fell by 42 per cent worldwide, and international tourist arrivals were 1 billion fewer – worst year in tourism history ever (UNWTO, 2021a).This is especially detrimental to developing economies that rely heavily on tourism for employment and revenue generation.

In the first half of 2020, global trade volumes in goods and services showed sharp declines. With such a painful economic slump, an estimated 88 million to 115 million more people were pushed into extreme poverty in 2020, with the total rising to as many as 150 million people by 2021; an equivalent of 255 million full-time jobs was lost (ILO, 2021). Though the post-COVID-19 era has yet to come, world trade has started its recovery since the third quarter of 2020. In the first quarter of 2021, global trade volume was 4.9 per cent higher than in the first quarter of 2020. After the 2009 and 2015 recessions, it took 9 and 13 quarters for international trade to recover, respectively. The pandemic-induced recession for world trade bounced back after only four quarters. However, this recovery remains fragile and uneven.

The socioeconomic fallout of the pandemic may be a lot more devastating for LDCs than the health shock. Limited export diversification has heightened their vulnerability to the impact of the pandemic on global trade. International tourism remains at a standstill almost one year into the crisis, with severe impacts on employment in many LDCs. Manufacturing exports have improved more recently, but it is still too early to assess the consistency of the rebound. Falling prices of commodities as oil and gas have had a lasting impact on several LDCs (United Nations, 2021b). Hence, LDCs registered an annual decline of 10.3 per cent in merchandise exports in 2020, much less than the 22 per cent decline in 2009 after the 2008 global financial crisis (UNCTAD, 2021a).

Trade openness of developing economies and LDCs

As shown in figure 1, developing and developed economies' trade openness indices are converging. LDCs' trade openness, i.e. the ratio of exports and imports to GDP, has been consistently lower than in other developing economies. The global dip of 2009, associated with the financial crisis, was followed by a short recovery in trade openness for developing economies, but since 2011 their trade openness has drifted downward, bouncing back only slightly after 2016. In 2019, their trade openness index plummeted from 60.5 to 56.5, which is the lowest point ever seen since 2005.

From 2014 to 2017, LDCs experienced a persistent decline in trade openness with the index dropping from 59 to 47.9 per cent (see figure 1). From 2018 to 2019, trade openness dropped from 54.1 to 51.6 per cent.

Figure 1. Trade openness index

(Percentage)

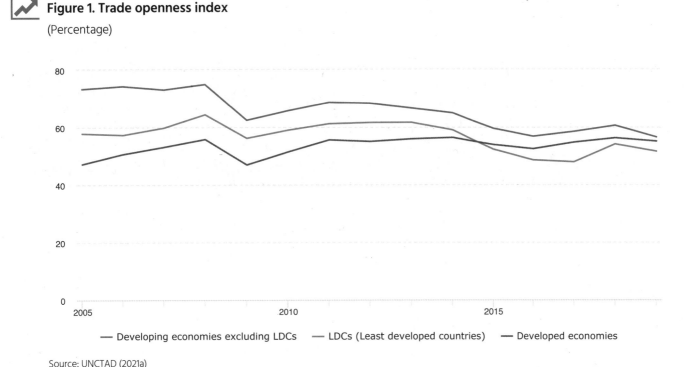

Source: UNCTAD (2021a)

Notes: This index measures the relative importance of international trade in goods relative to the domestic economic output of an economy. Exports are given equal weight to imports. Economy groups refers to the April 2020 classification as specified in UNCTAD (2021b)

Current drift of trade in developing economies

After the 2008 global financial crisis and the more recent trade downturn in 2014-2016, developing economies have seen a strong recovery since 2017. This was offset by the economic impact of the pandemic in 2020. Goods trade in developing countries decreased at an annual rate of 2.4 per cent in 2019 and by 6.1 per cent in 2020 (figure 2). Trade in services grew by 3.2 per cent in 2019 and dropped by 24.8 per cent in 2020.

In 2019, total exports of goods and services amounted to US$10.4 trillion in developing economies and only US$9.4 trillion in 2020. Thus, in 2020, exports of goods and services decreased to US$8.0 trillion and US$1.4 trillion, respectively.

In 2020, developing economies' trade fell by 9.5 per cent compared to a 7.5 per cent decline globally as the pandemic disrupted economic activity around the world. The disruptions will have profound implications for the most vulnerable economies, including developing economies and LDCs. However, some signs of recovery can be observed since the start of 2021. Global merchandise trade values and volumes and global services trade values look set to continue their recovery into the second quarter of 2021 after the sharp contractions experienced in the first half of 2020. In the second quarter of 2021, services trade is nowcast to continue to grow by 7.4 per cent from the previous quarter, compared with 11.6 and 4.7 per cent for merchandise trade values and volumes, respectively. (UNCTAD, 2021d).

 Figure 2. Trends of goods and services trade in developing economies
(Millions of United States dollars)

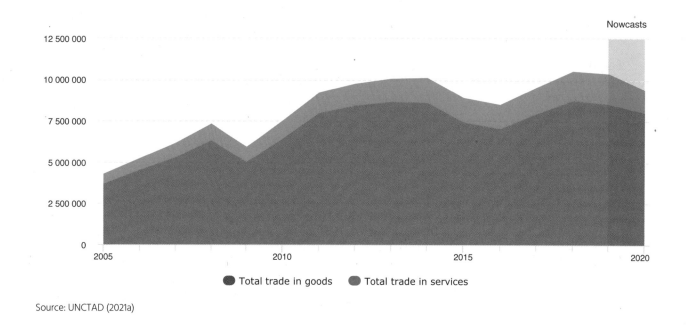

Source: UNCTAD (2021a)

Developing countries' performance with respect to SDG 17.11.1

The evaluation of progress towards SDG target 17.11, to significantly increase the exports of developing countries, and to double the LDCs' share of global exports by 2020, requires a choice of a baseline year. According to the IAEG-SDGs (United Nations, 2019), the default baseline year for each indicator should be 2015. However, some exceptions may be necessary to allow a longer review of trends.

Five years is hardly enough time to double the LDCs' share of global exports. Therefore, for SDG 17.11.1, an earlier baseline year is arguably more appropriate. Yet, whatever the baseline is for the past 20 years, developing countries' share of global exports has not increased significantly, nor has LDCs' share doubled. However, at a country level, performances differ and will vary depending on the chosen baseline year (see map 1). The baseline selected for MDGs, for instance, was 1990 – ten years before their adoption in 2000. This gave time for countries to achieve progress and allowed for a more ambitious agenda. If a similar approach was applied to the SDGs, a comparable baseline (ten years prior to adoption) would be 2005.

Table 1. Evolution of LDCs' and developing economies' share of global trade

(Different baselines scenario, in percentage)

Group of economies	Measure	Alternative baselines Share of global trade (percentage)				2020 Change from baseline (percentage points)		
		2005	2010	2015	2020	2005-2020	2010-2020	2015-2020
LDCs	Service exports	0.44	0.60	0.74	0.63	0.18	0.02	-0.11
	Goods exports	0.76	1.03	0.97	1.03	0.27	0.00	0.06
	Total exports	0.69	0.94	0.92	0.94	0.25	0.00	0.02
Developing economies	Service exports	22.79	27.71	29.79	27.95	5.17	0.24	-1.83
	Goods exports	35.97	42.84	45.68	46.16	10.19	3.32	0.47
	Total exports	33.22	39.66	41.94	42.09	8.87	2.44	0.15

Source: UNCTAD (2021a).

Another measurement issue to consider is the composition of LDCs. Several LDCs are likely to graduate from this status in the coming years. Vanuatu is now graduated from LDCs and according to the UNDESA (2021), several others will follow after the end of the target year, 2020. MacFeely (2020) has discussed the implications of the changing group composition for assessing progress towards the SDG target. Will the rates of change be calculated using the original composition of LDCs or developing economies at the baseline (say 2010/2011 or 2015), or the group as it is composed in 2020? Some soon-to-graduate countries have only a marginal contribution to the group performance, and whether they are included or not will have little impact, whereas the weight of some other countries is considerable, like that of Bangladesh (see map 1) and will have a significant impact on the performance of the group as a whole. Of course, the COVID-19 pandemic impacts are likely to delay the achievement to the target even further.

For the reasons outlined above, 2010 has been selected as a baseline for the scenario discussed in this chapter. Data for additional years are available also. Map 1 shows developing countries' share of global exports of goods and services by country.

Map 1.a Developing countries' share of global exports of goods

(Percentage of total trade)

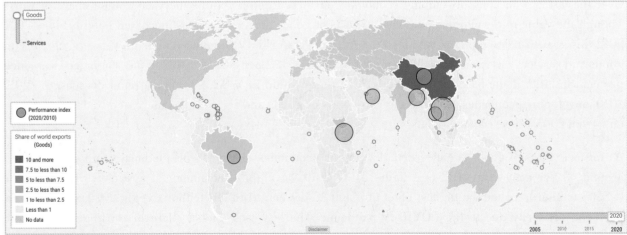

Source: UNCTAD (2021a).

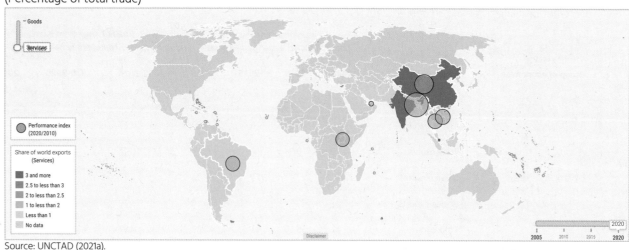

Map 1.b. Developing countries' share of global exports of services

(Percentage of total trade)

Source: UNCTAD (2021a).

Several countries doubled their share of global trade from 2010 to 2020. Viet Nam's share of world exports of goods grew from 0.47 per cent in 2010 to 1.6 per cent in 2020. Its share of world exports of services also grew from 0.19 per cent to 0.45 per cent. Thailand almost doubled its share of world services exports (from 0.87 to 1.34 per cent), and the United Arab Emirates quadrupled their share of services exports (from 0.3 to 1.2 per cent). Bangladesh almost doubled their share of total services exports as well as total goods exports (from 0.13 to 0.20 per cent for goods and from 0.06 to 0.1 for services). However, the pandemic has ceased

By 2019, **Vietnam** had **doubled** their share of world **goods exports** and **tripled** their share of world **services exports** from 2010

the increasing trends. In 2020, Viet Nam's and Thailand's shares of world service exports are estimated to fall to 0.14 per cent and 0.629 per cent. On the contrary, Bangladesh's share in world's services exports is likely to rise to approximately 0.127 per cent, though its share in world's merchandise exports has decreased slightly to 0.19 per cent.

Developing economies struggle to keep pace with world exports

Over the last two decades, developing economies have recorded a notable increase in their share of world trade. Though the value of developing countries' exports of goods and services has increased notably since 2000, since 2012 this growth has no longer outpaced the developed world. Developing countries' share of global exports of goods and services has risen from 29.7 per cent in 2000 to 42.2 per cent in 2012 but has stagnated ever since to 41.5 per cent in 2019. If the baseline selected is 2015, there would be a 0.2 percentage point decrease by 2019. From 2010, developing economies' share of global exports of goods and services has increased by 1.8 percentage points and, from 2005, 7.6 percentage points.

As far as exports of goods is concerned, developing economies' share in world exports of goods has plateaued at around 45 per cent since 2012 (see figure 3). In 2019, developing economies' share of world services exports (US$6.1 trillion) reached the highest point of about 30 per cent (US$1.83 trillion), yet in 2020, this figure fell to 28 per cent, primarily due to the COVID-19 pandemic. The highest regional share of world services exports was recorded by developing Asia and Oceania at more than 24 per cent in 2019. The top three services exporters are China (4.6 per cent), India (3.4 per cent) and Singapore (3.5 per cent). They account for more than 40 per cent of developing economies' services exports.

Figure 3. Developing economies' shares of global exports (SDG 17.11.1) of goods and services

(Percentage)

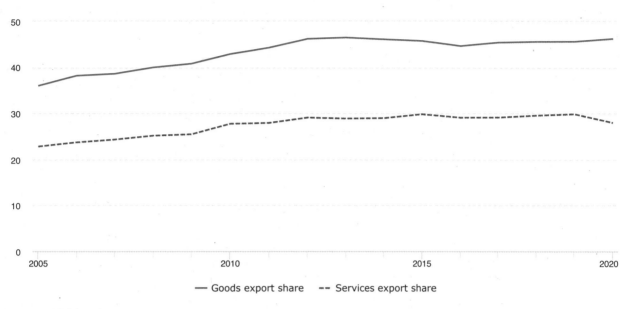

Goods export share   ‑‑ Services export share

Source: UNCTAD (2021a).
Note: Statistics on trade in services are preliminary, annual estimates based on the most recent quarterly figures (BPM6). Statistics on trade in goods are estimates based on Comtrade, international and national sources.

LDCs are a small player in world trade with a 0.96 per cent share of global goods and services exports in 2020. The 2030 Agenda sets a target to double LDCs' share in global exports by 2020. LDCs' share of global exports of goods and services was 0.92 per cent in 2010, slightly below the 2020 level. Taking 2005 as the base, their share in global exports of goods and services increased by 0.3 percentage points from 0.66 per cent to 0.96 in 2019. LDCs have a long way to go before doubling their share, and the target was not reached by 2020.

In 2020, the value of merchandise exports from LDCs was US\$172.6 billion, accounting for less than one per cent of world exports (0.98 per cent), signaling the failure of the 2020 target in doubling LDCs' merchandise exports. Their share in world merchandise exports almost doubled from 0.54 per cent in 2000 (US\$35 billion) to over one per cent in 2011-2013 (see figure 4). Since then, this trend has reversed slightly. LDCs' share of global services exports has increased gradually to reach 0.80 per cent by 2019, but dropping again to 0.63 per cent in 2020.

Figure 4. LDCs' share of global exports (SDG 17.11.1) of goods and services

(Percentage)

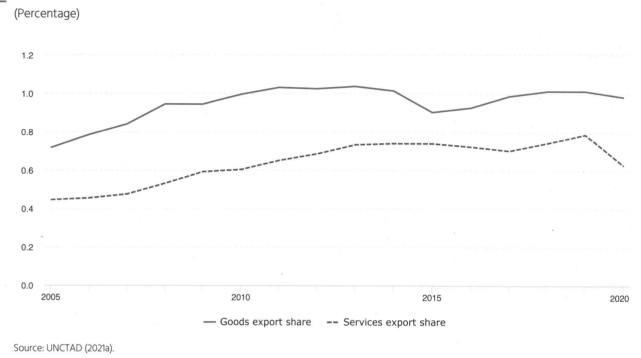

Goods export share   -- Services export share

Source: UNCTAD (2021a).

The key driver of export growth over this period (2000-2019) was the massive rise in the price of fuels, ores and metals, reflecting high demand in developing countries, most notably China. With 2005 taken as the baseline, the growth is more notable, 0.3 percentage points from 0.5 per cent to 0.8 in 2019 (UNCTAD, 2016b). However, in 2020, the massive fall in international trade negatively affected the price of commodities. The decline of the UNCTAD Commodity Price Index in 2020 in the second quarter of 2020 was comparable to the declines experienced in 2015 and 2016 When fuels are excluded, year-on-year changes are much more muted (UNCTAD, 2021c).

China, EU28 and the United States of America are the top trading partners of LDCs

In 2019, developing economies shipped most of their exports to the United States of America (US$1. trillion), China (US$1.1 trillion) and other Asian economies. The value of merchandise exports of developing countries to EU28 in 2019 amounted to almost US$1.3 trillion. For LDCs, the top export destinations in 2019 were EU28 (US$36.4 billion), China (US$679.8 million) and the United States of America (US$15.2 million).

By 2019, LDCs in Africa and Haiti delivered goods worth US$29.9 billion to China, more than to any other economy in the world (see figure 5). LDC exports in Asia were oriented towards China and the United States of America in 2018 and 2019. The importance of the European Union as a trading partner for LDCs in Asia has increased significantly since the turn of the century, with exports reaching US$53.4 billion in 2019. Intra-regional trade is also high for LDCs from East Asia and the Pacific, and low but rising for LDCs from most other regions.

As merchandise exports of LDCs are concentrated in a few markets, including those worst affected by the COVID-19 health crisis, which makes them vulnerable to decline in demand in these countries. For example, in 2019, Angola exported around 57.6 per cent of its merchandise to China, Benin around 41 per cent to India, Burkina Faso around 54 per cent to Switzerland, Haiti around 82 per cent to the United States of America and Rwanda around 65 per cent to the United Arab Emirates (UNCTAD, 2021b).

Figure 5. Top 5 partners for LDCs in merchandise exports
(Ranked by 2019, US$ billions)

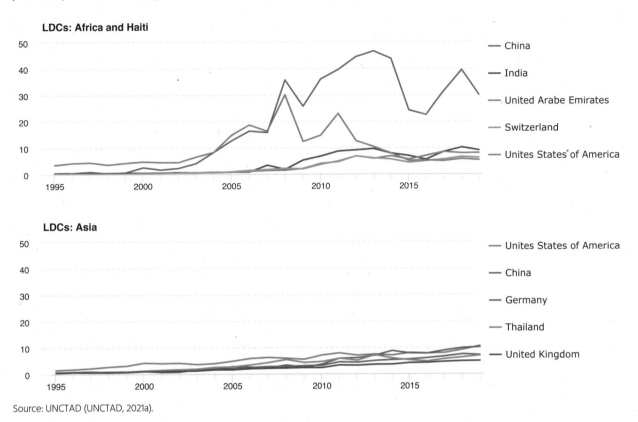

LDCs: Africa and Haiti

— China
— India
— United Arabe Emirates
— Switzerland
— Unites States of America

LDCs: Asia

— Unites States of America
— China
— Germany
— Thailand
— United Kingdom

Source: UNCTAD (UNCTAD, 2021a).

Finally, it's worth noting that the current health crisis has also challenged developing economies to boost their intra-regional trade and strengthen international trade agreements to harmonize their trade-related regulations, customs controls, and reduce both tariff and non-tariff barriers (see New protectionism versus inclusive trade).

Developing economies' trade hit by the downswing of the Chinese economy

The coronavirus pandemic has instigated a global economic downturn the likes of which the world has not experienced since the Great Depression. GDP in the world's second largest economy – China, fell by 6.8 per cent year-on-year in January-March 2020 (WEF, 2020). In the first quarter of 2020, China's exports dropped in volume terms by 11 per cent, year-on-year, but have been recovering since the third quarter of 2020. In the first quarter of 2021, China's exports grew by 38.8 per cent from the low first quarter of 2020 (UNCTAD, 2021b). The economic consequences of the economic downturn in China were quickly felt in other economies.

China is a major player in international trade as a manufacturer and exporter of consumer products, and as a key supplier of intermediate inputs for manufacturing companies globally. Today about 20 per cent of global trade in manufactured intermediate products originates in China (up from 4 per cent in 2002). UNCTAD (2020) has analysed the UN Comtrade dataset for about 200 countries and 13 manufacturing sectors to measure each country's and industry's integration with the Chinese economy using the GLI of intra-industry trade.

According to this analysis, the economic downturn in China will lead to disruptions in GVCs and diverse spill-over effects across economic sectors and countries. The crisis may impact the supply of critical parts from Chinese producers, affecting economic output and trade in any country depending on their dependency of the Chinese economy. These impacts may spread faster than expected due to the common strategy of limited inventories and just-in-time production.

While Asian developing economies occupy the top of the list of countries most directly linked to China through GVCs, the effects would also be felt in Mexico (US$1.3 billion), Turkey (US$0.4 billion) and Brazil (US$0.08 billion). In Mexico and Brazil, the automotive industry is most directly linked with Chinese value chains, while in Turkey the sector taking the brunt of the Chinese downturn would be textiles and apparel. Considering the wide-ranging impacts, the quick recovery of the Chinese trade brought some good news.

LDCs' export product mix becoming more diverse

The concentration of LDCs' exports, as measured by the Herfindahl-Hirschman Index[1], increased from 2001 to 2008. Since then concentration has gradually declined, converging with patterns typical of developing economies (see figure 6). Developing economies excluding LDCs have followed a similar trend. In other words, their export mix has become more diverse with a slight sustained set-back from 2016 to 2018 and a continued diversification in 2019.

South Sudan, Botswana, Angola and Guinea-Bissau are the four developing African countries with the highest concentration index, approaching or even exceeding an index value of 0.9 in 2019, which indicates that their trades are concentrated on a very few products. South Sudan and Angola are highly dependent on trade in petroleum, Botswana on precious stones, and Guinea-Bissau on fruits and nuts.[2] In 2019, LDCs as a group recorded an average index of 0.21. Yemen had a relatively high export concentration index in 2019 (0.42), the highest index among Asian LDCs (UNCTAD, 2021a). Of developing economies, the product mix of exports is most concentrated in African countries. The export mix is more varied in the developing economies of America, with Guatemala, Mexico and Panama recorded the lowest concentration index in 2019, and Asia, where Turkey, Thailand and China are the top three most diversified countries.

It is worth mentioning that diversifying the strategic economic sectors of LDCs, such as food and health sectors, and empowering both productions and services, such as banking, retailing, and public services with high-level of digitization, represent possibilities for these countries to build more resilient and sustainable economies (World Bank, 2020).

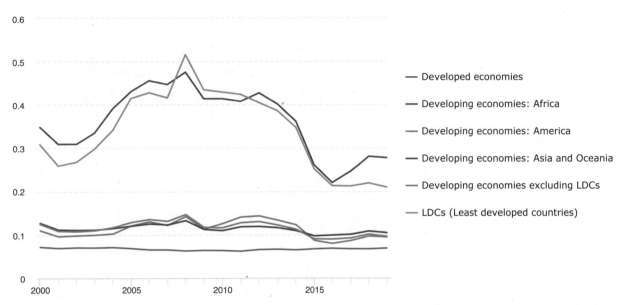

Figure 6. Product concentration index of exports in LDCs and developing economies

(Percentage)

Legend:
— Developed economies
— Developing economies: Africa
— Developing economies: America
— Developing economies: Asia and Oceania
— Developing economies excluding LDCs
— LDCs (Least developed countries)

Source: UNCTAD (2021a).
Notes: An index value closer to one indicates that a country's exports or imports are highly concentrated in a few products. On the contrary, values closer to zero reflect a more homogeneous distribution of exports or imports among a series of products.

The structure of exports by product group has changed significantly in LDCs and developing economies over the last ten years (see figure 7). In 2019, manufactured goods accounted for 36.7 per cent of total exports in LDCs – a notable increase from 2009 (23.1 per cent). However, only six LDCs—Bangladesh, Cambodia, Haiti, the Gambia, Nepal and Lesotho—received more than 50 per cent of their export revenue from exporting manufactured goods in 2018. Fuels formed the second largest product group in 2019 (26 per cent), while in 2009 they accounted for over half of the exports. The share of ores, metals, precious stones and non-monetary gold increased from 12 per cent to 20.1 per cent in the ten years from 2009 to 2019. The proportion of food items in exports also increased from 10.2 to 13.7 per cent during the same period.

Figure 7. Export structure by product group in LDCs and developing countries

(Percentage)

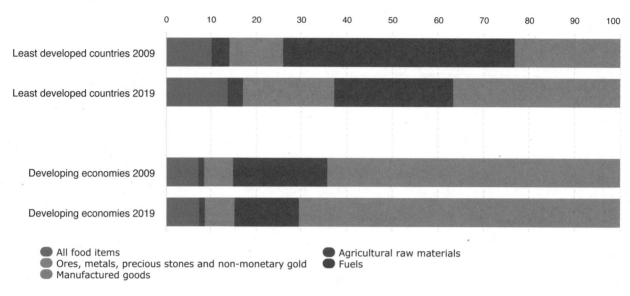

Source: UNCTAD (2021a).

Notes: For the composition of product groups please refer to UNCTAD (2021e).

In 2019, manufactured goods accounted for about 70 per cent of total merchandise exports from developing economies – almost as much as from developed economies. The share of fuels has reduced from 21 per cent in 2009 to 14.4 per cent in 2019. Food continues to be strongly represented in the exports of some economies in South America and Eastern Africa in particular, and ores, metals, precious stones and non-monetary gold in the exports of several Southern and Western African and Central Asian economies.

Figure 8. Commodities price index and LDC's total exports

(Percentage)

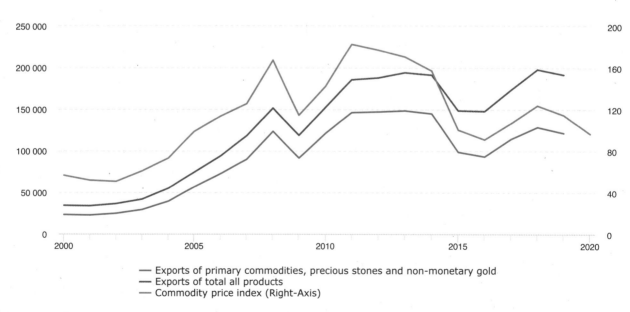

Source: UNCTAD (2021a).

Notes: Total all products refer to (SITC 0 to 8 + 961 + 971). Primary commodities, precious stones and non-monetary gold refer to (SITC 0 + 1 + 2 + 3 + 4 + 68 + 667 + 971).

LDCs are oriented towards commodity exports, accounting for more than 63 per cent of their goods exports. The periods when LDCs' exports declined more strongly than world exports (2008-2009 and 2014-2016) coincided with falls in commodity prices.

During the period between 2000 and 2020, LDCs recorded a first peak of exports in 2008 with more than US$151 billion followed by a strong decrease caused by the financial crisis in 2008-2009. The second peak was recorded in 2013 with almost US$194 billion. Thus, the global financial crisis of 2008 did not cause sustained declines (even though the commodity prices was connected with the financial crisis). Nevertheless, LDCs' exports seem to follow commodity price index trends (see figure 8). The decline in commodity prices has caused a more persistent decrease since 2014. The current situation with the COVID-19 pandemic should play out similarly, as the increase of commodity price index (56.1 in in March 2021) (UNCTAD, 2021d) will impact LDCs' exports. LDCs will need to diversify their exports to reduce their exposure to such crises.

Services exports had been increasing across economies

Before services were severely affected by the COVID-19 pandemic, the growth of services exports was a general trend across all economic regions, but mainly benefiting developed economies. In 2019, this group still accounted for 69.7 per cent of all traded services. With US$1.86 trillion worth of services exported in 2019, developing economies took only 30 per cent of the global services market. LDCs' share amounted to almost 0.81 per cent of total services exports.

2019 recorded an increase of 23 per cent in exports of services compared 2015 (UNCTAD, 2021a). This trend might be explained by factors, such as the increasing commercialization of intangibles, the larger role of services in global value chains and the gradual liberalization of this sector.

Among broad service categories, travel has the most prominent role in developing economies' exports. At more than US$583 billion, it accounted for 31.4 per cent of the services supplied internationally by developing economies. Transport is also an important export sector for the developing world, worth US$374 billion in 2019. Grouping together other services, including insurance and financial services, and business and intellectual-property-related services account for US$825.0 billion of developing economies' exports.

Smaller in dollar value than transport and travel, but linked to travel, – exports of personal, cultural and recreational services have been the most dynamic sector in LDCs' services exports. They grew, on average, by over 13 per cent annually between 2010 and 2020. In the same period, notable annual average increases were recorded for charges for the use of intellectual property, transport and travel services (11.5 per cent, 9.7 per cent, and 6.8 per cent, respectively). Of the broad services items (Other service sector) which accounts for almost 45 per cent of the total traded services in the region in 2020, only construction services saw a downturn in the same period (-4.6 per cent).

Figure 9. Annual average growth of services exports in LDCs, by service category, 2010-2020
(Percentage)

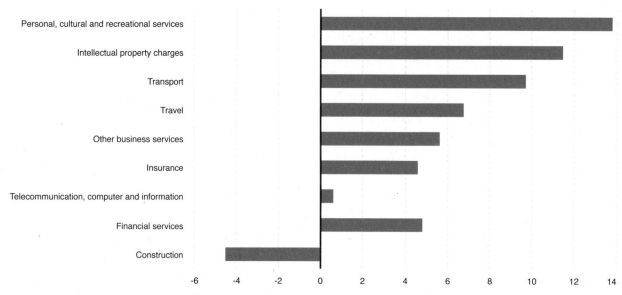

Source: UNCTAD (2021a).

Travel is the only type of service export where LDCs and other developing economies have a revealed comparative advantage[3]. The revealed comparative advantage of travel services for LDCs reached 1.75 in 2019 and was 1.3 for other developing economies (see figure 11). The value is also slightly greater than 1.34 for LDCs' transport services.

Figure 10. Revealed comparative advantage in service exports, 2019
(Proportion)

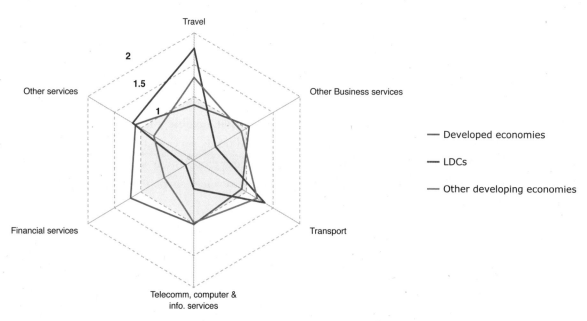

Source: UNCTAD calculations based on data from UNCTAD (2021a).
Notes: The revealed comparative advantage is measured as the proportion of a country group's exports by service category, divided by the proportion of world exports in each category. A country or region is considered to have a revealed comparative advantage for a product or sector if the index is greater than one.

Exports of services requiring proximity worst hit in the time of COVID-19

There are four different modes of supply for traded across borders: (mode 1) cross-border trade mainly for services transacted via the internet; (mode 2) consumption abroad covering mainly health and education service for foreigners; (mode 3) commercial presence which is specific to locally-established entities like hotels, banks and construction; and finally (mode 4) movement of natural persons which involve for example foreign IT consultants or health workers[4].

Figure 11 shows the distribution of global service trade by mode of supply. The data refer to 2017 but an indication about the mode of supply of services worldwide. More than US$10 billion are exported via mode 1 and 3. Naturally, a big part of services provided by mode 1 continue to be exported in the time of COVID-19, but these services, including telecommunications, computer and information services account for less than 10 per cent of total service exports of developing countries.

The three other modes require proximity between importers and exporters. Thus, the related service sectors will be severely affected and most likely will take longer to recover.

As mentioned above, travel and transport are key sectors in driving developing countries' service exports, accounting for more than 50 per cent of total service trade of the group. Those sectors are delivered mainly via mode 2, 3 and 4 and covering services such as education, travel, tourism and associated hotels, and restaurant services, as well as air passenger transport services and construction and other business services that require the movement of skilled and unskilled professionals across borders.

Figure 11. Composition of global services trade by modes of supply, 2017

(US$ billions)

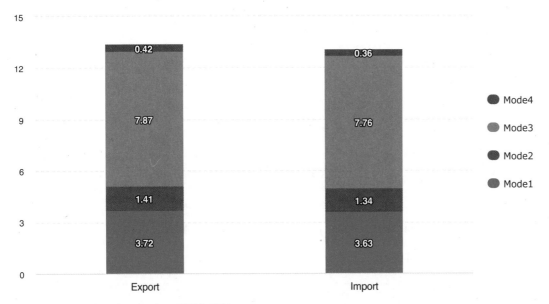

UNCTAD calculations based on data from WTO (2020b).

Travel and transport restrictions due to COVID-19 are likely to negatively affect the trade in services in 2020. Possible scenarios point to declines of 60 per cent to 80 per cent in international tourist arrivals in 2020. According to CCSA (2020), countries with the highest number of reported cases of COVID-19 (see In focus: COVID-19) account for about 55 and 68 per cent of global inbound and outbound tourism expenditure, respectively. The Joint Report (CCSA, 2020) warns that the effect of the crisis will spill out and be significantly more devastating for countries heavily dependent on tourism.

Tourism makes a significant contribution to sustainable development

One of the most important contributors to international trade in services is tourism. In addition to the direct service itself, tourism has large multiplier effects that extend to the domestic economy. It promotes growth and employment in a multitude of economic sectors, such as transportation, hotels and restaurants, retail trade, financial services and cultural services. It also attracts domestic and foreign investment and promotes the development of the private sector. For this reason, UNCTAD has recognized that touristic services, if properly harnessed, can become an important engine for inclusive and sustainable economic growth in developing countries (UNCTAD, 2017).

For many developing countries, tourism is one of the most important exports and an essential source of revenue. Figure 12 shows that, on average, tourism contributes to the economy at comparable rates in developing, developed and transition economies. However, for LDCs and especially SIDS, this sector is responsible for a larger share of total economic activity. During 2017-2019, tourism accounted for, on average, 12 per cent of SIDS' GDP. Moreover, the contribution of tourism to the economy seems to be increasing over time.

Figure 12. Direct contribution of tourism to GDP by country group, average
(Percentage of total GDP)

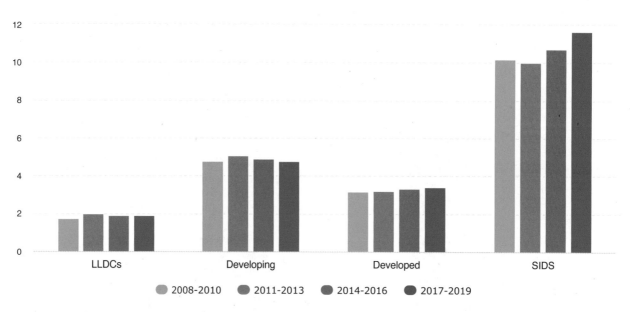

Source: UNCTAD calculations from UNWTO (2021b)
Note: Averages include only countries with available data. Data cover approximately 40 per cent of SIDS' total GDP, and about 50 per cent of LLDCs' total GDP. The coverage is over 90 per cent for developing economies and 100 per cent for developed economies.

As mentioned above, tourism has a multiplier effect on the domestic economy through several channels. One of these, depicted on map 2, is through its direct contribution to employment creation. In addition to SIDS, many countries in all geographic regions, including South-East Asia (Cambodia, Philippines), North Africa (Tunisia, Morocco), the Caucasus (Georgia), the Americas (Belize, Uruguay, Mexico), Europe (Croatia, Montenegro, Iceland, Greece) and Oceania (New Zealand), benefit greatly from the employment generated across the tourism industries. Overall, current estimates place tourism's direct contribution to worldwide GDP at 3.3 per cent and to global employment at 3.9 per cent (World Travel & Tourism Council data gateway, 2021)[5].

🌎 Map 2. Direct tourism contribution to employment, 2019

(Percentage of global employment)

Source: UNWTO (2021b).

Despite its increasing economic weight, touristic service supply is still relatively concentrated. Around 43 per cent of all international tourists were still travelling to European countries in 2019. As illustrated in figure 14, other regions of the world received a comparatively small share of international tourist arrivals. This is the case of Oceania, Central Asia, Sub-Saharan Africa and Latin America and the Caribbean, regions where many developing economies are located, including many LDCs. In many regions of the world, tourism still has unexploited potential as a means of development.

(Percentage)

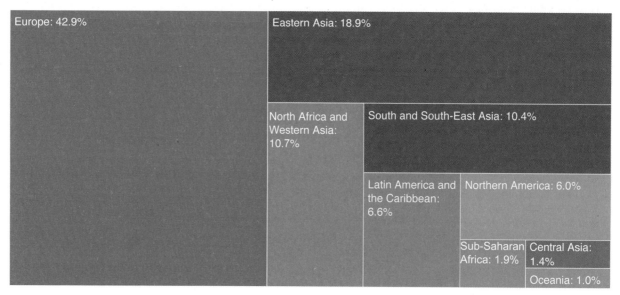

Source: UNCTAD calculations based on data from UNWTO (UNWTO, 2021b).

However, this is gradually changing. Worldwide tourist arrivals increased by almost 50 per cent between 2010 and 2018. While tourists travelling to Europe and Northern America increased by only 41 and 32 per cent, respectively, over the same period they increased by 93 per cent in South and South-East Asia and by a remarkable 243 per cent in Central Asia. The only developing region that did not benefit from this dynamism in tourism was Sub-Saharan Africa, where the number of tourists fell by nine per cent over the period.

Tourism remains vulnerable to global and regional risks

SDG target 8.9 aims to develop and implement policies to promote sustainable tourism that will result in more jobs and support of local cultures and products. However, even if tourism can bring substantial revenues and economic opportunities, it can also bring challenges for sustainable development. For example, tourism can help finance the preservation of historical and environmental treasures, but if poorly managed could also have reverse effects (UNCTAD, 2016b). Tourists also directly contribute to greenhouse gas emissions and climate change in many ways: through transportation by air, rail, road and sea, and by consumption of goods and services whose production is intensive in energy, water or other resources.

Tourism is a labour-intensive sector that could provide employment for a large share of people, including women and other underrepresented groups. It is also a sector with a high concentration of small and medium enterprises, self-employment and family businesses. For these segments, tourism-related economic activity could provide sustained livelihood opportunities and paths towards poverty reduction for women and local communities in developing countries (UNWTO and ILO, 2014).

100 to 120 million direct tourism jobs at risk due to COVID-19

(UNWTO, 2020)

However, as revealed by the precipitous decline in international travel and tourism in the aftermath of the COVID-19 outbreak, this is a pro-cyclical sector with high elasticity to global and regional economic trends. In addition, it is very sensitive to perceived security, health and environmental risks. Figure 14 shows the daily evolution of commercial flights during the first half of 2021 in comparison with 2019 and 2020. COVID-19 pandemic severely hit the global commercial aviation because of lockdowns and bans restricting flights across the globe. As of the end of June 2021, the number of commercial flights worldwide was down by 74 per cent compared to the same period of 2019. However, commercial flights record a steady recovery in recent months with an average positive growth of 10 per cent in June 2021 compared to the previous month.

Indeed, recent figures already show a catastrophic year for the sector. Tourist arrivals to Thailand fell by 52 per cent in the first four months of 2020, compared to the same period in 2019 (UNCTAD calculations based on data from (Refinitiv, 2021). Over the same period, the Republic of Korea recorded a fall of 62 per cent in the number of visitor arrivals (Korea Tourism Organization, 2020).

These figures show that, while international tourism could provide substantial opportunities for many developing economies, it remains exposed to high global and regional volatility.

Figure 14. Worldwide number of commercial flights, 2019-2021

(Number of flights)

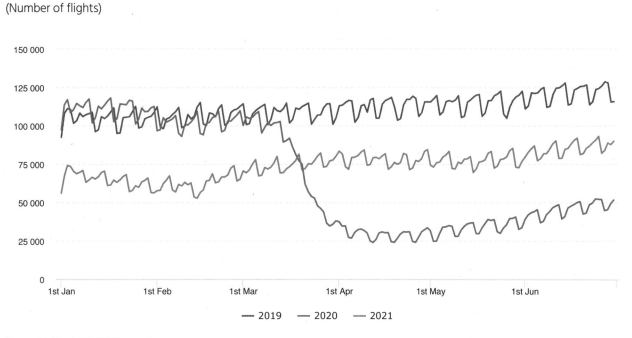

Source: Flightradar24 (2020)

Considering the vulnerabilities of developing economies and especially LDCs exposed by the COVID-19 crisis and the longer-term implications, international support will be essential not only for responding to immediate recovery needs, but also for accelerating structural transformation, trade support and assistance and development of resilience to external shocks.

Notes

1. The Herfindahl-Hirschman Index (HHI) is a measure of market concentration. A higher index value indicates a more concentrated export structure.
2. Products classification refers to three-digit level of SITC Revision 3.
3. The revealed comparative advantage is measured as the proportion of a country group's exports by service category, divided by the proportion of world exports in each category.

4. Examples of the four Modes of Supply (from the perspective of an "importing" country A) (WTO, 2020c)

- Mode 1: Cross-border
  A user in country A receives services from abroad through its telecommunications or postal infrastructure. Such supplies may include consultancy or market research reports, tele-medical advice, distance training, or architectural drawings.

- Mode 2: Consumption abroad
  Nationals of A have moved abroad as tourists, students, or patients to consume the respective services.

- Mode 3: Commercial presence
  The service is provided within A by a locally-established affiliate, subsidiary, or representative office of a foreign-owned and – controlled company (bank, hotel group, construction company, etc.).

- Mode 4: Movement of natural persons
  A foreign national provides a service within A as an independent supplier (e.g., consultant, health worker) or employee of a service supplier (e.g. consultancy firm, hospital, construction company).

5. WTTC also calculates that the total contribution of tourism to the economy. This includes, in addition to the direct impacts, the indirect contribution (tourism-related investment spending, government collective spending and domestic supply chain purchases of goods and services) plus the induced contribution (spending of those directly and indirectly employed by the tourism sector). According to these estimates, the total contribution of tourism is 10.4 per cent of GDP and 9.8 per cent of employment. For details on the methodology of these estimates, see WTTC and Oxford Economics (2018).

6. A country is considered to be export-commodity-dependent when more than 60 per cent of its total merchandise exports are composed of commodities.

References

- CCSA (2020). How COVID-19 is changing the world: A statistical perspective. Available at https://unstats.un.org/unsd/ccsa/documents/covid19-report-ccsa.pdf (accessed 8 June 2020).

- Doshi P (2011). The elusive definition of pandemic influenza. Bulletin of the World Health Organisation. *WHO Bulletin*. 89(7):532–538.

- ILO (2021). ILO Monitor: COVID-19 and the world of work. Seventh edition. Updated estimates and analysis. Available at https://www.ilo.org/wcmsp5/groups/public/@dgreports/@dcomm/documents/briefingnote/wcms_767028.pdf (accessed 29 March 2021).

- Korea Tourism Organization (2020). Monthly statistics of tourism. Available at https://kto.visitkorea.or.kr/eng/tourismStatics/keyFacts/KoreaMonthlyStatistics/eng/inout/inout.kto (accessed 6 April 2020).

- MacFeely S (2020). Measuring the Sustainable Development Goal Indicators: An Unprecedented Statistical Challenge. *Journal of Official Statistics*. 361–378.

- Refinitiv (2021). Eikon. (accessed 1 June 2021).

- Tipping A and Wolfe R (2016). Trade in Transforming Our World: Options for Follow-Up and Review of the Trade-Related Elements of the 2030 Agenda for Sustainable Development.

- UN DESA (2021). Graduation from the LDC category. Available at https://www.un.org/development/desa/dpad/least-developed-country-category/ldc-graduation.html (accessed 30 June 2021).

- UNCTAD (2016a). *World Investment Report 2016: Investor Nationality: Policy Challenges*. United Nations publication. Sales No. E.16.II.D.4. Geneva.

- UNCTAD (2016b). Development and globalization: Facts and figures 2016. Available at https://stats.unctad.org/Dgff2016/ (accessed 6 April 2020).

- UNCTAD (2018). Indicators explained #1: Export Market Concentration Index. UNCTAD/STAT/IE/2018/1 June. Available at https://unctadstat.unctad.org/EN/IndicatorsExplained.html (accessed 18 June 2020).

- UNCTAD (2020). Coronavirus outbreak has cost global value chains $50 billion in exports. Available at https://unctad.org/en/pages/newsdetails.aspx?OriginalVersionID=2297 (accessed 30 June 2021).

- UNCTAD (2021a). UNCTADStat. Available at https://unctadstat.unctad.org/EN/Index.html (accessed 21 April 2021).

- UNCTAD (2021b). UNCTADStat: Classifications. Available at https://unctadstat.unctad.org/EN/Classifications.html (accessed 10 June 2021).

- UNCTAD (2021c). Commodity Price Bulletin - March 2021. (accessed 30 June 2021).

- UNCTAD (2021d). Global merchandise and services trade nowcast. (accessed 30 June 2021).

- UNCTAD (2021e). UNCTAD product groups and composition (SITC Rev. 3) June. Available at https://unctadstat.unctad.org/EN/Classifications.html.

- UNIDO (2021). Available at http://stat.unido.org (accessed 2 June 2021).

- United Nations (2019). Sustainable Development Goals Progress Chart 2019. Available at https://unstats.un.org/sdgs/report/2019/progress-chart.pdf (accessed 30 June 2021).

- United Nations (2021a). *Financing for Sustainable Development Report 2021: Inter-Agency Task Force.* United Nations. S.l.

- United Nations (2021b). Comprehensive Study on the Impact of COVID-19 on the Least Developed Country Category. Committee for Development Policy.

- UNWTO (2021a). 2020: Worst year in tourism history with 1 billion fewer international arrivals. Available at https://www.unwto.org/news/2020-worst-year-in-tourism-history-with-1-billion-fewer-international-arrivals (accessed 18 June 2021).

- UNWTO (2021b). UNWTO database. Available at https://www.unwto.org/tourism-statistics-data (accessed 30 June 2021).

- UNWTO and ILO (2014). *Measuring Employment in the Tourism Industries: Guide with Best Practices.* Madrid and Geneva.

- WEF (2020). Embracing the New Age of Materiality: Harnessing the Pace of Change in ESG. Available at https://www.weforum.org/whitepapers/embracing-the-new-age-of-materiality-harnessing-the-pace-of-change-in-esg/ (accessed 17 June 2021).

- WHO (2020). Q&A on coronaviruses (COVID-19). Available at https://www.who.int/emergencies/diseases/novel-coronavirus-2019/question-and-answers-hub/q-a-detail/q-a-coronaviruses (accessed 11 May 2020).

- World Bank (2020). How will COVID-19 impact Africa's trade and market opportunities? Available at https://blogs.worldbank.org/africacan/how-will-covid-19-impact-africas-trade-and-market-opportunities (accessed 30 June 2020).

II. Towards inclusive trade in a post-COVID world

SDG indicators

SDG target 17.10: Promote a universal, rules-based, open, non-discriminatory and equitable multilateral trading system under the World Trade Organization, including through the conclusion of negotiations under its Doha Development Agenda.
SDG indicator 17.10.1: Worldwide weighted tariff-average (Tier I)

SDG target 17.12: Realize timely implementation of duty-free and quota-free market access on a lasting basis for all least developed countries, consistent with World Trade Organization decisions, including by ensuring that preferential rules of origin applicable to imports from least developed countries are transparent and simple, and contribute to facilitating market access.
SDG indicator 17.12.1: Average tariffs faced by developing countries, LDCs and SIDS (Tier I)

SDG target 10.a: Implement the principle of special and differential treatment for developing countries, in particular least developed countries, in accordance with World Trade Organization agreements
SDG indicator 10.a.1: Proportion of tariff lines applied to imports from LDCs and developing countries with zero-tariff (Tier I)

The Addis Ababa Action Agenda (United Nations, 2015) acknowledges that international trade is an engine for inclusive economic growth and poverty reduction. Target 17.10 is of paramount importance to advancing economic growth and fostering global competitiveness as it promotes a universal, rules-based, open, non-discriminatory and equitable multilateral trading system. Market access conditions are an important factor for the effectiveness of trade, and tariffs are an important determinant of market access.

Do trade reforms promote economic growth?

Recent research in trade theory suggests that trade reforms which significantly reduce import barriers have on average a positive effect on economic growth, although the economic effect of such trade policies vary across countries Dutt and Gallagher (2020). Falvey et al. (2013) report that economic growth is roughly 1.7 percentage points higher after trade reforms than a benchmark (compared to the situation without any trade reforms). Easterly (2019) finds that the positive correlation between a good trade policy and economic outcomes has increased since the 1990s. Piketty (2014) notes that free trade and economic openness are ultimately in everyone's interest. Safaeimanesh and Jenkins (2021), taking the case of the ECOWAS, estimate that from 15 to 26 per cent of the average annual value of net official assistance received by coastal ECOWAS members could be achieved through trade facilitation across borders. This ratio is even higher for Nigeria: around 31 to 46 per cent of net official assistance.

On the other hand, as underlined by Dutt and Gallagher (2020), developing countries need to be mindful of the potential impacts of trade and investment liberalization on the ability to mobilize domestic resources for development. Revenues accrued from tariffs may constitute a significant portion of a government's public revenue, particularly in low-income countries, where the need for coordination of tariff liberalization with other tax policies is of particular importance.

Trade agreements

In 1947, major economies involved in international trade signed the GATT, an agreement through which countries entered into "reciprocal and mutually advantageous arrangements aimed at the substantial reduction of tariffs and other barriers to trade and to the elimination of discriminatory treatment in international commerce" (WTO, 2021a). The conclusion of the "GATT-94" multilateral trade negotiations led to the creation of the WTO in 1995, with a mandate to develop an integrated, more viable and durable multilateral trading system. The WTO TFA was the first multilateral trade agreement concluded since the establishment of the WTO. It came into force in 2017 with the aim of boosting the speed and efficiency of cross-border trade procedures while reducing cost. Full implementation of the TFA could cut global trade costs by 10-18 per cent (OECD, 2018) and increase gains from exports up to US$ 3.6 trillion per year (WTO, 2015a).

Article 1 of the "GATT-94" stipulates that members set their tariffs on a MFN basis in such a way that any advantage, favour, privilege or immunity granted to any product originated in and destined for other countries becomes immediately and unconditionally applicable to all contracting parties (WTO, 2021a). Article 24 of the GATT, Article 5 of the GATS and the Enabling Clause (Paragraph 2(c)) allow WTO members to conclude RTAs as a special exception,

350 RTAs (Regional Trade Agreements) in force as of 1st June 2021

provided the agreements help trade flow more freely among the countries in the RTA without barriers being raised on trade with the outside world (WTO, 2021b). Since the inception of the GATT/WTO system, most economies across the world have negotiated bilateral or multilateral trade agreements with the objective of reducing barriers to trade and promoting exchanges among members. Nowadays, practically all countries participate in at least one RTA, with some countries forming more bilateral and regional RTAs than others. More than 50 per cent of global trade now takes place between countries that are members to PTAs, and one third under DTAs that go beyond traditional tariffs and existing WTO agreements (UNCTAD, 2021a). According to the WTO RTA Database, as of 1 June 2021 , 350 RTAs were in force for both goods and services, as compared to 137 in June 2005 (WTO, 2021b) (Figure 1).

▊▋▊ Figure 1. Evolution of RTAs, 1970-2021

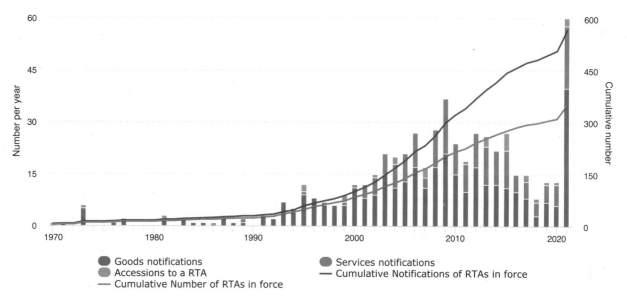

- ● Goods notifications
- ● Accessions to a RTA
- — Cumulative Number of RTAs in force
- ● Services notifications
- — Cumulative Notifications of RTAs in force

Source: WTO (2021b)
Note: Goods, services and accessions to an RTA are counted separately. The cumulative lines show the number of RTAs currently in force (by year of entry into force).

The coverage of PTAs has also expanded. While the average PTA in the 1970s covered less than ten policy areas, since the 2000s most new PTAs included between 10 and 20 policy areas (figure 2). Such agreements with larger scope tend to include not only traditional trade policy, such as tariff liberalization, but also trade-related regulations like subsidies or technical barriers to trade, as well as areas not related to trade, for example, labour, environment, and migration (Mattoo et al., 2020).

▊▋▊ Figure 2. Number of policy areas covered by PTAs, 1970-2019

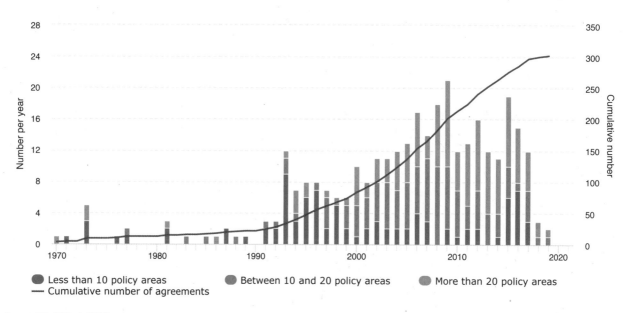

- ● Less than 10 policy areas
- — Cumulative number of agreements
- ● Between 10 and 20 policy areas
- ● More than 20 policy areas

Source: World Bank (2021)
Note: Number of policy areas covered in an agreement is calculated as the count of policy areas included in a PTA, a maximum number of policy areas being 52.

Making non-discriminatory tariff reforms work for development

In 2019, **SIDS imposed** some of the **highest import duties**

Even though most developed countries have pushed for lower tariffs in recent years, there are still many parts of the globe where they remain high. In 2019, the country with the highest weighted average tariff worldwide was Palau, classified as an LDC, at 118.2 per cent, followed by Bermuda at 103.2 per cent. Among major global economies, India imposed a weighted tariff-average of 6.6 per cent, while China's average rate was 2.5 per cent. The United States of America applied a weighted average tariff of 13.8 per cent on its imports, representing an increase of more than 8.6 times compared with 2018. The weighted average tariff applied in the EU was 1.8 per cent in 2019. The lowest weighted average tariffs, at zero per cent, were recorded in Hong Kong SAR, China; Macao SAR, China and Brunei.[1]

Map 1. Worldwide weighted average tariff, latest available data (SDG 17.10.1)

(Percentage)

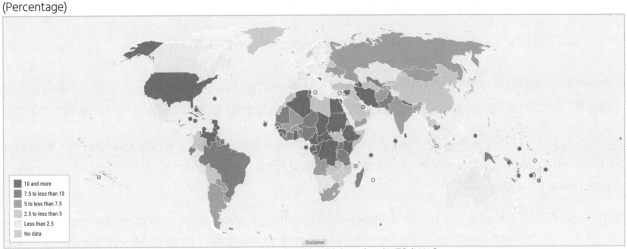

Source: World Bank estimates (World Bank, 2021), based on UNCTAD (2021b), WTO (2021c) and WTO (2021d).

Since 2010, tariffs have been trending downwards, mostly on a preferential basis. MFN tariffs on agriculture, manufacturing and natural resources have remained largely constant and amounted in 2019 to almost 17 per cent, 7 per cent, and 3 per cent, respectively (figure 3). The proliferation of PTA schemes has contributed to about 2 percentage points to the reduction of simple agricultural tariffs and to about 1 percentage point to manufacturing tariffs. On the other hand, preferential tariffs have increased on a trade weighted basis, indicating an increase of tariffs among some of the major trading nations. In the natural resources sector the liberalization occurred both in MFN and preferential terms, and, in 2019, amounted on a simple average basis to 2.6 per cent and 1.3 per cent, respectively (UNCTAD, 2021a) (see figure 3).

Figure 3. Multilateral and preferential tariff liberalization

(Percentage)

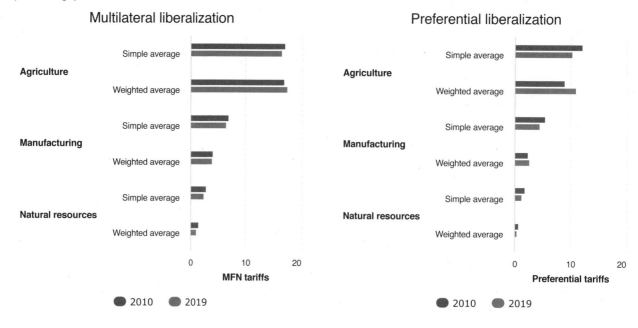

Source: UNCTAD, ITC and WTO calculations based on UNCTAD (2021b), ITC (2021) and WTO (2021c).

Tariffs applied to exports of LDCs and developing countries are slowly reducing

The average level of customs tariff rates (indicator 17.12.1) faced by developing countries and LDCs illustrates the pace at which the multilateral system is advancing toward the implementation of duty-free and quota-free market access (United Nations, 2021).

SDG target 17.12 aims to "realize timely implementation of duty-free and quota-free market access on a lasting basis for all least developed countries...". Recognizing LDCs' special economic situation, developed countries and other economies[2] agreed to grant LDCs duty-free and quota-free preferential market access.

Preferential market access for developing countries has been initiated by most developed countries since the early 1970s under the aegis of UNCTAD (2021c). These unilateral trade preferences called the GSP allow developed countries to apply different tariffs between different groups of trading partners without violating Article I of the GATT requiring non-discriminatory and equal treatment of trading partners.

Trade preferences under the GSP program are granted, not only by the so-called QUAD countries, namely the EU, United States, Japan and Canada, but also by Australia, New Zealand, Norway, Belarus, Iceland, Kazakhstan, Russian Federation, Switzerland, and Turkey.

Figure 4 shows that in 2019 import tariffs applied by developed countries to all products from LDCs registered a slight decline since 2015 and amounted to 1.1 per cent in 2019 . Tariffs, including preferences, faced by LDCs vary across product groups. Tariffs for clothing and textiles in 2019 amounted to about six per cent and nine per cent, while tariffs for industrial products remained low, at 0.4 per cent.

In 2019, developed countries applied on average 1.1% tariff rates to imports from LDCs

(Percentage)

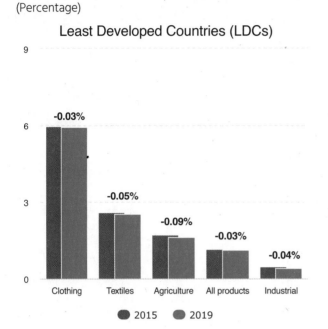

Least Developed Countries (LDCs)

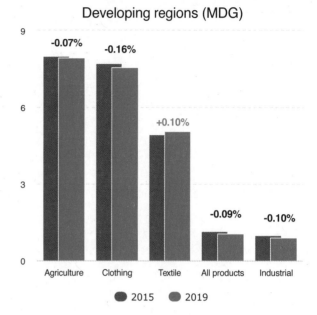

Developing regions (MDG)

Source: UNCTAD (2021d)

The true value of developing countries' export competitiveness that is granted duty free treatment can be in part measured by the magnitude of the preferential tariff margin, that is the difference between the preferential tariff rates applicable to the developing countries' exports and the non-preferential tariff rates. The higher margin indicates the greater market shares of these countries in preference granting countries. Figure 5 shows that LDCs' preferential margins are the strongest in low-skill manufactures, such as clothing, providing a tariff advantage of six percentage points in entering developed countries markets vis-à-vis foreign competitors. Preferential margins for LDCs are also substantial for textiles and agricultural products (between three and six percentage points). For developing countries, a substantial share of exports of clothing is bound to markets where countries have preferences (four percentage points). For SIDS, the highest preferential margins of more than 15 percentage points are registered for exports of agricultural products.

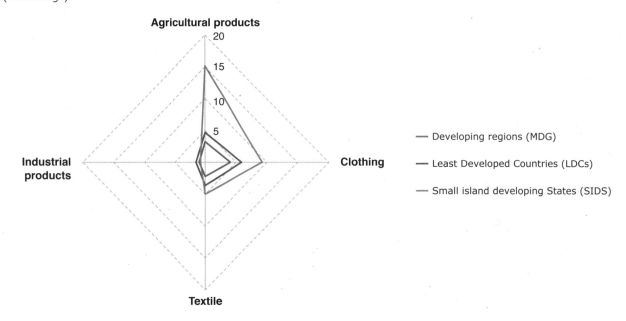

Figure 5. Preferential tariff margins for developing countries, LDCs and SIDS exports in developed-country markets, 2019

(Percentage)

- Developing regions (MDG)
- Least Developed Countries (LDCs)
- Small island developing States (SIDS)

Source: UNCTAD, ITC and WTO calculations based on UNCTAD (2021b), ITC (2021), and WTO (2021c)

To assist LDCs in the elaboration of studies on DFQF market access, UNCTAD produced two Handbooks on Duty-Free and Quota-Free Market Access and Rules of Origin For Least Developed Countries, (UNCTAD, 2018b) and a database (UNCTAD, 2021e) on utilization of trade preferences.

Import restrictiveness differs substantially across countries, and even within the same region. Table 1 presents a matrix of the average tariff levels imposed on trade flows between regions in 2019. Intraregional trade is generally subject to lower tariff trade restrictiveness than interregional trade. However, a large number of South-South trade flows are still burdened by relatively high tariffs. This is the case, for example, for trade between Latin America and South Asia, which face an average tariff of about 10 per cent. Market access for sub-Saharan Africa and South Asian countries often enjoys better interregional trade

Sub-Saharan Africa   South Asia

faced the highest intraregional tariffs in 2019

conditions than for intraregional trade. South Asia, and Western Asia and North Africa faced the highest intraregional tariffs, with tariffs of 5.7 per cent and 4.8 per cent respectively, in 2019 (UNCTAD, 2021a).

North-North tariffs are on average lower than North-South tariffs because of tariff peaks within product groups, which are of significant export interest to developing countries, such as agriculture and apparel. However, low income countries, within product categories, do receive higher preference margins, averaging three percentage points above other countries. Lesotho and Afghanistan, receive preference margins as much as ten percentage points. In contrast, such countries as Cuba and the Democratic People's Republic of Korea face tariffs about 5 percentage points higher than other countries (World Bank, 2020).

Table 1. Tariff restrictiveness, matrix by region, 2019

(Percentage)

Importing Region	Exporting Region					
	Developed economies	East Asia	Latin America	South Asia	Sub-Saharan Africa	Western Asia and North Africa
Developed economies	**2.0**	**5.7**	**1.1**	**2.2**	**0.6**	**1.2**
	0.3	3.4	0.4	-0.6	0.2	0.6
East Asia	**5.4**	**1.9**	**5.2**	**3.5**	**2.6**	**1.8**
	-0.6	-1.5	1.2	-0.1	0.6	-0.1
Latin America	**3.6**	**8.2**	**1.2**	**10.2**	**3.8**	**3.2**
	-0.1	-0.3	-0.2	-0.1	1.6	-0.1
South Asia	**10**	**7.0**	**10.2**	**5.7**	**5.6**	**5.7**
	0.8	-1.4	3.1	-1.4	-1.1	-0.8
Sub-Saharan Africa	**7.3**	**10.4**	**8.7**	**8.5**	**2.5**	**6.3**
	1.2	-0.2	1.6	0.8	0.7	1.3
Western Asia and North Africa	**6.6**	**7.1**	**7.8**	**4.5**	**3.4**	**4.8**
	1.4	0.5	1.7	0.6	-1.2	2.0

Source: UNCTAD (2021a)
Note: Changes between 2010 and 2019 are shown in smaller font.

Tariffs are particularly high for products of interest to low-income countries, such as agricultural products, as well as apparel, textiles and tanning. For example, tariffs on about 8 per cent of global trade in food products (and 26 per cent of the products in this group) are above 15 per cent. Some 10 per cent of world trade (and 21 per cent of the products in this group) in apparel is subject to tariff peaks of 15 per cent or more (figure 6).

About 8% of international trade in food products is subject to tariffs above 15%

Figure 6. Tariff peaks, by product groups, 2019

(Percentage)

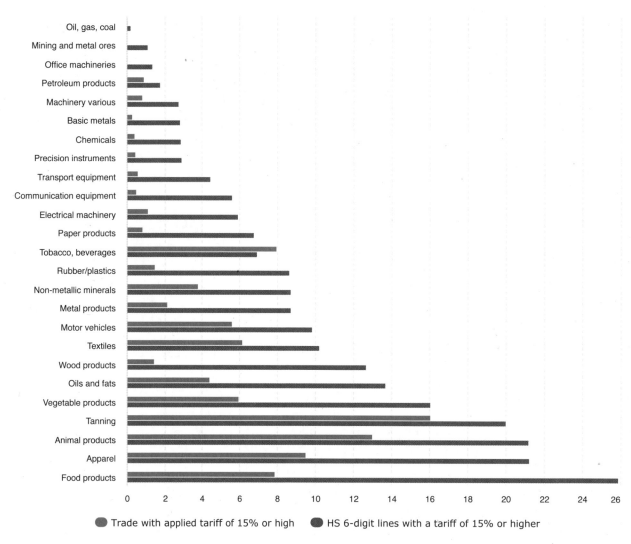

● Trade with applied tariff of 15% or high   ● HS 6-digit lines with a tariff of 15% or higher

Source: UNCTAD, ITC and WTO calculations based on UNCTAD (2021b), ITC (2021) and WTO (2021c).

The objective to improve market access conditions for LDCs' exports by giving special and differential treatment to LDCs in accordance with the WTO agreements was not only outlined in SDG target 17.12, but also in SDG target 10.a.

More than half of merchandise exports from developing countries benefit from duty-free market access

Most developed countries grant either full or nearly full duty-free and quota-free, i.e. DFQF market access for LCDs, and an increasing number of developing countries are in the process of extending similar treatment to most imports from LDCs. Australia, New Zealand, Norway and Switzerland provide full duty-free access through preferential LDC schemes. For Canada, Chile, the EU and Japan, 97 per cent of tariff lines are free of duty for products originating from LDCs. China and India grant duty-free access for LDCs on more than 94 per cent of their tariff lines. Iceland, the Republic of Korea and Montenegro have a duty-free coverage of around 90 per cent or higher (WTO, 2020c).

However, progress on export expansion from LDCs is slow. Despite considerable growth of LDCs' exports since 2000, their share in world trade in 2020 remained less than 1 per cent, whereas the share of LDCs in world population was more than 13 per cent (UNCTAD, 2021f).

Tariff barriers remain an issue in some countries, notably the United States. In 2018, some 60 per cent of LDC exports were dutiable under the United States' GSP scheme for LDCs, in dollar terms, with a trade-weighted average tariff of over ten per cent. Nevertheless, some LDCs enjoy significant duty-free access to the United States of America under the AGOA and the CBERA (WTO, 2020c).

Share of zero tariffs applied to LDCs exports
0%
amounted to 66% in 2019

SDG indicator 10.a.1 shows the extent to which special and differential treatment has been applied through import tariffs.[3]

LDCs were granted duty-free market access on more than 66 per cent of tariff lines in 2019 (figure 6); the respective share for all developing countries was around 52 per cent. [4]

The highest proportion of products from LDCs, excluding oil, in the zero-duty trade were the trade in agricultural products, followed by the trade in industrial products, 75.1 per cent and 74.4 per cent, respectively. In the case of developing countries, almost 54 per cent of agricultural products and 54.4 per cent of industrial products entered world markets duty free (See figure 7).

Figure 7. Share of duty-free products (exported products) to world from developing countries and LDCs, by product, 2019 (#SDG 10.a.1)

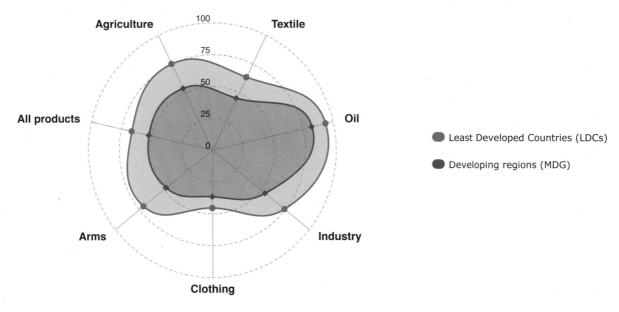

Least Developed Countries (LDCs)

Developing regions (MDG)

Source: UNCTAD (2021d)

Figure 8 shows that almost 68 per cent of international trade of agricultural products in 2019 was duty-free, with 19 per cent of this accounting for duty-free on the MFN basis and the rest under preferential tariffs. The remaining tariffs for agriculture are fairly high, averaging to 20.7 per cent. Preferential access is also important for trade in manufacturing products, for which it accounted for more than 33 per cent. The simple average tariff for manufacturing products is also high and stood, in 2019, at almost 10 per cent. For natural resources, preferential access is less important, as trade in these goods is largely tariff-free under MFN rates. The remaining tariffs are generally very low, with tariffs averaging 5.8 per cent.

Preferential access continued to play a key role in agricultural trade, but remaining tariffs were more than 20%

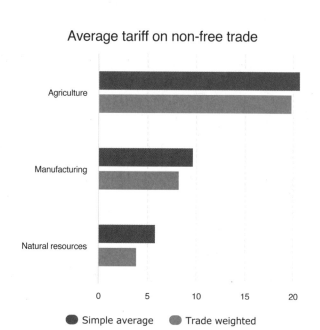

📊 **Figure 8. Free trade and remaining tariffs, by broad category**

(Percentage)

Duty free trade

Average tariff on non-free trade

● MFN ● Preferential

● Simple average ● Trade weighted

Source: UNCTAD, ITC and WTO calculations based on UNCTAD (2021b), ITC (2021), and WTO (2021c)

The rise of non-tariff measures

NTMs, often impede imports more than border duties. Trade costs associated with NTMs are estimated to account for as much as 1.6 per cent of global GDP, or US$1.4 trillion (United Nations, 2020), more than double that of ordinary customs tariffs. According to UNCTAD (2019) estimates for Asia and the Pacific, NTMs are now affecting around 58 per cent of trade in the region. For intra-African trade, the average import-weighted tariff is almost 7 per cent, while ad-valorem equivalent cost of non-tariff barriers is estimated to be 14.3 per cent (UNECA, 2020).

NTMs, as policy instruments, can be either directly or indirectly linked to sustainable development. Direct linkages include policies that have an immediate impact on social and environmental issues and help achieve SDGs: food security (SDG 2); nutrition and health (SDG 3); protect endangered species and the environment (SDGs 14 and 15); ensure sustainable production and consumption (SDG 12); energy (SDG 7); and combat climate change (SDG 13). On the other hand, indirect linkages may arise from trade policies that influence trade, which in turn can restrict economic growth and create negative spillover effects on sustainability objectives (UNCTAD, 2021h).

Today, a considerable number of NTMs are regulatory measures, which respond to a public demand for protection against environmental and health hazards (UNCTAD, 2021g) [5]. Technical NTMs, such as TBT, which includes labelling, standards on technical specifications and quality requirements, as well as all conformity-assessment measures, affect more than 30 per cent of product lines and almost 70 per cent of world trade (figure 9). SPS, which typically prevail in agriculture, affect almost 20 per cent of world trade. Figure 9 shows that agricultural sector is

Technical barriers to trade affect 30% of product lines and almost 70% of world trade

more often regulated than manufactures and natural resources, with most of world agricultural trade subject to forms of SPS and TBT. Almost 40 per cent of all exports are subject to at least one export measure (UNCTAD and World Bank, 2018).

Figure 9. NTMs in world trade, by type and broad category, 2019
(Percentage)

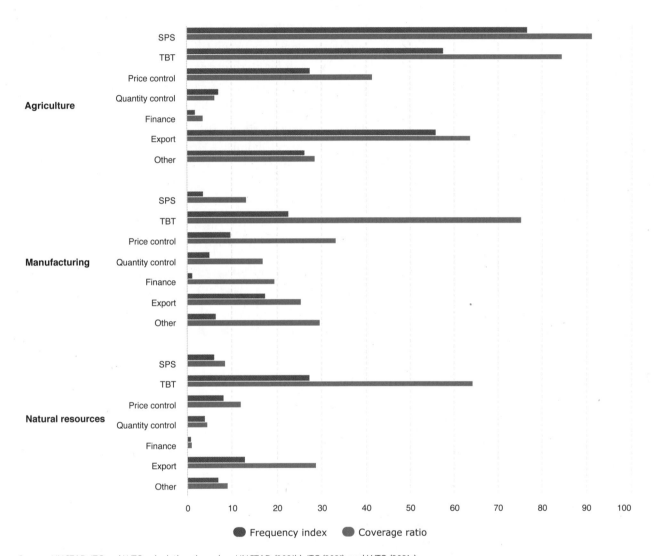

Source: UNCTAD, ITC and WTO calculations based on UNCTAD (2021b), ITC (2021), and WTO (2021c)
Note: The frequency index is defined as the percentage of HS six--digit lines covered; and coverage ratio is defined as the percentage of trade affected.

In LDCs and developing countries, about 40 per cent of imports are subject to NTMs. This is less than half as much as in developed countries. NTMs in developing countries and LDCs are less diversified than in developed countries. On average, developing countries use two different NTMs on any regulated product, and LDCs one, compared to four in developed economies (UNCTAD and World Bank, 2018).

In LDCs and developing countries, about 40% of imports are subject to NTMs

Statistics on NTMs are still incomplete. As of today, TRAINS (UNCTAD, 2021b) database developed by UNCTAD in partnership with several regional and international organisations is the most complete collection of publicly available data on NTMs at the HS six-digit level. As of 2018, UNCTAD has collected comprehensive and comparable NTMs data covering 109 countries and containing more than 65 000 measures.

Trade measures and COVID-19

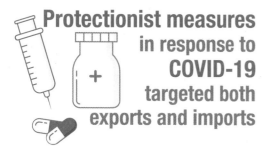

Protectionist measures in response to COVID-19 targeted both exports and imports

(Grizold and Jaklic, 2020)

The COVID-19 pandemic emerged in the context of already increasing protectionism and faltering globalization, with Brexit and the trade war between China and the United States of America, for instance. It highlighted major ongoing shifts in the objectives of countries and companies and put considerable pressure on multilateral rule-based trading system. Axioms of free trade, free movement of capital, or freedom of energy supplies have often been questioned against a cruder metric: "What's in it for me?"

Trade policy saw a rise of protectionist measures worldwide in response to COVID-19. Many countries sought to increase their self-sufficiency in strategic industries and reduce their reliance on single sources of supply, thus triggering the reconfiguration of value chains around the world and fueling a damaging spiral of trade restrictions (Anaya et al., 2020).

Trade measures targeted both exports and imports. As of the end of May 2021, WTO members had submitted a total of 371 COVID-19 related notifications. TBT and SPS measures made up the bulk of them, 162 and 94, respectively, along with quantitative restrictions aimed at ensuring domestic food and medical supplies (64) (figure 10).

Figure 10. WTO members' COVID-19 related notifications, by type

(Percentage)

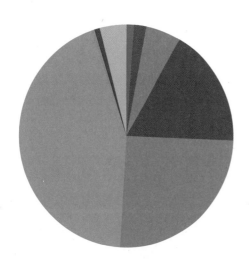

- Council forTrade in Goods
- Export restrictions
- Market access of goods
- Quantitive restrictions
- Sanitary and phytosanitary measures (SPS)
- Technical Barriers to Trade (TBT)
- Trade-Related Aspects of Intellectual Property Rights (TRIPS)
- Government Procurement Agreement (GPA)
- Agriculture

Source: WTO (2021f)

While most tariff measures were aimed at facilitating trade and concerned imports with over 100 countries either reducing or eliminating tariffs on essential goods, NTMs, although for the most part adopted on a temporary basis, were largely used to restrict trade and applied to exports, in particular of medical goods (Lee and Prabhakar, 2021). The EU placed export restrictions on medical equipment exports to non-EU countries. India, the world's largest pharmaceutical producer, enacted restrictions on the export of dozens of drugs, including various antibiotics. Personal protection equipment products, such as, aprons, medical masks and protective clothing were subject to tariffs of over ten per cent. In some countries, for example in Iran, tariffs on medical masks and protective clothing were as high as 65 per cent and 100 per cent of the import value, respectively (Espitia et al., 2020).

While the majority of trade measures were introduced as countermeasures against COVID-19, some do not seem to be directly linked to managing the health emergency, while others appear to primarily seek to protect domestic industries (Louise Curran et al., 2021). Examples of such measures include the increased tariffs on petrol imports in Fiji, restrictions of cement imports in Kazakhstan, and bans on imports of tobacco products in Botswana, on all non-essential goods in Sri Lanka, and on used clothing in Kenya.

WTO estimated that 2.8 per cent of G20 trade was affected by import-restrictive measures implemented from the mid-October 2019 to mid-May 2020. Import-restrictive measures applied since 2009 and still in force affect an estimated 10.3 per cent of G20 imports (US$1.6 trillion) (WTO, 2020b).

The inability of some countries to produce and export domestically manufactured equipment during the pandemic led to high procurement costs and delays elsewhere. For instance, the global supply of ventilators is highly concentrated: only seven countries account for 70 per cent of ventilators exports, hence exports ban from even one of them could lead to up to a 10 per cent temporary increase in prices and adversely affect billions of lives across importing countries (Zanhouo, 2021). Moreover, trade restrictions negatively impacted the access to other basic care services, other than those needed to target COVID-19, including vaccines needed for mass immunization campaigns (Barlow et al., 2021).

Governments have been challenged to find the right balance between the need to import medical supplies and protective equipment against the loss of tariff revenues associated with them. In order to facilitate timely availability of essential medical supplies, for example, the EU set up the COVID-19 clearing-house for medical equipment and abolished temporary controls on exports of essential equipment (de la Mata, 2020). To speed up the release of goods, China employed "green lanes" for fast customs clearance (UNCTAD, 2020b). Pakistan, for example, exempted medical equipment from import duties, and Brazil introduced new legislation that simplifies the customs clearance process for articles used to combat the spread of COVID-19. Argentina streamlined the import clearance process of certain critical medical products, and Iran removed an import ban on ethanol, used to produce sanitiser (Baldwin and Evenett, 2020).

The current health crisis has the potential to further exacerbate tensions and to create more segmented and polarized global trade relationships, with obvious negative consequences for many countries (UNCTAD, 2020c). A recent report estimated that high tariffs and trade restrictions could slow economic recovery from the COVID-19 crisis and reduce global GDP by US$10 trillion per year unless repealed or reduced by governments (Anaya et al., 2020). In the post-pandemic era, the recovery will be much faster and stronger if society strengthens international cooperation, countries work together to open their economies and to reduce trade costs through better connectivity and logistics, and to build up new areas of consensus on issues of common ground, such as climate change, cybersecurity risks, the need for building transformative productive capacities, and many others (UNCTAD, 2020a).

Notes

1. Data are classified using the Harmonized System of trade at the six- or eight-digit level. Tariff line data were matched to the SITC revision 3 codes to define commodity groups and import weights. To the extent possible, specific rates have been converted to their ad valorem equivalent rates and have been included in the calculation of Weighted mean applied tariff. Import weights were calculated using the UNSD's Commodity Trade (Comtrade) database. Effectively applied tariff rates at the six- and eight-digit product level are averaged for products in each commodity group. When the effectively applied rate is unavailable, the most favoured nation rate is used instead.

2. Following the WTO Hong Kong Ministerial Decision in 2005 (WTO, 2015b).

3. Limitations of this indicator include the following: (i)Tariff-based measures are only a part of trade limitation factors. (ii) Inability to comply with rules of origin criteria limits the utilization of preferential treatments. (iii) Using data on zero-tariff lines assumes full utilization of benefits. (iii) Low MFN tariffs mean that duty-free treatment is not always preferential (United Nations, 2019).

4. Proportion of total number of tariff lines applied to products imported from least developed countries and developing countries is presented in per cent, corresponding to a 0 per cent tariff rate in HS chapter 01-97. This indicator allows observing on how many products developing countries and LDCs will have free access to Developed countries markets.

5. According to WTO, for non-agricultural products the product coverage of tariff binding by developed country members was 100 per cent, while that of developing country members was around 73 per cent (WTO, 2021g).

References

- Anaya P et al. (2020). The $10 Trillion Case for Open Trade. Available at https://www.bcg.com/publications/2020/ten-trillion-dollar-case-for-open-trade (accessed 12 May 2021).

- Baldwin R and Evenett SJ, eds. (2020). *COVID-19 and Trade Policy: Why Turning Inward Won't Work*. CEPR Press. London.

- Barlow P, CI van Schalkwyk M, McKee M, Labonté R and Stuckler D (2021). COVID-19 and the collapse of global trade: building an effective public health response. Article No. DOI: 10.1108/cpoib-05-2020-0041. Elsevier The Lancet Planetary Health Volume 5, Issue 2.

- Doshi P (2011). The elusive definition of pandemic influenza. Bulletin of the World Health Organisation. *WHO Bulletin*. 89(7):532–538.

- Dutt D and Gallagher KP (2020). Does Protectionism Matter in the Time of Pandemic? Available at https://www.bu.edu/gdp/files/2020/07/GEGI_WorkingPaper_040_Final.pdf (accessed 31 May 2021).

- Easterly W (2019). In Search of Reforms for Growth: New Stylized Facts on Policy and Growth Outcomes. NBER Working Paper No. 26318. National Bureau of Economic Research.

- Espitia A, Rocha N and Ruta M (2020). Database on COVID-19 trade flows and policies. World Bank. Available at https://public.tableau.com/profile/alvaro.espitia#!/vizhome/Covid19-TradeStatistics/Home (accessed 25 May 2021).

- Falvey R, Foster-McGregor N and Khalid A (2013). Trade liberalisation and growth: a threshold exploration. *Journal of the Asia Pacific Economy*. 18(2):230–252.

- Grizold A and Jaklic A (2020). Changing International Relations After the COVID-19 Pandemic: Managing the Growing Gap Between National and Multilateral Responses. *Teorija in Praksa, Ljubljana: University of Ljubljana, Faculty of Social Sciences*. Teorija in Praksa, Ljubljana: University of Ljubljana, Faculty of Social Sciences. Vol. 57 (4).

- ITC (2021). Market Access Map. Available at https://www.macmap.org/ (accessed 15 May 2021).

- Jenkins GP and Safaeimanesh S (2021). Trade Facilitation and Its Impacts on the Economic Welfare and Sustainable Development of the ECOWAS Region. *Sustainability*. 13(1):.

- Lee S and Prabhakar D (2021). COVID-19 Non-Tariff Measures: The Good and the Bad, througha Sustainable Development Lens. WB Policy Research Working Paper No. 60. UNCTAD.

- Louise Curran, Eckhardt J and Lee J (2021). The Trade Policy Response to COVID-19 and its Implications for International Business. Article No. DOI: 10.1108/cpoib-05-2020-0041. Critical Perspectives on International Business, Bradford, Vol 17, issue 2.

- de la Mata I (2020). European Solidarity during the COVID crisis. Article No. DOI: 10.1108/cpoib-05-2020-0041. Eurohealth 2020; 26(2). (accessed 26 May 2021).

- Mattoo A, Rocha N and Ruta M (2020). The Evolution of Deep Trade Agreements. WB Policy Research Working Paper No. 9283. WB.

- OECD (2018). Implementation of the WTO Trade Facilitation Agreement - The Potential Impact on Trade Costs. Available at https://issuu.com/oecd.publishing/docs/implementation_of_the_wto_trade_fac (accessed 1 June 2021).

- Piketty T (2014). *Capital in the Twenty-First Century*. Belknap Press. Cambridge, Mass.

- UNCTAD (2018a). *Trade and Development Report 2018: Power, Platforms and the Free Trade Delusion*. United Nations publication. Sales No. E.18.II.D.7. New York and Geneva.

- UNCTAD (2018b). Available at https://unctad.org/en/Pages/MeetingDetails.aspx?meetingid=1864 (accessed 9 June 2020).

- UNCTAD (2019). Trade costs of non-tariff measures now more than double that of tariffs. Available at https://unctad.org/news/trade-costs-non-tariff-measures-now-more-double-tariffs (accessed 5 June 2021).

- UNCTAD, ed. (2020a). *Transforming Trade and Development in a Fractured, Post-Pandemic World: Report of the Secretary-General of UNCTAD to the Fifteenth Session of the Conference*. United Nations publication. Sales No. E.20.II.D.39. New York and Geneva.

- UNCTAD (2020b). Case Study: China's Trade Facilitation responses to the COVID-19 Pandemic. Available at https://unctad.org/news/case-study-chinas-trade-facilitation-responses-covid-19-pandemic (accessed 26 May 2021).

- UNCTAD (2020c). A new take on trade by Mukhisa Kituyi, Secretary-General of UNCTAD. Available at https://unctad.org/news/new-take-trade (accessed 2 June 2021).

- UNCTAD (2021a). *Key Statistics and Trends in Trade Policy 2020: The Regional Comprehensive Economic Partnership*. United Nations publication. Sales No. UNCTAD/DITC/TAB/2020/3. Geneva.

- UNCTAD (2021b). TRAINS: The global database on Non-Tariff Measures. Available at https://trains.unctad.org/ (accessed 4 May 2021).

- UNCTAD (2021c). Preferential market access and the Generalized System of Preferences. Available at https://unctad.org/en/Pages/DITC/GSP/Generalized-System-of-Preferences.aspx (accessed 10 May 2021).

- UNCTAD (2021d). SDG Trade Monitor. Available at https://sdgtrade.org/en (accessed 15 May 2021).

- UNCTAD (2021e). https://unctad.org/topic/trade-agreements/trade-preferences-utilization. Available at https://unctad.org/topic/trade-agreements/trade-preferences-utilization (accessed 15 May 2021).

- UNCTAD (2021f). UNCTADStat. Available at https://unctadstat.unctad.org/EN/Index.html (accessed 21 April 2021).

- UNCTAD (2021g). Classification of Non-Tariff Measures. Available at https://unctad.org/en/Pages/DITC/Trade-Analysis/Non-Tariff-Measures/NTMs-Classification.aspx (accessed 15 May 2021).

- UNCTAD (2021h). NTMs and SDGs. Available at https://unctad.org/en/Pages/DITC/Trade-Analysis/Non-Tariff-Measures/NTMs-and-SDGs.aspx (accessed 11 May 2021).

- UNCTAD and World Bank (2018). *The Unseen Impact of Non-Tariff Measures: Insights from a New Database*. Geneva.

- UNECA (2020). Trade Policies for Africa to Tackle Covid-19. Available at https://www.uneca.org/publications/trade-policies-africa-tackle-covid-19 (accessed 15 May 2021).

- United Nations (2015). Report of the third international conference on financing for development. A/CONF.227/20. Addis Ababa. 3 August. (accessed 20 April 2020).

- United Nations (2019). E-handbook on SDG Indicators. Available at https://unstats.un.org/wiki/display/SDGeHandbook/Home (accessed 15 May 2021).

- United Nations (2020). *Report of the Inter-Agency Task Force on Financing for Development: Financing for Sustainable Development Report 2020*. United Nations publication. Sales No. E.20.I.4. New York.

- United Nations (2021). SDG indicators: Metadata repository. Available at https://unstats.un.org/sdgs/metadata/ (accessed 20 April 2021).

- WHO (2020). Q&A on coronaviruses (COVID-19). Available at https://www.who.int/emergencies/diseases/novel-coronavirus-2019/question-and-answers-hub/q-a-detail/q-a-coronaviruses (accessed 11 May 2020).

- World Bank (2020). *World Development Report 2020: Trading for Development in the Age of Global Value Chains*. World Bank Group. Washington, DC.

- World Bank (2021). Tariff rate, applied, weighted mean, all products (%). Available at https://data.worldbank.org/indicator/tm.tax.mrch.wm.ar.zs (accessed 12 May 2020).

- WTO (2015a). Speeding up trade: benefits and challenges of implementing the WTO Trade Facilitation Agreement: World Trade Report 2015. Available at https://www.wto.org/english/res_e/publications_e/wtr15_e.htm (accessed 12 May 2021).

- WTO (2015b). Ministerial declaration. WT/MIN(05)/DEC. Hong Kong. 22 December. Available at https://www.wto.org/english/thewto_e/minist_e/min05_e/final_text_e.htm (accessed 1 June 2021).

- WTO (2020a). The basic rules for goods. Available at https://www.wto.org/english/tratop_e/region_e/regatt_e.htm (accessed 15 May 2020).

- WTO (2020b). WTO report on G20 trade measures (mid-October 2019 to mid-May 2020) June. Available at https://www.wto.org/english/news_e/news20_e/report_trdev_jun20_e.pdf (accessed 1 June 2021).

- WTO (2020c). Market access for products and services of export interest to least developed countries. Working documents of the Sub-Committee on Least-Developed Countries to the General Council No. WT/COMTD/LDC/W/68.

- WTO (2021a). The General Agreement on Tariffs and Trade (GATT 1947). Available at https://www.wto.org/english/docs_e/legal_e/gatt47_01_e.htm (accessed 18 April 2021).

- WTO (2021b). Regional Trade Agreements Database. Available at http://rtais.wto.org/UI/PublicMaintainRTAHome.aspx (accessed 15 May 2021).

- WTO (2021c). WTO Integrated Data Base. Available at http://tariffdata.wto.org/ (accessed 15 April 2021).

- WTO (2021d). Consolidated Tariff Schedules database. Available at http://tariffdata.wto.org/ (accessed 15 May 2021).

- WTO (2021e). Glossary - a guide to 'WTO speak.' Available at https://www.wto.org/english/thewto_e/glossary_e/glossary_e.htm (accessed 1 July 2021).

- WTO (2021f). WTO members' notifications on COVID-19. Available at https://www.wto.org/english/tratop_e/covid19_e/notifications_e.htm (accessed 25 May 2021).

- WTO (2021g). Market access for goods. Available at https://www.wto.org/english/tratop_e/markacc_e/markacc_e.htm (accessed 30 May 2020).

- Zanhouo AK (2021). Does Protectionism Matter in the Time of Pandemic? Available at https://case-research.eu/files/?id_plik=6729 (accessed 31 May 2021).

III. Trade, food security and sustainable agriculture

SDG indicators

SDG target 2.b: Correct and prevent trade restrictions and distortions in world agricultural markets, including through the parallel elimination of all forms of agricultural export subsidies and all export measures with equivalent effect, in accordance with the mandate of the Doha Development Round
SDG indicator 2.b.1: Agricultural export subsidies

SDG target 2.c: Adopt measures to ensure the proper functioning of food commodity markets and their derivatives and facilitate timely access to market information, including on food reserves, in order to help limit extreme food price volatility
SDG indicator 2.c.1: Indicator of (food) price anomalies

Goal 2 of the 2030 Agenda sets out to "End hunger, achieve food security and improved nutrition and promote sustainable agriculture". As with other SDGs, realizing this goal will require a multifaceted approach. One part of the equation is the necessity for properly functioning food commodity markets. To ensure that markets around the world have access to nutritious food requires international trade and cross-border cooperation. In the context of climate change, with risks of decreased predictability of harvests and uncertainty regarding the sustainability of many regional crops, the importance of trade in food commodities may well increase rather than diminish.

Two targets belonging to SDG 2 deal with the proper functioning of food markets. Target 2.c, limits or reduces price volatility through better access to market information. Furthermore, target 2.b aims to avoid market distortions by eliminating export subsidies and equivalent measures. Cooperation via multilateral trade has an important role to play in order to alleviate hunger, complementing other efforts, such as, increasing ODA and OOFs to the agricultural sector (see Official support for sustainable development).

Increasing food insecurity due to COVID-19 calls for more international cooperation

The Global Report on Food Crisis (FSIN and Global Network Against Food Crises, 2021) counts 155 million people living under conditions considered a food crisis or worse. This is the highest number in that publication's five-year history. Food crises are characterized as situations where people struggle to meet minimum food needs and where levels of acute malnutrition are above-normal. The report counts another 208 million people living under stressed conditions where they can still get necessary nutrition, but only by forgoing some essential non-food expenditures.

The causes of food crises are often multifaceted with several factors reinforcing each other. The most common primary driver is conflict. In June 2021, the Famine Early Warnings Systems Network (2021) categorized South Sudan, Yemen, Nigeria and Ethiopia as countries of highest concern; all areas where people are fleeing violence. However, the number of food crises where the primary factor was considered an economic shock doubled to 17 in 2020

In 2020, 360 million people's access to food was stressed, in crisis or worse

(FSIN and Global Network Against Food Crises, 2021). These economic shocks include shocks due to the COVID-19 pandemic. The food crises report points out that the pandemic has threatened many vulnerable people's livelihoods but also disrupted supply chains which in turn have led to food price anomalies. Ahead of the fifteenth session of UNCTAD and the Twelfth Ministerial Conference of WTO, UNCTAD recommends that the international trade architecture is enhanced to ensure that international trade can do its part in increasing food security (UNCTAD, 2021a). These recommendations include counteracting export restrictions of essential food and more favorable trade terms for developing economies.

Through Article XI of GATT-94 parties agree, in principle, to not apply export bans or restrictions. However, members are allowed to apply temporary restrictions to safeguard products such as food, and in early 2020 several WTO members introduced export prohibitions and restrictions on food to ensure food stability within their territories (WTO, 2020). This raised fears that if the number of export restrictions continues to grow, they could disrupt the global food supply chain, and "imperil global food security, especially in atomized net food-importing developing countries" (Coke Hamilton and Nkurunziza, 2020). By the end of 2020, new export restrictions on food were uncommon (ITC, 2021) and measures introduced in the beginning of the year had been terminated (International Food Policy Research Institute, 2020b).

The WTO Agreement on Agriculture (2021b) requires countries to give due consideration to the food security needs of others while considering temporary export restrictions on food. Furthermore, an argument that trade restrictions on food lacks utility is the fact that the world as a whole has a sufficient inventories of staple foods (International Food Policy Research Institute, 2020a). Past food crises have made the world more prepared for the current one. Figure 1 shows that in 2020 global stocks-to-use ratios for key staples were still substantially higher than in 2008, when the market conditions for these products were tight.

Figure 1. World stocks-to-use ratio of select food commodities

(Percentage)

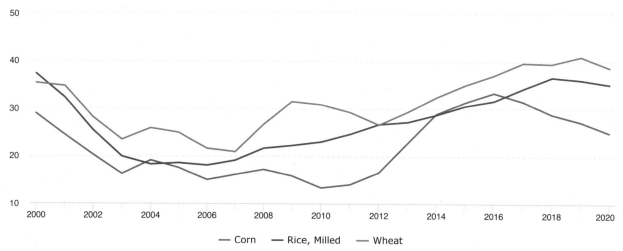

— Corn — Rice, Milled — Wheat

Source: UNCTAD calculations based on United States Department of Agriculture (2021).
Notes: Years are standard international trade years that depend on hemisphere and that does not correspond exactly to calendar years. The selected commodities are the most commonly recorded staple foods in the dataset. The world total is based on the sum of domestic consumption and the sum of ending stocks for individual economies for a given year. Included economies are those with data on both measures for a given commodity since the year 2000. This number is 118 for corn, 113 for rice and 117 for wheat.

Increasing trade in food – small change in actors

85% of imports of basic food to Africa comes from outside of the region

85%

In the period 2015 – 2019 the median for individual economies was that 11 per cent of merchandise imports consisted of basic food[1]. However, at country level, the importance of food to individual countries' import basket can vary considerably. In Haiti and Somalia, food comprised 42 per cent of the total value of merchandise imports. Merchandise exports exceeded 30 per cent in Benin, Yemen, American Samoa, Eritrea, South Sudan and Guinea-Bissau (UNCTAD calculations based on UNCTAD, 2021b).

The median of economies' net imports of basic food, defined as imports minus exports of these products, was 4.6 per cent of total merchandise imports for the period 2015 – 2019. South America is home to several net food-exporting countries while many net-importing countries are found in the Middle East and Africa (see map 1). Another prominent group of net food importers are the SIDS. Net imports of basic food exceeded 10 per cent of merchandise imports for half of SIDS. At the same time, many

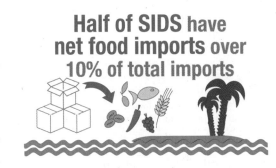

Half of SIDS have net food imports over 10% of total imports

islands and other economies with access to oceans are net exporters of basic food – the extreme being the Falkland Islands where an estimated 95 per cent of exports in 2019 were crustaceans, mollusks and aquatic invertebrates (UNCTAD, 2021b). At the regional level, Latin America and the Caribbean together with Oceania are net food exporters while Africa and Asia are net food importers (see table 1).

Map 1. Net import of food as a ratio to total imports, 2015-2019

(Percentage)

40%

10%

0%

-10%

-40%

No data

Disclaimer

Source: UNCTAD calculations based on UNCTAD (2021b).
Notes: Net food imports are calculated as imports minus exports of basic food excluding tea, coffee, cocoa and spices (SITC 0 + 22 + 4 less 07) during the years 2015-2019. The percentage displayed is reached by dividing net food imports with total imports of all goods for the economy in the same period.

Economies turn to partners outside their own geographical region for much of the food that they import. Europe stands out as a region with high intra-regional food trade. Only a quarter of the US$0.5 trillion of the food imported by European economies originates from outside the region. This is in stark contrast to Africa, where 85 per cent of food imports are extra-regional. There has been little change in these patterns over the recent decade (see table 1).

Table 1. Total imports of basic food and the share of intra-group imports by geographical region

(Billions of US$ in current prices and associated percentages)

Group of economies	Food imports[a]	Extra-group imports[b]		Net food imports[c]	
	2019 (Billion of US$)	2005 - 2009 (per cent)	2015 - 2019 (per cent)	2005 - 2009 (per cent)	2015 - 2019 (per cent)
Africa	74.4	86.7	84.5	6.7	6.7
Northern America	145.5	64.4	70.2	-1.6	-1.4
Latin America and the Caribbean	75.0	60.1	61.6	-10.8	-13.2
Asia	474.7	60.9	64.6	5.0	7.3
Europe	513.0	28.1	26.3	3.2	0.7
Oceania	17.8	70.3	73.3	-11.1	-13.6

Source: UNCTAD calculations based on UNCTAD (2021b).
Notes: Food, basic excluding tea, coffee, cocoa and spices (SITC 0 + 22 + 4 less 07).
[a] Billions of US$ in current prices.
[b] As a ratio to total food imports.
[c] As a ratio to total imports of all products.

For several of individual economies that constitute the top net importers of basic food, net imports have increased over the past decade (see figure 2). Most significant among these are Yemen, and Wallis and Futuna Islands. Eritrea and Timor-Leste have moved in the other direction, both because of significantly growing exports of vegetables (UNCTAD, 2021b).

Figure 2. Net food imports as ratio to total imports, 2015 – 2019 compared to 2005 – 2009

(Percentage)

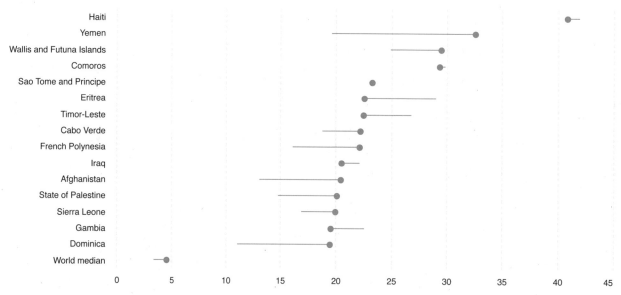

Source: UNCTAD calculations based on UNCTAD (2021b).
Notes: The point represents values for 2015 – 2019 while the line segment reaches the value for 2005 – 2009. Net food imports are calculated as imports minus exports of the product group "food, basic excluding tea, coffee, cocoa and spices (SITC 0 + 22 + 4 less 07)". The percentage displayed is reached by dividing net food imports with total imports of all products in the corresponding period. Included economies are the top fifteen net importers of import food in 2015 – 2019 after excluding South Sudan for which data are not available before 2011.

A noticeable change has occurred over time in total food trade; the value of exports in basic food in constant 2019 prices has doubled since 2000, reaching almost US$1.3 trillion in 2019, up from US$610 billion in 2000. This is in large part driven by a general increase in merchandise trade, but while 5.4 per cent of merchandise trade was basic food in 2000, this proportion grew to 6.8 per cent in 2019. The growth in trade value has been accompanied by a slow and steady decrease in the export concentration index for basic food from 0.154 in 2000 to 0.125 in 2019. This indicates that economies that previously were not big exporters of food now participate more in the global trade of these products. Indeed, the export concentration of basic food has decreased more than the concentration index for total exports during this period (UNCTAD, 2021b).

Trade in fruits and vegetables, the most traded food-product group, has grown steadily over the last two decades and accounted for 22 per cent (US$ 282 billion) of all exports in total basic food in 2019 (see figure 3). Cereals accounted for 14 per cent of exports of basic food.

Figure 3. Total world export of selected food product groups

(Billions of US$ at constant 2019 prices)

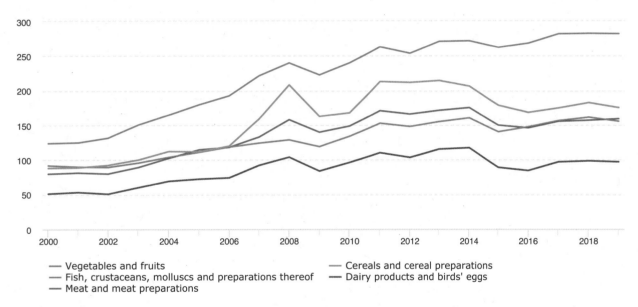

Source: UNCTAD calculations based on UNCTAD (2021b).
Note: Product groups are SITC product groups 01 - 05. These five groups together constituted 67 per cent of the world export in basic food in 2019. All product groups except dairy products and birds' eggs are in the top five in total export value. Fruits also includes nuts. See UNCTAD (2021c) for the product classification used.

Price information is valuable and is being gathered more often

Like other commodities, the price of food has increased over the last two decades. Stable increases in prices give consumers and producers a theoretical chance to budget and plan, whereas volatile prices are more disruptive to the livelihoods of people on both sides of the market. The price of food has been increasing in the second half of 2020, especially in the first months of 2021. There is a strong correlation between food prices and commodity prices generally, though food prices have tended to be less volatile than, for example, non-edible agricultural raw materials or metals (see figure 4). However, sharp rises in food prices between 2007 and 2008 and again in 2011 highlighted the need to develop methods to track price volatility as advance warnings of food crises (Baquedano, 2015).

Figure 4. Growth rate for selected subindices of UNCTAD's Free market commodity price index

(Percentage, monthly, year-on-year)

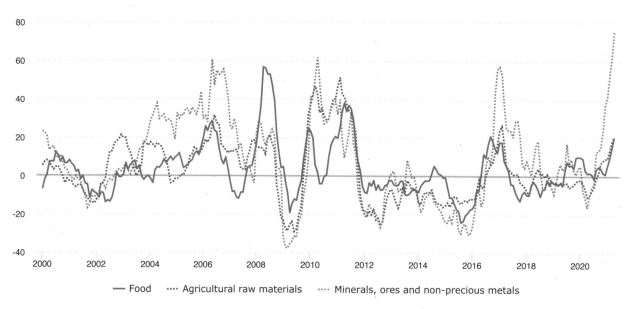

— Food   ···· Agricultural raw materials   ···· Minerals, ores and non-precious metals

Source: UNCTAD (2021b)

Spikes in food prices can deny low-income families' access to sufficient nutritious food. Abnormalities in food prices are in themselves strong indicators of potential threats to food security and provide valuable warning signs, signaling the need for action. Prices carry broad information about recent changes in supply and demand as well as signals about expectations and risks for future food markets. They can be observed easily and frequently (Kalkuhl et al., 2016).

The methodology for the SDG indicator of food price anomalies[2] relies on identifying food prices with growth rates that differ from the historical average (United Nations, 2021a; Baquedano, 2015). Grains are some of the most tracked or monitored food products, most particularly rice (see table 2).[3]

 Table 2. Food price anomalies, 2020 (SDG 2.c.1)

Type of product	Number of economies with price data	Categorization of price		
		Abnormally low	Normal or moderately low/high	Abnormally high
Maize	47	0	41	6
Millet	10	0	8	2
Rice	55	1	49	5
Sorgum	17	0	17	0
Wheat	42	2	34	6

Source: UNCTAD calculations based on United Nations (2021b)

Notes: Abnormal prices are defined as a compound growth rate of one standard deviation or more from the historical mean (United Nations, 2021a). Products are not comparable since product prices are recorded in different economies.

Food price anomalies and volatility are often combined with losses in agricultural income, climate extremes, reduced food access and extreme changes in the quantity, quality and diversity of food consumed (FAO, 2018). The episodes of high food price volatility pose a major threat to food access, especially in developing economies, including LDCs. These episodes are expected to become more frequent with the rising number of extreme climate-related events.

Agricultural export subsidies are vanishing but production is still supported

International trade in open and transparent markets may alleviate the effects of external shocks. UNCTAD has long called for increased transparency and tighter regulation of commodity markets to help avoid speculative bubbles (UNCTAD, 2012). Applying these initiatives in food markets can contribute to food security.

WTO members have agreed that export subsidies may have harmful effects on international trade (see GATT Article XVI, WTO, 2021a). Agricultural subsidies were originally intended to aid domestic producers and farmers in areas where agricultural production costs were high and to ensure the production of enough food to meet domestic needs. Agricultural export subsidies are a form of government intervention to modify a country's terms of trade. They protect producers from international market competition; i.e., economies where the costs of production, such as labour or land, are cheaper. As such, subsidies may have many spillover effects for the global economy where they can exacerbate price volatility and food price spikes. They allow exporters to gain market share without the efficiencies that should accompany such growth.

The WTO Agreement on Agriculture, which came into force in 1995 (WTO, 2021b), has placed limits on export subsidies that distort agricultural trade in order to prevent the disposal or dumping of surplus commodities on global agricultural markets. Following the 2015 Nairobi Ministerial Conference, WTO members have taken steps to phase out export subsidy entitlements from their WTO schedule of commitments in order to level the playing field between developed and developing economies. Apart from a few selected agricultural products, developed countries agreed to remove export subsidies with immediate effect, and most developing countries agreed to do so by 2018. However, developing countries will retain the flexibility to cover marketing and transport costs for agriculture exports until the end of 2023, while the poorest and food-import dependent developing countries will be granted more time to reduce export subsidies (WTO, 2021c).

Notifications of agricultural export subsidies were between US$ three and four trillion in the early years of the 2000s but have since decreased substantially. The 2015 Nairobi package has further strengthened WTO members' commitment to abolish trade-distorting subsidies in agricultural markets. In 2018, only five economies notified WTO about agricultural export subsidies to a total value of US$138 million (see figure 5).

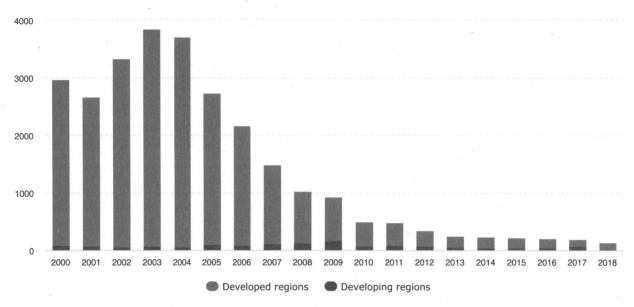

Figure 5. Notifications to WTO of agricultural export subsidy outlay (SDG 2.b.1)
(Millions of US$)

Source: United Nations (2021b).

Notes: Only export subsidies notified to WTO by members who are required to do so are included (United Nations, 2021a).

However, governments still provide substantial support to agricultural producers through budgetary transfers and policy measures that amount to a market price support (OECD, 2020). In OECD countries, these forms of support sum to about US$231 billion in 2019, which accounts for about 18 per cent of gross farm receipts. In 2000, this figure was 31 per cent (OECD, 2021b). Agricultural markets are further supported by budgetary transfers to consumers and by general service supports that are not paid

18% of receipts for **agricultural producers in OECD countries are a result of government support**

directly to producers but has the agricultural sector as its main beneficiary. A report by the Food and Land Use Coalition (2019) estimates that, globally, the agricultural sector is supported to the tune of US$700 billion per year.

The report of the Food and Land Use Coalition (2019) found that the current use of agricultural subsidies leads to inefficient land use and that there are huge opportunities in reorienting subsidies away from high carbon-emitting production and incentives for deforestation and redirecting them towards more sustainable practices. The positive effects would be manifold, including improving global health and combatting climate change. Especially among OECD economies there is a push towards payments to producers that are conditional on production practices that preserve public goods, such as, biodiversity. The OECD notes that policy approaches to support sustainable agriculture are available but remain underutilized (OECD, 2020).

Other intervention measures

Governments have a wide range of policy instruments at their disposal, including tariffs and NTMs. As mentioned in Barriers to trade tariffs on agricultural products are generally considerably higher than those for manufactured products or natural resources. Tariffs are slowly being reduced and NTMs, besides export subsidies, are playing an ever-greater role in international trade.

There are multiple links between NTMs and the SDG goals. NTMs threaten trade openness, but not all measures are harmful. Some measures relate to health and environmental protection. Transparent technical import measures can encourage exporters to fulfill requirements that in turn promote sustainable agriculture. Meeting the challenge of navigating the competing ways that NTMs can affect food security is part of UNCTAD's work in this area (UNCTAD, 2021e).

Most countries impose some form of technical import measure to at least one food product. The most common measures are sanitary and phytosanitary. Of the 91 economies with NTMs recorded in the TRAINS database (UNCTAD, 2021f), 72 have some measure imposed on basic food. All of the 72 have some sanitary and phytosanitary measures and most have more than 50 such measures (see table 3).

OECD (2020) found that government support for agriculture is predominately provided via measures that distort production and trade. Forty per cent of support to agricultural producers, in 2017 – 2019, was in the form of market price supports. These create gaps between effective producer prices and international market prices. The resulting price distortions vary widely between economies but have generally been decreasing over the last two decades. In 2000, agricultural producers received 30 per cent more for their products than international market levels, compared with only 9 per cent in 2019 (OECD, 2021b).

GTA systematically documents trade interventions by traded product and classifies their probable effect as harmful or liberalizing[4]. There is a tendency towards more liberalization of tariffs, but the overwhelmingly biggest category of new measures, 2016 – 2020, are non-technical import measures; of which 2 576 are categorized as harmful[5]. It is also worth noting that though export subsidies seem to be disappearing in figure 5, GTA lists 795 new interventions classified as harmful export subsidies on basic food. The difference between this observation and official SDG data, shown in figure 5, can be explained by differing

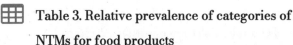

Table 3. Relative prevalence of categories of NTMs for food products

NTM category	Number of economies imposing	Median number of measures per economy
Technical import measures	72	92.5
Sanitary and phytosanitary measures	72	69.5
Technical barriers to trade	70	18
Pre-shipment inspection	59	3
Non-technical import measures	72	12.5
Contingent trade protective measures	3	2
Quantity control measures	68	8
Price control measures	64	4
Other non-technical import measures	35	2
Export measures	71	25

Source: UNCTAD calculations based on UNCTAD (2021f).
Notes: Measures in force as of May 2021. Only measures affecting all countries are included (bilateral measures are excluded). Product groups considered are HS chapter 01-24 excluding 05 – Products of animal origin, not elsewhere specified or included, 06 – Live trees and other plants; bulbs, roots and the like; cut flowers and ornamental foliage, 09 – Coffee, tea, mate and spices, 13 – Lac; gums, resins and other vegetable saps and extracts, 14 – Vegetable plaiting materials; vegetable products not elsewhere specified or included, 22 – Beverages, spirits and vinegar, and 24 – Tobacco and manufactured tobacco substitute. There are, in total, 91 economies in the database.

Non-technical import measures are currently the most common new harmful trade intervention on food products

definitions and by the fact that economies that have pledged to not use export subsidies are not required to notify the WTO if they do (United Nations, 2021a).

Figure 6. Trade interventions implemented between 2016 and 2020 for food products by type and effect

(Number of documented interventions)

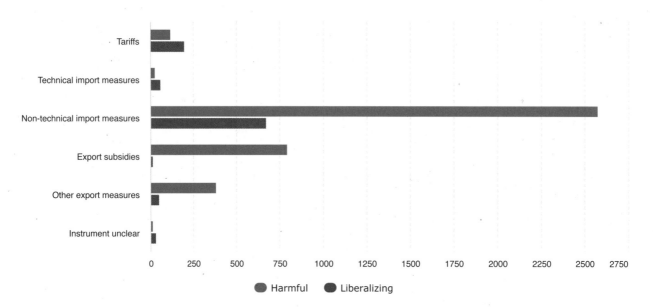

Source: UNCTAD calculations based on Global Trade Alert (2021).
Notes: Included products are HS codes 01-24 minus 05, 06, 09, 13, 14, 22 and 24. The database also contains a total of 42 interventions evaluated "potentially harmful" not displayed.

A review of trade policy changes since 2006 by Bellmann and Hepburn (2017) showed a resurgence of market access protection and government subsidies in order to maintain domestic farm incomes. Indeed, after correcting for the fact that newer interventions have had a shorter time to be documented, analysis of the interventions in the GTA database shows an uneven but upward trend in harmful measures imposed on food products. Moreover, there have been more harmful than liberalizing measures each year since GTA started documenting trade interventions, with the sole exception of 2011 (see figure 7).

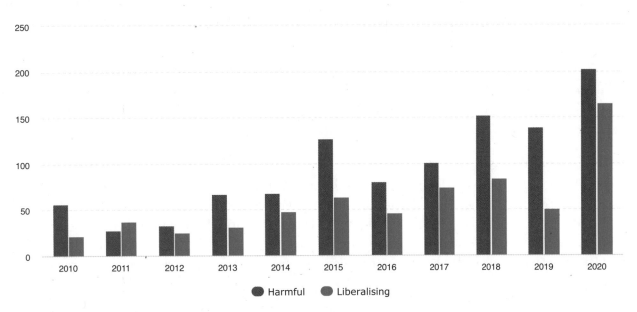

📊 Figure 7. Trade intervention by year and effect

(Number of documented interventions)

Source: UNCTAD calculations based on Global Trade Alert (2021).
Notes: To ensure comparability between years, only interventions documented in the database before the end of the same year are included.

UNCTAD work on trade in biodiversity-related products

Trade in agricultural or food products is only part of total trade on products based on biodiversity (biotrade). This category comprises all products with a biological origin, including vegetable and animal species found on land, water or air. Since 1996, UNCTAD's BioTrade Initiative has fostered trade as an incentive for biodiversity conservation and improved economic and social welfare, particularly in developing countries, through sustainable trade activities. UNCTAD and BioTrade partners focus on enhancing biodiversity-based sectors, creating an enabling policy environment and sustainable sourcing capacities for BioTrade companies, access and benefit-sharing, and increased trade in value-added (UNCTAD, 2021g).

In response to the 2030 Agenda and the SDGs, as well as to reflect evolving legal and policy frameworks, and building on partners' decade-long experience, UNCTAD completed a new version of the BioTrade P&C in early 2020 (UNCTAD, 2007, 2020a). The P&C is a set of guidelines for businesses, governments and civil society wishing to support the conservation and sustainable use of biodiversity, as well as the fair and equitable sharing of benefits through trade.[6] These are promoted under the Global BioTrade programme, launched by UNCTAD in 2018 with the support of the Swiss State Secretariat for Economic Affairs SECO (UNCTAD, 2021h).

BioTrade is being implemented in over 80 countries worldwide in sectors, such as, personal care, phytopharma, food, fashion, handicrafts, textiles and natural fibres and sustainable tourism, among others (UNCTAD, 2016). Sales by BioTrade companies and initiatives reported in 2020 amounted to €9 billion, an increase of nearly 75 per cent from 2019 (UNCTAD, 2020b). New companies implementing the P&C, particularly transnational companies, contributed to this increase in sales despite the challenges linked to the COVID-19 pandemic. The BioTrade Initiative directly supports SDGs 1, 2, 5, 8, 10, 12, 14, 15 and 17 and

Sales by UNCTAD BioTrade entities grew by nearly 75% from 2019 to 2020

additionally contributes to the post-2020 global biodiversity framework to be adopted during the 15th Conference of the Parties to the Convention on Biological Diversity, scheduled for October 2021 (UNCTAD, 2021i).

BioTrade in practice: Supporting the SDGs in the Mekong region

For years, megadiverse countries in the Mekong region have been leaders in developing products and services based on the sustainable use of biodiversity. The regional BioTrade project in Southeast Asia, implemented by Helvetas Swiss Intercooperation, has been supporting companies in implementing the BioTrade P&C in Lao PDR, Myanmar and Viet Nam since 2016 (Helvetas, 2021a).

BioTrade is contributing significantly to the 2030 Agenda by conserving biodiversity, generating livelihoods and food security for rural populations and vulnerable groups, and helping developing countries increase their exports. From January to August 2020, the total exports of BioTrade companies connected to the Regional Biotrade Project reached US$14.7 million for biodiversity-related products. This value is higher than the total annual exports of US$ 12.2 million in 2019. Similarly, 17,575 people (54 per cent of whom are women) in Viet Nam, Myanmar and Lao PDR were employed or enjoyed increased incomes due to the Regional Biotrade Project (Helvetas, 2021b).

Providing the latest data on trade in biodiversity-related products

UNCTAD is also developing a statistical tool providing updated trade flows for biodiversity-based products and will host information from BioTrade partners under a set of "Trade and biodiversity profiles". A pilot exercise was conducted to identify trade flows of BioTrade priority species and products (grouped in over 140 HS Codes) from 2010 to 2018 in 14 BioTrade beneficiary countries in Africa, Latin America and Southeast Asia.

The results of this exercise for Myanmar, Lao PDR and Viet Nam show an increase in exports for the three countries from US$1.6 billion in 2010 to US$5.2 billion in 2018. The top six biodiversity/BioTrade export products were edible fruits, fish meat, non-alcoholic beverages, nuts and other seeds, food preparations, and cosmetics and toilet preparations. As shown in figure 8, BioTrade has grown at a faster rate than overall exports in Myanmar. In Viet Nam BioTrade and general exports have followed similar trends, and did so also in Lao PDR between 2011 and 2016.

Figure 8. Trade value indices for trade in biodiversity-based products and total exports, Lao PDR, Myanmar and Vietnam

(Index, 2010 = 100)

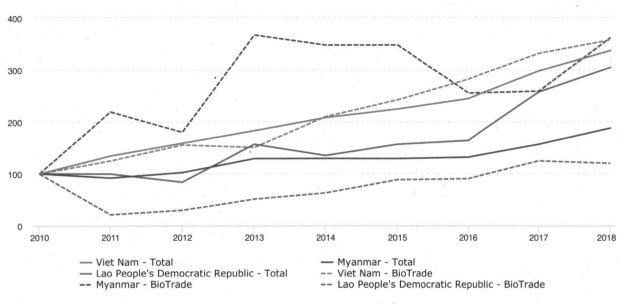

Source: UNCTAD calculations based on United Nations (2021b).

BioTrade products still have a small weight in the total exports for these countries, but this share has shown a growing trend in Myanmar, and since 2011 in Lao PDR. For example, from 2010 to 2018, Myanmar registered a 262 per cent growth in the exports of the selected BioTrade products, three times faster than for overall exports. As a result, the share of BioTrade in total exports in this country increased from 1.5 per cent in 2010 to 2.8 per cent in 2018 (with a maximum of 4.2 per cent in 2013) (see figure 9).

The increasing demand among consumers worldwide for natural and environmentally friendly products continues to offer growing opportunities for BioTrade. The UNCTAD BioTrade initiative is continuously enhancing data availability and more data will become publicly available in 2021 on UNCTADstat under the "Trade and Biodiversity database" (UNCTAD, 2021b).

 Figure 9. Share of BioTrade products in total trade, Myanmar

(Percentage)

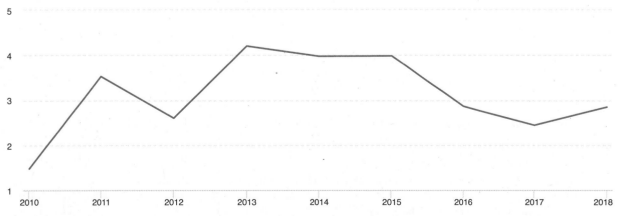

Source: UNCTAD calculations based on United Nations (2021c).

Notes

1. Basic food refers here to a category of food products that excludes beverages and tobacco, tropical beverages (such as coffee and tea) and spices. When SITC codes are used, the included codes are 0 - *Food and live animals*, 22 - *Oil seeds and oleaginous fruits*, 4 - *Animal and vegetable oils, fats and waxes* with the exclusion of 07 - *Coffee, tea, cocoa, spices, and manufactures thereof*. When HS codes are used, basic food refers to chapter 1-24 excluding 05 - *Products of animal origin, not elsewhere specified or included*, 06 - *Live trees and other plants; bulbs, roots and the like; cut flowers and ornamental foliage*, 09 - *Coffee, tea, mate and spices*, 13 - *Lac; gums, resins and other vegetable saps and extracts*, 14 - *Vegetable plaiting materials; vegetable products not elsewhere specified or included*, 22 - *Beverages, spirits and vinegar*, and 24 - *Tobacco and manufactured tobacco substitute*.

2. SDG indicator 2.c.1.

3. The FAO collects and disseminates food commodity prices via the Food Price Monitoring and Analysis database (FAO, 2021). The prices tracked differs from economy to economy. In May 2020 there were annual indicators of food price anomaly for five cereal products from 2015 and 2020 in the Global SDG Database (United Nations, 2021b).

4. A small portion of measures documented in the GTA database are evaluated as "potentially harmful". These are excluded from the present analysis.

5. It is important to note that the number of interventions does not necessarily represent the proportional impact of exports affected by them.

6. The BioTrade P&C are also aligned to the objectives of multilateral environmental agreements, including the Convention on Biological Diversity, the Convention on International Trade in Endangered Species and Wild Fauna and Flora, the Ramsar Convention on Wetlands, and others.

References

- Baquedano FG (2015). Developing an indicator of price anomalies as an early warning tool: A compound growth approach. FAO. Available at http://www.fao.org/giews/food-prices/research/detail/en/c/235685/ (accessed 10 June 2021).

- Bellmann C and Hepburn J (2017). The Decline of Commodity Prices and Global Agricultural Trade Negotiations: A Game Changer? International Development Policy | Revue internationale de politique de développement [Online] 8.1. Available at http://journals.openedition.org/poldev/2384 (accessed 18 June 2020).

- Bobenrieth E, Wright B and Zeng D (2013). Stocks-to-use ratios and prices as indicators of vulnerability to spikes in global cereal markets. *Agricultural Economics*. 44(s1):43–52.

- Coke Hamilton P and Nkurunziza J (2020). COVID-19 and food security in vulnerable countries. Available at https://unctad.org/en/pages/newsdetails.aspx?OriginalVersionID=2331 (accessed 10 June 2021).

- Doshi P (2011). The elusive definition of pandemic influenza. Bulletin of the World Health Organisation. *WHO Bulletin*. 89(7):532–538.

- Famine Early Warnings Systems Network (2021). FEWS NET. Available at https://fews.net/ (accessed 10 June 2021).

- FAO (2018). *The State of Agricultural Commodity Markets 2018: Agricultural Trade, Climate Change and Food Security*. FAO. Rome.

- FAO (2021). FPMA Tool: A web–based tool for analysis and dissemination of price data. Available at http://www.fao.org/giews/food-prices/price-tool/en/ (accessed 10 June 2021).

- Food and Land Use Coalition (2019). Growing better: Ten critical transitions to transform food and land use. The Global Consultation Report of the Food and Land Use Coalition. September. Available at https://www.foodandlandusecoalition.org/global-report/ (accessed 13 June 2021).

- FSIN and Global Network Against Food Crises (2021). Global Report on Food Crises 2021. Rome. Available at https://www.fsinplatform.org/ (accessed 10 June 2021).

- Global Trade Alert (2021). GTA database. Available at https://www.globaltradealert.org/ (accessed 8 June 2021).

- Helvetas (2021a). Vietnam, Laos, Myanmar: Ethical trade in botanicals. Available at https://www.helvetas.org/en/switzerland/what-we-do/how-we-work/our-projects/asia/vietnam/vietnam-laos-myanmar-regional-market (accessed 13 June 2021).

- Helvetas (2021b). Personal communication, July 2021.

- International Food Policy Research Institute (2020a). COVID-19: Trade restrictions are worst possible response to safeguard food security. Available at https://www.ifpri.org/blog/covid-19-trade-restrictions-are-worst-possible-response-safeguard-food-security (accessed 10 June 2021).

- International Food Policy Research Institute (2020b). Covid-19 food trade policy tracker. Available at https://www.ifpri.org/project/covid-19-food-trade-policy-tracker (accessed 10 June 2021).

- ITC (2021). COVID-19 temporary trade measures. Available at https://www.macmap.org/covid19 (accessed 10 June 2021).

- Kalkuhl M, von Braun J and Torero M (2016). Volatile and Extreme Food Prices, Food Security, and Policy: An Overview. In: Kalkuhl M,, von Braun J, and Torero M, eds. *Food Price Volatility and Its Implications for Food Security and Policy*. Springer International Publishing. Cham: 3–31.

- OECD (2020). *Agricultural Policy Monitoring and Evaluation 2020*. OECD Publishing. Paris.

- OECD (2021a). DAC glossary of key terms and concepts. Available at http://www.oecd.org/dac/dac-glossary.htm (accessed 20 April 2021).

- OECD (2021b). OECD Data: Agricultural support. Available at https://data.oecd.org/agrpolicy/agricultural-support.htm (accessed 9 June 2021).

- UNCTAD (2003). Course on Dispute Settlement - Module 3.9. WTO: SPS Measures. UNCTAD/EDM/Misc.232/Add.13. Available at https://unctad.org/en/Pages/DITC/TNCD/Dispute-Settlement-in-International-Trade.aspx (accessed 29 June 2020).

- UNCTAD (2007). *UNCTAD BioTrade Initiative: BioTrade Principles and Criteria*. UNCTAD/DITC/TED/2007/4. New York and Geneva.

- UNCTAD (2012). Don't blame the physical markets: Financialization is the root cause of oil and commodity price volatility. UNCTAD Policy Brief No. 25. UNCTAD/PRESS/PB/2012/1. Geneva. (accessed 10 June 2021).

- UNCTAD (2016). *20 Years of BioTrade: Connecting People, the Planet and Markets*. UNCTAD/DITC/TED/2016/4. Geneva.

- UNCTAD (2018). Indicators explained #1: Export Market Concentration Index. UNCTAD/STAT/IE/2018/1 June. Available at https://unctadstat.unctad.org/EN/IndicatorsExplained.html (accessed 18 June 2020).

- UNCTAD (2020a). *BioTrade Principles and Criteria for Terrestrial, Marine and Other Aquatic Biodiversity-Based Products and Services*. UNCTAD/DITC/TED/2020/2. Geneva.

- UNCTAD (2020b). Global BioTrade Programme: Annual progress report 2019-2020 (internal document).

- UNCTAD (2021a). Towards a new trade agenda for the right to food. UNCTAD Policy Brief No. 83. UNCTAD/PRESS/PB/2021/1. Geneva.

- UNCTAD (2021b). UNCTADStat. Available at https://unctadstat.unctad.org/EN/Index.html (accessed 21 April 2021).

- UNCTAD (2021c). UNCTADStat: Classifications. Available at https://unctadstat.unctad.org/EN/Classifications.html (accessed 10 June 2021).

- UNCTAD (2021d). Classification of Non-Tariff Measures. Available at https://unctad.org/en/Pages/DITC/Trade-Analysis/Non-Tariff-Measures/NTMs-Classification.aspx (accessed 15 May 2021).

- UNCTAD (2021e). NTMs and SDGs. Available at https://unctad.org/en/Pages/DITC/Trade-Analysis/Non-Tariff-Measures/NTMs-and-SDGs.aspx (accessed 11 May 2021).

- UNCTAD (2021f). TRAINS: The global database on Non-Tariff Measures. Available at https://trains.unctad.org/ (accessed 4 May 2021).

- UNCTAD (2021g). BioTrade. Available at https://unctad.org/en/Pages/DITC/Trade-and-Environment/BioTrade.aspx (accessed 13 June 2021).

- UNCTAD (2021h). Global BioTrade Facilitation Programme: Linking trade, biodiversity and sustainable development. Available at https://unctad.org/en/Pages/DITC/Trade-and-Environment/BioTrade/BT-Initiative-Linking-programme.aspx (accessed 13 June 2021).

- UNCTAD (2021i). Post-2020 global biodiversity framework. Available at https://unctad.org/en/Pages/DITC/Trade-and-Environment/BioTrade/BT-Post2020.aspx (accessed 13 June 2021).

- United Nations (2021a). SDG indicators: Metadata repository. Available at https://unstats.un.org/sdgs/metadata/ (accessed 20 April 2021).

- United Nations (2021b). Global SDG Indicators Database. Available at https://unstats.un.org/sdgs/indicators/database/ (accessed 2 April 2021).

- United Nations (2021c). UN Comtrade Database. Available at https://comtrade.un.org/ (accessed 1 January 2021).

- United States Department of Agriculture (2021). Production, Supply and Distribution. Available at https://apps.fas.usda.gov/psdonline/app/index.html#/app/home (accessed 26 May 2021).

- WHO (2020). Q&A on coronaviruses (COVID-19). Available at https://www.who.int/emergencies/diseases/novel-coronavirus-2019/question-and-answers-hub/q-a-detail/q-a-coronaviruses (accessed 11 May 2020).

- WTO (2020). Export prohibitions and restrictions: Information note. April. Available at https://www.wto.org/english/news_e/news20_e/rese_23apr20_e.htm (accessed 10 June 2021).

- WTO (2021a). The General Agreement on Tariffs and Trade (GATT 1947). Available at https://www.wto.org/english/docs_e/legal_e/gatt47_01_e.htm (accessed 18 April 2021).

- WTO (2021b). Agreement on Agriculture. Available at https://www.wto.org/english/docs_e/legal_e/14-ag_01_e.htm (accessed 10 June 2021).

- WTO (2021c). Export subsidies and other export support measures. Available at https://www.wto.org/english/tratop_e/agric_e/factsheetagric17_e.htm (accessed 10 June 2021).

- WTO (2021d). Nairobi Package. Available at https://www.wto.org/english/thewto_e/minist_e/mc10_e/nairobipackage_e.htm (accessed 10 June 2021).

IV. Policies to promote trade (International cooperation and multilateral mechanisms)

SDG indicators

SDG target 8.a: Increase Aid for Trade support for developing countries, in particular least developed countries, including through the Enhanced Integrated Framework for Trade-related Technical Assistance to Least Developed Countries.
SDG indicator 8.a.1:
for Trade commitments and disbursements (Tier I)

What is Aid for Trade?

The Aid for Trade initiative was launched at the 2005 WTO Ministerial Conference in China, Hong Kong (SAR) (WTO, 2015). It is aimed at helping developing countries, particularly LDCs, to build the supply-side capacity and trade-related infrastructure that they need to assist them to implement and benefit from WTO agreements and, more broadly, to engage in international trade. The assistance is targeted at enhancing national trade policy and regulations, developing infrastructure and building productive capacity (UNCTAD, 2016, Target 8.a).

The 2019 joint OECD-WTO Aid for Trade monitoring and evaluation exercise highlighted the importance of diversification, with a focus on promoting growth in the manufacturing sector for African countries. Export diversification is an indispensable part of economic growth and structural transformation, and remains an important development objective for many developing countries (OECD and WTO, 2019). Export demand for manufactured products facilitates growth of the manufacturing sector, thus giving an impetus for structural transformation (see Sustainable industrialization and technology). Industrialization is also paramount for LLDCs as "a thriving labour-intensive manufacturing base is best at generating productive employment" (Bolesta and Tateno, 2019).

Academic research and donor evaluation programmes provide evidence of the positive impact of Aid for Trade (OECD and WTO, 2019). Such evaluation can be limited by scarcity of useful data and methodological challenges (Razzaque and te Velde, 2013). According to OECD and WTO (2013), for every dollar of Aid for Trade, on average eight dollars in exports is generated; this reaches up to twenty dollars for the poorest countries. A recent study on the effectiveness of Aid for Trade suggests that a one per cent increase in Aid for Trade for policies and regulations (as a percentage of GDP) induces a 0.15 per cent decline in tariff volatility (Gnangnon, 2019). The latter study supports the finding that Aid for Trade has a more positive impact on countries with higher economic and political stability (OECD and WTO, 2013).

Increase in Aid for Trade levelled off in the last few years

Aid for Trade commitments and Aid for Trade disbursements have increased by 37 and 65 per cent, respectively, during the last ten years. In 2019, Aid for Trade commitments totalled US$52.9 billion and disbursements US$45.7 billion in constant 2019 prices. The corresponding figures in 2009 were US$38.6 billion and US$27.7 billion. While there has been an overall positive trend in annual Aid for Trade commitments, their volatility has increased somewhat in recent years, mitigating that growth. In 2014, 2016 and 2018, Aid for Trade commitments declined by 2, 8 and 5 per cent from the previous year, respectively, while they grew in 2015 and 2017 by about 12 per cent. In 2019, they declined again by about 6 per cent, marking a relatively steady decline in the last few years since 2017. Realised disbursements remained more stable (see figure 1).

In 2019, Aid for Trade disbursements totalled US$45.7 billion

LDCs 30%

LDCs' share ticked back up to 30% in 2019

ılıl Figure 1. Aid for Trade flows to developing economies

(Billions of US$ in constant 2019 prices)

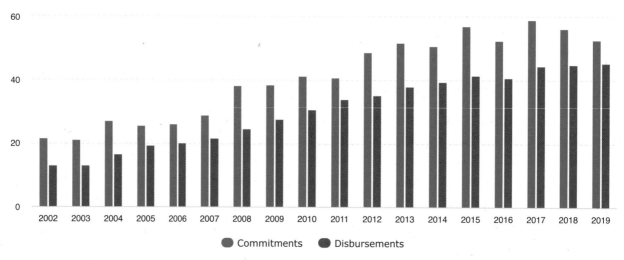

Source: UNCTAD calculations based on data from OECD (2021b).

The disbursements to LDCs grew by almost 70 per cent in ten years from US$8.2 billion in 2009 to US$13.9 billion in 2019 (OECD, 2021b), with growth somewhat slowing down in the last couple of years. LDCs' share of Aid for Trade peaked at just over 30 per cent of the total in 2009, after which it gradually declined to 25 per cent in 2016. After that, in 2017, 2018 and 2019, this share ticked back up to 30 per cent (see figure 2).

Figure 2. Aid for Trade disbursements by recipient

(Billions of US$ in constant 2019 prices)

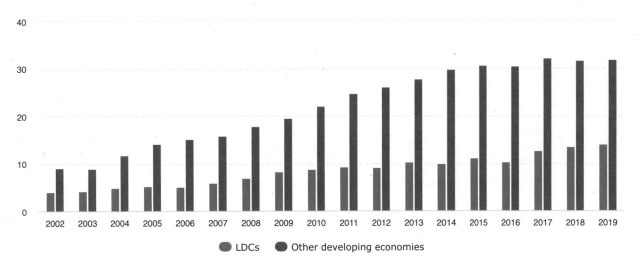

Source: UNCTAD calculations based on data from OECD (2021b) .
Note: Country grouping refer to country classification as per OECD (2021c). LDCs group includes Vanuatu. Please refer to OECD (2021b).

Asia and Africa remain the primary recipients of Aid for Trade

Africa receives the largest share of global Aid for Trade, US$17 billion in 2019

Asia and Africa received most of the global Aid for Trade disbursements in 2019, US$16.99 billion (37 per cent) and US$18.0 billion (39.5 per cent), respectively. Figure 3 shows the largest Aid for Trade recipient countries.

The top ten Aid for Trade recipients shared about 34 per cent of total country-specific disbursements in 2019. They comprise six Asian (Bangladesh, India, Uzbekistan, Pakistan, Philippines and Iraq) and four African countries (Kenya, Morocco, Egypt and Mozambique). Of these countries, Bangladesh and Mozambique are LDCs. To put the 34 per cent in perspective, it should be noted that the total population of these top ten recipients accounts for almost 34 per cent of the total population of developing economies.

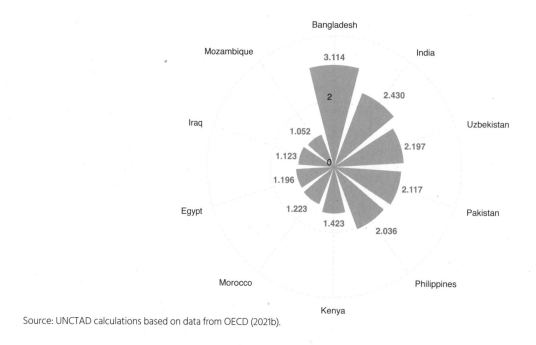

Figure 3. Top 10 recipients of total Aid for Trade disbursements, 2019

(Billions of US$ in constant 2019 prices)

Source: UNCTAD calculations based on data from OECD (2021b).

Official Development Assistance targets trade more often

The share of Aid for Trade in ODA has increased from 22.4 per cent in 2009 to 27.9 per cent in 2019. The share peaked in 2012 at 27.8 per cent but has plateaued since then, with 2019 again reaching that value (see figure 4). Aid for Trade is particularly important for countries whose trade depends on a narrow export basket. For example, in 2018, LDCs depended, on average, on only few products, mainly commodity products which represent 57.6 per cent of their exports. The share of primary commodities in total exports of LDCs decreased in 2019, down to 54.2 per cent. This was mostly due to the lower value of exports of fuels, ores and metals and non-ferrous metals in all LDC exports which decreased to 43.5 per cent in 2019, as compared to 50.3 per cent in 2018. The share of manufactured products in LDC exports, on the contrary, increased from 34.9 per cent in 2018 to 36.6 per cent in 2019, mainly due to a higher share of chemical products (1.8 per cent) and textiles (27.8 per cent) in LDC merchandise exports in 2019, as compared to the previous year (UNCTAD, 2021).

Figure 4. Aid for Trade, share of net ODA disbursements

(Percent)

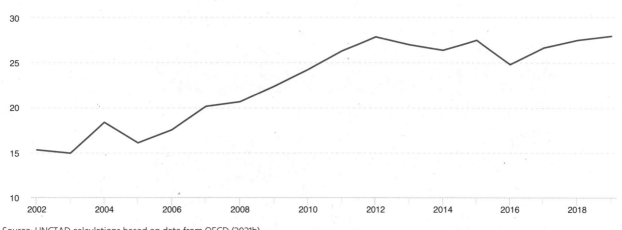

Source: UNCTAD calculations based on data from OECD (2021b).

Transport, energy and agriculture receive the majority of Aid for Trade

Aid for Trade provides support to economic infrastructure (55 per cent in 2019), productive capacity building (43 per cent) and trade policies (2 per cent). Economic infrastructure (transport, communication and energy) has consistently received over 50 per cent of Aid for Trade since 2010 (see figure 5). From 2009 to 2019, the share dedicated to transport and storage has remained rather constant at around 29 per cent of all Aid for Trade, whereas the share targeting energy has increased from 18 to 25 per cent.

Aid for productive capacity targets economic activities that produce goods and services for trade. Agriculture, forestry and fishing together account for almost half of the support for productive capacity, while aid targeting banking and financial services constitute about 27 per cent. Aid for banking increased between 2009 and 2019 from US$3.9 billion to US$5.1 billion.

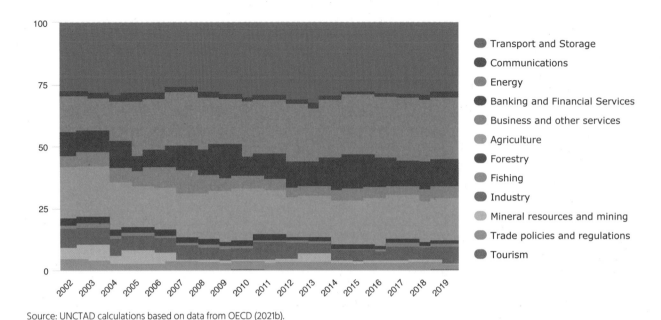

Figure 5. Distribution between sectors of total Aid for Trade disbursements

(Proportion of total)

Legend:
- Transport and Storage
- Communications
- Energy
- Banking and Financial Services
- Business and other services
- Agriculture
- Forestry
- Fishing
- Industry
- Mineral resources and mining
- Trade policies and regulations
- Tourism

Source: UNCTAD calculations based on data from OECD (2021b).

Energy and transport overtake agriculture as a target of Aid for Trade in Africa

The sectors receiving Aid for Trade disbursements vary across regions. About 43 per cent of the Aid for Trade disbursements to Asia and Oceania go to transport, and together with energy these account for over 69 per cent of Aid for Trade to this region. At nearly 27 per cent, energy, overtook agriculture, forestry and fishing (25 per cent) as the largest recipient sector of Aid for Trade in Africa, with transport closely following at 20 per cent. In Europe, on the other hand, banking and financial services receive the second largest share of Aid for Trade disbursements (24 per cent) after transport (27 per cent), while in America the largest sectors are energy (33 per cent) and transport (27 per cent).

In 2019, energy sector received 27% of the Aid for Trade in Africa

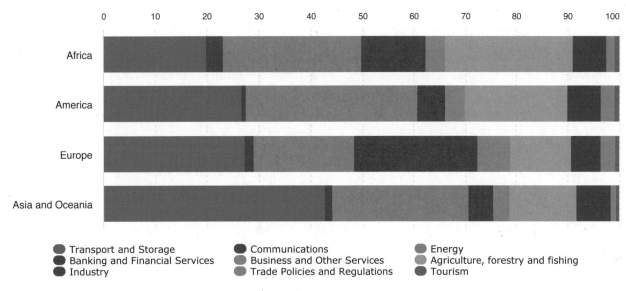

Figure 6. Aid for trade disbursements by sector and recipient region, 2019

(Proportion of total)

Legend:
- Transport and Storage
- Banking and Financial Services
- Industry
- Communications
- Business and Other Services
- Trade Policies and Regulations
- Energy
- Agriculture, forestry and fishing
- Tourism

Source: UNCTAD calculations based on data from OECD (2021b).

The COVID-19 related disruptions to global value chains - a major risk to LDCs

As noted earlier, LDCs often rely on a small set of export goods and, depending on the product mix, risk losing a significant portion of export revenues due to a sharp fall in demand caused by the COVID-19 pandemic and falls in prices (for commodity exporters). Global markets are severely impacted by the pandemic, which significantly increases the need for Aid for Trade to LDCs and other vulnerable countries. The disruptions to trade in LDCs relate to shortages of raw materials from China and other large economies, for example in the garment industry, and to widespread business closures in many countries affecting LDCs in sectors where they are involved as sub-contractors. Many LDCs also depend on services, which contribute a large share to their export revenue, GDP and employment, especially tourism and transport, which are badly hit by the pandemic.

By May 2021, more than 45 countries had above 70 export restrictions in force as the result of the COVID-19 pandemic

According to WTO (2021), as of end of May 2021, 7 export restrictions and 64 quantitative restrictions as a result of the COVID-19 pandemic had been notified by more than 45 countries. Most of these focus on medical supplies (e.g. facemasks and shields), pharmaceuticals and medical equipment (e.g. ventilators), but also additional products, such as foodstuffs and toilet paper.

Although it is too early to predict the impact of COVID-19 on Aid for Trade flows, they will be critical for the most vulnerable countries, such as LDCs and LLDCs, in helping a swift recovery from the economic impacts of the pandemic. There could be a temporary decline in Aid for Trade due to resources being channelled toward COVID-19 response efforts in donor countries (figure 7). Since Aid for Trade, as part of ODA (see Official support for sustainable development), is linked to the GNI of each donor country, a reduction in global economic activity will generally mean decreased Aid for Trade flows unless special efforts are undertaken.

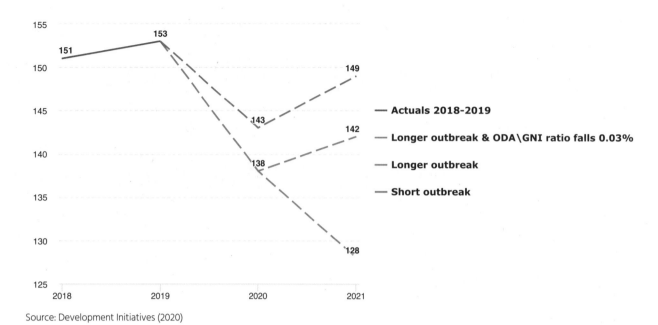

Figure 7. Possible impact of Covid-19 on 2021 ODA levels

(Billions of US$ in constant 2019 prices)

- **Actuals 2018-2019**
- **Longer outbreak & ODA\GNI ratio falls 0.03%**
- **Longer outbreak**
- **Short outbreak**

Source: Development Initiatives (2020)

Several developed and some developing countries have announced stimulus packages, such as additional funding to businesses or fiscal policy measures to support their economies, which may not be feasible for LDCs. Global collaboration is needed to pool financial support – including a recent Call to Action (IMF, 2020) to suspend debt payments for IDA countries. Analyses by the World Bank warns that COVID-19 could push up to an additional 60 million people into extreme poverty (the share of the world's population living on less than US$1.90 per day) (CCSA, 2020).

ODA levels are projected to fall in 2021 up to 16% as compared to 2019 levels as a result of the COVID-19

References

- AidFlows (2019). Glossary of AidFlows terms. Available at http://www.aidflows.org/about/ (accessed 17 June 2019).
- Bolesta A and Tateno Y (2019). Structural Transformation in Asia-Pacific Small Island Developing States. UNESCAP MPDD Policy Brief No. 100. UNESCAP.
- CCSA (2020). How COVID-19 is changing the world: A statistical perspective. Available at https://unstats.un.org/unsd/ccsa/documents/covid19-report-ccsa.pdf (accessed 8 June 2020).
- Development Initiatives (2020). Coronavirus and aid data: What the latest DAC data tells us. Briefing. April. Available at https://devinit.org/resources/coronavirus-and-aid-data-what-latest-dac-data-tells-us/ (accessed 24 June 2020).
- Doshi P (2011). The elusive definition of pandemic influenza. Bulletin of the World Health Organisation. *WHO Bulletin*. 89(7):532–538.
- Gnangnon SK (2019). Effect of Aid for Trade Policy and Regulations on Tariff Policy Volatility: Does Institutional and Governance Quality Matter? *Economies*. 7(1):6.
- IMF (2020). Joint Statement World Bank Group and IMF Call to Action on Debt of IDA Countries. Available at https://www.imf.org/en/News/Articles/2020/03/25/pr20103-joint-statement-world-bank-group-and-imf-call-to-action-on-debt-of-ida-countries (accessed 20 June 2021).
- Negin J (2014). Devpolicyblog. Available at http://www.devpolicy.org/understanding-aid-for-trade-part-one-a-dummys-guide-20140228/ (accessed 19 June 2019).

- OECD (2021a). DAC glossary of key terms and concepts. Available at http://www.oecd.org/dac/dac-glossary.htm (accessed 20 April 2021).

- OECD (2021b). Aid-for-trade statistical queries. Available at https://www.oecd.org/dac/aft/aid-for-tradestatisticalqueries.htm (accessed 17 June 2021).

- OECD (2021c). Available at https://www.oecd.org/dac/financing-sustainable-development/development-finance-standards/daclist.htm (accessed 17 July 2020).

- OECD and WTO (2013). *Aid for Trade at a Glance 2013: Connecting to Value Chains*. Aid for Trade at a Glance. OECD.

- OECD and WTO (2019). *AIDFORTRADE AT A GLANCE 2019: ECONOMIC DIVERSIFICATION AND EMPOWERMENT*. Aid for Trade at a Glance. WTO and OECD Publishing. Geneva and Paris.

- Razzaque MA and te Velde DW, eds. (2013). *Assessing Aid for Trade: Effectiveness, Current Issues and Future Directions*. Commonwealth Secretariat. London.

- UNCTAD (2016). Development and globalization: Facts and figures 2016. Available at https://stats.unctad.org/Dgff2016/ (accessed 6 April 2020).

- UNCTAD (2021). UNCTADStat. Available at https://unctadstat.unctad.org/EN/Index.html (accessed 21 April 2021).

- United Nations (2021). SDG indicators: Metadata repository. Available at https://unstats.un.org/sdgs/metadata/ (accessed 20 April 2021).

- WHO (2020). Q&A on coronaviruses (COVID-19). Available at https://www.who.int/emergencies/diseases/novel-coronavirus-2019/question-and-answers-hub/q-a-detail/q-a-coronaviruses (accessed 11 May 2020).

- WTO (2006). Aid for Trade Task Force - Recommendations of the Task Force on Aid for Trade. WT/AFT/1.

- WTO (2015). Ministerial declaration. WT/MIN(05)/DEC. Hong Kong. 22 December. Available at https://www.wto.org/english/thewto_e/minist_e/min05_e/final_text_e.htm (accessed 1 June 2021).

- WTO (2021). WTO members' notifications on COVID-19. Available at https://www.wto.org/english/tratop_e/covid19_e/notifications_e.htm (accessed 25 May 2021).

Productive Growth

"Exploration is the engine that drives innovation. Innovation drives economic growth".

— Edith Widder

Productive growth

Sustained and inclusive economic growth is an essential requisite for poverty eradication and sustainable development. Productive infrastructure, access to ICT and new technologies, and a stable macroeconomic environment are some of the most important determinants of long-term growth. These are some of the topics covered in this theme of SDG Pulse, along with the domestic and international mechanisms available to finance these policies.

As shown in the statistics and insights presented in SDG Pulse, there are great opportunities to use infrastructure, new technologies, sound economic policy and stable financing mechanisms as enablers of growth. However, these same areas, when not properly managed, could also become obstacles for development. The SDG indicators allow countries to monitor these areas and identify the most urgent priorities.

Available data on these SDG indicators show a mixed picture. On one hand, there has been significant progress in developing economies in many areas, including access to ICT technologies among the population and a growing weight as transport hubs for global trade. On the other hand, there are also important concerns in many countries in terms of access to international sources of financing for development and their financial sustainability, for instance external public and private debt. In terms of domestic resource mobilization, the topic of illicit financial flows is increasingly considered as a significant threat to sustainable development, one requiring concerted national and international efforts to contain it.

The **weight of international financing** sources for developing economies has decreased since 2005, but it still represents **4% of their GNI**.

UNCTAD & OECD SDG indicator 17.3.1

121 **countries** had signed a bilateral investment **treaty with an LDC** in 2020.

UNCTAD SDG indicator 17.5.1

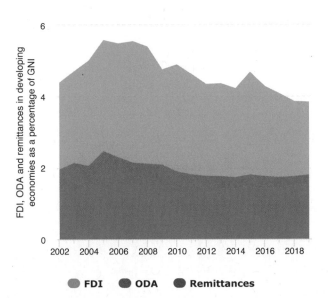

121 countries

Donor countries continue to fall short on their ODA commitments.

SDG indicator 17.2.1

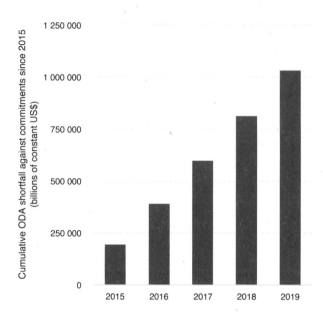

International maritime transport continues to increase in line with trade volume growth.

SDG indicator 9.1.2

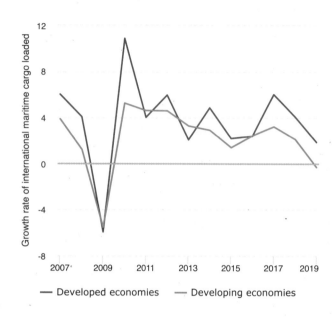

Access to ICT technologies, including broadband connections, continues to rise in developing countries, but they still lag behind the levels of developed economies.

SDG indicator 17.6.1

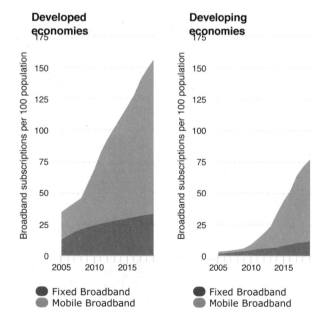

As external debt stocks in the developing world expand, debt service continues to rise, especially in low-income economies.

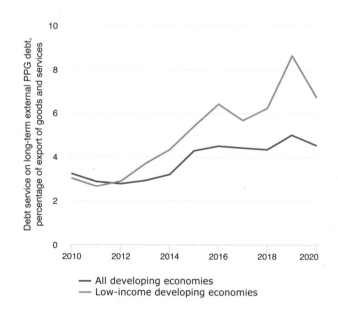

Pilots will help to find **feasible country-specific solutions** to applying the common framework for IFFs.

UNCTAD & UNODC SDG indicator 16.4.1

Pilots will help to find feasible country-specific solutions to applying the common framework for IFFs

I. Robust and predictable sources of financing for sustainable development

Many countries lack the capacity to mobilise sufficient funds under the right conditions to support programmes and implement reforms towards sustainable development. In addition, even at an aggregate level, there can be considerable fluctuation in resource flows from one year to the next (United Nations, 2017). These economic flows can also have a vastly different impact on short and long-term sustained development depending on their source, type and volume. For this reason, financing strategies for the 2030 Agenda receive a prominent role in all implementation strategies.

There are two crucial challenges when it comes to financing development programmes. First, there is a general need for more resources to achieve the SDGs. Second, it is important to find the right mix and adequate terms of financing in order to have a lasting effect and reach those individuals, households and communities with the most urgent needs and where the highest impact can be achieved.

Different external financing sources are better for different aspects of development

The outcome documents of the most recent United Nations International Conferences on Finance for Development (Monterrey Consensus: United Nations, 2003, Addis Ababa Action Agenda: 2015) state that the primary responsibility for financing development belongs to the countries themselves. Therefore, governments must enhance their domestic resource mobilization so that financing needs are met in a predictable and sustained manner. However, the international community also has an important role to play. Sources of external financing include international trade, FDI and other private flows (from businesses and individuals), international financial and technical cooperation, and external debt. These different forms of economic flows are, however, not assumed to be equal in their effect on development.

International trade has expanded significantly in previous decades under the existing multilateral trading system, while many new and longstanding challenges remain. These issues are covered in Multilateralism for Trade & Development. International trade is an important engine for economic growth. With adequate support and fostering mechanisms, trade can encourage long-term investments and higher productivity, create jobs and livelihoods for millions, and provide important resources to finance public services and policy interventions. However, a high dependence on international markets could increase exposure to global volatility and macroeconomic imbalances, as well as imperil vulnerable or immature domestic industries to excessive competition. If not managed properly, trade can create imbalanced development opportunities thus promoting inequality across population groups, as well as between women and men (see Luomaranta et al. (2020) and The Many Faces of Inequality).

Public debt is another essential financing mechanism for development. As long as funds raised by external or domestic borrowing support strategic productive investment, they can foster growth without threatening future financial stability. It is, therefore, important for countries to reach long-term debt sustainability. This topic is covered in depth in Developing countries' external debt sustainability.

LDCs received just more than 1% of global FDI inflows in 2019

FDI remains a vital source of financing for development. With inflows of US$790 billion in developing economies in 2019 (UNCTAD, 2021a), FDI was the largest source of external financing in these countries (UNCTAD, 2021b). Moreover, these flows are directly linked to the main drivers of productive growth and employment creation: establishment of new businesses and greenfield investments; expansion of operations; acquisition of machinery and equipment; upgrade of technology, knowledge and innovation; and others. However, FDI inflows are not distributed evenly among countries; instead, they are concentrated among countries with higher growth prospects, stronger rule of law and respect for contracts, and stable institutions. This means that some countries with urgent financing needs may be bypassed. FDI to LDCs represented only 1.3 per cent of global inflows in 2019, for example (UNCTAD, 2021b). In addition, this source of external financing remains tied to macroeconomic performance and the global economic climate. It is, therefore, typically a pro-cyclical flow that may be absent in times when sustained financing is most needed. FDI flows will be severely impacted by the global pandemic, with the expectation that 2020 levels will drop significantly lower than the trough attained during the 2008 financial crisis. LDCs and developing countries figure to be especially hard hit with their reliance on export and commodity-based investments, which have been hit especially hard during the pandemic.

Remittances lack the employment creation potential of FDI because they are managed directly by individuals and are mostly directed towards household consumption. Their capacity to raise productive investment is, therefore, limited. However, remittances are an indispensable source of income for many countries. In LDCs, for example, they are the most important source of external financing, remaining substantially higher than FDI in 2019 (US$51 billion compared with US$20 billion) (UNCTAD, 2021b). Remittances are also a stable source of income for families, contributing to housing, nutrition, health and education. Thus, they act as an important social safety net. In addition, in countries with an active support policy, remittances have become a significant source of funds for improving social and economic infrastructure.

Official international support plays a unique role when it comes to supporting global development, especially for LDCs and other vulnerable economies. In addition to its concessional nature, official support is the only source of financing available in many cases. Especially in situations of low rentability or high risk, official support can become important for mobilizing additional resources. This source of funding is described in greater detail in Official Support for Sustainable Development.

In this context, it is also important to monitor South-South Cooperation. Links and connections between countries of the Global South have expanded in volume and scope over the previous decades. This is explained to a certain extent by the increasing political and economic weight of several emerging and developing economies across Asia, Africa and Latin America. It is now recognized as an important source of finance for development. Its importance is emphasized in the 2030 Agenda and the Addis Ababa Action Agenda. However, for a variety of reasons, including the lack of a universally accepted definition and opacity regarding its scope and coverage, South-South Cooperation has proven hard to quantify (Besharati and MacFeely, 2019). For this reason, at the 51st session of the UN Statistical Commission in 2020, a special working group on the measurement of development support was established to develop an indicator for SDG target 17.3 (United Nations Statistical Commission, 2020). This work will include recommendations on how to measure South-South Cooperation.

Recent trends in external financing

Financing for development is a crucial element of the 2030 Agenda. SDG target 10.b seeks to "encourage official development assistance and financial flows, including foreign direct investment, to States where the need is greatest [...]" To this end, SDG indicator 10.b.1 measures total resource flows for development. Figure 1 presents recent trends in these flows for three groups of economies, LDCs, LLDCs and SIDS, that face heightened challenges in achieving their development goals.

Figure 1. Total resource disbursements for development (SDG 10.b.1)
(Billions of current US$)

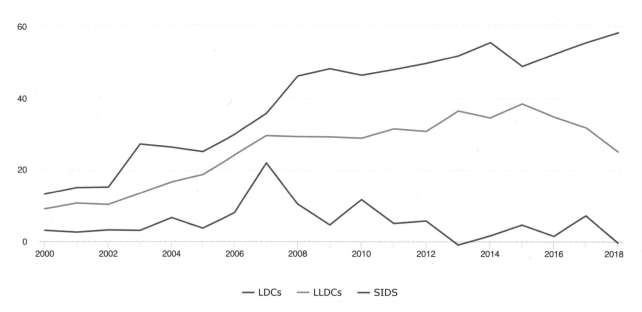

Source: UNCTAD calculations based on data from OECD (2021a).

Even expressed in current prices, the trends in external financing have not been homogeneous through time or across country groups. Resource flows to LDCs increased fourfold between 2000 and 2018. However, most of this increase was registered before 2010. Since then, total external funding for LDCs has increased at a slower rate and with some transitory reversals. Figure 1 shows a more disappointing evolution for LLDCs. The years from 2000 to 2007 showed sustained growth in funding, followed by several years of stagnation. An improvement during the years 2012 to 2015 was followed by three straight years of decline, falling back to 2006 levels in 2018. Funding for

SIDS has shown more modest volumes and greater volatility. After a peak of US$22 billion in 2007, external financing has seen steep declines, practically drying out in 2018.

The use of this variable as a measure of external financing for development for SDG indicator 10.b.1 has received some criticism. Some important sources of funds are missing. For example, remittances, an important flow in many developing countries, is not included. Furthermore, only the 30 DAC countries and 17 non-DAC countries are included. OECD (2019) acknowledge that the coverage of private sector flows from non-DAC donors should be expanded. This is a particularly important omission at a time when South-South Cooperation is increasingly important as a source of revenue and a driving force for collaboration among developing and transition economies. Thus, the official data of this indicator are likely to under-estimate total financial flows for development.

SDG indicator 17.3.1 examines financial support for development from multiple sources, but as a proportion to GNI. This transformation puts external financing in context with all sources of income in the national economy. Figure 2 shows the results for LDCs, LLDCs, and SIDS. The figure also includes remittances because, although not part of the official SDG indicator, they are an important revenue source for many countries.

 **Figure 2. FDI, ODA and remittances**

(Percentage of GNI)

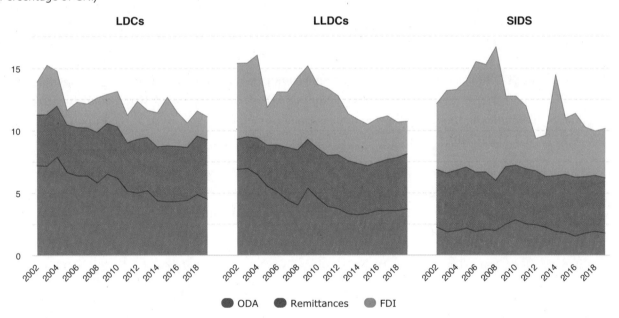

Source: UNCTAD calculations based on data from OECD (2021b) and World Bank (2021).

Between 2002 and 2019 FDI, ODA and remittances accounted for 13% of GNI for LLDCs on average, and 12% for SIDS

Figure 2 shows the importance of external financing flows to LDCs, LLDCs and SIDS. The three sources combined on occasion amount to 15 per cent or more of total GNI, though in recent years this share has been decreasing, driven mostly by slowdowns in FDI or ODA. In fact, although a sizable source of financial flows, FDI shows high volatility, in addition to a downward trend since 2008 for LLDCs and SIDS. Remittances for all three groups routinely account for more than 4 per cent of GNI and they are significant both in terms of high volume and low volatility. They have surpassed FDI for all three groups since 2013, apart from SIDS in 2014 and 2016. Remittances represent a more stable inflow than FDI, with a standard deviation almost 10 times lower over the period covered in figure 2. The observed downward trends for FDI and ODA in these groups of economies indicate room for policies to attract investment and other sources of funds to the places where they are most urgently needed.

There is a risk that the measures to contain the COVID-19 outbreak may put a brake on all the sources of financing described above. The global economic recession of 2020 will entail less available official and private resources, capital flight from developing economies and increased risk aversion, higher unemployment and lower wages, and rising financing costs.[2] A consequence of this may be reversals in hard-earned progress towards development goals. As described in each of the chapters cited above, it is crucial to implement measures aimed at sustaining the financing sources of the most vulnerable economies.

National and international investment policies of home countries promote investment in developing countries

SDG target 17.5 encourages countries to promote investment for LDCs. Developed economies have implemented some policies and measures to encourage outward FDI, including investment in LDCs and other developing countries. Emerging economies have also begun to do so. These policies include mainly investment guarantees protecting outward investors against certain political risks in a host country, financial and fiscal support, mostly in form of loans, or direct capital participation by a home state in an investment project abroad. The conclusion of IIAs is yet another policy tool. Furthermore, governments of countries receiving investment have also put in place investment policies and measures to attract inward FDI to their economies.

The intention of SDG indicator 17.5.1 is to measure the "number of countries that adopt and implement investment promotion regimes for developing countries, including LDCs". As a result of work done by UNCTAD, as the custodian of this indicator, the definitions and measurement methodologies were agreed upon in late 2019 by the IAEG-SDG (UNCTAD, 2021b).

Investment promotion instruments are generally available for outward investment in any foreign country or economy. Promotion tools targeted specifically at supporting investment in LDCs could not be identified, nevertheless a limited number of countries promote outward investment in selected developing or transition economies.

Even if most home countries do not yet have in place investment promotion regimes targeting specific groups of countries, such as LDCs, progress on these indicators can be assessed by looking at the number and amount of investment guarantees and financial and fiscal support that home countries and international institutions have provided to investors when investing in LDCs and other developing countries. In addition, one can count the number of BITs concluded with LDCs, as this type of IIAs are concluded bilaterally and can thus be allocated to LDCs.

In total, UNCTAD identified 22 countries that provide for at least one type of instrument for promoting outward investment in other countries, including LDCs in 2020. The most common policy instruments are investment guarantees or insurance policies (at least 16), but countries provide also loans for internationalization of local companies (at least 13). Almost half of identified countries offers minority equity participation as well (at least 11).

The COVID-19 outbreak has also affected the number of IIAs concluded in 2020, leading to a low number of IIAs with substantive investment protection standards. The conclusion of an IIA usually requires intensive negotiations involving the travel of government officials, organization of domestic consultation meetings and preparatory steps that vary from one country to another. While governments were able to shift some of these activities online, for example negotiations of the AfCFTA's Investment Protocol resumed in late 2020, treaty making activity in 2021 is likely to continue to be somewhat suppressed.

Modernizing international investment agreements slowed down

UNCTAD works with members states to modernize IIAs using the Investment Policy Framework for Sustainable Development first developed in 2012 and updated in 2015 (UNCTAD, 2015). Since then, over 150 countries have formulated new sustainable, development oriented and equitable IIAs. These modernized IIAs emphasize investment for sustainable development and focus on reforming investment policy.

Modernization of the stock of 2 500 old-generation IIAs in force today is still outstanding. Most recently, UNCTAD has launched the IIA Reform Accelerator (UNCTAD, 2020) to expedite this process. The Accelerator responds to the need for change of substantive aspects of the IIA regime by focusing on a selection of reform-oriented formulations for eight key IIA clauses (including fair and equitable treatment, and indirect expropriation provisions). The IIA Reform Accelerator identifies ready-to-use model language, accompanied by recent IIA and model BIT examples.

This work is further supported by UNCTAD "Action Packages" for investment to mainstream SDGs into IPAs and investment strategies (UNCTAD, 2018). Modern industrial policies often directly promote SDG-related industries, such as clean energy, electric vehicles, ecotourism, health care and education, but the process of modernizing industrial policies is slow. This progress has further slowed down, at least momentarily, due to the COVID-19 pandemic and the related slowdown in IIA negotiations.

In 2020, the number of effective treaty terminations exceeded the number of treaties concluded, with only 21 newly signed IIAs compared with 42 IIAs terminated. More than half of the newly signed IIAs were concluded by the United Kingdom as a consequence of leaving the European Union. Notable among the newly signed IIAs is the Regional Comprehensive Economic Partnership (RCEP) which covers 15 signatories in the Asia-Pacific region, including three LDCs. When reviewing investment promotion for LDCs, it is possible to analyse bilateral IIAs, namely BITs concluded with LDCs. According to UNCTAD (2021c), developed economies have 224 BITs in place with LDCs and developing economies (other than LDCs) about 283 BITs. In addition, LDCs have some 28 BITs in place with other LDCs (see figure 3).

Figure 3. Bilateral investment treaties with LDCs by development status of donor countries

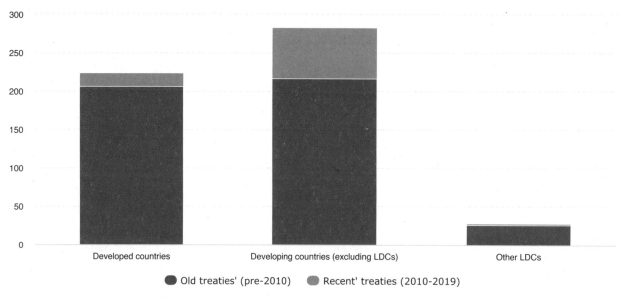

Source: UNCTAD (2021b).

Treaty making with LDCs peaked at the turn of the millennium but fell to a low point in 2019, when only three new BITs were signed and none entered in force. Thereafter, the pace of treaty making with LDCs began to revive slightly. The increase in developing countries' BITs after 2000 reflected a growing emphasis on investment in development strategies related to South-South cooperation, as well as the emergence of some developing country firms as global players (UNCTAD, 2006) (see figure 4). This pace, however, has slowed down since 2017.

Figure 4. Number of BITs with LDCs signed and entered in force each year

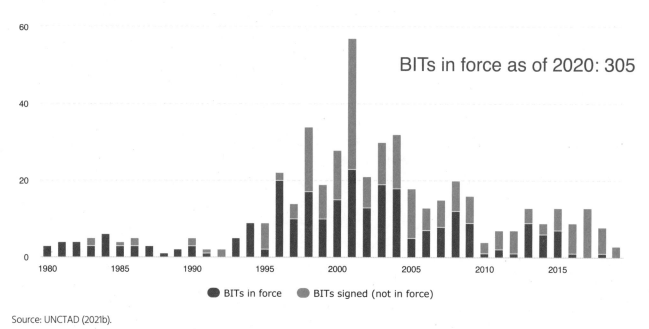

Source: UNCTAD (2021b).

Typically, LDCs' BITs with other countries are still "old generation" treaties that are in need of modernization so that they can help achieve more sustainability-oriented development outcomes. BITs and other IIAs could be reformed in five areas: (i) safeguarding the right to regulate, while providing protection; (ii) reforming investment dispute settlement; (iii) promoting and facilitating investment; (iv) ensuring responsible and sustainable investment; and (v) enhancing systemic consistency (UNCTAD, 2017). LDCs concluded 86 "new generation" BITs between 2010 and 2020, while 449 existing "old generation" BITs, dating from before 2010, have not yet been reformed. Most of these old generation BITs make little or no reference to sustainable development objectives or to the right of LDCs to regulate investment in the public interest. UNCTAD's Investment Policy Framework for Sustainable Development (UNCTAD, 2015), its Reform Package for the International Investment Regime (UNCTAD, 2018) and the newly released IIA Reform Accelerator (UNCTAD, 2020) can guide countries in reforming these old-generation IIAs.

Developed economies, including many EU member states, have the largest number of BITs with LDCs; for instance, Germany has 33. The top ten economies, listed in table 1, are also well placed to contribute to the modernization of investment agreements with LDCs to consider sustainable development and social responsibility. The LDCs with the most BITs in place with other economies comprise Yemen, Ethiopia and Sudan (see table 1). Efforts to modernize investment treaties would have a potentially large effect on these LDCs to promote investment for development.

 Table 1. Economies with the most BITs with LDCs, as of end-2020

Top 10 developed countries with most BITs with LDCs

Developed country	Number of BITs
Germany	33
Switzerland	25
France	18
Belgium and Luxembourg	17
United Kingdom	17
The Netherlands	16
Italy	15
Portugal	7
Spain	7
Sweden	7

Top 10 LDCs with BITs

LDC country	Number of BITs
Yemen	36
Ethiopia	32
Sudan	30
Bangladesh	29
Senegal	28
Mozambique	27
Cambodia	26
Guinea	24
Laos	23
Mali	22
Mauritania	22

Source: UNCTAD (2021b).
Note: Belgium/Luxembourg are included as a group because they negotiate treaties together as an economic union (Ministry of Foreign and European Affairs, Luxembourg, 2018).

Africa was the main recipient for development finance

OECD (2021c) collects data on funds mobilized from the private sector by development finance interventions, such as investment guarantees, syndicated loans, credit lines and direct investment in companies. According to preliminary data by OECD, a total of US$260 billion was mobilized globally from 2012 to 2019, with a drop of 10 per cent in 2019 from the previous year. In 2019, over nine per cent of the amounts mobilized supported LDCs, totalling US$4.4 billion. Support to LDCs increased by 14 per cent from 2018.

9% of private funds mobilized by **development finance targeted LDCs** in 2019

In the period 2017-2018, development finance was divided evenly across the five continents. Among LDCs, the top recipients were Uganda, Myanmar, Benin, Mauritania and Bangladesh, receiving half of the support to LDCs. The top sectors receiving development finance in LDCs were energy (US$677 million), banking (US$503 million), industry and construction (US$303 million) as well as communications (US$211 million).

Overall, investment guarantees were the instrument that mobilized the most funds for LDCs, US$2.6 billion according to preliminary figures for 2019, accounting for about 60 per cent of the total. Other financing tools included direct investment, syndicated loans, credit lines and co-financing. In 2017-2018, the largest bilateral providers were France, the United States of America, the United Kingdom, Finland and the Netherlands. The flows from Finland consisted of direct investment only; the Netherlands mainly offered syndicated loans; whereas the other three utilised more often investment guarantees.

LDCs received US$2.6 billion in investment guarantees in 2019

LDCs' own measures help to attract investment

A complete direct measure of SDG indicator 17.5.1 is not yet available. Instead, in addition to the data presented above, investment promotion regimes put in place by LDCs themselves, or other outward investment promotion measures directed to LDCs, can be examined. LDCs' own investment promotion regimes play an important role in attracting FDI (see figure 5).

Figure 5. Number of new national investment promotion and facilitation measures

(Number of policies)

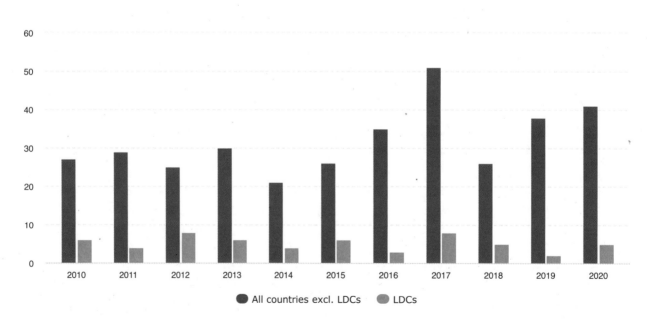

Source: UNCTAD (2021c).
Notes: This graph depicts data on positive investment measures (i.e., new investment promotion or facilitation schemes).

Between 2010 and 2020, at least 406 new investment promotion and facilitation measures were introduced around the world, of which 57 by LDCs. These measures mainly include investment facilitation, investment incentives and special economic zones. Investment incentives are the most common mechanism, accounting for almost half of all new measures (49 per cent). Investment facilitation was more common in countries other than LDCs. Africa (28 per cent) and Asia (37 per cent) accounted for the bulk of new promotion and facilitation measures introduced by all countries between 2010 and 2020. Africa also accounted for 79 per cent of all promotion and facilitation measures introduced by LDCs during this period, with Asia accounting for the rest.

Notes

1. Indicator 17.3.1 was changed from as a proportion of total domestic budget to as a proportion of GNI (United Nations, 2020a, 2020b).

2. For example, World Bank and KNOMAD (2020) expect a decline in global workers' remittances of 20 per cent in 2020.

References

- Besharati N and MacFeely S (2019). Defining and quantifying South-South Cooperation. UNCTAD Research Paper No. 30. UNCTAD/SER.RP/2019/2. Geneva.

- Doshi P (2011). The elusive definition of pandemic influenza. Bulletin of the World Health Organisation. *WHO Bulletin*. 89(7):532-538.

- ILO (2020). Unemployment rate. Available at https://www.ilo.org/ilostat-files/Documents/description_UR_EN.pdf (accessed 15 June 2020).

- IMF (2009). *International Transactions in Remittances: Guide for Compilers and Users (RCG)*. IMF. Washington, D.C.

- IMF (2014). *External Debt Statistics: Guide for Compilers and Users*. IMF. Washington, D.C.

- Luomaranta H, Cantu F, MacFeely S and Peltola A (2020). The impact of multinational and trading enterprises on gender equality - Case Finland. Available at https://unctad.org/en/PublicationsLibrary/ser-rp-2020d4_en.pdf (accessed 31 May 2020).

- Ministry of Foreign and European Affairs, Luxembourg (2018). Available at https://maee.gouvernement.lu/en/directions-du-ministere/affaires-europeennes/organisations-economiques-regcoop.html (accessed 20 April 2020).

- OECD (2019). *Geographical Distribution of Financial Flows to Developing Countries 2019: Disbursements, Commitments, Country Indicators*. OECD Publishing. Paris.

- OECD (2021a). DAC glossary of key terms and concepts. Available at http://www.oecd.org/dac/dac-glossary.htm (accessed 20 April 2021).

- OECD (2021b). Creditor reporting system (CRS). Available at https://stats.oecd.org/Index.aspx?DataSetCode=CRS1 (accessed 20 April 2021).

- OECD (2021c). Amounts mobilised from the private sector for development. Available at https://www.oecd.org/development/financing-sustainable-development/development-finance-standards/mobilisation.htm (accessed 1 June 2021).

- UNCTAD (2006). *Recent Developments in International Investment Agreements*. IIA Monitor No. 2, No. UNCTAD/WEB/ITE/IIT/2005/1. UN. Geneva.

- UNCTAD (2015). *Investment Policy Framework for Sustainable Development*. UNCTAD/DIAE/PCB/2015/5. Geneva.

- UNCTAD (2016). *World Investment Report 2016: Investor Nationality: Policy Challenges*. United Nations publication. Sales No. E.16.II.D.4. Geneva.

- UNCTAD (2017). *World Investment Report 2017: Investment and the Digital Economy*. United Nations publication. Sales No. E.17.II.D.3. Geneva.

- UNCTAD (2018). *World Investment Report 2018: Investment and New Industrial Policies*. United Nations publication. Sales No. E.18.II.D.4. Geneva.

- UNCTAD (2020). UNCTAD. Available at https://investmentpolicy.unctad.org/publications/1236/international-investment-agreements-reform-accelerator (accessed 27 April 2021).

- UNCTAD (2021a). UNCTADStat. Available at https://unctadstat.unctad.org/EN/Index.html (accessed 21 April 2021).

- UNCTAD (2021b). International Investment Agreements Navigator. Available at https://investmentpolicy.unctad.org/international-investment-agreements (accessed 20 April 2021).

- UNCTAD (2021c). Investment Policy Hub. Available at https://investmentpolicy.unctad.org/ (accessed 20 April 2021).

- United Nations (2003). Monterrey Consensus of the International Conference on Financing for Development. United Nations. A/CONF.198/11. Monterrey. (accessed 20 April 2020).

- United Nations (2015). Report of the third international conference on financing for development. A/CONF.227/20. Addis Ababa. 3 August. (accessed 20 April 2020).

- United Nations (2017). *The Sustainable Development Goals Report 2017*. United Nations publication. Sales No. E.17.I.7. New York.

- United Nations (2021). SDG indicators: Metadata repository. Available at https://unstats.un.org/sdgs/metadata/ (accessed 20 April 2021).

- United Nations Statistical Commission (2020). Report on the fifty-first session of the Statistical Commission (3-6 March 2020). E/2020/24-E/CN.3/2020/37. New York.

- UNOSSC (2020). About South-South and Triangular Cooperation. Available at https://www.unsouthsouth.org/about/about-sstc/ (accessed 29 April 2020).

- WHO (2020). Q&A on coronaviruses (COVID-19). Available at https://www.who.int/emergencies/diseases/novel-coronavirus-2019/question-and-answers-hub/q-a-detail/q-a-coronaviruses (accessed 11 May 2020).

- World Bank (2021). World Development Indicators. Available at http://data.worldbank.org/data-catalog/world-development-indicators (accessed 20 April 2021).

- World Bank and KNOMAD (2020). COVID-19 crisis through a migration lens. Migration and Development Brief No. 32. (accessed 27 May 2020).

II. Official international assistance plays a key role in financing for sustainable development

---

SDG indicators

SDG target 2.a: Increase investment, including through enhanced international cooperation, in rural infrastructure, agricultural research and extension services, technology development and plant and livestock gene banks in order to enhance agricultural productive capacity in developing countries, in particular least developed countries

SDG indicator 2.a.2: Total official flows (official development assistance plus other official flows) to the agriculture sector (Tier I)

SDG target 9.a: Facilitate sustainable and resilient infrastructure development in developing countries through enhanced financial, technological and technical support to African countries, least developed countries, landlocked developing countries and small island developing states

SDG indicator 9.a.1: Total official international support (official development assistance plus other official flows) to infrastructure (Tier I)

SDG target 17.2: Developed countries to implement fully their official development assistance commitments, including the commitment by many developed countries to achieve the target of 0.7 per cent of gross national income for official development assistance (ODA/GNI) to developing countries and 0.15 to 0.20 per cent of ODA/GNI to least developed countries; ODA providers are encouraged to consider setting a target to provide at least 0.20 per cent of ODA/GNI to least developed countries

SDG indicator 17.2.1: Net official development assistance, total and to LDCs, as a proportion of the OECD DAC donors' GNI

The Addis Ababa Action Agenda on Financing for Development (United Nations, 2015) clearly identifies ODA and OOFs as a relevant element in the financing of sustainable development programmes. As shown in Robust and predictable financing sources, these flows are relatively small when compared to domestic public resources or private flows. However, they still play an essential role since they frequently function as "seed funds" or catalysers of additional resource mobilization in sectors or projects where other funding options are limited, or where investors are

Net ODA to developing countries reached 0.33% of donor countries' GNI in 2019,

less than half of the 0.7% target

reluctant to participate. Furthermore, for some countries in vulnerable situations, official funds are frequently the only source of financing available.

For this reason, the importance of official flows is often highlighted in the 2030 Agenda. In fact, they are referred to in 11 targets, including sector-specific official support to agriculture[1], health[2], water and sanitation[3], clean energy[4], biodiversity[5] and others.

Gaps in official support affect financing for development

It is important to highlight the commitment of developed economies under SDG target 17.2 to dedicate 0.7 per cent of their GNI to ODA to developing countries, including 0.15 to 0.20 per cent exclusively to LDCs. As shown in figure 1, actual ODA funds made available for developing countries have yet to reach half of this commitment in any year, while those made available to LDCs fare relatively better, although reaching their target range only once since 2002. The increasing cumulative shortfall could compromise the financing of the 2030 Agenda.

 Figure 1. Net ODA to developing countries and LDCs (SDG 17.2.1)

(Percentage of GNI commitments and actual disbursements)

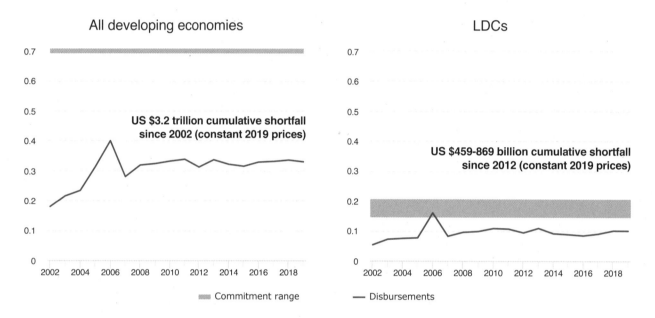

Source: UNCTAD calculations based on (OECD, 2021b).
Notes: Cumulative shortfall since 2002, the earliest availability of relevant data. Under SDG target 17.2, developed economies commit to dedicate 0.7 per cent of their GNI for ODA to developing countries, including a range between 0.15 to 0.20 per cent specifically to LDCs.

While there exists much debate around the efficacy of ODA in general, studies have found positive relationships with ODA in sectors such as agricultural productivity (Ssozi et al., 2019), water infrastructure (Botting et al., 2010) and infrastructure construction projects (Lee and Jeon, 2018). These and other studies note, however, shortcomings in how ODA is deployed and the difficulties in assessing its impacts.

Reflecting such assessments of the efficacy of official support, as well as changing priorities by both donors and recipients, the sectoral allocation of official support has changed substantially in the last 15 years. Figure 2 shows a shift in official support away from some social infrastructure sectors like education and civil society and into economic infrastructure related to energy, transport, banking and financial services and other areas. In terms of productive sectors, industry has been increasingly prioritised, while support to agriculture has declined.

■■■ Figure 2. Changes in the allocation of official international support by sector

(Percentage of total official support)

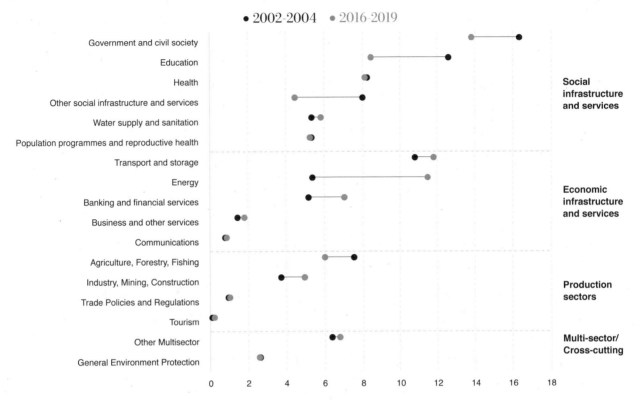

Source: UNCTAD calculations based on OECD (2020a).
Note: For a complete description of the sectors and their coverage, see OECD (2020b).

Official flows play an important role in supporting the response to the COVID-19 pandemic and its fallout on sustainable development, as the OECD (2020) underline. This applies in particular to LDCs and other countries with financing constraints. OECD also stresses the importance of safeguarding ODA budgets and ensuring the continuation of official support during this health and economic crisis.

This chapter covers concessional resources to two areas: economic infrastructure and agriculture. Although the role of this source of financing is essential everywhere, in these two areas they are directly linked with productive growth and its contribution to sustainable development.

Official flows remain supportive of infrastructure projects

Investment in modern and efficient economic infrastructure (transport, information and communication technologies, water supply, electrical power) is essential to achieving sustainable development objectives. Long-term strategies for economic growth, poverty reduction and environmental sustainability all have infrastructure development as a common element. A 2015 report (Bhattacharya et al., 2015) estimates that the global economy needs to invest between US$5 and 6 trillion (in constant 2010 prices) in economic infrastructure every year over the period from 2015 to 2030. Additional funds equivalent to US$600 to 800 billion per year will be necessary to make this investment sustainable. Developing countries will account for about two thirds of the investments required to accommodate higher growth and structural change. These figures do not take into account soft infrastructure, which also plays an important role in economic development, including, for example, national data infrastructure (UNCTAD, 2016).

Woetzel et al. (2017) estimate the sectoral breakdown of global infrastructure needs with a 2030 horizon as 38 per cent for transport, 30 per cent for power, 17 per cent for telecommunications, and 15 per cent for water. Given these needs and the current and expected investment trends, the largest infrastructure investment gaps will be concentrated in the generation and distribution of electricity, followed by transport infrastructure.[6] In addition, significant additional resources are needed across all sectors for climate change mitigation and adaptation (UNCTAD, 2019).

Even if most of the funds for infrastructure investment will come from the public sector and private actors, including through public-private partnerships and other forms of blended finance, ODA will also play a significant role, particularly for LDCs and countries in vulnerable situations. For this reason, SDG indicator 9.a.1 monitors "total official international support (official development assistance plus other official flows) to infrastructure".[7]

Figure 3 shows the evolution of total official flows and those directed to economic infrastructure. While the global financial crisis of 2007/2008 had a profound impact on overall concessional financing flows, those targeting infrastructure projects were sustained. This has led to an increase in the average annual share of infrastructure in total flows, from 14 per cent before the crisis (2002-2008) to 23 per cent after (2009-2019). From 2016, after a marked increase in 2015, official support flows increased only modestly each year. ODA and OOFs in support of infrastructure reached US$65 billion in 2019, their highest level ever, accounting for 24 per cent of total flows.

In 2019, **24%** of all **official** international **support** was **directed to infrastructure** in **economic sectors**

📊 **Figure 3. Official International support, total and to infrastructure (SDG 9.a.1)**

(Billions of constant 2018 US$)

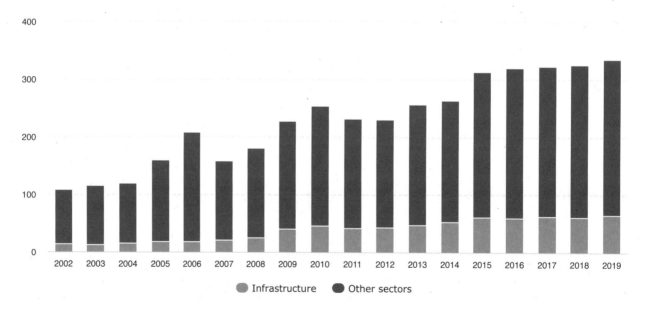

Source: UNCTAD calculations based on (OECD, 2021b).
Note: Official international support to infrastructure includes sector codes in the 200 series of the DAC classification (see note 7).

Of this amount, the majority was assigned to energy and transportation projects (see figure 4). Communications received a relatively low share, but this can be attributed to the large participation of the private sector as a source of financing in this area.

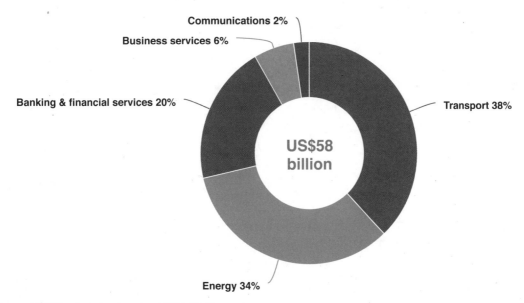

Source: UNCTAD calculations based on (OECD, 2021b).
Notes: Official international support to infrastructure includes sector codes in the 200 series of the DAC classification (see note 7).

An important source of funding for infrastructure in LDCs, LLDCs and SIDS

In 2019, just 13 countries received half of all official international support to infrastructure. The largest recipients were India (12.8 per cent of the total), Egypt (5.4 per cent), Bangladesh (4.6 per cent), China (4.3 per cent) and Indonesia (3.5 per cent). However, these are also among the largest developing economies and official support represents only a small share of their total sources of domestic and external financing.

For other countries, official international support has a higher weight relative to the size of their economies. In some cases, because of special needs in terms of economic infrastructure or lack of access to other sources of development financing, official support is fundamental. Figure 5 shows the international support to infrastructure relative to GDP by groups of economies. LDCs, LLDCs and SIDS receive a higher share of funds from ODA compared to other developing or transition economies.

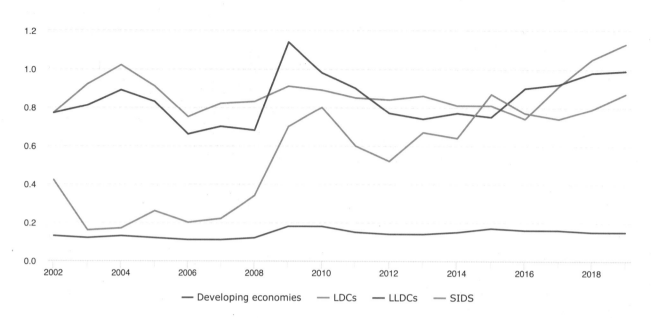

Figure 5. International official support to infrastructure by group of economies

(Percentage of GDP)

Legend: Developing economies — LDCs — LLDCs — SIDS

Source: UNCTAD calculations based on (OECD, 2021b) and (UNCTAD, 2021).
Notes: Official international support to infrastructure includes sector codes in the 200 series of the DAC classification (see note 7).

The need for infrastructure development, particularly transport, is of central importance for economic development in LLDCs due to their isolation from international markets. However, there is an important investment gap in this area (UN-OHRLLS, 2018). This points to the importance of all sources of funding for infrastructure projects. LLDCs were recipients of US$8.3 billion of development assistance to economic infrastructure in 2019, equivalent to one per cent of GDP. This continues an increasing trend in terms of volumes and share of GDP since 2015.

Due to their structural characteristics, such as small population size, geographic remoteness, economic reliance on trade and tourism, as well as high vulnerability to natural disasters and climate change, SIDS have significant infrastructure requirements, both in terms of building new facilities and maintaining and adapting existing ones (OECD, 2018). As seen in figure 5, the importance of official international support to economic infrastructure in these economies has grown in recent years, increasing from about 0.2 per cent of GDP in 2006 to 0.9 per cent in 2019.

Despite the growing infrastructure challenges, long-term investment in infrastructure for sustainable development in developing countries remains insufficient. Stronger consideration should be given to the positive impact of infrastructure, as developing countries will require large-scale investment to build high quality, resilient and inclusive infrastructure (United Nations, 2018). Official international support will remain a key component in the financing of the infrastructure investments required to achieve the SDGs.

Agriculture no longer a priority for ODA, even when challenges keep mounting

The agricultural sector employs a considerable share of the labour force and plays an essential role for food security and rural development. Agricultural products are traded internationally and constitute an important source of revenue for many countries. However, even if agriculture remains a crucial economic sector in many developing economies, agricultural productivity remained stagnant during the 1960s to 1980s and has only increased gradually since then. This could be attributed to several factors, including unsupportive policies and insufficient resources to develop this sector (Mattoo et al., 2020).

In addition to the urgent need for increases in productivity, agriculture must also embrace sustainable practices and adapt to climate change. On one hand, the sector contributes to greenhouse gas emissions, natural habitat loss and unsustainable use of water resources, among others (see Make or Break for Green Economy), and reducing its environmental impact would require important investments. On the other hand, agriculture is strongly affected by climate change and extreme climatological or meteorological events. Significant resources are needed for adaptation and mitigation. In many countries, official flows in the form of ODA and OOFs play a key role in financing agricultural development. In this sense, SDG indicator 2.a.2 measures "total official flows (official development assistance plus other official flows) to the agriculture sector".[8]

The agricultural sector receives only 3.6% of global official international support

During the 1970s and 1980s, agriculture was a major recipient of international assistance, accounting for 15 to 20 per cent of total ODA (Cabral and Howell, 2012). However, the relative importance of agriculture as a beneficiary of ODA has declined since then. Several factors are behind this shift, including changing donor priorities, pressure from environmental groups and insufficient evidence of its contribution to increasing productivity (Mattoo et al., 2020).[9]

As shown in figure 6, while ODA to agriculture has increased in absolute terms every year since 2012, its share of total concessional resources has remained stable, at a low level. Indeed, since 2005 the four-per-cent mark has not been exceeded. Flows in 2019 were higher than in 2018, reaching US$9.9 billion, equivalent to 3.6 per cent of total official international support.

📊 **Figure 6. Total official international support to agriculture (SDG 2.a.2)**

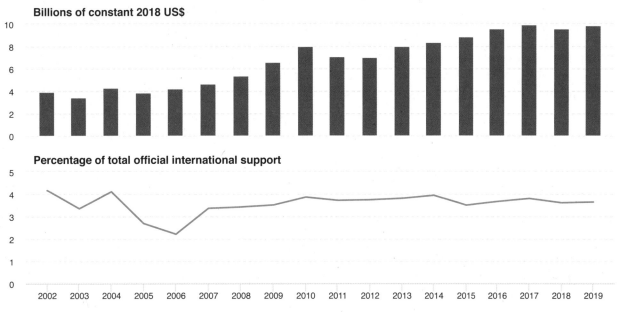

Source: UNCTAD calculations based on (OECD, 2021b).
Notes: Official international support to infrastructure includes sector codes in the 311 series of the DAC classification (see note 8).

Even if ODA to agriculture has remained stagnant relative to other sectors (see figure 2), it still represents an important source of funding for many developing economies. Map 1 shows the weight of these flows relative to the value added of the primary sector.[10] It can be seen that several economies in Central and West Africa, Central Asia and the Caucasus still rely on ODA as an important source of financing for the development of their agricultural sector.

The agricultural sector is facing mounting environmental challenges, including changing climatological patterns, water shortages, treatment-resistant plagues and increased incidence of natural disasters. These factors, combined with an increasing food demand caused by population growth and changing consumption preferences, could translate into important threats for food security in many parts of the world. The COVID-19 pandemic may have exacerbated these risks by restricting the mobility of people and products and disrupting trade and global value chains. This could lead to lower yields, scarcity of specific food commodities and food price increases (FAO, 2020). Given the importance of agriculture for people's life and livelihoods, this productive sector could well regain its priority in official support programs for sustainable development.

🌍 Map 1. Official international support to agriculture as a percentage of primary sector GDP, 2019

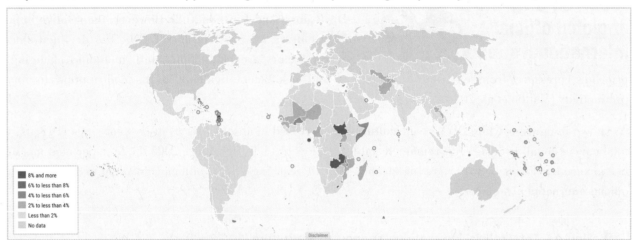

Source: UNCTAD calculations based on (OECD, 2021b) and (UNCTAD, 2021).
Notes: Official international support to infrastructure includes sector codes in the 311 series of the DAC classification (see Note 8). Countries in gray: developed economies or countries not included in the CRS database.

Are official international flows to the agricultural sector effective? A recent study on the effectiveness of agricultural ODA in Sub-Saharan Africa found that development assistance is positively related to agricultural productivity, in general terms. However, the specific effects vary according to the destination of the funds and the characteristics of the recipient economies. For example, it has been argued that ODA creates a substitution effect towards agricultural production activities related to the industrial or other export sectors, and away from food crop production. Furthermore, institutional factors such as government effectiveness, property rights and business freedom have been found to strengthen the positive impact of international support on agricultural productivity (Ssozi et al., 2019). For policymakers in both donor and recipient economies, it is important to consider the appropriate mix of funds and ensure supporting institutional reform in order to maximize the positive impact of ODA in agriculture.

Notes

1. SDG indicator 2.a.2: Total official flows (official development assistance plus other official flows) to the agriculture sector.

2. SDG indicator 3.b.2: Total net official development assistance to medical research and basic health sectors.

3. SDG indicator 6.a.1: Amount of water- and sanitation-related official development assistance that is part of a government-coordinated spending plan.

4. SDG indicator 7.a.1: International financial flows to developing countries in support of clean energy research and development and renewable energy production, including in hybrid systems.

5. SDG indicator 15.a.1: Official development assistance and public expenditure on conservation and sustainable use of biodiversity and ecosystems.

6. For more information on investment needs specific to transport infrastructure, see chapter Mitigating risks to build transport infrastructure.

7. Note that the definition of infrastructure for the purpose of this indicator could vary from other classifications. According to the DAC classification, official flows to infrastructure can be divided into social and economic sectors. The former includes education, health, population policies, water supply and sanitation, and government and civil society; the latter comprises transportation and storage, communications, energy, banking and financial services, and business services (OECD, 2021c). As specified in its official metadata, funding from all official international donors directed to infrastructure in economic sectors in developing countries is considered for SDG indicator 9.a.1 (United Nations, 2021).

8. According to the official metadata, this indicator measures funding from all official international donors to the agricultural sector in developing countries (United Nations, 2021). This corresponds to sector code 311 of the DAC classification, including sub-sectors such as agricultural development, agricultural policy, agricultural water and land resources, food crop production, livestock, industrial/exports crops, rural co-operatives, agricultural inputs, and agrarian reforms, among others (OECD, 2021c).

9. In order to reflect current practices in terms of ODA to the primary sector, a broader definition could also include other relevant sectors, such as rural livelihoods, rural development and food security, and take into account multi-sector ODA-financed projects (Cabral and Howell, 2012). However, even with this definition, ODA directed to agricultural projectsNstill shows a decline in relative terms, although at a slower rate.

10. The primary sector is broader than agriculture (it also includes hunting, forestry and fishing). It is used in map 1 as a denominator since data on value added for agriculture is not available for all countries.

References

- Bhattacharya A, Oppenheim J and Stern N (2015). Driving sustainable development through better infrastructure: Key elements of a transformation program. Global Economy & Development Working Paper No. 91. Brookings Institute. (accessed 20 April 2020).

- Botting MJ et al. (2010). Water and sanitation infrastructure for health: The impact of foreign aid. *Globalization and Health*. 6(12):.

- Cabral L and Howell J (2012). Measuring aid to agriculture and food security. Briefing Paper No. 72. Overseas Development Institute.

- Doshi P (2011). The elusive definition of pandemic influenza. Bulletin of the World Health Organisation. *WHO Bulletin*. 89(7):532–538.

- FAO (2020). Novel Coronavirus (COVID-19). Available at http://www.fao.org/2019-ncov/en/ (accessed 11 May 2020).

- *FutureStructure* (2013). What is soft infrastructure? November.

- Lee S-W and Jeon J-K (2018). Dynamic relationships between mega projects and official development assistance: Case of South Korean infrastructure construction projects in ASEAN's developing countries. *Sustainability*. 10(12):1–22.

- Mattoo A, Rocha N and Ruta M (2020). The Evolution of Deep Trade Agreements. WB Policy Research Working Paper No. 9283. WB.

- OECD (2015). *Frascati Manual 2015: Guidelines for Collecting and Reporting Data on Research and Experimental Development*. OECD Publishing. Paris.

- OECD (2018). *Making Development Co-Operation Work for Small Island Developing States*. OECD Publishing. Paris.

- OECD (2020). OECD and donor countries working to focus development efforts on Covid-19 crisis, building on a rise in official aid in 2019 April. Available at http://www.oecd.org/development/oecd-and-donor-countries-working-to-focus-development-efforts-on-covid-19-crisis-building-on-a-rise-in-official-aid-in-2019.htm (accessed 23 April 2020).

- OECD (2021a). DAC glossary of key terms and concepts. Available at http://www.oecd.org/dac/dac-glossary.htm (accessed 20 April 2021).

- OECD (2021b). Creditor reporting system (CRS). Available at https://stats.oecd.org/Index.aspx?DataSetCode=CRS1 (accessed 20 April 2021).

- OECD (2021c). Available at http://www.oecd.org/dac/financing-sustainable-development/development-finance-standards/dacandcrscodelists.htm (accessed 20 April 2021).

- Ssozi J, Asongu S and Amavilah V (2019). The effectiveness of development aid for agriculture in Sub-Saharan Africa. *Journal of Economic Studies*. 46(2):284–305.

- UNCTAD (2016). Development and globalization: Facts and figures 2016. Available at https://stats.unctad.org/Dgff2016/ (accessed 6 April 2020).

- UNCTAD (2019). SDG Investment Trends Monitor. UNCTAD/DIAE/MISC/2019. Geneva. (accessed 30 April 2020).

- UNCTAD (2021). UNCTADStat. Available at https://unctadstat.unctad.org/EN/Index.html (accessed 21 April 2021).

- United Nations (2015). Report of the third international conference on financing for development. A/CONF.227/20. Addis Ababa. 3 August. (accessed 20 April 2020).

- United Nations (2018). *Financing for Development: Progress and Prospects 2018*. United Nations publication. Sales No. E.18.I.5. New York.

- United Nations (2021). SDG indicators: Metadata repository. Available at https://unstats.un.org/sdgs/metadata/ (accessed 20 April 2021).

- United Nations, European Commission, IMF, OECD and World Bank (2009). *System of National Accounts 2008*. United Nations publication. Sales No. E.08.XVII.29. New York.

- UN-OHRLLS (2018). Financing infrastructure in the transport sector in landlocked developing countries: Trends, challenges & opportunities. Available at http://unohrlls.org/custom-content/uploads/2018/09/LLDCs_Report_18_digital_Final.pdf (accessed 20 April 2020).

- WHO (2020). Q&A on coronaviruses (COVID-19). Available at https://www.who.int/emergencies/diseases/novel-coronavirus-2019/question-and-answers-hub/q-a-detail/q-a-coronaviruses (accessed 11 May 2020).

- Woetzel J, Garemo N, Mischke J, Kamra P and Palter R (2017). Bridging infrastructure gaps. Has the world made progress? itemKey/KJW9URYV. Available at https://www.mckinsey.com/industries/capital-projects-and-infrastructure/our-insights/bridging-infrastructure-gaps-has-the-world-made-progress (accessed 26 April 2019).

III. Sustainable and resilient transport amidst rising uncertainty, disruptions and climate risks

SDG indicators

SDG target 9.1: Develop quality, reliable, sustainable and resilient infrastructure, including regional and transborder infrastructure, to support economic development and human well-being, with a focus on affordable and equitable access for all

SDG indicator 9.1.2: Passenger and freight volumes, by mode of transport (Tier I)

Infrastructure, including transport infrastructure, directly and indirectly influences the attainment of all the SDGs, including 92 per cent of the 169 individual targets (Thacker et al., 2018). With transport infrastructure being the lifeline linking global economies and societies, the sustainability and resilience of transport are critical for a sustainable development path.

Transport enables trade, supports global supply chains, propels growth and promotes social progress. While the continuity of freight movements and trade flows requires the use of multimodal transport networks including rail, road and inland waterways, maritime transport remains the backbone of globalization, handling over an estimated 80 per cent of global trade by volume and more than 70 per cent of its value (UNCTAD, 2020a). Apart from supporting globalized and production networks, maritime transport is an economic sector in its own right that generates economic and social gains (Rodrigue, 2020; Ministry of Transport, New Zealand Government, 2016; UNECE, 2015).

Increased transport activity exerts pressure on the sector's sustainability and heightens its exposure to global risks and disruptive shocks that dislocate transport networks and supply chains, including pandemics such as the COVID-19 and, the six-day blockage of the Suez Canal in March 2021 after the grounding of the 20 000 TEU container ship, the 'Ever Given'. Other major risks include inward-looking trade policies, geopolitical threats, unsustainable energy use, environmental degradation and climate change (UNCTAD, 2021a).

The COVID-19 disruption underscored the importance of transport, in particular maritime transport infrastructure as an essential sector for the continued delivery of critical supplies and global trade in time of crises, during the recovery stage and when resuming normality. The sector is now facing not only immediate concerns resulting from the pandemic but also longer-term wide-ranging considerations. These include shifts in supply chain design and globalization patterns, new consumption and spending habits, a growing focus on risk assessment, adaptation, resilience-building, and digital transformation, as well as a heightened global sustainability and low-carbon agenda (UNCTAD, 2020b).

Given the strategic role of the sector as a catalyst for growth and development, a full consideration of these challenges and risks is required to devise policies that promote sustainable and inclusive long-term growth (UNCTAD, 2018d). While access to affordable, reliable and cost-effective transport systems remains a challenge for many developing countries, especially for LLDCs and SIDS, mainstreaming sustainability and resilience, in particular climate criteria, into transport designs, development plans and management, is an imperative (UNCTAD, 2014a). In the wake of COVID-19, integrating criteria such as risks assessment and management, event and risk forecasting and business continuity plans has also become critical. As part of UN action in response to the COVID-19 pandemic, UNCTAD and the United Nations Regional Commissions are currently implementing a joint technical assistance project on "Transport and trade connectivity in the age of pandemics: Contactless, seamless and collaborative UN solutions" (UNCTAD, 2021b). Relevant outputs include, among others, advice and guidance on some of the complex commercial law issues that arise in the context of the pandemic and its aftermath for contracting parties to commercial contracts throughout the supply chain (UNCTAD, 2021c, 2021d). It also includes global and regional impact assessment reports and webinars disseminating information about the impact of COVID-19 on the maritime supply chain, response measures introduced to mitigate these impacts, and good practices in future proofing the maritime supply chain (UNCTAD, 2021e).

Bearing in mind the important role of transport for international trade and development, and its exposure to global risks, SDG target 9.1 seeks to improve infrastructure that supports economic activity and human well-being while promoting sustainability. Specific to transport infrastructure, SDG indicator 9.1.2 measures progress towards sustainable and resilient transportation and measures trends in "passenger and freight transport." Freight transportation is of direct relevance to UNCTAD's mandate on transport and trade logistics. This chapter highlights trends in critical maritime transport infrastructure and services that underpin trade, supply chain linkages and economic integration.

Maritime transport amidst heightened uncertainty and challenges ahead

Maritime transport remains the backbone of globalized trade and manufacturing supply chains as it is estimated that more than four fifths of world merchandise trade volumes are carried by sea (UNCTAD, 2021a). However, according to UNCTAD (2020a), growth in international maritime trade further weakened in 2019, owing to the lingering trade tensions and heightened uncertainty. Volumes reached 11.08 billion tons in 2019, reflecting a marginal increase of 0.5 per cent, after an annual growth of 2.8 per cent

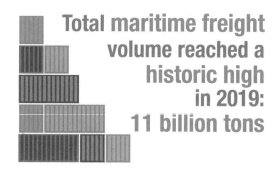

Total maritime freight volume reached a historic high in 2019: 11 billion tons

registered in 2018. In 2019, dry bulk commodities, such as coal and iron ore, together with containerised trade, continued to account for the largest share of total maritime trade. As shown in figure 1, this reflects the ongoing structural shift in maritime trade observed since 1980.

In 2020, maritime trade patterns were significantly impacted by the pandemic. Global port calls by all ship types fell by about 10 per cent compared with the previous year. The impact across maritime sectors was uneven. Container vessel port calls showed more resilience than port calls on average, with a drop of only 3.2 per cent (figure 2). UNCTAD expects maritime trade volumes to fall by 4.1 per cent in 2020, before recovering in 2021 (UNCTAD, 2020a).

Figure 1. Volume of international maritime trade by cargo type

(Billions of tons loaded)

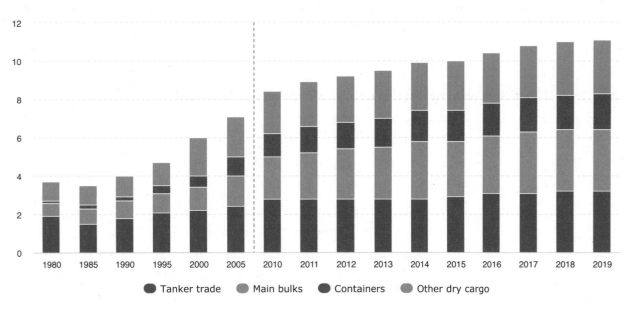

● Tanker trade   ● Main bulks   ● Containers   ● Other dry cargo

Source: UNCTAD (2020a).
Note: Calculations based on AIS weekly data on ship arrivals in ports provided by MarineTraffic.

Figure 2. Vessel port calls, change from 2019 to 2020

(Percentage)

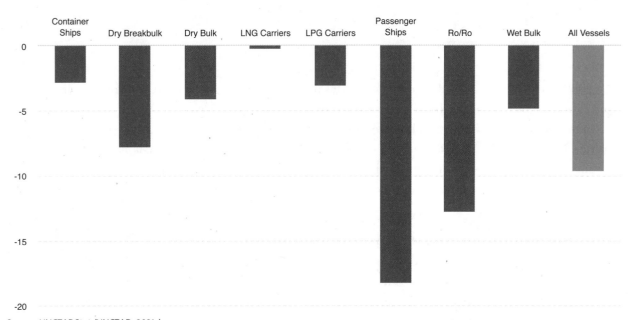

Source: UNCTADStat (UNCTAD, 2021a).
Note: Calculations based on weekly AIS data provided by MarineTraffic. Aggregated figures are derived from the combination of AIS data and port mapping intelligence by MarineTraffic, covering ships of 5 000 GT and above. Only arrivals have been taken into account to measure the number of port calls.

In 2019, global containerised trade expanded at a slower rate than in the previous year, rising by 1.1 per cent, down from 3.8 per cent in 2018, and bringing the total to 152 million TEUs. Much of the growth was driven by activity on non-mainland East–West, South–South and intraregional trade routes, involving mainly trade among developing countries. The prominence of Asia as the world's 'factory' continued boosting intra-Asian container trade, with a growing contribution from South-East Asia.

As shown in figure 3, developing economies account for most of global maritime trade flows, both in terms of goods loaded and goods unloaded. These economies loaded 58 per cent and unloaded 65 per cent of the total in 2019.

⊞ Figure 3. Participation of developing countries in global maritime trade

(Percentage share of global maritime trade volumes)

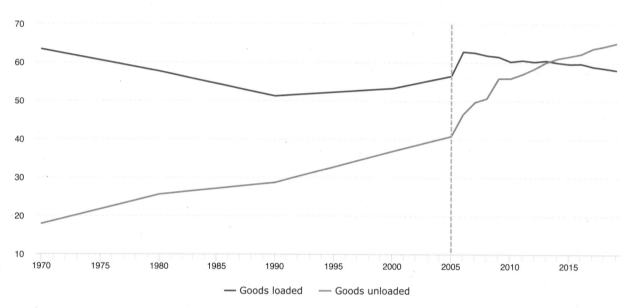

Source: UNCTADStat (UNCTAD, 2021a).

Since 2000, the contribution of developing countries to maritime trade has shifted, reflecting their growing role as major exporters of raw materials, as well as large exporters and importers of finished and semi-finished goods. Participation in containerised trade, however, has been concentrated in Asia, notably in China and neighbouring countries. Capitalizing on the fragmentation of globalized production processes, Asia has become a maritime hub that concentrates over 50 per cent of global maritime freight. Other developing regions do not contribute equally, reflecting their varying degrees of integration into global value chains and manufacturing networks.

The leading influence of Asia in maritime transport is also reflected in figure 4. In 2019, this region shipped 41 per cent and received 62 per cent of world maritime cargo. Corresponding figures for the Americas were 22 and 13 per cent, respectively, while 16 per cent of global goods were loaded and 19 per cent of global goods unloaded at European ports. The other regions were responsible for smaller shares of worldwide maritime cargo flows.

Asia shipped 41% **and received 62%** **of world maritime cargo**

Figure 4. International maritime trade by region, 2019

(Percentage share of global maritime trade volume)

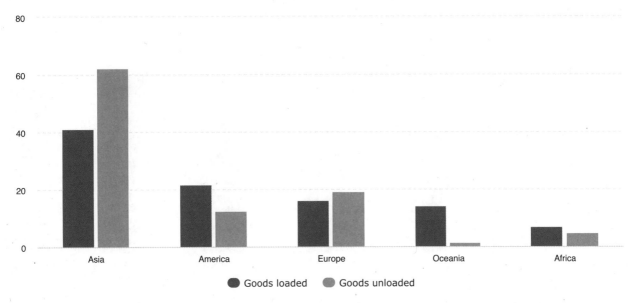

● Goods loaded   ● Goods unloaded

Source: UNCTADStat (UNCTAD, 2021a).

Logistical bottlenecks and insufficient infrastructure investment undermine maritime transport. They raise costs, extend delays, reduce access, constrain connectivity, and hinder effective participation in supply chains and transport networks. Beyond ports, road and rail networks are necessary for door-to-door transport of goods and to connect countries, especially LLDCs, overland. Infrastructural gaps and bottlenecks affecting inland networks can render transportation costly for these countries.

International freight costs in LDCs almost double than developed economies

Figure 5 shows that exports from LLDCs are inflicted with transport costs amounting to 15 cents per US dollar of the exported goods' value, a rate one half higher than for exports from other developing economies. Transporting goods from SIDS to their destination countries is almost equally expensive, estimated to cost on average 14 cents per US dollar. LDCs, by contrast, do not show significantly higher unit transport costs for their exports than developing and developed countries.

‖ıll Figure 5. Estimates of transport and insurance costs of international trade, 2016

(Percentage value of exports)

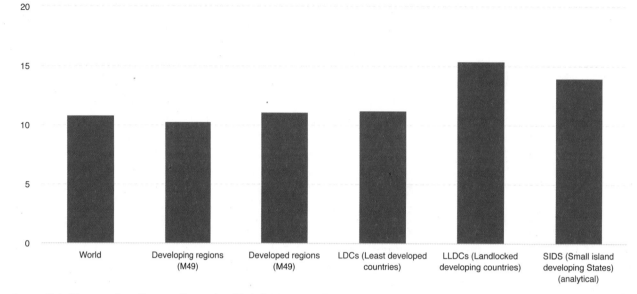

Source: Global Transport Costs Dataset of International Trade (UNCTAD, 2021f).
Note: FOB. Transport cost estimates measure the costs of transport from border to border, including insurance. Country coverage will be improved gradually and more recent data on transport costs will be made available in the database.

As trade volumes expand, the importance of port efficiency also increases

Ports are important and strategic nodes in the transport networks. Port performance indicators, such as port connectivity and waiting time at port, are useful measures of trade efficiency and competitiveness. Every hour of ship-time saved in a port saves money on port infrastructure investments, capital expenditure on ships and inventory holding costs. Port performance varies across ship segments and sizes, with vessels calling at ports in developing countries and LDCs recording relatively higher turnaround times. (UNCTAD, 2020a).

Significant positive correlation between port efficiency and connectivity

In ports receiving the highest number of vessel calls, the median turnaround time is seldom more than one hour. In ports with fewer calls, this time can often reach two to four hours. The causality goes both ways: shorter turnaround time means that the same number of berths can accommodate a larger number of port calls. At the same time, ports in countries with larger trade volumes and vessel port calls will generate higher income levels, thereby enabling more investment in efficient port operations. Reflecting the region's significant contribution to containerised trade, ports in Asia receive a large number of port calls (see map 1).

Productivity levels and efficient cargo handling operations explain some of the observed differences in port calls and connectivity across regions. There are, however, other factors at play such as geography. This is exemplified by ports in countries such as Egypt, Morocco, South Africa and Djibouti that are located on major East-West trade lanes).

Map 1. Container ship port calls and time in port, 2020

(Number of arrivals and median number of days in port)

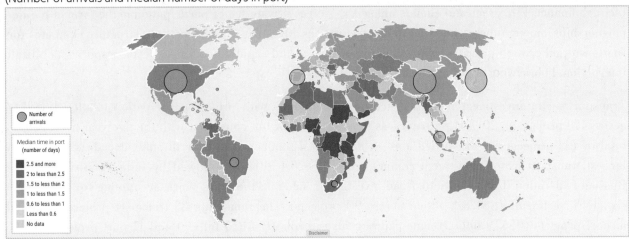

Source: UNCTADStat (UNCTAD, 2021a).

Note: Ships of 1 000 gross tons and above. For port arrivals, data refer to 2019 for Anguilla, Bermuda, Hungary, Montserrat, Slovakia and Tuvalu. For time spent in port, data refer to 2019 for Anguilla, Bermuda, Montserrat and Tuvalu. These figures are based on AIS data. The variable "median time in port" provide an estimation of overall time in port; however, it should not be considered as a precise measurement of efficiency in port since it does not distinguish between waiting time, berth time, and working and idle time.

Investing in transport efficiency, sustainability and resilience

The COVID-19 disruption and the pressing need for sustainability require scaling up investment in smart, green and resilient transport infrastructure and services. As infrastructure is set to play a key role in the global economic recovery, there is, therefore, an opportunity to advance objectives such as efficiency and resilience-building. Investing in risk assessment and preparedness will be crucial in a post COVID-19 world. Such measures include control towers and tools to effectively predict and analyse transport system disruptions and business continuity plans for different stages of a crisis. In the face of disruptions, it is also important to collect and share information on potential concentration and bottlenecks and accelerate greater uptake of technology as a proven mitigating tool. All in all, lessons learned from the pandemic should serve as guidance for informing preparedness and future-proofing of maritime transport.

Available estimates specific to the transport sector also reveal high investment needs over the coming decades.[1] Around US$95 trillion of investments, or US$6.3 trillion per year, not considering climate change concerns, are estimated to be required over the period from 2016 to 2030 in infrastructure (energy, transport, water and telecommunications). Transport accounts for 43 per cent, or US$41 trillion, of the required investments, with much of the needs concentrated in developing regions (OECD, 2017).

Investing in resilient and sustainable transport infrastructure generates important co-benefits. For example, decarbonizing and climate proofing transport infrastructure against increased risks such as climate-related shocks and natural disasters are found to be both sound and profitable. In addition to ensuring more reliable infrastructure with reduced impact on environment and climate, these investments generate financial gains. For example, net benefits of investing in climate resilient infrastructure in developing countries could amount to US$4.2 trillion over the lifetime of new infrastructure, meaning US$4 benefit for each dollar invested in resilience (World Bank, 2020a). In this context, and bearing in mind the prevailing sustainable transport infrastructure investment gap, it is crucial that traditional public funding be supplemented by additional and innovative sources of financing to scale up investment levels.

Alleviating the persistent transport infrastructure gap and ensuring proper service delivery require further mobilization of domestic resources, and taping into other financing sources and arrangements, including blended finance, FDI, green and climate finance, as well as private sector participation in the form of public-private partnerships, among others. However, in many countries, investing in transport infrastructure competes for public funds with other high-priority areas, while opportunities and capabilities for domestic resource mobilization and international borrowing are often constrained and limited.

Transport-sector investment in infrastructure commitments with private participation totalled US$47.8 billion across 123 projects in 2019, 11 per cent less than 2018 levels, but consistent with the five-year average. In 2020, a total of 122 projects were recorded, the second highest number seen over the past decade. China received the largest transport-sector investment commitments (US$28.4 billion), followed by India (US$6.7 billion) and the Russian Federation (US$3.4 billion). Road investments made up the lion's share, accounting for 59 per cent of the sector's investments (US$28.4 billion across 90 projects). The remaining 33 transport projects included seven airport projects (US$3.9 billion), nine railroad investments (US$10.6 billion) and 17 port projects worth US$4.9 billion. (World Bank, 2020b.)

Adapting transport infrastructure in times of climate change

UNCTAD has worked on the implications of climate change for maritime transportation since 2008, with an increasing focus on climate change adaptation and resilience building for seaports and other key coastal transport infrastructure (UNCTAD, 2021g). These are strategic nodes in the network of closely interconnected global supply chains. In keeping up with the global momentum of the 2030 Agenda for Sustainable Development, the Paris Agreement on Climate Change and the 2019 Climate Action Summit convened by the Secretary-General of the United Nations, UNCTAD is intensifying its efforts to promote sustainable and climate-resilient freight transport infrastructure and services.[2]

Transport infrastructure is affected directly and indirectly by climate change, with far-reaching consequences for international trade and the development prospects of the most vulnerable nations.[3] Seaports are key nodes in the network of global supply chains and critical for access to global markets. With global mean sea level continuously rising (WMO, 2021), climate resilience and adaptation for critical coastal transport infrastructure, such as ports, is a matter of strategic socio-economic importance (UNCTAD, 2020c, 2020d). This is the case for all countries, but particularly for SIDS, which depend on their coastal transport infrastructure as lifelines for external trade, food and energy security, and tourism, as well as in the context of disaster risk reduction (UNCTAD, 2019b, 2020e).

Climate-related extreme events and disasters can result in significant damage, disruption and delay, giving rise to extensive economic costs (WMO, 2021; UNCTAD, 2020e). In light of recent climate projections and the urgency to act (IPCC, 2018, 2019), they are considered the top global economic risks, with implications for additional infrastructure investment needs and climate adaptation (World Economic Forum, 2021).

Figure 6 illustrates the share of disasters over the past 20 years that have had an impact on infrastructure. The figure suggests that transport is the sector that is most vulnerable to disasters. On average, transport facilities have an 18 to 26 per cent probability to be impacted by geophysical, hydrological and meteorological events. Some of these events are expected to increase in frequency and intensity as a result of climate change, with severe consequences for infrastructure. Indeed, a recent study estimated that global damages due to sea-level rise and related extreme events might amount to US$10.8 trillion per year, about 1.8 per cent of global GDP, for a scenario of 1.5°C warming by 2100. For a scenario of 2°C or more, the costs could reach considerably higher levels (Jevrejeva et al., 2018). Despite a brief dip in carbon dioxide emissions caused by the COVID-19 pandemic, the world is still heading for a temperature rise in excess of 3°C this century – far beyond the Paris Agreement goals of limiting global warming to well below 2°C and pursuing 1.5°C (UNEP, 2020) (see Green economy). Therefore, accelerated action both on mitigation and adaptation will be key.

Figure 6. Share of disasters that had an impact on infrastructure, by sector, 2000-2019

(Percentage)

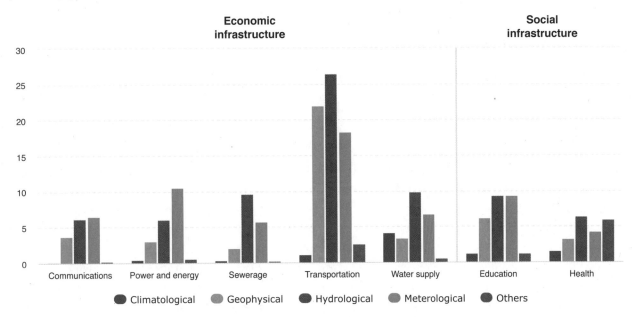

Source: UNCTAD calculations based on data from UNDRR (2020).
Notes: The share shown in this chart is calculated as the number of disasters that damaged infrastructure, divided by the total number of disasters. It is calculated for each infrastructure sector and type of disasters. The category "other" includes multi-hazard events. The source database provides an inventory of disasters and their effects for 155 economies during the period 2000-2019; however, given data gaps and coverage issues, it should be considered as indicative only. For more information on the database, including the classification of disasters, see UNDRR (2020).

Adaptation and resilience measures are not only essential to reducing the negative impacts of climate change on critical transport infrastructure; they are also key to achieving progress on several SDG targets. In view of the long service life of transport infrastructure and the potentially major consequences of inaction, effective adaptation and resilience requires an early re-thinking of established approaches and practices (UNCTAD, 2011b, 2019c, 2019b, 2020c, 2020d). However, a recent UNCTAD port-industry survey on climate change impacts and adaptation for ports shows important gaps in data on resilience and preparedness among seaports worldwide (UNCTAD, 2017). Relevant data are urgently needed for effective climate risk assessment and adaptation planning of coastal transport infrastructure, especially for ports in developing countries (UNCTAD, 2011a, 2011b, 2019c, 2019b, 2020c, 2020e). As noted in UNCTAD (2020c, 2020e), legal and regulatory approaches as well as policies and plans are key in facilitating effective risk and vulnerability assessments and providing a supportive framework for adaptation action. Guidance, standards, best practices, methodologies (UNCTAD, 2018a; PIANC, 2020) and other tools in support of adaptation (UNCTAD, 2020c, 2021h) are urgently required, especially for the most vulnerable countries.

Climate change adaptation is a particularly urgent imperative for SIDS (IPCC, 2019; Climate Ambition Support Alliance, 2020). These countries are often particularly exposed and vulnerable to the impacts of climate change while, at the same time, they are highly dependent on coastal transport infrastructure for external trade, food, energy and tourism. SIDS therefore suffer from a "double exposure" to external economic and environmental shocks (UNCTAD, 2021i). Climate-related extreme events, which are expected to increase in frequency and severity, may cause major disruptions to the connectivity of SIDS to international markets with broad ramifications for sectors such as tourism (UNCTAD, 2014b; IPCC, 2018; UNCTAD, 2019d, 2020e).

UNCTAD has recently conducted vulnerability assessments for eight seaports and coastal airports in two SIDS in the Caribbean: Saint Lucia and Jamaica (UNCTAD, 2018b, 2018c), as part of a technical assistance project on climate change adaptation for coastal transport infrastructure in SIDS (UNCTAD, 2021h). The results of the assessment, which focused on operational disruptions and marine inundation risk under different climate scenarios, suggest severe climate change impacts on coastal transport infrastructure and operations from as early as the 2030s unless further climate change adaptation is undertaken (Monioudi et al., 2018; IPCC, 2018, 2019). Because of SIDS' heavy reliance on maritime and air transport infrastructure, climate-change driven impacts on transport assets (or transportation demand) have significant impacts on livelihoods, economic, social, and environmental assets, and adversely affect the overall sustainable development prospects of these countries (UNCTAD, 2019b, 2020c, 2020e).

Priority actions to strengthen adaptation and resilience building include inspection and maintenance, monitoring systems and effective data management, as well as risk assessments, contingency plans and warning systems. In addition, flexible and adaptive infrastructure, systems and operations, and engineered redundancy to improve resilience are needed (PIANC, 2019, 2020). With regard to climate change adaptation and resilience-building for seaports, the latest UNFCCC Global Climate Action 'Transport' pathway action table includes a distinct impact area for adaptation with a focus on resilient transport systems, infrastructure and vehicles, setting out milestones towards 2050 (for 2020, 2030 and 2040) (UNFCCC, 2020a). Inter alia, these milestones, which have also been integrated into the cross-sectoral 'Resilience and Adaptation' pathway action table (UNFCCC, 2020b), envisage that, by 2030, policymakers must "ensure policies, governance, legal and institutional frameworks are in place to support the climate-resilience of all critical (transport, energy and other) infrastructure to (at least) 2050"; and, by 2040, "ensure the climate-resilience of all critical transport, energy and other infrastructure to at least 2100." A major acceleration of efforts will be required to put relevant measures in place to reach these targets.

Without timely planning and implementation of appropriate adaptation measures, the projected impacts on critical transport infrastructure may have broad economic and trade-related repercussions, and could severely compromise the sustainable development prospects of the most vulnerable nations (UNECE, 2020; Pacific Community, 2019; UNCTAD, 2020c, 2020d). However, important knowledge gaps remain concerning vulnerabilities and the specific nature and extent of the exposure that individual coastal transport facilities may be facing.

The potentially severe economic impacts of the global COVID-19 public health crisis might challenge the adaptation efforts of the transport sector in the short term – through a shift in budget allocations resulting in a decrease of infrastructure financing, for example. However, this pandemic underlines the critical importance of preparedness, risk assessment and resiliency building. Lessons learnt could provide renewed impetus to climate risk and vulnerability assessments of critical transport infrastructure and foster long-term planning essential to enhancing resiliency. Changing circumstances arising from the impacts of the pandemic, e.g., the need for health and safety measures at ports of entry; changes to tourism markets; greater reliance on local and national resources and supplies, will need to be taken into account in any strategy for infrastructure adaptation and resilience building. Addressing the impacts of climate change remains a major challenge, in particular for the most vulnerable groups of countries, such as SIDS which depend on their critical coastal transport infrastructure but face a high and growing risk of coastal flooding (Monioudi et al., 2018; IPCC, 2018, 2019).

While central to development, transport can also have detrimental effects on the environment through air pollution, GHG emissions, soil contamination, waste, noise, threats to land and water ecosystems and biodiversity, and others. Each mode of transport may entail a different combination of negative impacts on the environment

(UNECE, 2015). While maritime transport is the most CO_2-efficient mode of freight transport, the large volumes handled by this sector and its projected expansion in the coming decades make climate change efforts of the sector a priority. For instance, according to different scenarios, CO2 emissions from maritime transport are expected to increase by 50 to 250 per cent until 2050 (IMO, 2015, 2020; OECD, 2010).

The sector is making progress towards achieving the levels of ambition set out in the initial IMO strategy on reduction of GHG emissions from ships, including on ship energy efficiency, alternative fuels and the development of national action plans, to address GHG emissions from international shipping (UNCTAD, 2020a). However much more remains to be done. From the perspective of developing countries including SIDS, it is important that their legitimate interests be taken into account in the quest to reduce emissions from international shipping. UNCTAD is collaborating with IMO by providing an expert view about the potential impact of the proposed short-term IMO measures on GHG emission reduction across three 2030 scenarios. UNCTAD assessed the impact of the proposed measure on countries' trade, transport costs (UNCTAD, 2021f), connectivity and economic growth, in particular the economies of SIDS and LDCs (IMO, 2021).

Promoting sustainable transport involves balancing the economic, social and environmental dimensions of the sector. More specifically, it involves ensuring that transport infrastructure, services and operations be safe, socially acceptable, universally accessible, reliable, affordable, fuel-efficient, environmentally friendly, low-carbon and climate-resilient (OECD, 2011; UNCTAD, 2018d, 2020a, 2020f, 2020e; UNECE, 2015).[4] Given the potential for a broad range of climate-change induced impacts and the multi-dimensional nature of the sector, collaboration and participation of all relevant stakeholders, including public and private actors and academia, will be crucial to drive more systemic approaches to resiliency building (UNCTAD, 2019d, 2019a, 2020e).

Notes

1. For example, OECD (2012) forecasts global investment needs for airports, ports, rails and energy transportation of US$585 billion per year from 2015 to 2030. PwC and Oxford Economics (2015) estimate that investment requirements in transport infrastructure will increase from US$557 billion in 2014 to US$900 billion in 2025 globally. Finally, Woetzel et al. (2016) project cumulative investment needs in the sector over the period from 2016 to 2030 to amount to US$18.7 trillion.

2. For additional information, see UNCTAD (2020c), UNCTAD (2021g), UNCTAD (2020f) and UNCTAD (2021j).

3. For some recent studies on these topics, see Asariotis and Benamara (2012); Becker et al. (2013); UNCTAD (2017), UNCTAD (2020c) and UNCTAD (2021g) and UNECE (2013) and UNECE (2020).

4. For more information on UNCTAD's current work on sustainable and climate resilient freight transport, see UNCTAD (2021g) and UNCTAD (2021k).

References

- Asariotis R and Benamara H, eds. (2012). *Maritime Transport and the Climate Change Challenge*. Routledge. United Kingdom.

- Becker AH et al. (2013). A note on climate change adaptation for seaports: A challenge for global ports, a challenge for global society. *Climatic Change*. 120(4):683–695.

- Climate Ambition Support Alliance (2020). Climate science for Small Island Developing States. Available at https://casaclimate.org/wp-content/uploads/2020/04/CASA-guide-to-science-of-climate-and-oceans-FINAL-April-2020.pdf (accessed 24 April 2020).

- Doshi P (2011). The elusive definition of pandemic influenza. Bulletin of the World Health Organisation. *WHO Bulletin*. 89(7):532–538.

- IMO (2015). *Third IMO Greenhouse Gas Study 2014*. International Maritime Organization. London, United Kingdom.

- IMO (2020). Fourth Greenhouse Gas Study 2020. Available at https://www.imo.org/en/OurWork/Environment/Pages/Fourth-IMO-Greenhouse-Gas-Study-2020.aspx (accessed 11 May 2021).

- IMO (2021). Reduction of GHG Emissions from Ships. Comprehensive impact assessment of short-term measure approved by MEPC 75 – full report on the impacts on the fleet and on States. Note by the Secretariat No. MEPC 76/INF.68/Add.1. IMO.

- IPCC (2018). Global warming of 1.5°C. An IPCC Special Report on the impacts of global warming of 1.5°C above pre-industrial levels and related global greenhouse gas emission pathways, in the context of strengthening the global response to the threat of climate change, sustainable development, and efforts to eradicate poverty. Available at https://www.ipcc.ch/sr15 (accessed 11 May 2021).

- IPCC (2019). IPCC special report on the ocean and cryosphere in a changing climate. Available at https://www.ipcc.ch/srocc/ (accessed 11 May 2021).

- Jevrejeva S, Jackson LP, Grinsted A, Lincke D and Marzeion B (2018). Flood damage costs under the sea level rise with warming of 1.5 °C and 2 °C. *Environmental Research Letters*. 13(7):074014.

- Ministry of Transport, New Zealand Government (2016). Contribution of transport to economic development: Economic development and transport project. Summary report. Available at https://www.transport.govt.nz/assets/Uploads/Our-Work/Documents/4886c08ee6/edt-contribution-of-transport-lit-review.pdf (accessed 9 April 2020).

- Monioudi IN et al. (2018). Climate change impacts on critical international transportation assets of Caribbean Small Island Developing States (SIDS): the case of Jamaica and Saint Lucia. *Regional Environmental Change*. 18(8):2211–2225.

- OECD (2010). *Globalisation, Transport and the Environment*. OECD Publishing. Paris.

- OECD (2011). *Environmental Impacts of International Shipping: The Role of Ports*. OECD Publishing. Paris.

- OECD (2012). *Strategic Transport Infrastructure Needs to 2030: Main Findings*. OECD Publishing. Paris.

- OECD (2017). Investing in Climate, Investing in Growth. A synthesis. Available at https://www.oecd.org/env/investing-in-climate-investing-in-growth-9789264273528-en.htm (accessed 11 May 2021).

- OECD (2021). Glossary of statistical terms. Available at https://stats.oecd.org/glossary/index.htm (accessed 11 May 2021).

- Pacific Community (2019). Fourth pacific regional energy and transport ministers' meeting. Available at https://www.spc.int/updates/news/speeches/2019/09/fourth-pacific-regional-energy-and-transport-ministers-meeting (accessed 11 May 2021).

- PIANC (2019). Declaration on climate change. Available at https://www.pianc.org/uploads/files/COP/PIANC-Declaration-on-Climate-Change.pdf (accessed 11 May 2021).

- PIANC (2020). Climate Change Adaptation Planning for Ports and Inland Waterways. EnviCom WG 178. Available at https://www.pianc.org/publications/envicom/wg178 (accessed 12 May 2021).

- PwC and Oxford Economics (2015). Assessing the global transport infrastructure market: Outlook to 2025. Available at https://www.pwc.com/sg/en/publications/cpi-assessing-global-transportation-infrastructure-market-outlook-to-2025.html (accessed 9 April 2020).

- Rodrigue J-P (2020). *The Geography of Transport Systems*. Routledge. New York.

- Thacker S et al. (2018). *Infrastructure: Underpinning Sustainable Development*. UNOPS. Copenhagen, Denmark.

- UNCTAD (2011a). Ad hoc expert meeting on climate change impacts and adaptation: A challenge for global ports. Main outcomes and summary of discussions. UNCTAD/DTL/TLB/2011/3. Geneva. (accessed 12 May 2021).

- UNCTAD (2011b). Ad hoc expert meeting on climate change impacts and adaptation: A challenge for global ports. Information note by the UNCTAD Secretariat. UNCTAD/DTL/TLB/2011/2. Geneva. (accessed 12 May 2021).

- UNCTAD (2014a). *Closing the Distance: Partnerships for Sustainable and Resilient Transport Systems in SIDS*. UNCTAD/DTL/TLB/2014/2. New York and Geneva.

- UNCTAD (2014b). Small island developing states: Challenges in transport and trade logistics. TD/B/C.I/MEM.7/8. Geneva. 15 September. (accessed 12 May 2021).

- UNCTAD (2016). *World Investment Report 2016: Investor Nationality: Policy Challenges*. United Nations publication. Sales No. E.16.II.D.4. Geneva.

- UNCTAD (2017). Port industry survey on climate change impacts and adaptation. UNCTAD Research Paper No. 2017/18. UNCTAD/SER.RP/2017/18. Geneva. December.

- UNCTAD (2018a). *Climate Risk and Vulnerability Assessment Framework for Caribbean Coastal Transport Infrastructure. Climate Change Impacts on Coastal Transport Infrastructure in the Caribbean: Enhancing the Adaptive Capacity of Small Island Developing States (SIDS).*

- UNCTAD (2018b). *Climate Change Impacts on Coastal Transport Infrastructure in the Caribbean: Enhancing the Adaptive Capacity of Small Island Developing States (SIDS). Saint Lucia: A Case Study.* UNCTAD/DTL/TLB/2018/3. New York and Geneva.

- UNCTAD (2018c). *Climate Change Impacts on Coastal Transport Infrastructure in the Caribbean: Enhancing the Adaptive Capacity of Small Island Developing States (SIDS). Jamaica: A Case Study.* UNCTAD/DTL/TLB/2018/2. New York and Geneva.

- UNCTAD (2018d). Sustainable freight transport in support of the 2030 Agenda for Sustainable Development. TD/B/C.I/MEM.7/17. Geneva. 12 September.

- UNCTAD (2019a). *Review of Maritime Transport 2019.* United Nations publication. Sales No. E.19.II.D.20. New York and Geneva.

- UNCTAD (2019b). High-level Panel discussion at COP 25, Madrid: Climate resilient transport infrastructure for sustainable trade, tourism and development in SIDS. Available at https://unctad.org/meeting/unfccc-cop-25-side-event-climate-resilient-transport-infrastructure-sustainable-trade (accessed 12 May 2021).

- UNCTAD (2019c). Ad hoc expert meeting on climate change adaptation for international transport: Preparing for the future. Available at https://unctad.org/en/pages/MeetingDetails.aspx?meetingid=2092 (accessed 12 May 2021).

- UNCTAD (2019d). Outcome document, High-level Panel discussion at COP 25, Madrid: Climate resilient transport infrastructure for sustainable trade, tourism and development in SIDS. Available at https://unctad.org/system/files/official-document/unfcc_cop25_outcomedocument_dec2019_en.pdf (accessed 12 May 2021).

- UNCTAD (2020a). *Review of Maritime Transport 2020.* United Nations publication. Sales No. E.20.II.D.31. New York and Geneva.

- UNCTAD (2020b). Impact of the COVID-19 pandemic on trade and development: transitioning to a new normal. Available at https://unctad.org/webflyer/impact-covid-19-pandemic-trade-and-development-transitioning-new-normal (accessed 19 May 2021).

- UNCTAD (2020c). *Climate Change Impacts and Adaptation for Coastal Transport Infrastructure: A Compilation of Policies and Practices.* UNCTAD/DTL/TLB/2019/1. Geneva.

- UNCTAD (2020d). Climate Change Adaptation for Seaports in Support of the 2030 Agenda for Sustainable Development. Available at https://unctad.org/meeting/multi-year-expert-meeting-transport-trade-logistics-and-trade-facilitation-eighth-session (accessed 12 May 2021).

- UNCTAD (2020e). Report of the multi-year expert meeting on transport, trade logistics and trade facilitation on its eighth session. No. TD/B/C.I/MEM.7/24. Geneva, 17. (accessed 12 May 2021).

- UNCTAD (2020f). Sustainable freight transport and finance: Toolkit. Available at https://unctadsftportal.org/sftftoolkit/ (accessed 12 May 2021).

- UNCTAD (2021a). UNCTADstat: Port call and performance statistics. Available at http://stats.unctad.org/PortCall (accessed 13 May 2021).

- UNCTAD (2021b). Transport and trade connectivity in the age of pandemics. Available at https://unctad.org/project/transport-and-trade-connectivity-age-pandemics (accessed 12 May 2021).

- UNCTAD (2021c). COVID-19 implications for commercial contracts: Carriage of goods by sea and related cargo claims. No. UNCTAD/DTL/TLB/INF/2021/1. Geneva. (accessed 12 May 2021).

- UNCTAD (2021d). COVID-19 implications for commercial contracts: International sale of goods on CIF and FOB terms. No. UNCTAD/DTL/TLB/INF/2021/2. Geneva. (accessed 12 May 2021).

- UNCTAD (2021e). *COVID-19 and Maritime Transport: Impact and Responses. UNCTAD/DTL/TLB/2021/1. Geneva.* Transport and Trade Facilitation Series, No. 5.

- UNCTAD (2021f). UNCTADstat: Transport cost database. Available at https://unctadstat.unctad.org/wds/ReportFolders/reportFolders.aspx (accessed 24 May 2021).

- UNCTAD (2021g). Climate change and maritime transport. Available at https://unctad.org/topic/transport-and-trade-logistics/climate-change-and-maritime-transport (accessed 12 May 2021).

- UNCTAD (2021h). Climate change impacts and adaptation for coastal transport infrastructure in the Caribbean. Available at https://sidsport-climateadapt.unctad.org/ (accessed 12 May 2021).

- UNCTAD (2021i). UNCTAD Development and Globalization: Facts and Figures 2021: Small Island Developing States. Available at https://unctad.org/statistics (accessed 10 June 2021).

- UNCTAD (2021j). Transport infrastructure and services. Available at https://unctad.org/topic/transport-and-trade-logistics/infrastructure-and-services (accessed 12 May 2021).

- UNCTAD (2021k). UNCTAD Framework for Sustainable Freight Transport. Available at https://www.sft-framework.org/ (accessed 12 May 2021).

- UNDRR (2020). DesInventar Sendai. Available at https://www.desinventar.net (accessed 13 May 2021).

- UNECE (2013). *Climate Change Impacts and Adaptation for International Transport Networks.* Expert Group Report. ECE/TRANS/283. New York and Geneva.

- UNECE (2015). *Transport for Sustainable Development - The Case of Inland Transport.* Transport Trends and Economics Series, No. ECE/TRANS/251. UNECE.

- UNECE (2020). *Climate Change Impacts and Adaptation for Transport Networks and Nodes.* ECE/TRANS/283. Geneva.

- UNEP (2020). Emissions gap report 2020. Available at https://www.unep.org/emissions-gap-report-2020 (accessed 13 May 2021).

- UNFCCC (2020a). Marrakech Partnership for Global Climate Action. Climate action pathway: Transport. Action table. Available at https://unfccc.int/sites/default/files/resource/Action_table_Transport_.pdf (accessed 11 May 2021).

- UNFCCC (2020b). Marrakech Partnership for Global Climate Action. Climate action pathway: Resilience and adaptation. Action table. Available at https://unfccc.int/sites/default/files/resource/Action_table%20_Resilience.pdf (accessed 11 May 2021).

- WHO (2020). Q&A on coronaviruses (COVID-19). Available at https://www.who.int/emergencies/diseases/novel-coronavirus-2019/question-and-answers-hub/q-a-detail/q-a-coronaviruses (accessed 11 May 2020).

- WMO (2021). *State of the Global Climate 2020.*

- Woetzel J, Garemo N, Mischke J, Hjerpe M and Palter R (2016). Bridging global infrastructure gaps. Available at https://www.mckinsey.com/industries/capital-projects-and-infrastructure/our-insights/bridging-global-infrastructure-gaps (accessed 9 April 2020).

- World Bank (2020a). 3 Things You Need to Know About Adaptation and Resilience. Available at https://www.worldbank.org/en/topic/climatechange/brief/3-things-you-need-to-know-about-adaptation-and-resilience (accessed 13 May 2021).

- World Bank (2020b). Private participation in infrastructure (PPI). Annual PPI Database Global Report, 2019. Available at https://ppi.worldbank.org/en/ppi (accessed 9 April 2020).

- World Economic Forum (2021). *The Global Risks Report 2021.* World Economic Forum. Geneva.

IV. Digitalization offers great potential for development, but also risks

SDG indicators

SDG target 9.c: Significantly increase access to information and communications technology and strive to provide universal and affordable access to the Internet in LDCs by 2020
SDG indicator 9.c.1: Proportion of population covered by a mobile network, by technology (Tier I)

SDG target 17.6: Enhance North-South, South-South and triangular regional and international cooperation on and access to science, technology and innovation and enhance knowledge-sharing on mutually agreed terms, including through improved coordination among existing mechanisms, in particular at the United Nations level, and through a global technology facilitation mechanism
SDG indicator 17.6.1: Fixed Internet broadband subscriptions per 100 inhabitants, by speed (Tier I)

SDG target 17.8: Fully operationalize the technology bank and science, technology and innovation capacity-building mechanism for LDCs by 2017 and enhance the use of enabling technology, in particular information and communications technology
SDG indicator 17.8.1: Proportion of individuals using the Internet (Tier I)

Information and communications technologies (ICTs) have led to important economic changes over recent decades, transforming value chains and the production and trade of goods and services. ICTs have become an increasingly important tool for development, providing access to information for science, technology and innovation, fostering and enhancing regional and international cooperation and knowledge-sharing. While this has led to substantial improvements in productivity, it has also created new barriers to entry. Only those individuals with the requisite skills and those firms with access to the right tools can reap benefits from the digital revolution. Moreover, the ICT sector is characterized by constant and rapid changes. It has the potential to bring large benefits in terms of productivity and economic development, but it can also by disrupting the status quo lead to inequality and exclusion.

While the COVID-19 pandemic has had a sweeping impact on economic activity, it has also resulted in an exceptional surge in the use of various digital solutions. Workers around the world have shifted to telework and online conferencing, while many students have had to follow their classes remotely, supported by a variety of digital technologies. Use of e-commerce, digital entertainment (streaming, e-media and web-based news services) and social media accelerated in 2020 (UNCTAD, 2021b). In addition to enabling continued business in many areas, digital solutions have also helped social and cultural activities to continue during the pandemic, thus contributing to maintaining a better quality of life while in isolation.

While this will likely have lasting effects on the adoption of ICTs in many areas, even beyond the crisis, there are also growing concerns about the unequal access to these digital goods and services, both between and within countries. Before the COVID-19 outbreak, there were already persistent differences in access between men and women, urban and rural sectors, low- and high-skilled workers, large and small firms, public and private schools, and others. The measures taken by the governments to contain the pandemic have the potential to increase these existing inequalities (UNCTAD, 2021b). In addition, privacy and data protection concerns have multiplied. In order to meet the SDG targets of universal access to ICTs, efforts to bridge existing and emerging digital divides should be reinforced in order to allow more countries and all sectors of the population to take advantage of digital technologies.

Access to ICTs continues to improve

While SDG 9 encourages innovation and infrastructural improvements, including through ICT, it also recognises the risk that many people and businesses could be left behind. To address this, SDG target 9.c calls for increased access to ICT, striving to achieve universality and affordability. To this end, SDG indicator 9.c.1 proposes to measure the proportion of the population covered by a mobile network, broken down by technology.

Fast mobile network coverage is virtually universal in Eastern Asia

Figure 1 illustrates how mobile networks now cover most of the population in all regions of the world. Except for Sub-Saharan Africa, the share of the population lacking mobile telephony coverage does not exceed six per cent in any region. For many people in developing countries, mobile phones are often the only way of accessing the Internet and they have allowed the poorest to become connected. Increasingly, they are being directly used for economic purposes, supporting entrepreneurship, empowerment and financial inclusion. For example, the number of registered mobile money accounts worldwide surpassed one billion in 2019, about 45 per cent of them in Sub-Saharan Africa. Daily transaction by mobile money were worth almost US$2 billion in 2019 (GSMA, 2020).

Faster and more reliable Internet and mobile services are important for access to more sophisticated digital content that can add more value for business. Except for Sub-Saharan Africa, 4G or newer wireless systems are now prevalent in all regions.

Figure 1. Distribution of population by mobile network coverage, by technology, 2019 (SDG 9.c.1)

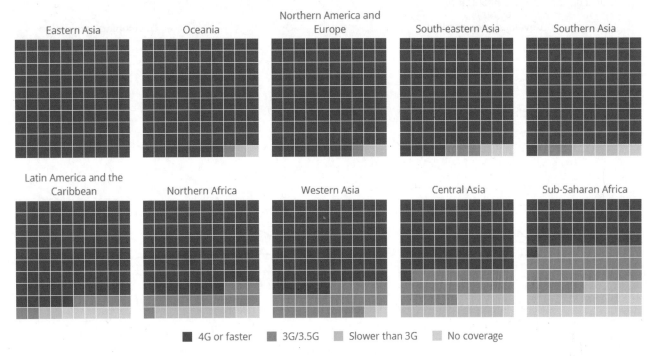

Source: UNCTAD calculations based on ITU (2020a).
Notes: Geographic regions follow UNSD (2020). Missing values estimated by logistic regression models by mobile technology.

This indicator, however, only reflects a minimum requirement for ICT access, since population coverage does not necessarily mean that those covered are actually able to use the services, for example because of technological or affordability constraints. A more complete picture can be obtained by the number of subscribers to ICT services relative to the population, and this is shown in the graph below.

Mobile cellular networks have expanded rapidly in recent years and this has helped to overcome the infrastructure barriers to fixed telephony (United Nations, 2015). Figure 2 shows that, in contrast to the global decline in the number of fixed telephone subscriptions, mobile telephony is booming, especially in developing countries, where the number of subscriptions per 100 inhabitants increased from 23 in 2005 to 103 in 2019. In the LDCs, the increase was particularly fast, from 5 in 2005 to 75 in 2019.

In 2019, for the first time there were more than one mobile telephone subscription per person in developing countries

Figure 2. ICT access indicators

(Subscriptions per 100 inhabitants)

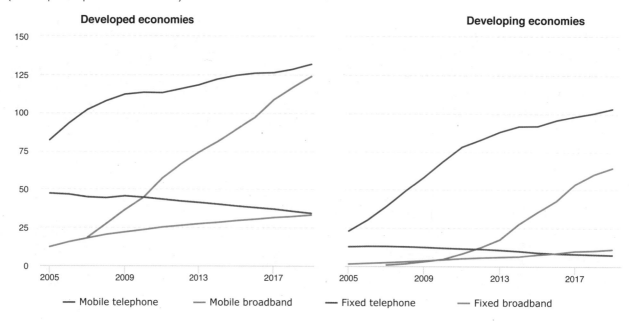

Source: ITU (2020a).
Notes: Developing and developed regions follow UNSD (2020). Figures for 2019 are estimates.

High-speed Internet access plays an important enabling role in the digital economy. The rapid development of broadband networks is widely considered essential if developing countries are to leverage the benefits available through ICT and avoid the widening of the digital gaps (UNCTAD, 2015). Therefore, the number of individuals and businesses using broadband technology is a good indicator of the extent to which the private sector is leveraging the Internet. As shown in figure 2, while the number of broadband subscriptions per capita has increased globally, developing countries are lagging behind in the adoption of this technology. Mobile connections are the prevailing way to access broadband technology in both developing and developed economies.

Furthermore, these global averages hide large variations across regions. Figure 3 presents the number of fixed broadband subscriptions relative to the population disaggregated by speed, as specified in SDG indicator 17.6.1. While broadband, in general, is widespread in Northern America, Europe, Oceania and Eastern Asia, other regions have much lower subscription rates. For example, Southern Asian countries had, on average, only 2.1 subscriptions per 100 inhabitants in 2019, and Sub-Saharan African countries only 0.8.

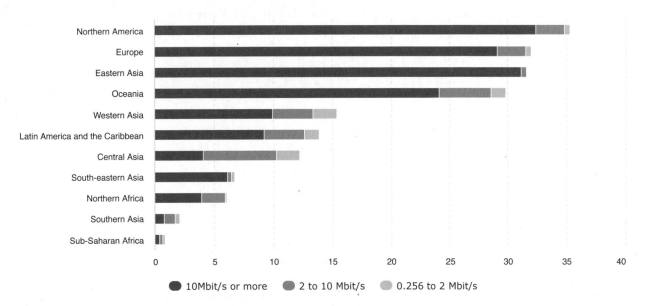

📊 **Figure 3. Fixed broadband subscriptions by speed, 2019 (SDG 17.6.1)**

(Subscriptions per 100 inhabitants)

Source: UNCTAD calculations based on ITU (2020a).

Notes: Geographic regions follow UNSD (2020). Some missing values estimated by regression models by speed and region.

There is also some variability in terms of speed, influencing the quality and functionality. While in some regions most broadband connections provide high-speed access, in others the problem of limited fixed broadband subscriptions is compounded by lower broadband speeds, which constrain the potential benefits of ICT use. This is the case, for instance, in Northern Africa or Central Asia.

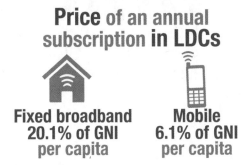

Price of an annual subscription in LDCs

Fixed broadband
20.1% of GNI
per capita

Mobile
6.1% of GNI
per capita

It is useful to examine the cost of broadband in different country groups as a possible determinant of the extent of its uptake. Although the monthly subscription charge for fixed broadband has fallen considerably all over the world, it remains high in many developing countries, including LDCs. Indeed, the median annual cost of a fixed broadband subscription (5GB basket or equivalent) in developed countries during 2020 was equivalent to only 1.2 per cent of per capita GNI, while it reached 20.1 per cent of GNI per capita in LDCs. The yearly median cost of mobile broadband subscriptions (1.5GB basket or equivalent) reached 0.6 and 6.1 per cent of GNI per capita in developed countries and LDCs, respectively.[1] A high-speed internet connection, therefore, remains a luxury good for most people in LDCs.

More people are using Internet, but access is unequal

UNCTAD has long drawn attention to the importance of the digital divide in broadband capacity and quality, noting that it creates new divisions in terms of the extent to which individuals, businesses, economies and societies are able to take advantage of new ICT innovations and applications (UNCTAD, 2013). As mentioned above, the COVID-19 pandemic could exacerbate this digital divide (UNCTAD, 2021b). Ideally, there should be universal coverage of high-speed broadband, with regular upgrading of infrastructure and reduced regulatory barriers to service providers. In addition, the international regulatory environment for ICT infrastructure and related services should be open, competitive and transparent (UNCTAD, 2016).

As a way to monitor the use of ICT, SDG indicator 17.8.1 measures the proportion of individuals that use the Internet, rather than just have access to it. ITU estimates that 87 per cent of the population in developed economies were using the Internet in 2019, compared to 44 per cent in developing economies and 19 per cent in LDCs (ITU, 2020b). Although Internet use in LDCs is growing rapidly (from 1.4 per cent of the population in 2005), the percentage is still low compared to other developing regions.[2] In addition, important disparities still exist between different population groups. For example, the percentage of women using Internet is lower than that of men, especially in less advanced economies. Additionally, a large gap is still observed between individuals living in urban and rural areas.[3]

ICT is now an essential element of business

Disparities also exist between countries in the proportion of businesses that use the Internet. Official data on ICT use in business is limited, particularly in LDCs. But available figures show that most firms in developed economies use the Internet, while this proportion varies considerably for developing countries. Within countries, there is a persistent gap in Internet use between small and large enterprises, and between enterprises in rural and urban locations.[4]

Internet use by employees has been positively correlated with productivity (World Bank, 2016). It is also a condition for e-commerce, which could contribute to poverty reduction, innovation and financial inclusion. It also facilitates the participation in global value chains and, in this way, promotes exports (UNCTAD, 2017a). Businesses that fail to develop digital tools for reaching out to customers may be at a higher risk, as it became evident during the COVID-19 pandemic.

E-commerce sales (B2C and B2B) were estimated to be worth US$26.7 trillion in 2019 (UNCTAD, 2020e), about 30 per cent of global GDP. This amount has increased continuously in recent years, and it was four per cent higher than in 2018. An indication of the rapid expansion of e-commerce is the number of online shoppers in the world, which rose from less than 600 million in 2010 to about 1.48 billion in 2019. However, the distribution is highly unequal, with China accounting for 42 per cent of the total and LDCs responsible for only a small share of Internet shoppers (UNCTAD, 2020e).

E-commerce sales in 2019 were equivalent to 30% of global GDP

The COVID-19 crisis has resulted in spikes in B2C and B2B online sales, as business and consumer replaced their traditional channels for retail and wholesale trade with e-commerce alternatives. In addition, many traditional businesses rapidly deployed an e-commerce presence to continue their business during the containment measures. Data for countries accounting for 65 per cent of global B2C e-commerce suggest that online retail sales as a share of total retail sales jumped by 3 percentage points in 2020 (from 16 per cent to 19 per cent) compared to a two percentage point rise between 2018 and 2019 (UNCTAD, 2021b). However, e-commerce has also faced restrictions and delays imposed by limited capacity of traditional distribution networks, as well as by disrupted trade channels, supply chain bottlenecks and regulations affecting logistics services (UNCTAD, 2021b).

In order to help countries gain insight into their preparedness for e-commerce, UNCTAD has developed the B2C e-commerce index. This index evaluates the prerequisites for the development of e-commerce, such as payment methods, cyber security, postal reliability, and Internet use amongst the population.[5] Map 1 displays the 2020 values of the B2C e-commerce index. Most developed economies, but also some developing countries such as the United Arab Emirates and Malaysia, have developed all the fundamentals of e-commerce and, therefore, receive a high score in this indicator. Most LDCs are toward the bottom of the ranking: Out of the 20 economies with the lowest value in the 2020 index, 18 are LDCs, with Congo and Syrian Arab Republic being the only non-LDCs in this group. This suggests that LDCs are still not fully prepared for the adoption of e-commerce and similar development opportunities stemming from ICT.

Map 1. UNCTAD B2C e-commerce index, 2020

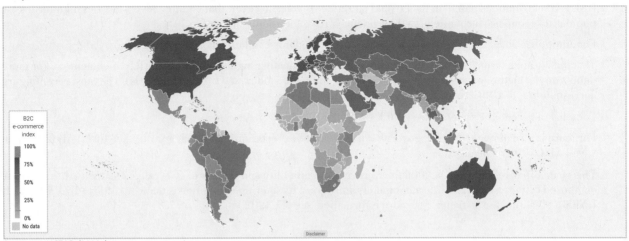

Sources: UNCTAD (2020a).

UNCTAD takes an active role in promoting ICT as a tool for development

The rapid changes taking place as a result of e-commerce and other ICT developments require new approaches to accelerate readiness to adapt to and maximize opportunities from these changes. UNCTAD is implementing several initiatives to respond to this need. An example is the "eTrade for all" program (UNCTAD, 2020b), a global partnership comprising around 30 organizations that work together to support an enabling environment for sustainable development through e-commerce. At the heart of this initiative is an online knowledge-sharing platform that allows countries to navigate the supply of technical and financial assistance from partnering institutions in key policy areas, such as ICT infrastructure and services, payments, trade logistics, regulatory frameworks, skills development and finance.

UNCTAD has undertaken 25 Rapid eTrade Readiness Assessments of LDCs in the past few years.[6] These assessments analyze what needs to be addressed in various policy areas in order to increase the capacity of countries to participate effectively in e-commerce. For most LDCs, these assessments can help to overcome a significant market failure: the fact that LDCs have lacked the information and awareness to formulate effectively their needs for development assistance in the area of e-commerce, and that donors as a result have witnessed limited demand for such assistance. UNCTAD also works with a number of developing countries to develop e-commerce strategies and policies, such as for Egypt (UNCTAD, 2017b), Botswana, Myanmar, Oman and Rwanda.

In addition to the B2C e-commerce index, UNCTAD has launched several initiatives to improve the measurement of ICT-related contributions to the economy and trade. UNCTAD has responded to the need to boost work in this area by establishing the Intergovernmental Group of Experts on E-commerce and the Digital Economy, which on its third session (2019) created the Working Group on Measuring E-commerce and the Digital Economy.[7] UNCTAD is also an active and founding member of the Partnership on Measuring ICT for Development.[8] Capacity-building efforts to strengthen the capacity of developing countries to measure e-commerce and the digital economy are supported by UNCTAD (see UNCTAD, 2021c).

Notes

1. UNCTAD calculations based on data from ITU (2020a).

2. UNCTAD estimates based on data from ITU (2020a).

3. UNCTAD calculations based on data from ITU (2020a). Note, however, that country-level statistics on Internet use by population group are incomplete, so the evidence presented is only indicative.

4. For additional details, see figures on the information economy available in UNCTAD (2021a).

5. This index ranges from zero to 100, with higher values indicating higher readiness for B2C e-commerce. For more details on the methodology of the UNCTAD B2C e-commerce index, see UNCTAD (2020a). The most recent figures, corresponding to 2019, are available in UNCTAD (2020a).

6. For a list of recent assessments, see UNCTAD (2020c).

7. For more information on the intergovernmental group of experts and the working group, see UNCTAD (2020d) and UNCTAD (2019), respectively.

8. This is an initiative launched in 2004 to improve the availability and quality of ICT-related statistics. It is currently composed of 14 regional and international organizations. Its steering committee is made up of ITU, UNCTAD and UNESCO Institute for Statistics. For more information, see ITU (2020c).

References

- Doshi P (2011). The elusive definition of pandemic influenza. Bulletin of the World Health Organisation. *WHO Bulletin.* 89(7):532–538.

- GSMA (2010). Mobile money definitions July. Available at https://www.gsma.com/mobilefordevelopment/resources/mobile-money-definitions (accessed 28 May 2020).

- GSMA (2020). State of the industry report on mobile money. Available at https://www.gsma.com/sotir/wp-content/uploads/2020/03/GSMA-State-of-the-Industry-Report-on-Mobile-Money-2019-Full-Report.pdf (accessed 28 May 2020).

- ITU (2014). *Manual for Measuring ICT Access and Use by Households and Individuals.* International Telecommunication Union. Geneva.

- ITU (2020a). World telecommunication/ICT indicators database. Available at https://www.itu.int/en/ITU-D/Statistics/Pages/publications/wtid.aspx (accessed 25 April 2021).

- ITU (2020b). Measuring digital development facts and figures 2020. ITU, 19. (accessed 23 April 2021).

- ITU (2020c). Partnership on measuring ICT for development. Available at https://www.itu.int/en/ITU-D/Statistics/Pages/intlcoop/partnership/default.aspx (accessed 28 May 2020).

- OECD (2021). Glossary of statistical terms. Available at https://stats.oecd.org/glossary/index.htm (accessed 11 May 2021).

- UNCTAD (2013). *Information Economy Report 2013: The Cloud Economy and Developing Countries.* United Nations publication. Sales No. E.13.II.D.6. New York and Geneva.

- UNCTAD (2015). *Implementing WSIS Outcomes: A Ten-Year Review.* UNCTAD/DTL/STICT/2015/3. Geneva.

- UNCTAD (2016). Aid for eTrade: Unlocking the potential of e-commerce in developing countries. Draft call for action. UNCTAD/DTL/ICT4D/2016/CFA. Geneva. 18 March. (accessed 28 May 2020).

- UNCTAD (2017a). *Information Economy Report 2017: Digitalization, Trade and Development.* United Nations publication. Sales No. E.17.II.D.8. New York and Geneva.

- UNCTAD (2017b). *ICT Policy Review: National E-Commerce Strategy for Egypt.* UNCTAD/DTL/STICT/2017/3. New York and Geneva.

- UNCTAD (2019). Working group on measuring e-commerce and the digital economy, first meeting. Available at https://unctad.org/en/Pages/MeetingDetails.aspx?meetingid=2259 (accessed 28 May 2020).

- UNCTAD (2020a). UNCTAD B2C e-commerce index 2020. UNCTAD Technical Notes on ICT for Development No. 17. TN/UNCTAD/ICT4D/14. Geneva. 2 December. (accessed 22 January 2021).

- UNCTAD (2020b). eTrade for all. Available at https://etradeforall.org/ (accessed 28 May 2020).

- UNCTAD (2020c). Rapid eTrade readiness assessment of least developed countries (eT Ready). Available at https://unctad.org/en/Pages/Publications/E-Trade-Readiness-Assessment.aspx (accessed 28 May 2020).

- UNCTAD (2020d). Available at https://unctad.org/en/Pages/Meetings/Group-of-Experts-Ecommerce-Digital-Economy.aspx (accessed 28 May 2020).

- UNCTAD (2020e). UNCTAD estimates of global e-commerce 2018. UNCTAD Technical Notes on ICT for Development No. 15. TN/UNCTAD/ICT4D/15. Geneva. 27 April. (accessed 28 May 2020).

- UNCTAD (2021a). UNCTADStat. Available at https://unctadstat.unctad.org/EN/Index.html (accessed 21 April 2021).

- UNCTAD (2021b). COVID-19 and e-commerce: a global review. (accessed 20 April 2021).

- UNCTAD (2021c). Manual for the Production of Statistics on the Digital Economy 2020. (accessed 11 May 2021).

- UNESCO Institute for Statistics (2020). Glossary. Available at http://uis.unesco.org/en/glossary (accessed 15 March 2021).

- United Nations (2015). Report of the partnership on measuring information and communications technology for development: Information and communications technology statistics. E/CN.3/2016/13. New York. 18 December. (accessed 28 May 2020).

- UNSD (2020). Standard country or area codes for statistical use (M49). Available at https://unstats.un.org/unsd/methodology/m49/ (accessed 28 May 2020).

- WHO (2020). Q&A on coronaviruses (COVID-19). Available at https://www.who.int/emergencies/diseases/novel-coronavirus-2019/question-and-answers-hub/q-a-detail/q-a-coronaviruses (accessed 11 May 2020).

- World Bank (2016). *World Development Report 2016: Digital Dividends*. The World Bank.

V. Developing country external debt: From growing sustainability concerns to potential crisis in the time of COVID-19

SDG indicators

SDG target 17.4: Assist developing countries in attaining long-term debt sustainability through coordinated policies aimed at fostering debt financing, debt relief and debt restructuring, as appropriate, and address the external debt of highly indebted poor countries to reduce debt distress.

SDG indicator 17.4.1: Debt service as a proportion of exports of goods and services (Tier I)

Debt is a key component of long-term financing for sustainable development and structural transformation. The most important criterion for the long-term sustainability of debt obligations is that borrowing serves the purpose of increasing productive investment significantly with regard to the average interest rate and maturity of the debt stock. If this condition is met, increases in domestic income and export earnings are expected to cover the servicing of outstanding debt obligations. A second key criterion concerns the contractual conditions of (re-) financing such debt. The more closely lending conditionalities are aligned with the objective of mobilizing debt finance for structural transformation in developing countries, the higher the chances the debt can be serviced promptly.

External indebtedness poses important challenges for developing countries, particularly in a context of floating exchange rate systems, open capital accounts and fast integration into international financial markets. The historical position of developing countries as debtors in foreign currency has been a recurrent source of vulnerability to external shocks, for example during a commodity price slump. This is because the servicing of external debt obligations ultimately requires generating sufficient export earnings (or other forms of income). At the same time, exchange rate volatility is likely to affect the value of debt owed externally and that of export earnings in opposite directions. Thus, a depreciation of the local currency against hard currencies may result in increased export earnings (provided that the fall in the dollar price of local exports is compensated by a commensurate increase in export volumes),) but will automatically imply an increase in the value of foreign-currency denominated debt obligations in local currency.

Against a backdrop of insufficient international public finance flows and limited access to concessional resources,[1] developing economies have increasingly raised development finance on commercial terms in international financial markets. They have also opened their domestic financial markets to non-resident investors, and they have allowed their citizens and firms to borrow and invest abroad. While increased access to international financial markets can help capital-scarce countries to quickly raise much-needed funds, it also exposes them to higher risk profiles of debt contracts, i.e. shorter maturities and more volatile financing costs, as well as to sudden reversals of private capital inflows. In conjunction with other exogenous shocks, such as natural disasters, pandemics or episodes of political instability, external debt burdens deemed sustainable by international creditors can quickly become unsustainable.

External debt grew to a record high in 2020, with worsening risk profiles

In the wake of the COVID-19 pandemic, external debt stocks of developing countries reached US$10.6 trillion, their highest level on record, more than twice their value of US$4.4 trillion registered in 2009, and more than four-fold their level of US$2.3 trillion in 2000 (see figure 1). Given the sluggish growth since the global financial crisis of 2007-2008, this translated into a renewed increase in the average ratio of external debt to GDP from 23 per cent in 2008 (its lowest point in the last 20 years) to 31 per cent in 2020, as shown in figure 2. Moreover, 2020 has seen the highest annual increase since the financial crisis, probably as a result of the COVID-19 crisis.

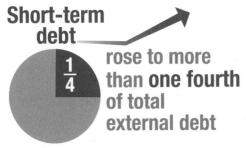

External debt of developing economies reached 31% of their GDP in 2020

These trends are largely influenced by China, whose economy accounted for 23 per cent of total external debt stocks of developing economies and 44 per cent of their GDP in 2020. During the period 2009-2020 China's external debt stock grew at a slightly higher rate than the developing countries average, but its GDP grew much faster. As a result, the average ratio of external debt to GDP for developing economies excluding China is 13 percentage points higher, reaching 44 per cent of their GDP in 2020. This gap between China and the rest of the developing countries has widened in 2020. At the same time, the public-private composition of long-term external debt changed, with the share of private (PNG) debt in overall external debt surpassing that of public (PPG) debt from 2011 to 2016 and practically remaining at similar levels since then. In addition, the share of short-term debt (characterised by higher risk profiles) increased, from 16 per cent of overall external debt in 2000 to 26 per cent in 2020, with a peak at 33 per cent in 2013.

Short-term debt rose to more than **one fourth** of total external debt

▩ Figure 1. External debt stocks, developing economies

(Billions of current US$)

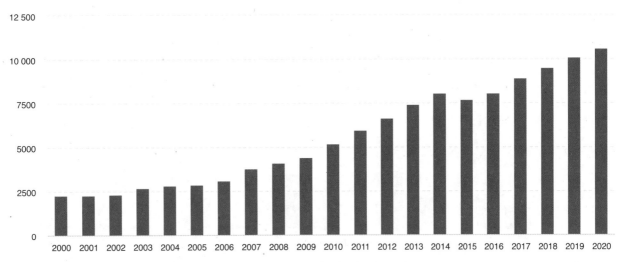

Source: UNCTAD calculations based on data from World Bank (2021), IMF (2021) and national sources.
Note: Figures for 2020 are UNCTAD estimates.

ılıl Figure 2. External debt stocks as a percentage of GDP, developing economies

(Percentage)

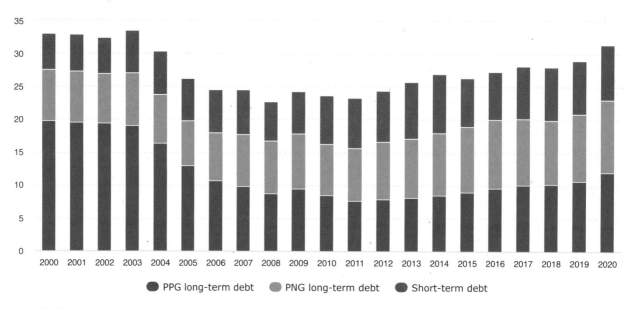

Source: UNCTAD calculations based on data from World Bank (2021), IMF (2021) and national sources.
Note: Figures for 2020 are UNCTAD estimates.

As figure 3 shows, over the past two decades, overall external debt stocks have not only risen markedly across all developing regions, but this increase has also been accompanied by a rising share of short-term debt and PNG long-term debt in total external debt. Given their deeper financial systems, the majority of international private lending into developing countries went to high-income and upper-middle income economies, particularly in Asia and Latin America. But the trend has also been upward in other developing regions, including those with a large share of low-income economies, such as Sub-Saharan Africa.

ılıl Figure 3. External debt stocks, developing economies, by region

(Billions of current US$)

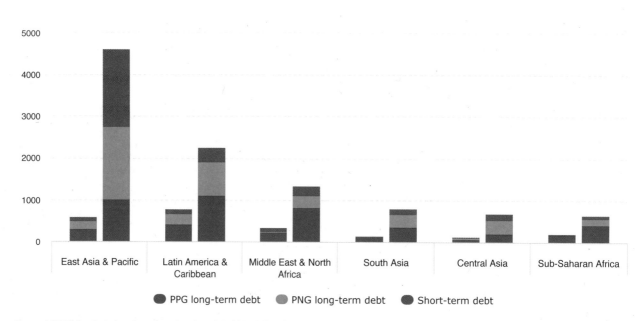

Source: UNCTAD calculations based on data from World Bank (2021), IMF (2021) and national sources.

This increase of private sector participation in developing country PPG external debt accelerated after 2009 (see figure 4) and this trend has not always been warranted by positive developments in these economies' domestic financial and banking systems. Instead, the driving forces have mostly been global "push factors", such as the impact of accommodative monetary policies in many developed economies in the aftermath of the global financial crisis. High levels of private external indebtedness are of concern since they represent a large contingent liability on public sector finances, ultimately backed by international reserves held in the domestic economy. In the event of wide-spread private sector debt distress, governments will have little choice but to transfer the bulk of distressed private debt to public balance sheets.

Figure 4. Long-term external PPG debt by creditor, developing economies
(Percentage of total PPG debt)

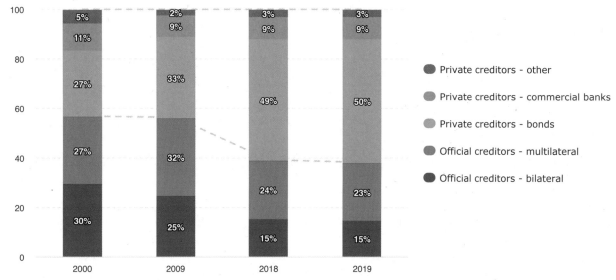

UNCTAD calculations based on data from World Bank (2021).
Notes: Averages by group of economies. Only countries with available data were included.

Public debt in bond markets almost doubled its share of total debt between 2000 and 2019 **x2**

The fragility of developing countries' debt positions prior to the COVID-19 outbreak was further increased by accompanying changes to the ownership of long-term external PPG debt. As shown in figure 4, the share of PPG external debt of developing governments owed to private creditors reached 62 per cent of the total in 2019, compared to around 20 per cent in the 1970s and 43 per cent in 2000. Its most volatile component, public bond finance, is clearly on the increase relative to financing through commercial bank loans and other private creditors. This reflects the growing reliance of developing country governments on refinancing their external debt obligations in international financial markets with strong speculative features rather than borrowing from official bilateral and multilateral creditors, which is generally more stable and in more favourable terms.

Debt service costs on public external debt continue to pose a serious challenge

Rising external debt burden along with increased risk profiles of such debt translate into rising servicing costs. Debt service ratios are considered important indicators of a country's debt sustainability. In this sense, SDG indicator 17.4.1 measures "debt service as a proportion of exports of goods and services". This indicator reflects a government's ability to meet external creditor claims on the public sector through export revenues. A fall (increase) in this ratio can result from increased (reduced) export earnings, a reduction (increase) in debt servicing costs, or a combination of both. A persistent deterioration of this ratio signals an inability to generate enough foreign exchange income to meet external creditor obligations on a country's PPG debt, and thus potential debt distress in the absence of multilateral support or effective sovereign debt restructuring.

Figure 5. Debt service on long-term external PPG debt by groups of economies (SDG 17.4.1)

(Percentage of exports of goods and services)

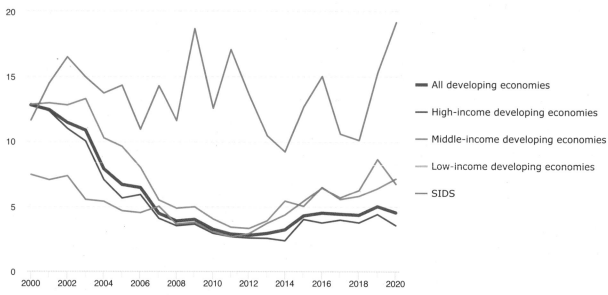

Source: UNCTAD calculations based on data from World Bank (2021), IMF (2021) and national sources.
Notes: Figures for 2020 are UNCTAD estimates. Income groups follow World Bank's definition.

As figure 5 shows, only high-income developing countries have maintained a stable ratio of external long-term PPG debt to export revenues of around two to four per cent in the last decade. This is largely due to their greater capacity to issue domestic public debt, with a view to avoid currency mismatches. However, while greater reliance on local-currency denominated public debt reduces the vulnerability to exchange rate volatility, it frequently creates maturity mismatches. Even governments in high-income developing countries are often unable to issue long-term government securities at a sustainable rate of interest, yet they need to be able to pay off or roll over maturing short-term obligations. In contrast, a marked increase of debt service ratios has been registered since 2012 across all other income categories: in middle-income countries this ratio rose from 3.3 per cent in 2012 to 7.1 per cent in 2020 and in low-income countries from 2.9 to 6.7 per cent. SIDS saw this ratio rise from a low point of 9.2 per cent in 2014 to 19.2 per cent in 2020. As these economies increasingly tapped into international capital markets, this reflects rising external public debt stocks since 2012 in a context of commodity price volatility, sluggish global economic growth and rising debt service.

Moving beyond SDG indicator 17.4.1, the share of government revenues dedicated to servicing PPG debt rose sharply over recent years, particularly in the poorest developing economies. As figure 6 illustrates, whereas in 2012 low-income developing countries spent 3.3 per cent of their government revenues to meet external public debt obligations, this figure rose to 9.4 per cent in 2019, falling slightly to an estimated 6.6 per cent in 2020. The squeeze on government revenues from service payments on external PPG debt was particularly drastic in Sub-Saharan Africa, where this ratio jumped from a low point of 3.3 per cent in 2011 to 10 per cent in 2020.

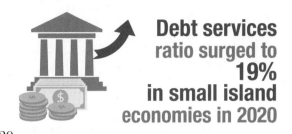

Debt services ratio surged to 19% in small island economies in 2020

 Figure 6. Debt service on long-term external PPG debt, selected groups of developing countries
(Percentage of government revenue)

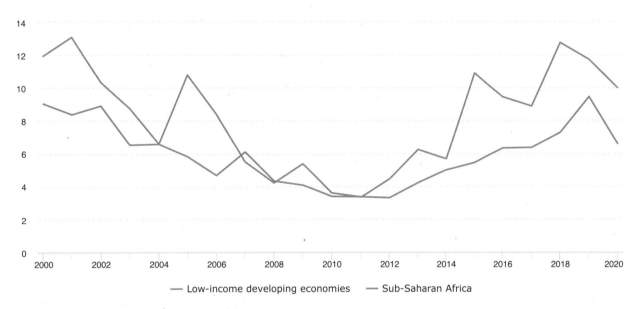

Source: UNCTAD calculations based on data from World Bank (2021), IMF (2021) and national sources.
Note: Figures for 2020 are UNCTAD estimates.

This is of concern since low-income developing countries still rely predominantly on public financing to mobilise resources for structural transformation, yet also struggle the most with limited fiscal space given their shallow domestic financial and banking systems and limited options to refinance maturing debt obligations in the international financial markets.

The challenges posed by the COVID-19 shock

The COVID-19 pandemic has translated into a shock that has put a glaring spotlight on the rapidly deteriorating debt sustainability in many developing countries, since it threatens to turn what was already a dire situation prior to the pandemic into a series of sovereign defaults.

While developed countries are putting together massive stabilisation packages to flatten both the pandemic curve and the curve of economic and financial crisis, this is not an option open to many developing economies, at least not at the required scale. On one hand, developing countries cannot easily lock down their largely informal economies effectively without more people being affected by hunger rather than by illness. On the other, they face substantive limitations on their fiscal space to mount rescue packages comparable to those currently under way in developed economies.

Developing economies are expected to face a "wall of maturity" for their public external debt in the 2020-2021

To pay for imports and to meet external debt obligations, the vast majority of developing countries are heavily reliant on access to hard currencies, earned primarily through commodity and service exports, such as food, oil and tourism, or received through remittances, as well as access to further concessional and market-based borrowing. Their central banks cannot act as lenders of last resort to their governments to the extent central banks in developed economies can without risking a large depreciation of their local currencies and its effects in terms of steep increases in the value of foreign-currency denominated debt. This has the potential to unleash destructive inflationary pressures. But with volumes of international trade experiencing a sharp contraction, core commodity prices in free fall, tourism at a virtual standstill, remittances drying up and private capital outflows from developing countries reaching unprecedented levels in recent history, many developing economies are increasingly cut off from conventional sources of income when they need them most.[2]

It is against this backdrop that already existing debt vulnerabilities and distress in developing countries require decisive action to avoid liquidity constraints turning into wide-spread insolvency crises. Well-designed debt relief – through a combination of temporary standstills with sovereign debt reprofiling and restructuring – will therefore be essential to address not only immediate liquidity pressures, but also to restore long-term external debt sustainability in many developing countries, not least with a post-COVID-19 view of achieving the 2030 Agenda for Sustainable Development.[3]

Notes

1. For more information on this topic, see Robust and predictable financing sources and Official support for sustainable development.

2. See UNCTAD (2020a) for more detail.

3. See UNCTAD (2020b) for more detail.

References

- Doshi P (2011). The elusive definition of pandemic influenza. Bulletin of the World Health Organisation. *WHO Bulletin*. 89(7):532–538.

- IMF (2009). *International Transactions in Remittances: Guide for Compilers and Users (RCG)*. IMF. Washington, D.C.

- IMF (2014). *External Debt Statistics: Guide for Compilers and Users*. IMF. Washington, D.C.

- IMF (2021). World Economic Outlook (WEO) database. Available at https://www.imf.org/en/Publications/SPROLLs/world-economic-outlook-databases#sort=%40imfdate%20descending (accessed 5 February 2021).

- UNCTAD (2020a). The Covid-19 shock to developing countries: Towards a "whatever it takes" programme for the two-thirds of the world's population being left behind. UNCTAD/GDS/INF/2020/2. Geneva.

- UNCTAD (2020b). From the Great Lockdown to the Great Meltdown: Developing country debt in the time of Covid-19. Available at https://unctad.org/en/PublicationsLibrary/gdsinf2020d3_en.pdf (accessed 10 May 2020).

- WHO (2020). Q&A on coronaviruses (COVID-19). Available at https://www.who.int/emergencies/diseases/novel-coronavirus-2019/question-and-answers-hub/q-a-detail/q-a-coronaviruses (accessed 11 May 2020).

- World Bank (2021). International debt statistics. Available at https://databank.worldbank.org/data/source/international-debt-statistics (accessed 10 May 2021).

VI. Recent conceptual and methodological developments on measuring illicit financial flows for policy action

SDG indicators

SDG target 16.4: By 2030, significantly reduce illicit financial and arms flows, strengthen the recovery and return of stolen assets and combat all forms of organized crime

SDG indicator 16.4.1: Total value of inward and outward illicit financial flows (in current United States dollars) (Tier II)

As the world searches for the funds needed to recover from the COVID-19 pandemic and achieve the 2030 Agenda for Sustainable Development (United Nations, 2015b), potentially billions of dollars of IFFs slip through the cracks every year. IFFs stemming from organized crime, trade in illegal goods, corruption and illegal and illicit tax and commercial practices move across borders, often in the direction of financial havens.

These flows weaken state institutions by encouraging corruption and undermine the rule of law and the functioning of the criminal justice systems. They also divert resources that are needed for essential services. UNCTAD's Economic Development in Africa Report (2020) found that some countries with high IFFs spend on average 25 per cent less on health and 58 per cent less on education compared with countries with low IFFs. By eroding the tax base and discouraging public and private investment, they hamper structural transformation, economic growth and sustainable development.

The ability to achieve the SDGs remains fragile when undermined by IFFs. The 2030 Agenda underscores the need for increased mobilization of financial resources for sustainable development, including through the improved capacity for revenue collection, and more resources dedicated to investment. The 2030 Agenda identifies the reduction of IFFs as a priority area, as reflected in target 16.4: "by 2030, significantly reduce illicit financial flows and arms flows, strengthen the recovery and return of stolen assets and combat all forms of organised crime". The Addis Ababa Action Agenda (United Nations, 2015a) on financing for development also calls for a redoubling of efforts to substantially reduce IFFs, with a view to eventually eliminating them.

Absence of complete and consistent statistics hampers policy action to curb IFFs

In July 2017, the United Nations General Assembly adopted the indicator framework for the monitoring of progress towards SDGs (United Nations, 2017b). Indicator 16.4.1, "total value of inward and outward illicit financial flows", was selected as one of two indicators to measure progress towards target 16.4. At the time, there was no universal agreement on the definition of IFFs, what should be included within their scope or how the component parts could be measured. Without reliable statistics on IFFs the high uncertainty about the size of these flows, their origins and impact on development hampers policy action to combat IFFs.

Conceptual development of SDG indicator 16.4.1

UNCTAD and UNODC, assigned by the General Assembly as custodians of indicator 16.4.1, lead the methodological work to develop statistical definitions and methods to measure IFFs. As a result of this work, UNCTAD and UNODC (2020) published a *Conceptual Framework for the Statistical Measurement of Illicit Financial Flows*, reflecting concepts and standards approved by the IAEG-SDGs and the United Nations Statistical Commission.[1]

In February 2021, these concepts were subsequently adopted by the FACTI Panel (United Nations, 2021), noting that UNCTAD and UNODC together "developed the first statistical definition of the term to contribute to the development of SDG indicators". This was followed by a reaffirmed agreement by the cluster on IFFs of the Financing for the Development in the Era of COVID-19 and Beyond Initiative on the *Conceptual Framework* and the United Nations definition of what constitutes IFFs for statistical purposes. Cluster 5 will contribute to the development and refinement of methodologies to measure IFFs.

Pioneering countries across continents are testing the *Conceptual Framework* and guidance by UNCTAD and UNODC to measure IFFs. Pilots are carried out in Africa, Asia and the Pacific, Europe and Latin America in coordination with Regional Commissions.

The agreed *Conceptual Framework* builds on a series of expert consultations and a stock taking of research, knowledge and experience with different types of IFFs, carried out from 2017 to 2019 (UNODC, 2017; UNCTAD, 2018). The expert consultations involved experts from national statistical offices, financial intelligence units, tax authorities, academia, non-governmental organisations, international organisations and other IFF experts.

Common definition of IFFs for statistics reached

The consultations highlighted an urgent need to agree on concepts and definitions and recommended further engagement with national statistical authorities in line with the General Assembly resolution (United Nations, 2017a) [2]. To this end, UNCTAD and UNODC established a statistical Task Force in January 2019 to define concepts, assess data availability, develop statistical methods, and guide country-level activities. [3]

The IAEG-SDG endorsed the resulting methodological proposal in October 2019 and reclassified indicator 16.4.1 from Tier III to Tier II, meaning that the indicator is conceptually clear and based on internationally established standards, while data are not yet available from countries.

Statistical definition of IFFs for SDG indicator 16.4.1

For the purpose of the SDG indicator, IFFs are defined as *financial flows that are illicit in origin, transfer or use that reflect an exchange of value and cross country borders*. This definition implies that IFFs have the following features:

- **Illicit in origin, transfer or use**. A flow of value is considered illicit if it is illicitly generated (e.g. originates from criminal activities or tax evasion), illicitly transferred (e.g. violating currency controls) or illicitly used (e.g. for financing terrorism). The flow can be legally generated, transferred or used, but it must be illicit in at least one of these aspects. Some flows that are not strictly illegal may fall within the definition of IFFs, e.g. cross-border tax avoidance which erodes the tax base of a country where that income was generated.

- **Exchange of value, rather than money or purely financial transfers**. Exchanges of value include not only currency exchanges, but also exchanges of goods and services, and financial and non-financial assets.

- **IFF measure a flow of value over a given time**, as opposed to a stock measure, which would be the accumulation of value.

- **Flows that cross a border.** This includes assets where the ownership changes from a resident of a country to a non-resident, even if the assets remain in the same jurisdiction.[4]

IFFs can be classified from many angles: sources, channels, impacts, actors involved, motives, etc. Figure 1 presents the main categories of activities that may generate IFFs.

Figure 1. Categories of activities that may generate IFFs

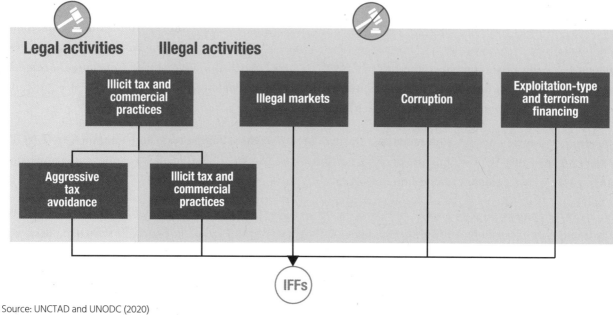

Source: UNCTAD and UNODC (2020)

According to this typology, four main categories of IFFs are distinguished:

1. **Illicit tax and commercial IFFs.** This category includes illicit practices by legal entities as well as arrangements and individuals with the objective of concealing revenues, reducing tax burden, evading controls and regulations and other purposes. This category can be divided into two components:

   - IFFs from illegal commercial and tax practices. These include illegal practices such as tariff, duty and revenue offences, tax evasion, corporate offences, market manipulation and other selected practices. Some activities that are non-observed, hidden or part of the so-called shadow economy, the underground economy or the informal economy may also generate IFFs. Related activities included in the ICCS comprise tax evasion, tariff, duty and revenue offences, competition offences, import/export offences, acts against trade regulations, restrictions or embargoes and investment or stack/shares offences.

   - IFFs from aggressive tax avoidance. Illicit flows can also be generated from legal economic activities through what is sometimes called harmful or aggressive tax avoidance (see box 1 for more detail on the distinction between legal and illegal illicit flows). Aggressive tax avoidance can take place through a variety of forms, such as manipulation of transfer pricing, strategic location of debt and intellectual property, tax treaty shopping, and the use of hybrid instruments and entities. For the purposes of the measurement of the indicator, these flows need to be carefully considered, as they generally arise from licit business transactions and only the illicit part of the cross-border flows belongs to the scope of IFFs.

2. **IFFs from illegal markets.** These include trade in illicit goods and services, when the money flows generated cross country borders. Such processes often involve a degree of criminal organisation aimed at creating profit. They include any type of illegal trafficking of goods, such as drugs and firearms, or services, such as smuggling of migrants. IFFs are generated by the flows related to international trade of illicit goods and services, as well as by cross-border flows from managing the illicit income from such activities.

3. **IFFs from corruption.** The United Nations Convention against Corruption (UNODC, 2004) defines acts considered as corruption, which are consistently defined in the ICCS. These include bribery, embezzlement, abuse of functions, trading in influence, illicit enrichment and other acts. When the economic returns from these acts directly or indirectly generate cross-border flows, they are considered IFFs.

4. **IFFs from exploitation-type activities and financing of crime and terrorism.** Exploitation-type activities are illegal activities that entail a forced and/or involuntary transfer of economic resources between two actors. Examples include slavery and exploitation, extortion, trafficking in persons, and kidnapping. In addition, terrorism financing and financing of crime are illicit, voluntary transfers of funds between two actors with the purpose of funding criminal or terrorist actions. When the related financial flows cross country borders, they constitute IFFs.

Four types of activities may generate IFFs

Illicit tax and commercial activities

Corruption

Illegal markets

Theft, financing of crime and terrorism

Box 1: Aggressive tax avoidance and IFFs

A specific conceptual challenge is to specify what kinds of activities should be designated as illicit or licit. It is noteworthy that SDG target 16.4 refers to 'illicit' instead of 'illegal' financial flows. Aggressive tax avoidance, including by MNEs, although usually legal, can drain resources and be considered illicit.

The inclusion of tax avoidance in the definition of IFFs creates some challenges, as it blurs the line between legal and illegal activities. Noting that the boundary between legal and illegal tax practices may be unclear, the European Commission (2017) described the continuum of activities from legal tax planning to illegal tax evasion (see figure 2). In this context, aggressive tax planning is described as "taking advantage of the technicalities of a tax system or of mismatches between two or more tax systems for the purpose of reducing tax liability."

 Figure 2. Boundaries of aggressive tax planning

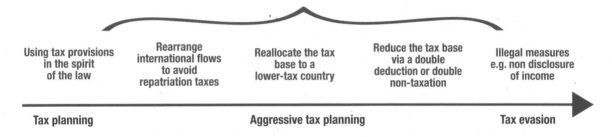

Using tax provisions in the spirit of the law	Rearrange international flows to avoid repatriation taxes	Reallocate the tax base to a lower-tax country	Reduce the tax base via a double deduction or double non-taxation	Illegal measures e.g. non disclosure of income
Tax planning		**Aggressive tax planning**		**Tax evasion**

Source: European Commission (2017).

IFFs stemming from aggressive tax avoidance are considered in detail in OECD (2013), and can include BEPS through interest payments, strategic location of intangible assets, abuse of tax treaties, artificial avoidance of permanent establishment and transfer pricing manipulation. The BEPS package, released in 2015 by OECD and G20 countries, delivers guidance for governments to close gaps in existing international rules that allow corporate profits to be artificially shifted to low-tax jurisdictions where companies have little or no economic activity. Work to address outstanding BEPS issues by the Inclusive Framework is ongoing (OECD, 2020).

As part of the OECD Inclusive Framework on BEPS, progress has also been made in improving data availability to support the measurement of MNE tax avoidance. Country-by-country reporting statistics are released publicly in an aggregated and anonymised form and can be analysed at the microdata level by country authorities.

IFFs need to be classified using a discrete, exhaustive and mutually exclusive statistical classification aligned with existing statistical frameworks and principles (OECD, 2021). The ICCS (UNODC, 2015) is a good point of departure for defining some of the activities that could generate IFFs, such as exploitation-type activities and terrorism, illicit trafficking and corruption, as well as many activities related to tax and commercial malpractices. However, IFFs that are not part of illegal activities may not be covered and an extended classification is being developed. Table 1 provides examples of such activities and how to link the main categories of IFFs to activities that generate them.

Table 1. Examples of activities generating IFFs from crime, by ICCS categories

Categories of IFFs	Examples
Tax and commercial practices	08041 Tariff, taxation, duty and revenue offences
	08042 Corporate offences including competition and import/export offences; acts against trade regulations
	08045 Market manipulation or insider trading, price fixing
Exploitation-type activities and terrorism financing (parts of sections 02, 04, 09)	020221 Kidnapping
	0203 Slavery and exploitation
	0204 Trafficking in persons
	0302 Sexual exploitation
	02051 Extortion
	0401 Robbery
	0501 Burglary
	0502 Theft
	09062 Financing of terrorism
Illegal markets.	ICCS includes a long list of activities, including for example drug trafficking (060132), firearm trafficking (090121), illegal mining (10043), smuggling of migrants (08051), smuggling of goods (08044), wildlife trafficking (100312)
Corruption (section 0703)	07031 Bribery
	07032 Embezzlement
	07033 Abuse of functions
	07034 Trading in influence
	07035 Illicit enrichment
	07039 Other acts of corruption

Source: UNODC (2015).
Note: This list is only intended to provide some examples and it is not exhaustive.

Data availability and the selection of statistical methods are likely to depend on the type of activity generating IFFs.

Defining statistical methodologies to measure IFFs

IFFs are deliberately hidden and, as they take many forms and use varying channels, their measurement is challenging both conceptually and in practice. The challenges differ across countries, depending on main types of IFFs affecting the country, data availability, mandates of national institutions, statistical capacity and national policy priorities. This calls for space for country-specific solutions and the flexible application of methods in line with the common framework.

There is a relevant stream of literature that proposes methods to measure IFFs from illegal economic activities, and illicit tax and commercial practices. The methods proposed can be grouped in two general approaches:

1. **Top-down methods** attempt to measure IFFs by interpreting or modelling inconsistencies in different types of aggregated data, such as currency demand, international trade, and capital account of BoP.

2. **Bottom-up approaches** attempt to measure IFFs starting from the analysis of a given illicit activity, defining the set of flows that can be identified as IFFs and then producing estimates for each of them. Overall estimates are obtained by aggregating from a lower to a higher level.

Consistently with the statistical framework presented here, where different types of IFFs are defined in relation to the activity generating them, a bottom-up and direct measurement approach is preferred. [5] The UNCTAD (2021) *Methodological Guidelines to Measure Tax and Commercial IFFs* for pilot testing [6] identify main types of tax and commercial IFFs and methods for their pilot measurement (see table 2).

Table 2. Activities that may generate tax and commercial IFFs and types of flows

Categories	Activities	Flows
A. IFFs from illegal commercial and tax activities	**A1** Acts against public revenue provisions [08041]	**F1** Transfer of wealth to evade taxes, i.e., flows related to undeclared offshore wealth
	A2 Acts against commercial or financial regulations [08042]	• Outright undeclared (concealed e.g., in secrecy jurisdictions)
	A3 Market manipulations or insider trading [08045]	• Undeclared via instruments (Phantom corporations or shell companies, tax havens)
	A4 Acts of commercial fraud [07019]	
	A5 Other illegal commercial and tax acts [08049+]	**F2** Misinvoicing
		• Under/over pricing
		• Multiple invoicing
		• Over/under reporting of quantities
		• Misclassification of tariff categories
B. IFFs from aggressive tax avoidance	**B1** Acts departing from the arm's length principle	**F3** Transfer mispricing
	B2 Acts related to strategic location of debt, assets, risks, or other corporate activities	**F4** Debt shifting
	B3 Other acts of aggressive tax avoidance	• Intracompany loans
		• Interest payments
		F5 Assets and intellectual property shifting
		• Strategic location of intellectual property
		• Strategic location of other assets
		• Cost-sharing agreements
		• Royalty payments

Source: UNCTAD (2021).
Note: Activities in category A are based on level-3 categories of the ICCS (with corresponding codes in brackets).

The *Methodological Guidelines* are aimed at statistical and other national authorities with a mandate to collect and access relevant information. Microdata available to national authorities enable the compilation of more reliable estimates. However, simpler methods are proposed in parallel with more sophisticated methods to enable IFFs' estimation also where less data are available. The UNCTAD guidelines provide a suite of methods for pilot testing the measurement of three main types (a-c) of tax and commercial IFFs:

1. **Trade misinvoicing by entities** (flow F2, table 2)
   - Method #1 – Partner Country Method •
   - Method #2 – Price Filter Method •
2. **Aggressive tax avoidance or profit shifting by MNEs** (flows F3-F5, table 2)
   - Method #3 – Global distribution of MNEs' profits and corporate taxes
   - Method #4 – MNE vs comparable non-MNE profit shifting
3. **Transfer of wealth to evade taxes by individuals** (flow F1, table 2)
   - Method #5 – Flows of undeclared offshore assets indicator
   - Method #6 – Flows of offshore financial wealth by country

The above methods are tier classified, allowing United Nations member States to exercise flexibility and select a feasible method reflecting on national capacity, existing data, feasible statistical methods, legal and regulatory frameworks, and other conditions. A three-tier classification is proposed, with tier 1 as the preferred method based on the soundness of methodology, data requirements, and expected quality of estimates. Tier 2 is proposed as a fallback option if tier 1 method cannot be applied. If neither are applicable, a tier 3 method could be used.

An important distinction is made to avoid double counting and link to the SNA between two different stages leading to IFFs: [7]

1. **IFFs linked to income generation**, as the set of cross-border transactions that are performed in the context of the production of illicit goods and services or the set of cross-border operations that directly generate illicit income for an actor during a non-productive illicit activity. Inward or outward IFFs occur when the operation in question is performed across a border.
2. **IFFs linked to income management**, as the set of cross-border transactions finalised to use the (illicit) income for investment in (legal or illicit) financial and non-financial assets or for consuming (legal or illegal) goods and services. If spent abroad, the operation is an outward IFF. If stemming from illicit activity outside a jurisdiction but is spent in the domestic jurisdiction, an inward IFF is generated.

In sum, this approach considers the multi-dimensional nature of IFFs, comprising several different kinds of activities, including flows originating from illicit activities, illicit transactions to transfer funds that have a licit origin, and flows stemming from licit activity being used in an illicit way. It identifies the main types of IFFs to be measured and lays out a framework based on existing statistical definitions, classifications and methodologies, in line with the SNA and BoP.

Data requirements for measuring IFFs

National statistical systems already have some of the data needed for the measurement of IFFs, but these data are scattered across a range of authorities and statistical domains. For instance, existing national accounts and BoP statistics include estimates of illegal economic activities and the non-observed economy; they provide a good starting point for the measurement of IFFs.

Relevant data may be held by the police and ministries and councils of justice, financial intelligence units and other government agencies collecting information on seizures and criminal offences. In addition, tax authorities collect relevant data for assessing the tax gap, and they exchange country-by-country reporting data on multinational enterprises. Customs' data and statistics on international trade in goods and services provide useful information on commercial IFFs.

Over 60 per cent of national statistical offices collate relevant data on underground, illegal and informal activities using surveys, administrative sources, mirror statistics, international studies and expert assessment (IMF, 2018). While these activities are largely domestic, many of them also generate cross-border flows. There are also systematic data collections on crime and related IFFs; UNODC, for instance, compiles statistics on drugs as reported directly by countries, including detailed data on demand, supply, prices, drug characteristics, seizure data, etc.

Initial measures of IFFs will be based on existing data and be aligned with national accounts and balance of payments

Compiling statistics on IFFs requires access to many data sources held by different authorities. Central banks, customs, tax authorities and national statistical offices often have the strongest mandate to collect and access such data. Several global databases also contain relevant data for the compilation of IFF estimates, for instance the OECD country-by-country reporting data, UNCTAD Global Transport Costs Dataset for International Trade, the United Nations Comtrade database and the locational banking statistics by the Bank of International Settlements.

Eventually, the many types of IFFs should be measured in one indicator. That will require close collaboration within the national statistical system and with administrative data providers. The compilation of SDG indicator 16.4.1 is a technical, statistical activity to be based on statistical considerations only in line with the Fundamental Principles of Official Statistics (United Nations, 2014). National statistical offices, as the focal point for coordinating the compilation of SDG indicators, should lead and coordinate the work to bring the necessary stakeholders together to measure IFFs.

Country pilots to measure illicit financial flows

While some elements of IFFs are more readily measurable, others are highly challenging to estimate, including bribery, abuse of functions, illicit enrichment and illicit tax practices. Country pilots are central to building the capacity to measure IFFs and testing the feasibility of selected methodologies starting from types of IFFs for which data are available. Coverage of different IFFs will be improved gradually along with data improvements.

Pilots will help to find feasible country-specific solutions to applying the common framework for IFFs

In 2021-2022, UNCTAD and UNODC, with partner organizations UNECA, ESCAP and ECLAC, will support countries in improving their statistical capacity to estimate IFFs. A series of pilot studies will provide critical information to refine the *Conceptual Framework* and guidance on statistical methods to measure IFFs.

The first pilots carried out in Latin America between 2018 and 2020, by UNODC, show the way forward for other countries. In the first pilots, Columbia, Peru, Ecuador, and Mexico measured IFFs from selected illegal markets, such as drugs trade and smuggling of migrants. [8] First estimates in Mexico, for instance, show that outward IFFs from smuggling of migrants increased from US$10 million in 2017 to almost US$14 million in 2018. A similar pilot in Afghanistan estimated illicit gross income of the opiate economy to be worth between US$1.2 and US$2.2 billion in 2018, a value corresponding from 6 to 11 per cent of the country's GDP, and more than its officially recorded exports of goods and services, estimated at 4.3 per cent of GDP. Pilots also addressed the measurement of IFFs from illegal gold mining and trafficking in persons, even if data in such cases did not allow for a sufficiently robust estimate.

In 2021, interested African countries will pilot test the measurement of IFFs with UNCTAD and UNECA focusing on tax and commercial IFFs. UNCTAD and UNODC are also pilot testing IFFs' measurement with ESCAP and six countries in Asia and the Pacific in 2021–2022. See map 1 for pilot countries, confirmed as of June 2021.

 Map 1. IFF pilots carried out and in progress

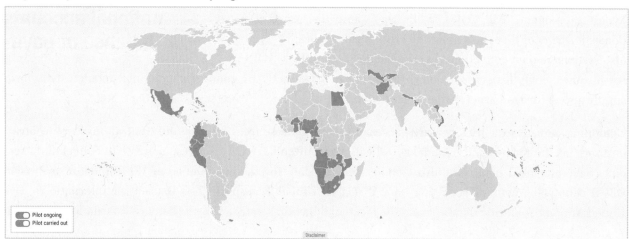

Note: Situation reflected on the map as in June 2021.

Pilot testing starts by a review of national circumstances in the form of an IFF risk assessment, followed by a mapping of relevant national stakeholders, a review of data availability and data quality; and finally, the pilot calculation of IFF estimates with one or two selected methods. Challenges and opportunities encountered in the pilots will help refine the *Methodological Guidelines* and contribute to the reporting of progress towards SDG target 16.4 in the future.

UNCTAD and UNODC invite all interested countries to test the measurement of IFFs that affect their economies most. Estimating IFFs will not only provide clarity on the scope of IFFs, but also help improve the quality of key macroeconomic statistics, such as GDP.

The statistical Task Force will continue its work to support countries in the pilot testing of the measurement of IFFs with a view to developing a *Statistical Framework for the Measurement of Illicit Financial Flows* with practical and methodological guidance in line with the *Conceptual Framework*. This will include a classification of activities generating IFFs, linked to the SNA and BoP concepts, and recommended methods to measure different types of IFFs and aggregate them into SDG indicator 16.4.1.

Further work will also aim at developing nuanced measurement of IFFs to support policy action and at the same time developing methods to aggregate estimates of different types of IFFs into one SDG indicator, e.g., to adjust for double counting. In the future, the measurement of IFFs as a satellite account taking into consideration national accounts concepts and definitions could be worth exploring.

Notes

1. This chapter is an abridged version of an UNCTAD and UNODC *Conceptual Framework* (UNCTAD and UNODC, 2020) with selected references to the *Methodological Guidelines* (UNCTAD, 2021).

2. The General Assembly resolution "stresses that official statistics and data from national statistical systems constitute the basis needed for the global indicator framework, recommends that national statistical systems explore ways to integrate new data sources into their systems to satisfy new data needs of the 2030 Agenda for Sustainable Development, as appropriate, and also stresses the role of national statistical offices as the coordinator of the national statistical system" (United Nations, 2017a).

3. The Task Force is composed of statistical experts from Brazil, Finland, Ireland, Italy, Peru, South Africa and the United Kingdom, representing national statistical offices, central banks, customs or tax authorities. The Task Force also includes experts from international organisations with recognised expertise in this field. ECLAC, ESCAP, Eurostat, IMF, OECD, UNECA, UNSD, UNCTAD and UNODC are represented.

4. The proposed bottom-up measurement approach considers domestic illicit financial flows as part of the illegal economy. These flows would not fall under the definition of IFFs for SDG indicator 16.4.1 but are of high relevance to understanding organised cross-border illicit flows.

5. This approach is consistent with Eurostat (2018).

6. The *Methodological Guidelines* suggest methods for pilot testing and will be refined during and after the pilot tests.

7. This basic typology is coherent with the main concept of national accounts. Indeed, income generation refers to the set of operations that in national accounts relate to production account, and generation and distribution of income account, while income management refers to the set of operations that in national accounts refer to capital and use of income account.

8. Preliminary estimates of IFFs from illegal activities resulting from pilot testing in Latin America were presented at a meeting in Latin America in March 2021 (UNODC, 2021).

References

- Doshi P (2011). The elusive definition of pandemic influenza. Bulletin of the World Health Organisation. *WHO Bulletin.* 89(7):532–538.

- European Commission (2017). Aggressive tax planning indicators: Final report. Taxation Papers No. 71–2017. European Commission. (accessed 17 May 2021).

- Eurostat (2018). Handbook on the compilation of statistics on illegal economic activities in national accounts and balance of payments, 2018 edition. Available at https://ec.europa.eu/eurostat/documents/3859598/8714610/KS-05-17-202-EN-N.pdf/eaf638df-17dc-47a1-9ab7-fe68476100ec (accessed 17 May 2021).

- IMF (2018). Preliminary report of the task force on informal economy. Available at https://www.imf.org/external/pubs/ft/bop/2018/pdf/18-10.pdf (accessed 17 May 2021).

- IMF (2019). Final report of the task force on informal economy. Available at https://www.imf.org/external/pubs/ft/bop/2019/pdf/19-03.pdf (accessed 10 February 2020).

- Medina L and Schneider F (2018). Shadow economies around the world: What did we learn over the last 20 years? IMF Working Papers No. WP/18/17. (accessed 9 June 2020).

- OECD (2012). Measuring the non-observed economy: A handbook. Available at https://www.oecd.org/sdd/na/measuringthenon-observedeconomy-ahandbook.htm (accessed 17 May 2021).

- OECD (2013). Action plan on base erosion and profit shifting. Available at https://www.oecd.org/ctp/BEPSActionPlan.pdf (accessed 17 May 2021).

- OECD (2020). Statement by the OECD/G20 Inclusive Framework on BEPS on the two-pillar approach to address the tax challenges arising from the digitalisation of the economy. Available at https://www.oecd.org/tax/beps/statement-by-the-oecd-g20-inclusive-framework-on-beps-january-2020.pdf (accessed 17 May 2021).

- OECD (2021). Glossary of statistical terms. Available at https://stats.oecd.org/glossary/index.htm (accessed 11 May 2021).

- UNCTAD (2018). Available at https://unctad.org/en/Pages/MeetingDetails.aspx?meetingid=1864 (accessed 9 June 2020).

- UNCTAD (2020). Economic Development in Africa Report 2020. Tackling Illicit Financial Flows for Sustainable Development in Africa. Available at https://unctad.org/webflyer/economic-development-africa-report-2020 (accessed 17 May 2021).

- UNCTAD (2021). Methodological Guidelines to Measure Tax and Commercial IFFs for pilot testing. Available at https://unctad.org/statistics (accessed 15 June 2021).

- UNCTAD and UNODC (2020). Conceptual framework for the measurement of illicit financial flows. Available at https://www.unodc.org/documents/data-and-analysis/statistics/IFF/IFF_Conceptual_Framework_for_publication_15Oct.pdf (accessed 30 January 2021).

- United Nations (2014). Fundamental Principles of Official Statistics. General Assembly resolution. A/RES/68/261. Available at https://unstats.un.org/unsd/dnss/gp/fundprinciples.aspx (accessed 17 May 2021).

- United Nations (2015a). Report of the third international conference on financing for development. A/CONF.227/20. Addis Ababa. 3 August. (accessed 20 April 2020).

- United Nations (2015b). Transforming our world: the 2030 Agenda for Sustainable Development. A/RES/70/1. New York. 21 October.

- United Nations (2017a). Resolution adopted by the General Assembly on 6 July 2017 on the Work of the Statistical Commission pertaining to the 2030 Agenda for Sustainable Development. A/RES/71/313. New York. (accessed 17 May 2021).

- United Nations (2017b). Global indicator framework for the Sustainable Development Goals and targets of the 2030 Agenda for Sustainable Development. A/RES/71/313. New York. 10 July.

- United Nations (2021). Financial Integrity for Sustainable Development. Report of the High Level Panel on International Financial Accountability, Transparency and Integrity for Achieving the 2030 Agenda. Available at https://www.factipanel.org/reports (accessed 17 May 2021).

- United Nations, European Commission, IMF, OECD and World Bank (2009). *System of National Accounts 2008*. United Nations publication. Sales No. E.08.XVII.29. New York.

- United Nations Statistics Division (2020). Tier classification for global SDG indicators. Available at https://unstats.un.org/sdgs/iaeg-sdgs/tier-classification/ (accessed 15 May 2020).

- UNODC (2004). United Nations Convention Against Corruption. A/RES/58/4. New York.

- UNODC (2015). International Classification of Crime for Statistical Purposes, Version 1.0. UNODC. Vienna.

- UNODC (2017). Expert consultation on the SDG indicator on illicit financial flows (IFFs). Available at https://unctad.org/en/pages/MeetingDetails.aspx?meetingid=1879 (accessed 9 June 2020).

- UNODC (2021). Meeting on Measuring Illicit Financial Flows from Illegal Markets. Presentation of the results of the pilot studies in four Latin American countries. Available at https://www.unodc.org/unodc/en/data-and-analysis/iff_Lac.html (accessed 17 May 2021).

- WHO (2020). Q&A on coronaviruses (COVID-19). Available at https://www.who.int/emergencies/diseases/novel-coronavirus-2019/question-and-answers-hub/q-a-detail/q-a-coronaviruses (accessed 11 May 2020).

THEME 3

Structural Transformation

"We are the last people who can prevent
catastrophe on the planet.
We have no excuse for failure.".

– UN Deputy Secretary General, Amina J. Mohammed

Structural transformation

Sustainable long-term growth that provides economies opportunities for everyone can only be achieved through a shift to higher value-added productive activities. This requires investment, the adoption of technological advancements, and a skilled workforce. To avoid further ecological degradation and climate change, this also calls for a shift to more efficient and less environmentally damaging economic activities.

Transforming to more sustainable consumption and production patterns, will not only be good for the economy, but also a necessity for the environment. This theme of SDG Pulse looks at two aspects of structural transformation:

- We look for evidence of a shift towards Sustainable industrialization and higher technology and more skills-intensive economic activities, and
- We consider whether it is Make or break for green economy in the face of serious climate concerns.

According to UNFCCC, to achieve the objectives of the Paris Climate Agreement, the world needs to deploy climate technologies on a much greater scale, and innovation plays a key role. The climate challenge is immediate, and as statistics in the SDG Pulse demonstrate, we can reduce carbon intensity of the economy through technological and economic transformation, but the challenge is urgent.

> *We are the last people who can prevent catastrophe on the planet. We have no excuse for failure.*
>
> — UN Deputy Secretary General, Amina J. Mohammed

LDCs' **pace too slow** to double their manufacturing share in value added by 2030: +0.7 percentage points neededN between 2019 and 2030 to make up lost ground vs. +0.42 in 2019.

SDG indicator 9.2.1

Share of manufacturing employment in total employment **increased in LDCs by 87%** since 2005 – on track for 2030.

SDG indicator 9.2.2

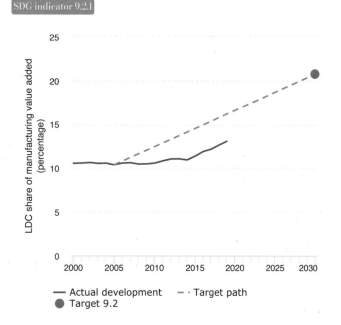

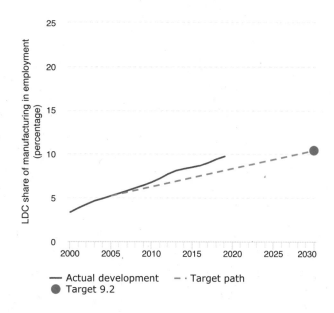

Medium and high-tech manufacturing share **very slowly increasing** in developing economies.

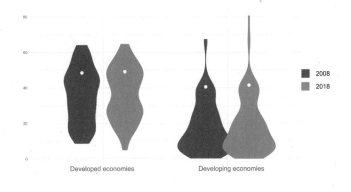

High income countries spend **almost 10 times more** than low income countries on R&D as a percentage of GDP.

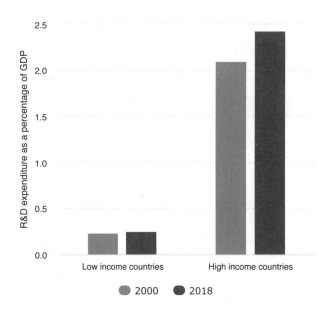

CO_2 emissions estimated to have declined by **7%** in 2020, largely due to COVID-19, and **the same pace** needs to continue to reach the Paris 1.5°C target.

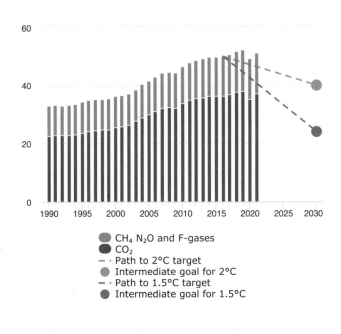

World **carbon intensity of GDP decreasing** – most of all in Europe and Sub-Saharan Africa, but less so in Latin America and the Caribbean.

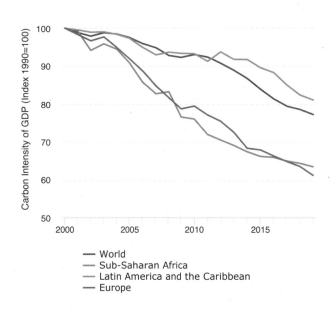

SDG Pulse shares preliminary results of company sustainability reporting across the World based on a sample of two global databases.

Energy intensity reducing faster than before, almost **2% per year** since 2008.

Sustainability reporting increasing

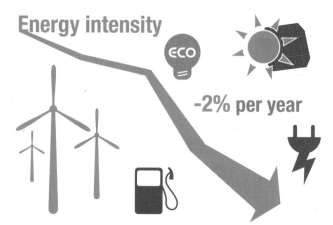

Energy intensity

ECO

-2% per year

I. Towards sustainable industrialization and higher technologies

SDG indicators

Target 9.2: Promote inclusive and sustainable industrialization and, by 2030, significantly raise industry's share of employment and gross domestic product, in line with national circumstances, and double its share in least developed countries.

Indicator 9.2.1: Manufacturing value added as a proportion of GDP and per capita (Tier I)

Indicator 9.2.2: Manufacturing employment as a proportion of total employment (Tier I)

Target 9.b: Support domestic technology development, research and innovation in developing countries, including by ensuring a conducive policy environment for, inter alia, industrial diversification and value addition to commodities.

Indicator 9.b.1: Proportion of medium and high-tech industry value added in total manufacturing value added (Tier I)

Target 9.5: Enhance scientific research, upgrade technological capabilities of industrial sectors in all countries, in particular developing countries, including, by 2030, encouraging innovation and increasing the number of research and development workers per 1 million people and public and private research and development spending.

Indicator 9.5.1: Research and development expenditure as a proportion of GDP (Tier I)

Indicator 9.5.2: Researchers (in full-time equivalent) per million inhabitants (Tier I)

Structural transformation has been an important driving force of economic development over the last decades. According to the theory of structural transformation (Kuznets, 1957; Chenery, 1960; Fourastié, 1963), development is driven by a shift from the extraction of raw materials and primary sector activities to increasingly complex technical transformation processes, commonly referred to as manufacturing. On the supply side, the sources of that transition include the development of know-how, increase in high-skilled labour and technological advancement, and enabling the application of new production methods. On the demand side, the rising standard of living induces a shift from the consumption of food and other primary commodities towards consumer goods, that are usually manufactured. This transformation leads to higher value added and greater economic welfare. In line with this thinking, SDG target 9.2 promotes inclusive and sustainable industrialization and aims to significantly raise industry's share of employment and GDP by 2030.

During the later phases of economic development, a sectoral shift from manufacturing to services has typically been observed. Once a certain standard of living is reached, the demand for services increases relative to the demand for physically produced goods. According to Haraguchi and Rezonja (2010) this level is reached when GDP per capita amounts to around US$13 000 at 2005 prices. At that stage, manufacturing usually accounts for around one fifth of value added. Based on these estimates, UNIDO (2017) considers countries to be industrialized when their manufacturing value added, adjusted to purchasing power parities, exceeds US$2 500 per capita.

Rapid industrialization in developing economies of Asia and Oceania

In 2019, manufacturing value added per capita amounted to US$5 108 at constant 2015 prices in developed economies (see figure 1). It was 2.7 times higher than in developing Asia and Oceania (US$1 423) and 3.6 times higher than in developing Latin America and the Caribbean (US$1 074). It exceeded the value in Africa (US$212) by almost 23 times.

In developing Asia and Oceania, real manufacturing value added per head almost tripled from 1999 to 2019

Over the last 20 years, manufacturing value added per capita in developing Asia and Oceania has steadily increased – by two and a half times since 1999 – with the result that the region overtook Latin America and the Caribbean in 2015. In Latin America and the Caribbean, the indicator has remained constant. Africa has seen a slight increase, by one fifth over 20 years. Developed economies have recorded modest steady growth over the last 20 years, disrupted only by the economic downswings from 2000 to 2002 and from 2007 to 2010.

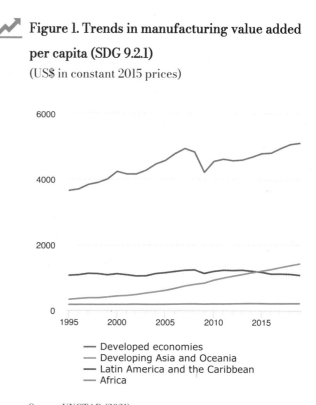

Figure 1. Trends in manufacturing value added per capita (SDG 9.2.1)

(US$ in constant 2015 prices)

— Developed economies
— Developing Asia and Oceania
— Latin America and the Caribbean
— Africa

Source: UNCTAD (2021).

Dropping industrial output after the outbreak of COVID-19

The outbreak of COVID-19 led to considerable disruptions of those long-term trends in manufacturing all over the world. According to ILO (2020, 2021a), manufacturing was among the economic sectors worst hit by the pandemic, alongside retail trade, accommodation, food services and other sectors. The impact by industry depended on the effects of the containment measures introduced on supply and demand. Some sectors were hit mainly from the demand side, for example due to restrictions concerning modes of consumption and the distribution of goods, and others more from the supply side, for example due to disrupted supply chains. It seems that certain sectors have also benefited from an increased demand for their products as a direct or indirect consequence of the pandemic. Some businesses have managed to make a digital leap to recover some lost revenue, enable new ways of working, such as telework and digital trade, and apply new methods to quickly adjust production according to rapidly changing demand and supply conditions. Accordingly, medium and high-tech industries have recovered faster from the crisis than lower-technology industries (CCSA, 2021).

Manufacturing was hit by the COVID-19 pandemic at different times across the world (see figure 2). China came first, experiencing a sharp drop in the PMI of the manufacturing sector in February 2020 (seasonally adjusted), showing how the economic outlook deteriorated, as Wuhan and other regions were locked down. Already in late February, Chinese manufacturing started to recover, with PMI levels returning to above 50 already in March 2020.

Manufacturing output hit hard by the pandemic in spring and summer 2020

In the Eurozone and the United States of America, manufacturing output started falling in March 2020. This fall was most pronounced in the Eurozone, where many countries introduced full or partial lockdowns by the middle of the month. During March and April, production in manufacturing, as measured by the IIP, dropped in the Eurozone by 30 per cent and in the United States by 20 per cent, after a longer period of stability. In both economies, the index returned to 5 per cent below pre-crisis levels by July, and it took until November in the Eurozone and until January 2021 in the United States for it to fully recover. The PMI of February and March 2021 lies well above 50 in both economies, heralding further growth of manufacturing output in the coming months, if conditions do not change.

Developments in Brazil resembled that of the Eurozone, showing an equally strong contraction during February and March. However, unlike in the Eurozone, by the end of the year, the IIP returned to a level 8 per cent higher than before the outbreak of the pandemic.

In South Africa and the Russian Federation the downturn in manufacturing began two months later than in the Eurozone and the United States. In the Russian Federation, the IIP for manufacturing remained unchanged until March, but declined by 12 per cent in April, although not as deep a fall as in the Eurozone and the United States. In South Africa, index indicated the sharpest contraction amongst the six economies compared in figure 2, losing almost half of its value (44 per cent) within one month. However, the rebound was relatively quick and, by August 2020, the IIP already reached 96 per cent of its December 2019 level.

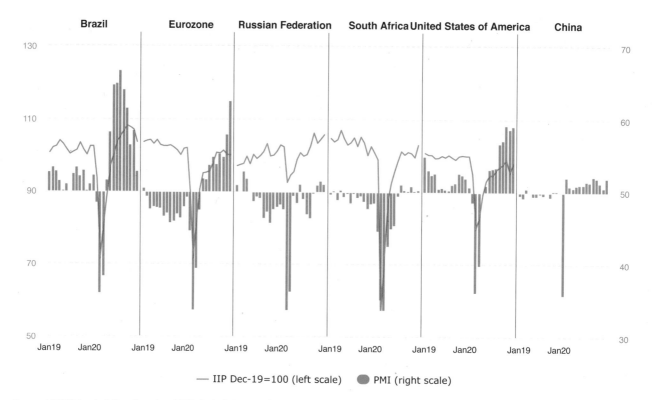

Figure 2. Industrial production (IIP) and purchasing manager's expectations (PMI) in manufacturing

Brazil   Eurozone   Russian Federation   South Africa   United States of America   China

— IIP Dec-19=100 (left scale)   ⬤ PMI (right scale)

Source: UNCTAD calculations based on OECD (2021a), Eurostat (2021) and Refinitiv (2021).
Notes: Series are seasonally adjusted. PMIs refer to manufacturing except for South Africa where it refers to agriculture, mining, construction, wholesale, retail and services in addition to manufacturing. IIPs are re-scaled to December 2019.

Intermittent catching up of LDCs

In 2019, LDCs' manufacturing sector produced on average US$137 per head, at 2015 prices, almost 40 times less than the average produced in the developed world. However, LDCs' manufacturing value added per capita has steadily increased over the last 20 years, at a higher rate than in developing countries in general. The level in 2019 was already more than three times higher than the level of 1999 (see figure 1).

The manufacturing share in value added, the focus of SDG target 9.2 for LDCs, increased from 10.5 per cent in 2000 to 13.1 per cent in 2019. Most of that progress was made in the last five years; until 2010, the share had remained constant at just below 11 per cent (see figure 3). Extrapolating the trend into the future, the growth achieved after 2005 on average appears to be too slow to achieve the SDG target of doubling the manufacturing share in value added by 2030.[1] From 2005 onwards, an average annual increase of 0.42 percentage points would have been required to reach the target. The actual annual average increase until 2019 was 0.19 percentage points. Since 2015, accruals comparable to the target path have indeed been recorded, but this accelerated growth has begun late too to be sufficient.

LDCs' pace of progress too slow to reach the SDG target of doubling the manufacturing

TARGET 9·2 **share in value added**

It is striking that the stagnation in the share of manufacturing in value added until 2014 was not reflected in a stagnation of the manufacturing share in employment. On the contrary, the employment share of manufacturing has seen a steady increase over the last 24 years, at a pace higher than required to reach by 2030 the SDG target

9.2.2 set up for employment. The findings above - in particular, the modest growth of manufacturing in value added compared to employment - suggest that new industrial innovations and policies are needed in LDCs to accelerate structural transformation.

 Figure 3. Development of the manufacturing share of value added (SDG 9.2.1) and of employment (SDG 9.2.2) in LDCs compared to the target

(Percentage)

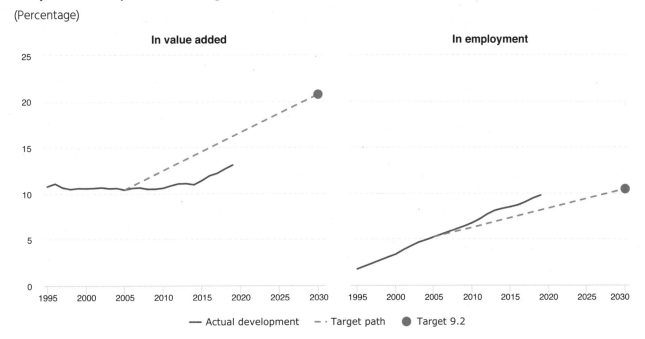

Source: UNCTAD (2021).
Note: Target and target path set with reference to the base year 2005.[1]

Diverging regional trends in structural transformation

How has structural transformation changed the sectoral distribution of employment and value added? Between 2000 and 2019, the share of manufacturing in employment increased only in developing Asia and Oceania (from 11.1 to 13.6 per cent) and in Africa (from 6.0 to 7.9 per cent) (see figure 4). In developing Asia and Oceania, in contrast to Africa, this increase was combined with an increase of the manufacturing share in value added (from 19.8 to 23.9 per cent). This highlights a growing disparity in productivity growth between the regions, in line with the above diverging trends in manufacturing value added per capita (see figure 1). In LDCs, increases in manufacturing value added per capita, discussed above, were strongly employment driven. The share of manufacturing in employment almost tripled in that group of economies, from 3.3 per cent in 2000 to 9.7 per cent in 2019.

These figures suggest that during the last two decades, among the broad regions compared, only Asian and Oceanian developing economies have gone through a process of structural transformation as described in the literature. The LDCs as a group have also followed that path. Latin America and the Caribbean, like the developed economies, recorded shrinking proportions of manufacturing in both employment and value added. This development is not what is aspired to by the SDG target, which aims at significantly raising industry's share of employment and value added. Many of these counties may nevertheless have changed their economic structure towards higher value-added activities, by raising the share of services, in particular telecommunication and ICT services or by a structural transformation within manufacturing from lower-tech to higher-tech production. Below, the analysis is extended to investigate to what extent such digitalization and transformation to higher technologies is happening.

📊 Figure 4. Share of manufacturing in value added (SDG 9.2.1) and employment (SDG 9.2.2)
(Percentage)

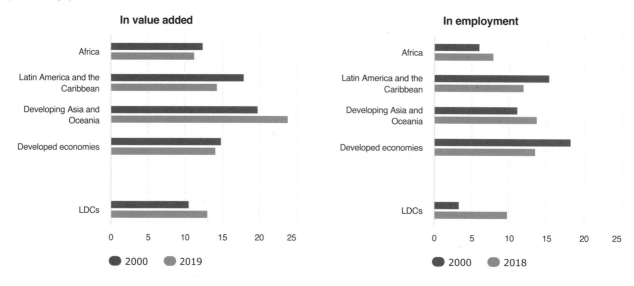

Source: UNCTAD calculations based on UNCTAD (2021), UNIDO (2021) and ILO (2021b).

Technology gap persists in manufacturing

The 2030 Agenda promotes technological development through research and innovation, especially in developing economies. Progress towards the achievement of that target is measured by the proportion of medium and high-tech industry value added in total manufacturing value added (SDG indicator 9.b.1). This indicator shows a shift from lower to higher technology value added, raising the average value added per worker. R&D and innovation play a crucial role in this transformation by providing the grounds for the use of new and more efficient technologies.

In the developed world, medium and high-tech industry accounts for higher shares of manufacturing value added than in developing (see figure 5). When looking at weighted regional averages, almost half of developed economies' manufacturing output is obtained in medium and high-tech industries. Among developing countries, the weighted rate varies considerably across regions. In developing Asia and Oceania, it was 43 per cent in 2018, almost as high as in developed economies, while the rate reached 32 per cent in developing America and only 21 per cent in Africa.

From 2008 to 2018, the gap between developing and developed economies has widened slightly. While developed economies managed to increase the share of medium and high-tech manufacturing slightly (from 48 to 49 per cent), the rate fell slightly in developing Asia and Oceania (from 44 to 43 per cent) and remained constant in developing America and Africa. Developed countries have cemented their lead, while developing economies have not managed to increase the share of higher technologies in manufacturing in the last 10 to 15 years, and some are shifting towards lower-technology sectors.

Figure 5 highlights the considerable variation across individual economies, especially in Asia. This region encompasses, on one hand, the two economies with the world's most innovative manufacturing sectors, namely,

Singapore (80 per cent in 2018) and Taiwan, Province of China (69 per cent); on the other hand, it includes several countries, primarily LDCs and SIDS, in which the share of medium and high-tech industries in value added has persistently remained below three per cent, such as Macao, SAR of China, Cambodia, Yemen, Maldives, Tajikistan and Kyrgyzstan.

 Figure 5. Proportion of medium and high-tech industry in manufacturing value added (SDG 9.b.1), by development status and region

(Percentage)

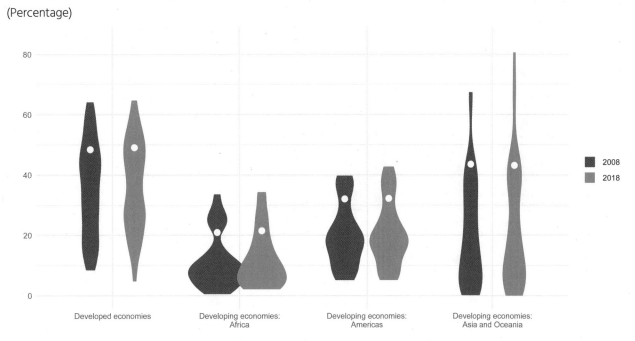

Source: UNCTAD calculations based on UNIDO (2021).

Notes: A violin plot shows the distribution of individual countries' medium and high-tech industry shares in manufacturing value added within each country group and year. The coloured areas depict the distribution of countries' rates smoothed by kernel density estimation, a non-parametric way to estimate the probability density function of a variable. The wider the violin shape, the higher the possibility to find an observation, in this case a country, in that location. The dots within the shapes represent the weighted average of countries' medium and high-tech industry shares in manufacturing value added.

Considerable spread in the medium and high-tech industry share of manufacturing value added is also found among developed economies. Some of them reach less than one third of the rates recorded by the developed countries at the highest ranks, such as, Switzerland (65 per cent) and Germany (62 per cent).

Many LDCs and SIDS are characterized by low shares of medium and high-tech manufacturing. However, this is changing. Noteworthy exceptions among SIDS include Trinidad and Tobago and Barbados, where the medium and high-tech share in manufacturing value added was at 40 and 38 per cent in 2018, respectively (see UNIDO, 2021).

Developing economies' medium and high-tech exports increasing

Looking at international trade, the share of medium and high-tech products in manufacturing exports has been increasing in developing countries recently, while it has remained almost constant in the developed world (see figure 6). In developing America and developing Asia and Oceania, the share of medium and high-tech exports reached almost 60 per cent in 2018, whereas in developed economies it stood at 62 per cent. Africa has increased its medium and high-tech export share from 34 to 39 per cent from 2008 to 2018. As a result, the region has been catching up in the structural transformation of manufactured exports, and the overall gap between the developing and developed world has narrowed.

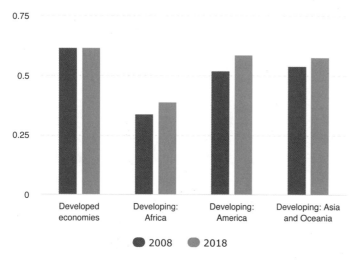

📊 **Figure 6. Share of medium and high-tech manufactured exports in total manufacturing exports**

(Percentage)

Source: UNCTAD calculations based on UNIDO (2021).

R&D investment and international cooperation are vital for fighting the COVID-19 pandemic

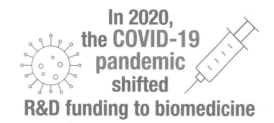

When it comes to R&D, the COVID-19 pandemic allotted unequivocal priority to biomedicine. The ICT sector benefitted from innovation investment as well. 2020 saw a strong and rapid international mobilization to develop treatment for COVID-19. Governments, the scientific community, and the private sector allocated resources to focus research on the global task of mitigating the effects of the pandemic and protecting populations. The OECD estimated that over US$7 billion of new or redirected funds were unlocked for COVID-19 related R&D during the first nine months of 2020. Despite some hitches, developing and distributing vaccines, tests, and treatments to millions of persons within 12 months has been a notable achievement. It would not have been possible without strengthened international coordination and improved transparency, including in R&D (OECD, 2021b). International cooperation and solidarity need to be reinforced for the treatment and vaccines to reach all countries and all vulnerable.

The extent of R&D investment in fighting COVID-19 is still difficult to gauge. Estimates from the OECD (2021b) suggest significant cuts in non-COVID-related research in 2020. Moreover, the lockdown measures disrupted R&D where access to laboratories, tools, and field work were necessary. As the social and economic consequences of the pandemic continue to unfold, further decline in research budgets can be expected, particularly from public funds (OECD, 2021b).

In 2018 and 2019, most industrial R&D targeted ICT hardware and electronic equipment, pharmaceuticals and biotechnology, automobiles, as well as software and ICT services. Which development can we expect in the post COVID-19 years? The Cornell University et al. (2020) suggest that ICT software, biomedicine, and alternative energy represent the three sectors that should not face difficulties in attracting innovation funding in the near future. They further estimate that the United States of America and China will see their R&D rebound more rapidly than other states, owing to: i) the fact that these two countries host some of the world's largest science and technology clusters (e.g. the Beijing cluster, or the San Jose - San Francisco cluster), and ii) recent government policies adopted to mitigate the shortage of R&D capital. In 2020, the EU has also promulgated additional programmes to financially support innovation and start-ups (see Cornell University et al., 2020).

Various international organizations have emphasized the importance of reinforcing public support for sustainable research targeting socially beneficial projects with wide spill-over effects. They also reiterated the significance of global cooperation and inter-disciplinary connections in science and innovation, aimed to build more resilient societies and avert future threats. Moreover, supporting innovation should facilitate progress towards achieving the SDGs (see UNCTAD, 2020).

Governments are encouraged to increase spending on R&D in the context of the 2030 Agenda. In 2018, the latest year with globally comparable innovation statistics, the world invested US$2.2 trillion in R&D, PPP-adjusted. Over the five-year period from 2013 to 2018, absolute R&D spending increased by 5.4 per cent each year on average. Not surprisingly, investment was highly concentrated in a few economies. In 2018, some 75 per cent of R&D investment was made by only 10 countries.

10 economies account for over 75% of total R&D spending in the world

In PPP-adjusted value terms, the leaders in R&D spending were the United States of America (US$582 billion), China (US$465 billion), Japan (US$171 billion) and Germany (US$141 billion). Remarkably, the United States and China accounted for almost half of global R&D investment (see figure 7 and table 1). Among developing economies, relatively high growth in R&D spending was recorded for Iran (the Islamic Republic of), Indonesia, Macao, SAR of China, El Salvador, and Panama: above 25 per cent average annual increase (UNESCO Institute for Statistics, 2021).

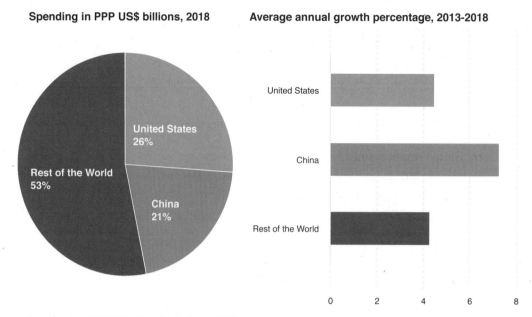

Figure 7. Dominance in global R&D spending, 2018 and growth from 2013-2018

(Spending in PPP US$ billions and average annual growth percentage)

Spending in PPP US$ billions, 2018

Average annual growth percentage, 2013-2018

United States
26%

Rest of the World
53%

China
21%

Source: UNCTAD calculations based on UNESCO Institute for Statistics (2021).

Despite the growth of world R&D investment in absolute terms, global R&D intensity – SDG indicator 9.5.1 – remained at 1.7 per cent of GDP from 2013 to 2018 (see figure 8). Israel (4.9 per cent) and the Republic of Korea (4.5 per cent) were the most prominent R&D investors relative to GDP, followed by Switzerland (3.4 per cent) and Sweden (3.3 per cent). The United States of America invested 2.8 per cent of its GDP in innovation, and China 2.1 per cent. Only a few developing economies have managed to develop into 'R&D powerhouses', such as China and the Republic of Korea. For some of these countries, that process took around two decades. Participation in global value chains and R&D networks is essential for moving-up the innovation ladder.

Global gross expenditure on R&D stagnant at 1.7% of GDP since 2013

Looking at regional averages, Northern America invested most in R&D in proportion to GDP. However, Eastern, South-Eastern and Western Asia were the regions in which R&D spending relative to GDP grew fastest from 2013 to 2018. The Cornel University et al. (2020) estimated that – besides China – most significant progress in R&D was achieved by India, the Philippines and Vietnam. Europe recorded only a slight increase in R&D funding. At 1.9 per cent of GDP in 2018, R&D intensity remained well below the three-per-cent goal set by the EU (European Commission, 2010). Only Austria, Denmark, Germany and Sweden reached or surpassed this target, as well as Switzerland (not an EU-member). The AU has also established an R&D intensity objective for its member states, set at one per cent (UNECA, 2018). According to available statistics, among AU member countries, only South Africa was close to that target, recording an R&D intensity of 0.8 per cent in 2018. Egypt and Tunisia registered R&D intensity of 0.7 and 0.6 per cent, respectively. Other African states remained below 0.5 per cent.

Table 1. Leading investors in R&D, ranked by PPP US$, 2018 (SDG 9.5.1)

(Ranked by GERD in PPP US$)

Investors	PPP US$ billions	Annual average growth, 2013-2018 [b]	Percentage of GDP	Percentage of world total
United States	582	5.0	2.8	26.0
China	465	7.3	2.1	20.8
Japan	171	0.2	3.3	7.7
Germany	141	6.7	3.1	6.3
Republic of Korea	98	7.5	4.5	4.4
Top 10 developing countries, excl. China and the Republic of Korea				
India	59	5.1	0.7	2.6
Brazil	36	-2.4	1.2	1.6
Turkey	22	9.9	1.0	1.0
Iran (Islamic Republic of)	12	24.5	1.0	0.6
Thailand	10	3.0	1.9	0.5
Malaysia[a]	10	...	0.8	0.5
Mexico[a]	9	5.5	1.0	0.4
Singapore[a]	8	10.8	1.3	0.4
Indonesia	8	5.1	0.7	0.4
Egypt	8	-2.6	0.3	0.4

Source: UNCTAD calculations based on UNESCO Institute for Statistics (2021).
Notes:
[a] refers to 2017.
[b] Growth is estimated for Malaysia, Singapore, Thailand, Turkey, United Arab Emirates

The developing economies of America spent on average 0.6 per cent of their GDP on innovation in 2018. At 1.2 per cent, Brazil's R&D intensity was more than two times higher than that of any other country in the region. In Oceania, R&D spending stood at 1.8 per cent of GDP, dropping from two per cent observed five years earlier. SIDS[2] allocated on average one per cent and LDCs some 0.2 per cent of GDP to R&D.

Brazil's R&D intensity over two times higher than in other Latin American countries x2

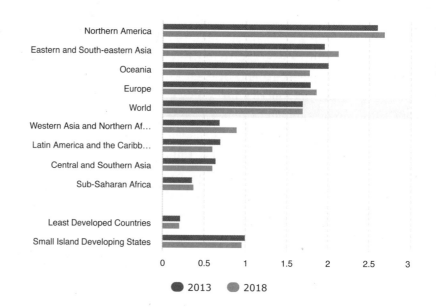

📊 **Figure 8. R&D expenditure as a proportion of GDP (SDG 9.5.1)**
(Percentage of GDP)

Source: UNESCO Institute for Statistics (2021).
Note: Based on UNESCO country classification

SDG indicator 9.5.2 looks at the number of persons directly employed in R&D, as FTE, per million inhabitants. According to this measure, the topmost performers come from Europe, led by Denmark and followed by Switzerland, Iceland and Luxembourg. Among non-European states, the Republic of Korea, Singapore, and New Zealand rank at the top. In 2018, Denmark reported over 11 000 per million employed on R&D, while the Republic of Korea and Switzerland recorded figures close to 10 000. These statistics include not only researchers, but also R&D technical and supporting staff. Between 2013 and 2018, stronger rise in R&D employment was observed in developing economies than in the developed world. Macao, SAR of China, Kuwait, and Iran recorded highest R&D job growth. According to figures available for 50 countries, on average 40 per cent of the R&D workforce were women. Interestingly, developing economies registered higher percentages of female R&D staff than developed economies (UNESCO Institute for Statistics, 2021).

About 40% of R&D employees are women – even more in developing economies

R&D services in international trade

Innovation is increasingly traded internationally. Global R&D services exports expanded by an estimated 6.6 per cent annually, between 2013 and 2018, outpacing the average growth of total trade in services (3.5 per cent). In 2018, countries exported about US$192 billion worth of R&D services. Again, innovation exports and imports were concentrated in a small group of economies. The top-ten R&D exporters accounted for 74 per cent of the total. The United States of America was the main R&D services supplier on the international markets, followed by Germany and France (see table 2). Seven out of ten leading R&D services exporters also belonged to the top-ten R&D services importers. They were also part of the world leading recipients of charges for the use of intellectual property. Among developing economies, prominent exporters of R&D services include China, India, the Republic of Korea, Singapore, Brazil and Malaysia.

Table 2. Leading ten R&D services exporters, 2018

(Countries ranked by exports value)

Country	Exports US$ billions	Annual average growth of exports, percentage, 2013-2018	Imports US$ billions	Ranking in GERD, PPP US$
United States	47	9.6	35	1
Germany	26	4.5	24	4
France	15	3.0	15	6
United Kingdom	14	6.3	10	8
Netherlands	8	6.0	8	16
Israel	8	7.5	2	19
Japan	7	9.9	20	3
Canada	5	0.7	2	12
Belgium	5	4.5	6	20
Sweden	5	19.1	7	18

Source: UNCTAD (2021).
Note: China belongs to leading R&D services exporters, according to estimates available for previous years. 2018 figures were not available.

Notes

1. In this report, progress in target 9.2 is measured with reference to the base year 2005. This is in line with the practice applied in the monitoring of the Millennium Development Goals, where the baseline was set to the year 1990, thus ten years before the adoption of the Millennium Development Declaration (United Nations, 2005). The 2030 Agenda for Sustainable Development does not specify any base year for target 9.2.

2. SIDS based on the UNESCO country classification: http://www.unesco.org/new/en/natural-sciences/priority-areas/sids/resources/sids-list/

References

- CCSA (2021). How COVID-19 is changing the world: A statistical perspective, vol 3. Available at https://unstats.un.org/unsd/ccsa/ (accessed 6 June 2021).
- Chenery HB (1960). Patterns of industrial growth. *American Economic Review*. 50(4):624–654.
- Cornell University, INSEAD and WIPO (2020). Global Innovation Index 2020. Available at https://www.wipo.int/publications/en/details.jsp?id=4514&plang=EN (accessed 19 April 2021).
- Doshi P (2011). The elusive definition of pandemic influenza. Bulletin of the World Health Organisation. *WHO Bulletin*. 89(7):532–538.
- European Commission (2010). *Europe 2020: A Strategy for Smart, Sustainable and Inclusive Growth*.
- Eurostat (2021). Eurostat database. Available at https://ec.europa.eu/eurostat/data/database (accessed 2 June 2021).
- Fourastié J (1963). *Le Grand Espoir Du XXe Siècle*. Gallimard. Paris.
- Haraguchi N and Rezonja G (2010). Search of general patterns of manufacturing development. Development Policy and Strategic Research Branch Working Paper No. 02/2010. UNIDO.
- ILO (2020). ILO Monitor: COVID-19 and the world of work. Second edition. Updated estimates and analysis. Available at https://www.ilo.org/wcmsp5/groups/public/---dgreports/---dcomm/documents/briefingnote/wcms_740877.pdf (accessed 25 May 2020).

- ILO (2021a). ILO Monitor: COVID-19 and the world of work. Seventh edition. Updated estimates and analysis. Available at https://www.ilo.org/wcmsp5/groups/public/@dgreports/@dcomm/documents/briefingnote/wcms_767028.pdf (accessed 29 March 2021).

- ILO (2021b). ILOStat. Available at https://www.ilo.org/ilostat (accessed 2 June 2021).

- Kuznets S (1957). Quantitative aspects of the economic growth of nations: II. Industrial distribution of national product and labor force. *Economic Development and Cultural Change*. 5(4):1–111.

- OECD (2015). *Frascati Manual 2015: Guidelines for Collecting and Reporting Data on Research and Experimental Development*. OECD Publishing. Paris.

- OECD (2021a). OECD Statistical Database. Available at https://stats.oecd.org/ (accessed 2 June 2021).

- OECD (2021b). OECD Science, Technology and Innovation Outlook 2021: Times of Crisis and Opportunity. Available at https://www.oecd.org/sti/oecd-science-technology-and-innovation-outlook-25186167.htm (accessed 2 June 2021).

- Refinitiv (2021). Eikon. (accessed 1 June 2021).

- UNCTAD (2020). The need to protect science, technology and innovation funding during and after the COVID-19 crisis. Available at https://unctad.org/webflyer/need-protect-science-technology-and-innovation-funding-during-and-after-covid-19-crisis (accessed 2 June 2021).

- UNCTAD (2021). UNCTADStat. Available at https://unctadstat.unctad.org/EN/Index.html (accessed 21 April 2021).

- UNECA (2018). Towards achieving the African Union's recommendation of expenditure of 1% of GDP on research and development. ECA Policy Brief. ECA/18/004. Addis Ababa.

- UNESCO Institute for Statistics (2020). Glossary. Available at http://uis.unesco.org/en/glossary (accessed 15 March 2021).

- UNESCO Institute for Statistics (2021). Available at http://uis.unesco.org/ (accessed 15 March 2021).

- UNIDO (2017). *Industrial Development Report 2018, Demand for Manufacturing: Driving Inclusive and Sustainable Industrial Development*. United Nations publication. Sales No. E.18.II.B.48. Vienna.

- UNIDO (2021). Available at http://stat.unido.org (accessed 2 June 2021).

- United Nations (2008). *International Standard Industrial Classification of All Economic Activities (ISIC) Revision 4*. United Nations publication. Sales No. E.08.XVII.25. New York, NY.

- United Nations (2010). International Recommendations for the Index of Industrial Production 2010. Available at https://unstats.un.org/unsd/industry/Docs/F107_edited.pdf (accessed 26 May 2020).

- United Nations (2021). SDG indicators: Metadata repository. Available at https://unstats.un.org/sdgs/metadata/ (accessed 20 April 2021).

- United Nations, European Commission, IMF, OECD and World Bank (2009). *System of National Accounts 2008*. United Nations publication. Sales No. E.08.XVII.29. New York.

- WHO (2020). Q&A on coronaviruses (COVID-19). Available at https://www.who.int/emergencies/diseases/novel-coronavirus-2019/question-and-answers-hub/q-a-detail/q-a-coronaviruses (accessed 11 May 2020).

II. Make or break for green economy

In light of recent scientific research (IPCC, 2019), choices in climate policy taken now will be critical for our future and for the future of the ocean and cryosphere. According to the IPCC (2014, p.6), climate change has already "caused impacts on natural and human systems on all continents and across the oceans". We are experiencing more frequent natural disasters and extreme weather events, rising sea levels and diminishing Arctic sea ice, among other changes (IPCC, 2018). In August 2019, the United Nations Secretary General, António Guterres, named 2020 a make-or-break year for climate policy, not anticipating that the COVID-19 pandemic would bring societies and economies to an abrupt halt, cutting emissions by an amount impossible to imagine under normal conditions.

Economic downturn in 2020 took pressure off the atmosphere

A growing concentration of the 'critical' greenhouse gases, mainly CO_2, CH_4, N_2O and F-gases, in the atmosphere has been identified as the main cause of increased temperatures on the planet (WMO, 2019). In 2019, greenhouse gas emissions reached a record high of 52.4 Gt of CO_2e. Emissions increased by 1.1 per cent from the previous year after a period of little or no growth from 2015 to 2016, a 1.3 per cent increase in 2017 and a 2.0 per cent increase in 2018. Including emissions from land-use change, which are difficult to measure, total emissions amounted to 57.4 Gt in 2019, according to a report from (Netherlands PBL, 2020). The report notes that this level is about 59 per cent higher than in 1990 and 44 per cent higher than in 2000 (see figure 1).

The COVID-19 pandemic had a major impact on global emissions. Estimates by the Global Carbon Project, a global consortium of experts, indicate a decrease of 7 per cent in total carbon dioxide emissions in 2020 (Carbon Brief, 2020). This is the largest reduction ever recorded and will bring us back to levels last seen almost 10 years ago. The previous record fall, caused by the global

COVID-19 cut CO_2 emissions by 7% in 2020

financial crisis, was a reduction of 1.2 per cent in 2009. In December 2020, energy-related CO_2 emissions have already rebounded, and they are expected to grow by almost 5 per cent in 2021 as demand for coal, oil and gas recovers with the economy (IEA, 2021).

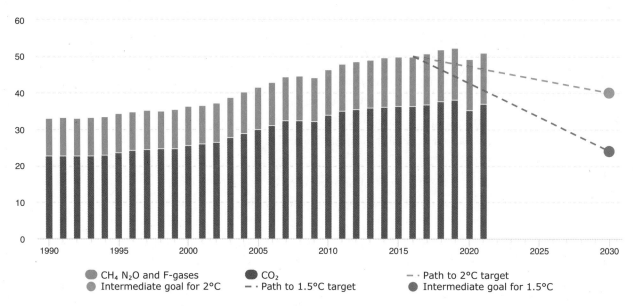

Figure 1. Greenhouse gas emissions and target reductions (SDG 9.4.1)

(Gt of CO₂e)

Legend:
- CH₄ N₂O and F-gases
- Intermediate goal for 2°C
- CO₂
- Path to 1.5°C target
- Path to 2°C target
- Intermediate goal for 1.5°C

Source: UNCTAD calculations based on Netherlands PBL (2020) and UNEP (2020).
Notes: Intermediate goals are shown as released by UNEP (2020). Emissions from land-use change are not included. The CO₂ emission estimate for 2020 by Carbon Brief (2020), and the estimate for 2021 by IEA (2021). The baseline for the path towards 2030 targets is set to 2016, when the Paris Agreement became effective.

What do these developments imply for global warming? The year 2020 was one of the three warmest on record, despite the unprecedented drop in emissions seen that year. The annual global temperature was already 1.2°C warmer than pre-industrial conditions (WMO, 2021). The 2015 Paris Climate agreement aims, by 2100, "to limit the temperature increase from pre-industrial levels to 2°C and pursue efforts to remain below 1.5°C" (UNFCCC, 2016). Even with a 1.5°C warming, climate scientists warn that the effects will be far greater than originally expected, including extinction of coral reefs, and many plants, insects and animals (IPCC, 2018).

According to simulations, reaching the Paris target of keeping global warming below 2°C required emissions of critical greenhouse gases to peak in 2020, and decline sharply thereafter. To remain below 2°C warming by 2100, global emissions should not exceed 40 Gt of CO₂e in 2030, and to achieve the below 1.5°C warming target, total emissions should remain below 24 Gt of CO₂e

Minor impact of COVID-19 on global warming: -0.01°C by 2050

by 2030. Remaining below the 2°C target requires a reduction from 2018 levels of nearly 25 per cent and nearly 55 per cent to remain below 1.5°C (UNEP, 2018). Thus, although record-breaking, the forecast reduction of CO₂ emissions caused by the COVID-19 outbreak will not be enough to achieve even the weakest of the targets set out by the Paris Climate agreement. Global emissions should be cut by almost 8 per cent every year for the next decade to keep us within reach of the 1.5°C target of the Paris Climate agreement. According to UNEP (2020), the estimated 2020 fall in emissions translates to only a 0.01°C reduction of global warming by 2050, due to the increasing concentrations of greenhouse gases in the atmosphere. While emissions dropped in 2020, earlier emissions remain in the atmosphere for long periods.

Most carbon dioxide emitted in Asia – per unit of GDP and in total

The most prevalent greenhouse gas is CO_2, as figure 1 reveals. It is a gas released through human activities, such as deforestation and burning of fossil fuels, and through natural processes, such as respiration and volcanic eruptions. Around 90 per cent of CO_2 emissions are generated by burning of fossil fuels in the form of coal, oil and natural gas. However, CO_2 concentrations in the atmosphere are also influenced by deforestation and other types of land-cover or land-use change, due to their impact on the land's potential to absorb or generate CO_2.

In recent years, CO_2 has accounted for almost three quarters of total greenhouse gas emissions. Thus, by focusing on CO_2, SDG indicator 9.4.1 helps monitor the largest part, although not the full amount of global greenhouse gas emissions.

The regional concentration of CO_2 emissions varies considerably across the globe. In 2019, many countries in Africa recorded emissions of less than 20 kg/km^2. In Latin American countries and in Australia, emissions were mainly between 20-100 kg/km^2. Much higher CO_2 emissions, typically more than 200 kg/km^2 and sometimes even higher than 2 000 kg/km^2, were common for countries located in a band that ranges from the United States of America and Central America over to Europe, excluding Iceland and most of Scandinavia, and over the Near East, to Southern, Eastern and South-Eastern Asia. Within that band, particularly high emission levels were recorded in Central Europe and Eastern Asia. Farther to the North, in Canada, Northern Europe and in Northern and Central Asia, emission levels were lower, usually ranging between 50 and 200 kg/km^2 on average per country.

Map 1. Geographic concentration of carbon dioxide emissions

(kg/km^2 per year)

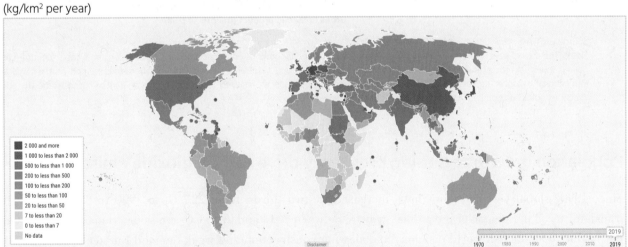

Source: UNCTAD calculations based on UNCTADStat (UNCTAD, 2021) and Crippa et al. (2020).
Notes: CO_2 emissions from fossil fuel use (combustion, flaring), industrial processes (cement, steel, chemicals and urea) and product use are included. Emissions from fuels burned on ships and aircrafts in international transport are not included.

As figure 2 shows, three regions of the world emitted most of the CO_2 from fuel combustion, industrial processes and product use: Eastern and South-Eastern Asia (15.5 Gt in 2019), Northern America (5.7 Gt) and Europe (6.6 Gt). Together, they accounted for about 75 per cent of global CO_2 emissions in 2019. In Europe, one tenth less emissions were associated with each unit of output in Europe than in Northern America. However, as the European economy is larger, measured in terms of GDP, it also accounts for a higher amount of CO_2 emissions than the economy of Northern America. Eastern and South-Eastern Asia was characterized by both higher GDP and higher carbon intensity than the other world regions shown in figure 2. The region alone emitted 41 per cent of world's emissions.

The least CO_2 emissions per unit of production were caused by the economies of Latin America and the Caribbean. The economies of Sub-Saharan Africa produced only slightly more CO_2 emissions per unit of production than European economies. Sub-Saharan Africa and Latin America and the Caribbean together only contributed 9 per cent of global CO_2 emissions, while Europe contributed 17 per cent. Fuels burned on ships and aircrafts involved in international transport, which cannot be allocated to economies, would add about 3 per cent to global CO_2 emissions (Crippa et al., 2020).

📊 **Figure 2. CO_2 emissions, emissions intensity and GDP, by region, 2019 (SDG 9.4.1)**

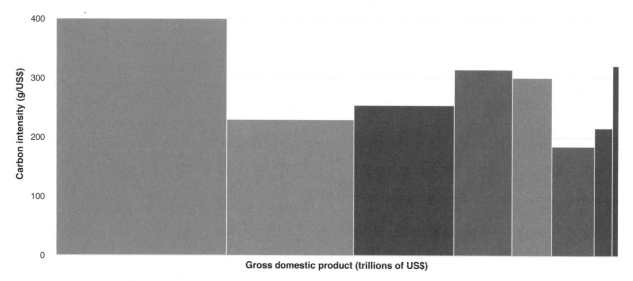

Source: UNCTAD calculations based on Crippa et al. (2020).

Notes: The area of bars measures CO_2 emissions. Regions are arranged by order of emissions amount. CO_2 emissions from fossil fuel use (combustion, flaring), industrial processes (cement, steel, chemicals and urea) and product use are included. Emissions from fuels burned on ships and aircrafts in international transport are not included. US$ values are in constant 2011 prices, adjusted to purchasing power parities based to the United States of America. Central and Southern Asia includes developing economies in Oceania.

Population growth and rising prosperity drive carbon dioxide emissions

Since 1990, global CO_2 emissions have increased by two thirds: from 22.7 Gt in 1990 to 38.0 Gt in 2019. This translates to 1.8 per cent average annual growth. Between 2014 and 2016 CO_2 emissions remained almost constant, partly due to a sluggish world economy and slowing construction and weak demand for steel. But from 2017 CO_2 emissions' growth resumed, and by 2018 the annual growth rate had returned to 2.3 per cent (Crippa et al., 2020). In 2019, the growth in emissions slowed down, before turning into negative in the face of the outbreak of COVID-19 (see above).

Much of the increase in CO_2 emissions observed over the last decades relates to world population growth and increased consumption per capita, since consumption relies on the production of goods and services. In fact, CO_2 emissions can be expressed as the product of population size, GDP per capita (GDP/population), and the carbon intensity of production (CO_2/GDP):

$$CO_2 = Population \left[\frac{GDP}{Population}\right]\left[\frac{CO_2}{GDP}\right]$$

An increase in GDP, the product of the first two factors in the equation above, leads to rising CO_2 emissions, unless carbon intensity, the third factor, decreases at a higher rate than the growth of GDP. Some studies suggest that carbon intensity decreases as a country's level of development rises, to the extent that GDP growth can be offset. This would result in a bell-shaped relationship between GDP and emissions – the so-called "environmental Kuznets curve". So far, research has provided mixed empirical evidence for the validity of this curve (see Stern, 2004; Victor, 2010; Hoffmeister, 2013; Pacini and Silveira, 2014).

At the global level, real GDP has more than doubled over the last quarter century – from US$49 trillion in 1990 to US$127 trillion in 2019.[1] This is the result of a 45 per cent increase in the world population (1971: 5.3 billion, 2019: 7.7 billion) and a three-quarters' increase in real GDP per capita (1990: US$9 290, 2019: US$16 470) (see figure 3).

Decreasing carbon intensity cannot offset GDP growth in the less developed regions

Global carbon intensity reduced by over one third from 1990 (458 g/US$) to 2019 (299 g/US$). That means, CO_2 emissions have grown at a slower pace than GDP. This decoupling of CO_2 emissions from GDP has been most significant in Europe, where carbon intensity fell by 55 per cent since 1990, and almost as much in Northern America (-49 per cent).

Carbon intensity of GDP down one third since 1990

Over the past 29 years, carbon intensity has decreased less in regions consisting mainly of developing economies. Eastern and South-Eastern Asia released over three times more CO_2 in 2019 than in 1990, reducing carbon intensity by only 27 per cent. Recently, their carbon intensity has been declining notably, from 2012 to 2017 at an annual rate well above 3 per cent. However, the reduction in carbon intensity over the last three decades did not compensate for the extraordinary increase in GDP per capita; it was just enough to offset the population growth.

In Sub-Saharan Africa carbon intensity of the economy dropped by 38 per cent from 1990 to 2019, compared to 17 per cent in Latin America and the Caribbean. In Australia and New Zealand, carbon intensity decreased by 34 per cent.

Growth contribution (*per cent*)

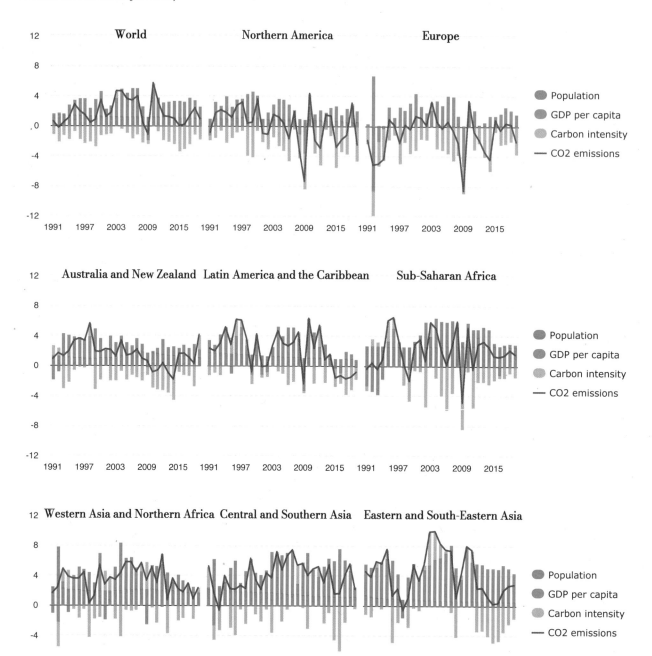

Source: UNCTAD calculations based on Crippa et al. (2020).
Notes: CO_2 emissions from fossil fuel use (combustion, flaring), industrial processes (cement, steel, chemicals and urea) and product use are included. Rates based on US$ values are in constant 2011 prices, adjusted to purchasing power parities based to the United States of America. Central and Southern Asia includes developing economies in Oceania.

Europe is the only region where the overall amount of CO_2 emissions is lower today than in 1990, by almost 30 per cent. Northern America is close to 1990 levels, but the remaining regions are well above.

CO$_2$ emissions in Europe

30% below 1990 levels

As countries are connected by global value chains and trade relations, the observed growth in carbon intensity of GDP in developing regions may be driven by demand for carbon-intensive final products in other regions. In fact, studies based on inter-country input-output tables prepared by the OECD (2018) find that demand-based CO$_2$ emissions of developed economies are generally higher than their production-based emissions, while most developing economies are net-exporters of CO$_2$ emissions embodied in final products (Wiebe and Yamano, 2016). As environmental policy is more stringent in some regions than in others, companies can save production costs by relocating carbon intensive production processes globally, a process described as "carbon leakage" (Lanzi E. et al., 2013).

Energy demand dropped in early 2020, but rebounded at the end of the year

Fuels are mostly burned to produce energy. For that reason, CO$_2$ emissions and energy supply are closely interlinked. According to the IEA (2019), this subcomponent of total CO$_2$ emissions, i.e. energy-related CO$_2$ emissions, accounts for two thirds of CO$_2$ emissions globally. Despite an extraordinary decline in energy demand in 2020, energy-related CO$_2$ emissions still reached 31.5 Gt, compared to 33.0 Gt in 2019, according to IEA (2021). They estimate that the global energy demand will increase by 4.6 per cent in 2021, due to the expected recovery from the COVID-19 pandemic.

Energy is an indispensable input for most processes generating value added in an economy. This means that energy intensity (Energy/GDP) is an important determinant of the carbon intensity of GDP (CO$_2$/GDP). The other determinant is the carbon intensity of energy supply (CO$_2$/energy), as the decomposition below shows:

$$\left[\frac{CO_2}{GDP}\right] = \left[\frac{Energy}{GDP}\right]\left[\frac{CO_2}{Energy}\right]$$

Figure 4 demonstrates the important role of efficient energy use in reducing the carbon intensity of GDP. From 2008 to 2018, energy intensity reduced on average by 1.7 per cent each year. During that time, developing and developed economies in Asia and Oceania achieved significant reductions in energy intensity, by 16 and 17 per cent respectively. However, due to rising emissions per unit of energy supplied, the reduction of carbon intensity of GDP was

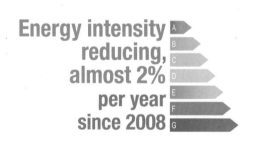

Energy intensity reducing, almost 2% per year since 2008

smaller: 8 per cent in developing and 13 per cent in developed Asia and Oceania. In Latin America and the Caribbean and in Africa, carbon intensity of energy supply remained almost unchanged. Cuts in energy intensity, however, enabled reducing the carbon intensity of GDP also in those regions by 4 and 11 per cent, respectively. By contrast, In Northern America and Europe, both energy intensity and carbon intensity of energy supply were considerably reduced. Due to higher saving in energy per unit of GDP, the overall reduction in carbon intensity of GDP was slightly higher in Northern America (-27 per cent) than in Europe (-23 per cent). Thus, if GDP did not grow, CO$_2$ emissions from fuel combustions would have declined in all regions of the world over the last decade.

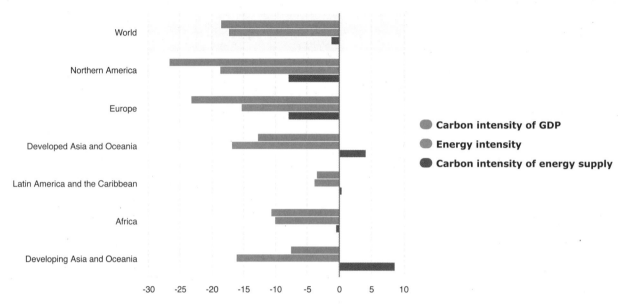

Figure 4. Changes in energy intensity (SDG 7.3.1) and carbon intensity, by region, 2008-2018

Growth rate (*per cent*)

Carbon intensity of GDP
Energy intensity
Carbon intensity of energy supply

Source: UNCTAD calculations based on OECD (2021b).

Notes: Emissions not caused by fuel combustion are not included. US$ values are in constant 2010 prices, adjusted to purchasing power parities based to the United States of America. Central and Southern Asia includes developing economies in Oceania.

Soon after the start of 2020, demand for energy fell sharply due to the measures taken against the COVID-19 pandemic around the world. China, hit by the pandemic first, saw their weekly energy demand fall by 15 per cent, whereas in the Republic of Korea and Japan the estimated impact of COVID-19 measures on energy demand remains below 10 per cent. In Europe, the periods of partial lock down cut weekly energy demand by 17 per cent on average, while countries with a higher share of services and greater stringency of lockdowns saw their energy demand reduce by as much as 25 to 30 per cent. India's full national lockdown reduced their weekly energy demand by almost 30 per cent. Overall, the IEA estimated that for each additional month of restrictions in place as of early April 2020, global annual energy demand would reduce by 1.5 per cent (IEA, 2021). In 2021, the pandemic continues to impact global energy demand.

The falling demand has been reflected in sinking oil and gas prices. In March 2020, the UNCTAD free market commodity price index for fuels recorded a historic drop of 33.2 per cent month-on-month (UNCTAD, 2021).

The impact of COVID-19 has been especially pronounced on transport. Since the outbreak of the pandemic, people have not been travelling much, and the global number of flights collapsed from mid-March 2020. The number of weekly commercial flights available was about 75 per cent lower in the first half of May compared with the start of January 2020. In January 2021, the number of commercial flights remained almost 40 per cent lower than in January 2020. But May 2021, is clearly, by 140 per cent, above the low levels of May 2020 (see Tourism section of Developing economies in international trade).

While air transportation generates about 2 per cent of global emissions, road transportation contributes almost 12 per cent (WRI, 2020). IEA (2021) expects road transport activity to recover to pre-COVID-19 levels only in the last months of 2021, while air transport demand would remain markedly below 2019 levels for all of 2021. They expect a partial recovery: CO_2 emissions from international aviation would remain one third below pre-pandemic levels in 2021, while emissions from road transport and domestic aviation would remain 5 per cent below 2019 levels.

The impact of COVID-19 brought large changes to the global energy mix in spring 2020. While the share of coal declined to below 23 per cent, renewables jumped to almost 13 per cent. Regional differences were large with major geographic variations (IEA, 2021). IEA notes that, in 2021, coal demand has rebounded strongly, reversing all the declines in 2020.

These developments led to notable short-term improvements in air quality, with NO_2 levels, a gas emitted from burning fossil fuels for transportation and electricity generation, dropping recently. First, in some areas of China, NO_2 concentrations dropped by 40 per cent from 2019 levels in January-February 2020. In March 2020, a 30 per cent drop was recorded in the North Eastern part of the United States of America, and the NO_2 levels halved in Europe by April 2020 (Carbon Brief, 2020; NASA, 2020; European Data Portal, 2020; CCSA, 2020). After a decline in the COVID-19 measures, air pollution levels are bouncing back to their pre-pandemic levels, according to satellite imagery (ESA, 2021).

A mixture of positive and negative trends – what will prevail?

Climate change continues to be a development issue, demonstrated particularly by the trends in Asia, where CO_2 emissions have dramatically increased in tandem with the rapid growth of GDP per capita over the last decades. Only decreasing energy intensity has limited the growth of CO_2 emissions in that region. This is a sobering message, considering the urgent need to limit the concentration of greenhouse gases in the atmosphere. At the same time, some statistics give hope: in most developed regions, CO_2 emissions have been diminishing for more than ten years, despite continuous GDP growth. This provides signs that a decoupling of emissions from the economic development is feasible.

The prolonged outbreak of COVID-19 has brought about an unexpected deviation from many long-term trends, leading to an unprecedented fall of greenhouse gas emissions in early 2020 and a faster shift to renewable energy sources. However, in light of latest data these changes seem temporary. Even if the pandemic has induced historical reductions of CO_2 emissions in 2020, it will not be enough in the fight against climate change, and a partial bounce back is expected in 2021. More effective and lasting efforts are needed to reduce CO_2 emissions and other greenhouse gases to limit global warming to below 2°C or especially below the 1.5°C target by 2100. As populations and GDP per capita continue to grow, a drastic reduction in carbon intensity will be required. Rising energy efficiency serves as an important step in that direction, as well as renewable and cleaner energy.

Involving the private sector in the sustainable development agenda

Recent global trends, not the least of which is the COVID-19 pandemic, emphasize the role of sustainability reporting in transitioning to a more sustainable economy. The business sector is identified in the Addis Ababa Action Agenda as a significant player in the financing of sustainable development (United Nations, 2015). Their actions contribute directly or indirectly to the attainment of all SDGs, including the state of the environment and greenhouse

Private business sector mentioned in only one SDG target: 12.6

gas emissions. Nonetheless, the business sector is mostly absent from the SDG targets and is explicitly mentioned in only one of them: target 12.6, which calls for a greater integration of sustainability information in the regular reporting cycle of firms.

This target and the related reporting are important for making companies' contribution to the 2030 Agenda visible and for encouraging them to review how their operations affect their stakeholders and the environment.

Sustainability reporting promotes transparency in the business sector and increases business accountability to society.

SDG indicator 12.6.1 aims to measure the number of companies that publish sustainability reports. Developing consistent reporting on the indicator requires aligning multiple reporting frameworks, including the International Integrated Reporting Council (IIRC, 2013) framework, the Global Reporting Initiative (GRI, 2019) standards, the standards proposed by the Sustainability Accounting Standards Board (SASB, 2018), the Climate-related financial disclosure recommendations (TCFD, 2017), the EU non-financial reporting directive (European Commission, 2014), the Framework on environmental, social and governance factors (WEF, 2020) and the UNCTAD (2018) Guidance on Core Indicators.[2]

To this end, UNCTAD and UNEP, as joint custodians of SDG indicator 12.6.1, identified four dimensions for sustainability reporting: economic, environmental, social and institutional. As a "minimum reporting requirement", only reports that cover certain elements in a meaningful way will be counted as sustainability reports for the SDG indicator. To further strengthen sustainable practices and accountability, the agencies also identified an "advanced reporting requirement" with more comprehensive reporting rules.

In September 2019, the IAEG-SDGs approved the concepts and methods developed by UNCTAD and UNEP, and data collection for the indicator began. The framework does not add new reporting requirements, instead it suggests a way to reconcile the existing frameworks.

Businesses striving to close large gaps in sustainability reporting

UNCTAD regularly convenes a Group of Experts on ISAR to discuss international accounting and reporting standards in order to improve the availability, reliability and comparability of financial and non-financial enterprise reporting, and especially to integrate sustainability information into business reporting.

Official statistics for SDG 12.6.1 are not yet available as companies are setting up the new sustainability reporting. However, an initial review is possible by looking at an unrepresentative sample of company sustainability reports as published by the United Nations Global Compact and GRI Sustainability Disclosure Database. In these samples, in 2020, 85 per cent of companies were reporting on the minimum requirements for SDG indicator 12.6.1 and 40 per cent on the advanced requirements the related UNCTAD Guidance (UNCTAD, 2018).

In March 2021, the preliminary review was based on a sample of almost 4 000 company reports in the two databases. Although this is a collection of voluntary reports and not representative of the world population of firms, the exercise still provides a first glimpse of current sustainability reporting practices and reveals some regional patterns.

Studying every single report would be time consuming. Instead, machine learning and natural language processing techniques have been used to analyse text syntax structures in the CoPs and identify keywords based on the 33 core elements listed in the UNCTAD Guidance, organised according to the four themes.[34]

Figure 5 shows that most companies reporting in line with the minimum requirements cover three out of the four reporting dimensions, i.e., economic, environmental, institutional and social dimensions, with the institutional dimension as the least covered dimension. Among companies following the advanced reporting requirements, the environmental dimension has been the most under-reported area.

The largest gaps in minimum reporting relate to indicators such as employee by contract type and gender; stakeholder engagement surrounding sustainability performance; materiality assessment, sustainability strategy and or principles related to sustainability; and employee training. While the largest gaps in advanced reporting include greenhouse gas emissions and waste intensity; material consumption, sourcing of materials and reclaimed or recycled materials used; biodiversity impacts; supplier and consumer engagement on sustainability issues; other local community impacts; supplier social assessment; details of remuneration; and supplier environmental assessment.

Figure 5. Sustainability reporting by dimension
(Number of reporting companies)

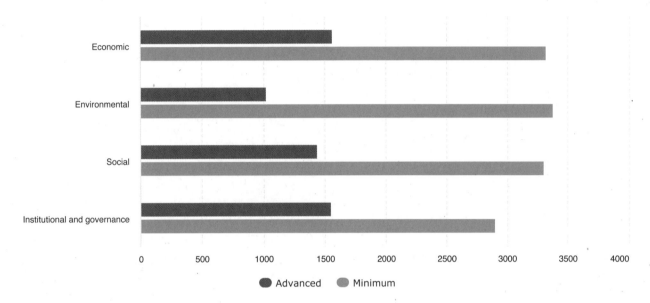

Source: Global AI Corporation with data from United Nations Global Compact (2020) and UNCTAD (2018).
Note: These are preliminary results from a non-representative sample. As much as the data on number of company reports reflect compliance with the minimum and advanced requirements, they also reflect current data gaps,

Figure 6 reflects the availability of sustainability reports by reporting requirements and region. The figure also reflects the large data gaps in some regions. Still, these data can be taken as an indication of the regional differences in voluntary reporting. It appears that in certain regions, such as, the Americas, Asia and Europe, firms demonstrate a higher compliance with the UNCTAD Guidance than in others. Larger gaps in reporting of some regions are evident, especially in Africa, Central, Western and Southern Asia and the Oceania.

Company reports in the Americas, Asia and Europe better aligned with SDG 12.6.1

Figure 6. Sustainability reporting, by region

(Number of reporting companies)

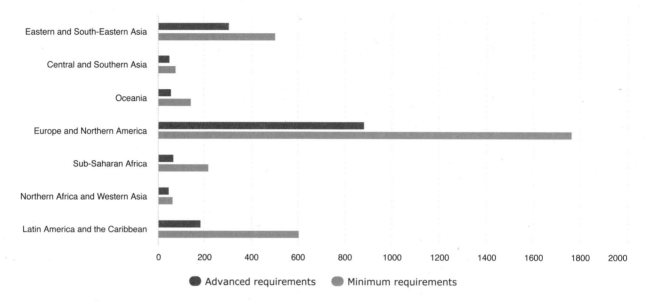

Source: Global AI Corporation with data from United Nations Global Compact (2020) and UNCTAD (2018).
Note: These are preliminary results from a non-representative sample. As much as the data on number of company reports reflect compliance with the minimum and advanced requirements, they also reflect current data gaps,

The overall quality of sustainability reports has improved across the world since the 2017 round of reports, especially in the environmental, social as well institutional and governance dimensions, where the ratio of reporting aligned with the minimum requirements almost doubled in these regions.

All in all, the 2030 Agenda has increased sustainability reporting among businesses and led to closer engagement of international organizations and businesses to develop a commonly agreed upon and harmonized set of indicators. The coming years will show if sustainability reporting will be used by an increasing number of firms to demonstrate commitment to sustainable development.

Notes

1. In constant 2017 prices adjusted to purchasing power parity based to the United States of America.

2. The Guidance on Core Indicators, developed by UNCTAD upon request by the 34th session of the Intergovernmental Working Group of Experts on ISAR, lists the main elements for entity reporting to monitor company-level contributions towards SDGs (UNCTAD, 2018).

3. Additional complexity is caused by the fact that the CoPs are reported in over 20 different languages and in different formats. Therefore, the algorithms use multiple data cleaning, noise reduction and filtering methods to better identify relevant content for each indicator.

4. The calculations were performed by Global AI Corporation.

References

- Carbon Brief (2020). Global Carbon Project: Coronavirus causes 'record fall' in fossil-fuel emissions in 2020. Available at https://www.carbonbrief.org/global-carbon-project-coronavirus-causes-record-fall-in-fossil-fuel-emissions-in-2020 (accessed 18 June 2021).

- CCSA (2020). How COVID-19 is changing the world: A statistical perspective. Available at https://unstats.un.org/unsd/ccsa/documents/covid19-report-ccsa.pdf (accessed 8 June 2020).

- Crippa M et al. (2020). Fossil CO_2 and GHG emissions of all world countries - 2019 Report. Available at https://edgar.jrc.ec.europa.eu/report_2020 (accessed 2 June 2021).

- Doshi P (2011). The elusive definition of pandemic influenza. Bulletin of the World Health Organisation. *WHO Bulletin*. 89(7):532–538.

- ESA (2021). Air pollution returning to pre-COVID levels. Available at https://www.esa.int/Applications/Observing_the_Earth/Copernicus/Sentinel-5P/Air_pollution_returning_to_pre-COVID_levels (accessed 27 June 2021).

- European Commission (2014). Corporate sustainability reporting. The Non-Financial Reporting Directive (NFRD). Directive 2014/95/EU . Available at https://ec.europa.eu/info/business-economy-euro/company-reporting-and-auditing/company-reporting/corporate-sustainability-reporting_en (accessed 17 June 2021).

- European Data Portal (2020). The COVID-19 related traffic reduction and decreased air pollution in Europe. Available at https://www.europeandataportal.eu/en/covid-19/stories/covid-19-related-traffic-reduction-and-decreased-air-pollution-europe (accessed 7 May 2020).

- GRI (2019). Available at https://www.globalreporting.org/information/sustainability-reporting/Pages/default.aspx (accessed 19 April 2019).

- Hoffmeister O (2013). Europäische Umweltpolitik im Zeichen der Finanz- und Wirtschaftskrise. *Umweltökonomische Probleme in Gesellschaft und Betrieb*. Merseburger Schriften zur Unternehmensführung(14):17–33.

- IEA (2019). CO_2 Emissions from Fuel Combustion 2019. Available at https://www.iea.org/reports/co2-emissions-from-fuel-combustion-2019 (accessed 25 April 2020).

- IEA (2021). Global Energy Review 2021. Available at https://www.iea.org/reports/global-energy-review-2021/co2-emissions (accessed 18 June 2021).

- IIRC (2013). The international <IR> framework. Available at http://integratedreporting.org/resource/international-ir-framework/ (accessed 4 June 2019).

- IPCC (2014). *Climate Change 2014, Synthesis Report, Contribution of Working Groups I, II and III to the Fifth Assessment Report (5AR) of the Intergovernmental Panel on Climate Change*. IPCC.

- IPCC (2018). Global warming of 1.5°C. An IPCC Special Report on the impacts of global warming of 1.5°C above pre-industrial levels and related global greenhouse gas emission pathways, in the context of strengthening the global response to the threat of climate change, sustainable development, and efforts to eradicate poverty. Available at https://www.ipcc.ch/sr15 (accessed 11 May 2021).

- IPCC (2019). IPCC special report on the ocean and cryosphere in a changing climate. Available at https://www.ipcc.ch/srocc/ (accessed 11 May 2021).

- Lanzi E., Damian M., Chateau J. and Dellink R. (2013). *Addressing Competitiveness and Carbon Leakage Impacts Arising from Multiple Carbon Markets: A Modelling Assessment*. OECD Environmental Working Papers, No. 58. OECD Publishing.

- NASA (2020). Satellite data show 30 percent drop in air pollution over Northeast U.S. Available at https://www.nasa.gov/feature/goddard/2020/drop-in-air-pollution-over-northeast (accessed 7 May 2020).

- Netherlands PBL (2020). Trends in Global CO2 and Total Greenhouse Gas Emissions; 2020 Report. Available at https://www.pbl.nl/en/publications/trends-in-global-co2-and-total-greenhouse-gas-emissions-2020-report (accessed 18 June 2021).

- OECD (2018). Inter-Country Input-Output (ICIO) Tables. Available at https://www.oecd.org/sti/ind/inter-country-input-output-tables.htm (accessed 18 June 2019).

- OECD (2021a). Glossary of statistical terms. Available at https://stats.oecd.org/glossary/index.htm (accessed 11 May 2021).

- OECD (2021b). OECD Statistical Database. Available at https://stats.oecd.org/ (accessed 2 June 2021).

- Pacini H and Silveira S (2014). Carbon Intensities of Economies from the Perspective of Learning Curves. *Challenges in Sustainability.* .

- SASB (2018). SASB standards application guidance. itemKey/Z5Y7LCYD. Available at https://www.sasb.org/company-use/key-resources-for-companies/ (accessed 4 June 2019).

- Stern DI (2004). The Rise and Fall of the Environmental Kuznets Curve. *World Development.* 32(8):1419–1439.

- TCFD (2017). Climate-related financial disclosure recommendations. Available at https://www.fsb-tcfd.org/ (accessed 17 June 2021).

- UNCTAD (2018). *Guidance on Core Indicators for Entity Reporting on the Contribution Towards the Attainment of the Sustainable Development Goals.* United Nations publication. Sales No. E.19.II.D.11. Geneva.

- UNCTAD (2021). UNCTADStat. Available at https://unctadstat.unctad.org/EN/Index.html (accessed 21 April 2021).

- UNEP (2018). *Emissions Gap Report 2018.* UNEP. Nairobi.

- UNEP (2020). Emissions gap report 2020. Available at https://www.unep.org/emissions-gap-report-2020 (accessed 13 May 2021).

- UNFCCC (2016). Paris Agreement. FCCC/CP/2015/10/Add.1. Paris. 29 January. (accessed 31 May 2019).

- United Nations (2015). Report of the third international conference on financing for development. A/CONF.227/20. Addis Ababa. 3 August. (accessed 20 April 2020).

- United Nations Global Compact (2013). UN Global Compact policy on communicating progress. Available at https://www.unglobalcompact.org/library/1851 (accessed 6 March 2019).

- United Nations Global Compact (2020). United Nations Global Compact Database. Available at https://www.unglobalcompact.org (accessed 6 February 2021).

- Victor PA (2010). Ecological Economics and Economic Growth, Annals of the New York Academy of Sciences. *Annals of the New York Academy of Sciences.* (1185):237–245.

- WEF (2020). Embracing the New Age of Materiality: Harnessing the Pace of Change in ESG. Available at https://www.weforum.org/whitepapers/embracing-the-new-age-of-materiality-harnessing-the-pace-of-change-in-esg/ (accessed 17 June 2021).

- WHO (2006). Air Quality Guidelines, Global Update 2005. Available at http://www.euro.who.int/__data/assets/pdf_file/0005/78638/E90038.pdf?ua=1 (accessed 11 May 2020).

- WHO (2020). Q&A on coronaviruses (COVID-19). Available at https://www.who.int/emergencies/diseases/novel-coronavirus-2019/question-and-answers-hub/q-a-detail/q-a-coronaviruses (accessed 11 May 2020).

- Wiebe KS and Yamano N (2016). *Estimating CO_2 Emissions Embodied in Final Demand and Trade Using the OECD ICIO 2015: Methodology and Results.* OECD Science, Technology and Industry Working Papers, No. 2016/5. OECD Publishing. Paris.

- WMO (2019). Available at https://public.wmo.int/en/our-mandate/focus-areas/environment/greenhouse%20gases (accessed 11 June 2019).

- WMO (2021). 2020 was one of three warmest years on record. Available at https://public.wmo.int/en/media/press-release/2020-was-one-of-three-warmest-years-record (accessed 18 June 2021).

- WRI (2020). World Greenhouse Gas Emissions: 2016. Available at https://www.wri.org/resources/data-visualizations/world-greenhouse-gas-emissions-2016 (accessed 5 May 2020).

UNCTAD technical cooperation in support of SDGs

UNCTAD technical cooperation in support of SDGs

UNCTAD gears its technical cooperation towards contributing to the achievement of the 2030 Agenda. UNCTAD's technical cooperation projects are delivered at an interregional, regional and country level (see figure 1).

Figure 1 – Distribution of project expenditures by region, 2020

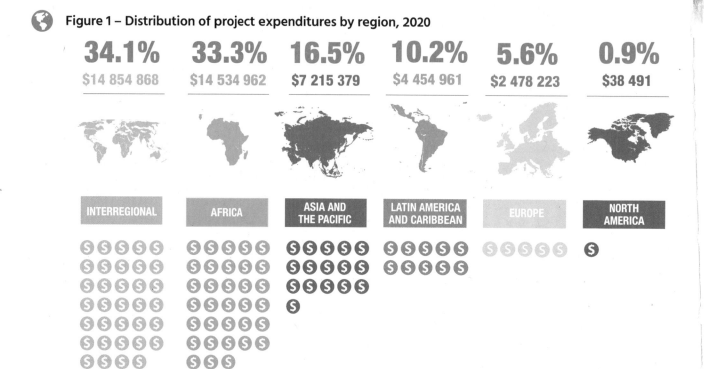

Source: UNCTAD (2021a).

The UNCTAD Toolbox (UNCTAD, 2015) has been developed to better align technical cooperation with the SDGs. See table 1 for a mapping of UNCTAD technical cooperation to SDGs by theme and product.

Table 1. UNCTAD technical cooperation, by theme and product, 2020

Cluster	Theme	Product	SDGs
	A	**Transforming economies, fostering sustainable development**	
VII	A1	Investment policy reviews	1, 8, 10, 17
I	A2	Services policy reviews	8, 9, 17
I	A3	Trade Policy Framework Reviews	17
XV	A4	Science, Technology and Innovation Policy Reviews	9
XIII	A5	E-commerce and the Digital Economy	8, 9, 17
VIII	A6	Investment Guides	9, 17
II	A7	Non-tariff Measures	3, 8, 17
I	A9	Trade Negotiations and the International Trading System	10, 17
III	A10	Sustainable Trade and the Environment	12, 13, 14, 15
VIII	A11	Investment Promotion and Facilitation	9, 17
All	A99	Others	
	B	**Tackling vulnerabilities, building resilience**	
XVI	B1	Support to Graduation from Least Developed Country Status	8
XI	B2	DMFAS - Debt Management and Financial Analysis System	17
XVII	B4	UNCTAD Contribution to the Enhanced Integrated Framework	9, 17
XVII	B5	Market Access, Rules of Origin and Geographical Indications for the Least Developed Countries	8, 10, 17
V	B6	Breaking the Chains of Commodity Dependence	8, 9
XII	B9	Sustainable and Resilient Transport and Logistic Services	8, 9, 13, 14
X	B93	Assistance to the Palestinian People	17
All	B99	Others	
	C	**Fostering economic efficiency, improving governance**	
IV	C1	Voluntary Peer Reviews of Competition and Consumer Protection Laws and Policies	8, 10
IV	C10	Competition and Consumer Protection Policies and Frameworks	8, 9, 10, 12, 17
VIII	C2	Business Facilitation	8, 16
XII	C3	Trade Facilitation	10, 16
XII	C4	ASYCUDA – Automated System for Customs Data	9, 15, 17
X	C5	Statistics	17
IX	C7	Enabling Accounting and Reporting on the Private Sector's Contribution to the SDG Implementation	12, 17
VI	C8	Investment and Public Health	3, 9
VII	C9	International Investment Agreements	17
IX	C96	Corporate Social Responsibility - the Sustainable Stock Exchanges Initiative	12
All	C99	Other	
	D	**Empowering people, investing in their future**	

Cluster	Theme	Product	SDGs
II	D1	Trade, Gender and Development	5, 8
IX	D3	Entrepreneurship for Sustainable Development	4, 8
XIV	D6	Train For Trade	8, 9, 14, 17
X	D94	The Virtual Institute	17
XIV	D95	Course on Key issues on the International Economic Agenda - paragraph 166	17
All	D99	Others	
All	E	Others	

Source: UNCTAD (forthcoming).

The UNCTAD toolbox currently features 28 technical cooperation projects, categorized into four overarching themes. In 2020, 204 projects, spread across 74 countries, and accounting for US$35 million were undertaken (see table 2).

Table 2. Technical cooperation expenditure by theme, product and SDG, 2020

Theme	Product	Multiple	1	3	4	5	7	8	9	10	12	13	14	15	16	17	Total
US$ thousands																	
A	Transforming economies, fostering sustainable development	14	-	6	309	59	68	1 124	605	61	226	177	269	850	160	1 006	**4 933**
B	Tackling vulnerabilities, building resilience	-	17	3	-	-	-	275	158	109	101	107	101	101	42	4 673	**5 686**
C	Fostering economic efficiency, improving governance	-	-	15	116	197	54	1 375	5 981	674	144	8	8	5 560	1 414	6 125	**21 670**
D	Empowering people, investing in their future	3	37	-	16	165	192	417	139	46	11	9	57	9	16	171	**1 289**
E	Others	1 460	-	-	-	-	-	-	-	-	-	-	-	-	-	-	**1 460**
		1 477	**54**	**24**	**441**	**422**	**314**	**3 194**	**6 883**	**889**	**482**	**300**	**435**	**6 520**	**1 633**	**11 974**	**35 039**
Percentage																	
A	Transforming economies, fostering sustainable development	0.0	0.0	0.0	0.9	0.2	0.2	3.2	1.7	0.2	0.6	0.5	0.8	2.4	0.5	2.9	**14.1**
B	Tackling vulnerabilities, building resilience	0.0	0.0	0.0	0.0	0.0	0.0	0.8	0.5	0.3	0.3	0.3	0.3	0.3	0.1	13.3	**16.2**
C	Fostering economic efficiency, improving governance	0.0	0.0	0.0	0.3	0.6	0.2	3.9	17.1	1.9	0.4	0.0	0.0	15.9	4.0	17.5	**61.8**
D	Empowering people, investing in their future	0.0	0.1	0.0	0.0	0.5	0.5	1.2	0.4	0.1	0.0	0.0	0.2	0.0	0.0	0.5	**3.7**
E	Others	4.2	0.0	0.0	0.0	0.0	0.0	0.0	0.0	0.0	0.0	0.0	0.0	0.0	0.0	0.0	**4.2**
		4.2	**0.2**	**0.1**	**1.3**	**1.2**	**0.9**	**9.1**	**19.6**	**2.5**	**1.4**	**0.9**	**1.2**	**18.6**	**4.7**	**34.2**	**100.0**

Source: UNCTAD (forthcoming).
Note: "Multiple" means that some technical cooperation cannot be mapped to a single SDG.

UNCTAD technical cooperation expenditure has been mapped to the SDGs, allowing readers to understand how each theme contributes to each SDG. Activities are also cross-classified by region to see where technical cooperation expenditure by SDG has occurred (see tables 2 and 3).

Table 3. Technical cooperation expenditure by region and SDG, 2020

Region	Multiple	1	3	4	5	7	8	9	10	12	13	14	15	16	17	Total
US$ thousands																
Africa	-	17	3	222	39	12	835	2 779	307	214	164	164	2 533	450	3 204	10 944
Asia & Pacific	-	-	6	63	60	69	213	1 643	116	16	10	10	1 620	84	2 050	5 961
Latin America & Caribbean	-	-	-	-	-	-	340	887	39	15	-	92	880	358	1 107	3 719
Europe	-	-	-	-	-	9	-	231	-	-	-	-	231	-	231	702
North America	-	-	-	-	-	-	-	-	-	-	-	-	-	-	-	-
Interregional	1 477	37	15	156	324	225	1 802	1 343	426	237	125	168	1 255	741	5 382	13 713
Total	**1 924**	**54**	**24**	**441**	**422**	**314**	**3 191**	**6 883**	**889**	**482**	**300**	**435**	**6 520**	**1 633**	**11 974**	**35 039**
Percentage																
Africa	-	0.0	0.0	0.6	0.1	0.0	2.4	7.9	0.9	0.6	0.5	0.5	7.2	1.3	9.1	31.2
Asia & Pacific	-	-	0.0	0.2	0.2	0.2	0.6	4.7	0.3	0.0	0.0	0.0	4.6	0.2	5.9	17.0
Latin America & Caribbean	-	-	-	-	-	-	1.0	2.5	0.1	0.0	-	0.3	2.5	1.0	3.2	10.6
Europe	-	-	-	-	-	0.0	-	0.7	-	-	-	-	0.7	-	0.7	2.0
North America	-	-	-	-	-	-	-	-	-	-	-	-	-	-	-	-
Interregional	4.2	0.1	0.0	0.4	0.9	0.6	5.1	3.8	1.2	0.7	0.4	0.5	3.6	2.1	15.4	39.1
Total	**4.2**	**0.2**	**0.1**	**1.3**	**1.2**	**0.9**	**9.1**	**19.6**	**2.5**	**1.4**	**0.9**	**1.2**	**18.6**	**4.7**	**34.2**	**100.0**

Source: UNCTAD (forthcoming).
Note: "Multiple" means that some technical cooperation cannot be mapped to a single SDG.

Table 4. Technical cooperation expenditure by theme, product and region, 2020

Theme	Product	SDGs	Africa	Asia & Pacific	Latin America & Caribbean	Europe	North America	Inter Regional	Total
US$ thousands									
A	Transforming economies, fostering sustainable development	1, 3, 8, 9, 10, 12, 13, 14, 15, 17	1 121	268	159	0	0	3 385	4 9335
B	Tackling vulnerabilities, building resilience	8, 9, 10, 13, 14, 17	1 119	303	113	0	0	4 151	5 686
C	Fostering economic efficiency, improving governance	3, 8, 9, 10, 12, 15, 16, 17	8 630	5 199	3 400	697	0	3 743	21 670
D	Empowering people, investing in their future	4, 5, 8, 9, 14, 17	74	191	46	4	0	973	1 289
E	Others		0	0	0	0	0	1 460	1 460
	Total		**10 9447**	**5 961**	**3 719**	**702**	**0**	**13 713**	**35 039**
Percentage									
A	Transforming economies, fostering sustainable development	1, 3, 8, 9, 10, 12, 13, 14, 15, 17	3.2	0.8	0.5	0.0	0.0	9.7	14.1
B	Tackling vulnerabilities, building resilience	8, 9, 10, 13, 14, 17	3.2	0.9	0.3	0.0	0.0	11.8	16.2
C	Fostering economic efficiency, improving governance	3, 8, 9, 10, 12, 15, 16, 17	24.6	14.8	9.7	2.0	0.0	10.7	61.8
D	Empowering people, investing in their future	4, 5, 8, 9, 14, 17	0.2	0.5	0.1	0.0	0.0	2.8	3.7
E	Others		0.0	0.0	0.0	0.0	0.0	4.2	4.2
	Total		**31.2**	**17.0**	**10.6**	**2.0**	**0.0**	**39.1**	**100.0**

Source: UNCTAD (forthcoming).

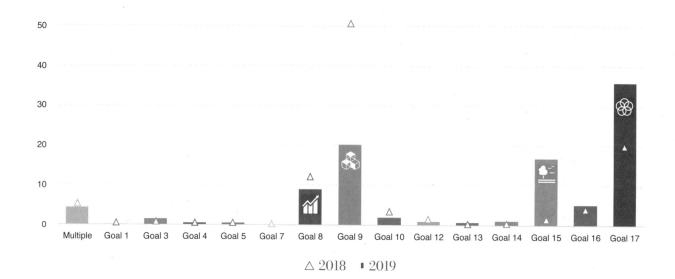

Figure 2. Percentage distribution of project expenditures by SDG

(In percentage of total expenditure)

△ 2018 ▪ 2019

Source: UNCTAD (forthcoming)

References

- OECD (2021). Glossary of statistical terms. Available at https://stats.oecd.org/glossary/index.htm (accessed 11 May 2021).

- UNCTAD (forthcoming). Review of the technical cooperation activities of UNCTAD and their financing. Report by the Secretary-General of UNCTAD. Annex II: Statistical table. Geneva.

- UNCTAD (2015). UNCTAD Toolbox: Delivering results. UNCTAD/TC/2015/1/iPub. Available at https://unctad.org/en/Pages/TC/TC-Products-in-the-Toolbox.aspx (accessed 7 June 2019).

- UNCTAD (2021a). UNCTAD Annual Report 2020 - Road to recovery. Available at https://unctad.org/webflyer/annual-report-2020-road-recovery-highlights (accessed 14 June 2021).

- UNCTAD (2021b). Classification of Non-Tariff Measures. Available at https://unctad.org/en/Pages/DITC/Trade-Analysis/Non-Tariff-Measures/NTMs-Classification.aspx (accessed 15 May 2021).

UNCTAD TrainForTrade – Strengthening knowledge for sustainable economic development

The UNCTAD TrainForTrade programme provides bespoke technical assistance to developing countries. The aim of the programme is to empower countries to participate in, and reap the benefits of, international trade in an equitable and sustainable manner. The programme has three goals:

1. Build sustainable networks of knowledge to enhance South-South cooperation and national ownership;
2. Promote digital solutions and innovative thinking to enhance capacities of international trade players;
3. Encourage development-oriented trade policy to reduce poverty and to promote transparency and good practices in trade.

> *The UNCTAD TrainForTrade programme is vitally important in achieving the 2030 Agenda for Sustainable Development and the Paris Climate Accords.*
>
> — President of Ireland, Mr. Michael D. Higgins (2018)

TrainForTrade contributes to the achievement of SDGs concerning life below water (SDG 14), industry innovation and infrastructure (SDG 9), decent work and economic growth (SDG 8), gender equality (SDG 5) and ending poverty in all forms (SDG 1). TrainForTrade also contributes to SDG 17, most directly to SDG Target 17.9, by building the capacity of developing countries to support the implementation of sustainable development goals in trade. Furthermore, in addition to timely management of the goods received, ports must prepare for the coming effects of climate change: rising temperatures, rising waters and extreme weather events; they must also ensure the environmental sustainability of their practices as part of global value chains. TrainForTrade also organises specialised workshops addressing climate change and the carbon market, thus contributing to SDG 13 also.

More than 5 000 participants from 2014 to 2018

Over the past five years, the programme has trained more than 5000 participants[1], completing, on average, nine full days of training. In total, between 2014 and 2018, participants received training equivalent to almost 45,000 full days, or 358,000 hours (see table 1).

Over 5000 participants over 5 years, completing on average 9 days of training

Table 1. Total capacity development provided by TrainForTrade

Year(s)	Number of participants total	Proportion female	Total amount of training in hours	Total amount of training in days	Number of countries receiving training
2014	1 258	38%	68 077	8 509	51
2015	1 066	29%	64 796	8 099	52
2016	836	36%	68 432	8 554	67
2017	1 332	32%	84 892	10 611	77
2018	893	37%	71 660	8 957	68
2014 - 2018	**5 385**	**34%**	**357 857**	**44 732**	**116**

Source: UNCTAD TrainForTrade.
Note: For detailed information, see appendix 1.

TrainForTrade trained participants from 116 different countries during this 5-year period (see map 1). Africa and Latin America and the Caribbean regions accounted for the bulk of this capacity development, with 55 per cent and 37 per cent of all persons trained, respectively (either face-to-face or via distance learning).

Map 1. Nationalities of participants in TrainForTrade courses, 2014-2018

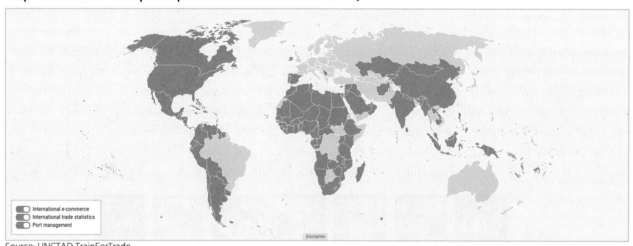

Source: UNCTAD TrainForTrade.

Focus on port management and international trade

During the last five years, TrainForTrade has focused on three areas: (1) port management; (2) international e-commerce; and (3) international trade statistics. Port management supports port communities in implementing efficient and competitive port management services. The e-commerce training covers legal aspects of e-commerce, best practices and digital identity, while the statistics training pertains to the compilation and use of trade-in-services statistics and merchandise trade statistics. Courses are currently offered in English, French and Spanish. Previously, courses were also completed in Portuguese – this option may again become available with funding.

TrainForTrade combines distance learning with face-to-face training. This is a an environmentally friendly and cost-efficient method of delivering high-quality training that offers considerable flexibility, making it a pragmatic approach for today's busy world (for more information, see UNCTAD (2020a)). Between 2014 and 2018, UNCTAD held a total of 150 TrainForTrade courses, either as face-to-face training or distance learning.

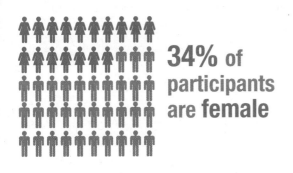

34% of participants are female

Overall, 34 per cent of all participants between 2014 to 2018 were female (table 1). The higher proportion of male participants is partly explained by the fact that some courses are aimed at work forces that are themselves male-dominated. This is especially true of port management, which heavily influences the overall ratio. Of course, participation in face-to-face training also depends on countries' nominations. In total, distance learning had more female participants (44 per cent) than face-to-face training (29 per cent). This is true even when only including courses that were offered as both face-to-face training and as distance learning (in that case the corresponding proportions of female participants were 44 and 36 per cent; see table 2 for gender distribution for each component and mode).

Table 2. Capacity development provided by TrainForTrade by programme component and mode of training, totals for the period 2014-2018

Programme area	Component	Mode	Number of participants total	Proportion female	Total amount of training in hours	Total amount of training in days	Number of countries receiving training
Port management	Port management	Face-to-face	2 318	25%	267 484	33 436	24
Port management	Port performance	Face-to-face	102	30%	3 264	408	18
Port management	Training the trainers	Face-to-face	453	32%	21 306	2 663	34
Port management	Training the trainers	Distance learning	33	33%	256	32	7
International e-commerce	E-commerce best practices	Distance learning	430	37%	12 252	1 532	18
International e-commerce	E-commerce for practitioners	Face-to-face	103	24%	2 713	339	11
International e-commerce	E-commerce for practitioners	Distance learning	363	19%	7 258	907	14
International e-commerce	Internet governance workshop	Face-to-face	75	41%	2 072	259	13
International e-commerce	Legal aspect of e-commerce	Face-to-face	183	43%	5 304	663	45
International e-commerce	Legal aspect of e-commerce	Distance learning	697	54%	17 808	2 226	43
International trade statistics	International merchandise trade statistics	Face-to-face	23	87%	736	92	14
International trade statistics	International merchandise trade statistics	Distance learning	140	69%	3 360	420	29
International trade statistics	International services trade statistics	Face-to-face	80	40%	3 024	378	47
International trade statistics	International services trade statistics	Distance learning	385	47%	11 020	1 378	85

Source: UNCTAD TrainForTrade.
Notes: For detailed information, see appendix 1.

As is evident in table 2, port management is the main programme area of TrainForTrade. This training accounts for 54 per cent of all participants and 82 per cent of training days. It is an intensive development programme designed to support ports to implement efficient and competitive port management services to increase trade flows and foster sustainable economic development.

> *One of the greatest successes of the UNCTAD program was to bring us together – the government with the private sector – to unite efforts and have the same vision for our ports*
> — Mr. Bismark Rosales, Port Manager - Jennefer, Bolivia, 2018

Capacity development relating to e-commerce accounted for 34 per cent of persons trained but only 13 per cent of training days. More recently, trade statistics have become an important aspect of capacity development and accounted for 12 per cent of persons trained. This includes courses in IMTS and SITS that both efficiently blend distance learning and face-to-face training. For example, SITS is jointly run by UNCTAD Statistics and TrainForTrade and begins with a six-week online training course run by a facilitator. Candidates who successfully complete the course and pass the online tests may be invited to regional face-to-face workshops to further develop their knowledge. The face-to-face workshops are often run in cooperation with the United Nations Statistics Division and the World Trade Organization.

Over 450 people trained and employed as trainers – promoting South-South cooperation

453 trainers' skills developed in 2014-2018

Training of trainers is an important component of the port management training. Between 2014 and 2018, 453 trainers were trained and employed as trainers. In most cases, these trainers were employed in their own countries. A particularly important element of this course is to develop trainers from the South, for each of the three language networks (English, French, Spanish), who then go on to train others from the South; i.e. a trainer from one developing country trains future trainers in another developing country. In doing so, TrainForTrade makes an important, albeit indirect, contribution to South-South Cooperation – an important ambition of SDG 17. Over the last five years, 78 trainers from the Global South were trained and subsequently provided training in other developing countries. Of these, 18 per cent were female (see table 3). The French-speaking network has trained the largest number of trainers from the South – these trainers largely serve Francophone West Africa.

Table 3. Total number of trainers trained by TrainForTrade, 2014-2018

		Total participants		Participants from one developing country employed in another	
		Total	Proportion female	Total	Proportion female
By language network	English	174	34%	17	35%
	French	181	33%	37	11%
	Spanish	98	29%	24	17%
By region	Asian	93	38%	10	50%
	African	243	30%	43	12%
	Latin America	117	32%	25	16%
Total		453	32%	78	18%

Source: UNCTAD TrainForTrade.

High certification and satisfaction rates among participants

TrainForTrade enjoys high certification and satisfaction rates, see table 4. Between 2014 and 2018, 82 per cent of participants received certificates after having completed their courses and passed online exams. The average satisfaction rate among participants was also high, at 84 per cent.

For additional testimonials, see the TrainForTrade Golden Book (UNCTAD, 2020b).

Certification and satisfaction rates both above 80%

Table 4. TrainForTrade certification and satisfaction rates

Year(s)	Total participants certified	Proportion female	Certification rate	Satisfaction rate
2014	859	44%	87%	-
2015	571	33%	82%	88%
2016	409	45%	80%	78%
2017	715	37%	81%	85%
2018	365	55%	76%	82%
2014-2018	**2 919**	**42%**	**82%**	**84%**

Source: UNCTAD TrainForTrade.
Notes: For detailed information, see appendix 1. Proportion female and satisfaction rate based on courses that have those figures recorded. The relatively low certification rate for 2018 is noteworthy. For some courses, a low certification rate does not reflect participants failing their tests, but rather not being able to attend the course due to administrative constraints. This is true for a SITS face-to-face workshop in 2018.

Notes

1. As some persons participate in more than one course, the number of participants does not equal the number of individuals.

References

- UNCTAD (2020a). TrainForTrade. See https://tft.unctad.org (accessed 12 June 2020).
- UNCTAD (2020b). Testimonials. Available at https://tft.unctad.org/tft_documents/testimonials/ (accessed 12 June 2020).

UNCTAD DMFAS programme – Strengthening debt management in support of good governance

Concerns regarding rising levels of debt and vulnerabilities in developing economies have drawn attention to problems with the transparency of debt statistics. There is broad consensus across the international community, including the G20 (World Bank and IMF, 2018) and the United Nations General Assembly (United Nations, 2020), that enhancing information sharing could help to avoid new episodes of debt distress.

Mandated by the UN General Assembly (United Nations, 2020) and UNCTAD member States (UNCTAD, 2016 para. 38.h), the UNCTAD DMFAS programme (UNCTAD, 2020) advises developing and transition economies in debt management and helps them to record and report reliable debt statistics for policy making. UNCTAD work on the recording, reporting and monitoring of debt statistics (the 'downstream' areas of debt management) complements the work of the World Bank and the IMF who focus primarily on data sustainability analysis and medium-term debt strategies ('upstream' debt management). The DMFAS programme follows a four-year strategic plan, currently focusing on the Programme's comparative advantages in technical assistance in the area of operational debt management, from debt data recording and statistical reporting up through basic debt analysis (UNCTAD, 2015).

The Programme is funded through bilateral donor contributions, cost-sharing by beneficiaries, which has steadily increased over the past 10 years, and UNCTAD's regular budget. The current donors include Germany, Ireland, the Netherlands, Switzerland and the European Union. Donors consider the DMFAS programme crucial for improving debt management:

> We congratulate the DMFAS program and the DMFAS user countries for the successful implementation of the 2016-2019 Strategy and the positive evaluation findings which demonstrate the effectiveness and clear added-value of the Programme.
>
> The DMFAS Programme provides a modern, effective and reliable system to register and store debt data, perform safe and accurate debt transactions and facilitate reporting and transparency. More importantly, the DMFAS program offers a comprehensive capacity development framework that accompanies users from the installation of the system up to the point of reporting and analysis.
>
> — Donor's statement, November 2019

> UNCTAD's DMFAS system contributes to improvements in governance by increasing data availability". "... DMFAS has contributed to more complete and transparent reporting on debt.
> — Assessment of UNCTAD: MI 9.3. (MOPAN, 2019)

Sustainable debt is important for sustainable development

Timely and comprehensive statistics on the levels and composition of debt are a prerequisite not only for the effective management of public liabilities but also for identifying risks of debt crises and limiting their impact (United Nations, 2020). Reliable debt statistics contribute to the formulation of financial policies and strategies, and consequently to improvement of financial stability and governance.

> *[The General Assembly] reiterates that timely and comprehensive data on the level and composition of debt are necessary for, inter alia, building early warning systems aimed at limiting the impact of debt crises, calls for debtor and creditor countries to intensify their efforts to collect and release data.*
>
> — United Nations (2020)

The DMFAS programme contributes directly to the achievement of SDG 17.4 of the 2030 Agenda as it assists "in attaining long-term debt sustainability through coordinated policies aimed at fostering debt financing, debt relief and debt restructuring". Training workshops, capacity-development and software tools enable better debt management and reporting that help developing countries to improve their financial policies. The work also contributes indirectly to poverty reduction (SDG 1) as better debt management and debt relief can help to take steps towards economic recovery for heavily indebted poor countries.

> *[The DMFAS Advisory Group] appreciates that the Programme continues to be highly relevant for developing countries, bilateral donors and other organizations, that it is highly responsive to the needs of debt management offices and that it is making an important contribution to the achievement of the Sustainable Development Goals.*
>
> — UNCTAD (2017 para 2)

DMFAS offers software, training and advisory services

The DMFAS programme offers countries a set of practical solutions for the management of public liabilities and the production of debt statistics. These include:

- DMFAS debt management and financial analysis software designed to meet the operational, statistical and analytical needs of debt managers and public debt strategies. This includes training in the installation, maintenance and use of the software.
- Capacity development in debt management skills through modules on debt data validation, statistics, debt portfolio analysis and operational risk management.
- Advisory services, including needs assessments and advice on technical, administrative, legal and institutional debt management. This includes assistance interfacing the DMFAS database with countries' integrated financial management systems.

Currently, 58 countries and 84 institutions around the world use DMFAS software for debt management. The software has been continuously improved and is now in its sixth edition since 1982. The software is available in four languages (English, French, Russian and Spanish).

DMFAS software is available in English, French, Russian and Spanish and used in 58 countries by 84 institutions

🌐 **Map 1. Geographical distribution of active DMFAS countries, December 2020**

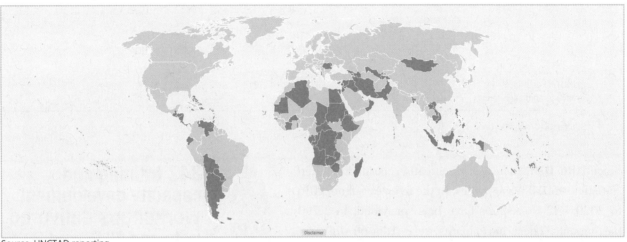

Source: UNCTAD reporting.

DMFAS has trained experts from 64 countries in debt management

Table 1 shows the number of officers that have benefited from training in debt management procedures and best practices between 2011 and 2020. In total, between 2011 and 2020, 5 755 people from 64 countries were trained by DMFAS. In addition, on average 370 experts participated in each UNCTAD Debt Management Conference held every second year since 2011.

Close to 5755 participants from debt offices over the last 10 years

Table 1. Number of participants in capacity development events organized by DMFAS

		2011	2012	2013	2014	2015	2016	2017	2018	2019	2020	2011 - 2020
Capacity development for debt offices	Training in debt validation, reporting and analysis	90	345	195	240	138	282	184	209	200	72	1 955
	Functional training in using DMFAS	324	276	192	245	120	244	134	233	159	91	2 001
	IT related training and advisory services	100	125	80	70	60	152	71	132	43	54	887
	Other advisory services	55	90	96	95	27	73	95	123	95	144	912
	Total	569	836	563	650	345	751	484	697	497	361	5 755
UNCTAD debt management conference		380	-	310	-	343	-	390	-	430	-	1 853

Source: UNCTAD reporting.

Since 2016, DMFAS has systematically recorded detailed statistics on DMFAS activities. In the five years from 2016 to 2020, 342 workshops have been provided, to 2 790 participants. These participants were from 64 different countries and 42 per cent were female (see table 2).

342 training and capacity development workshops delivered between 2016 and 2020

Table 2. Number of DMFAS capacity development events organized by UNCTAD and number of participants, 2016-2020

			Number of events	Total participant	Proportion female
Capacity development for debt offices	Training in debt validation, reporting and analysis	Data validation (initial)	22	263	52.5%
		Data validation (follow-up)	10	192	58.9%
		Debt statistics (initial)	9	132	41.7%
		Debt statistics (follow-up)	2	13	23.1%
		Debt portfolio analysis (initial)	8	119	37.8%
		Debt portfolio analysis (follow-up)	3	40	42.5%
		Other debt related training	13	188	34.6%
	Functional training in using DMFAS	Functional training in using DMFAS	69	844	47.6%
	IT related training and advisory services	DMFAS Installation and other IT workshops	44	204	27.0%
		Interfacing DMFAS with other systems[1]	33	248	39.5%
	Other advisory services	Implementation in partnership with DMF[2]	20	109	36.7%
		Workshops in coordination with partners	35	253	40.7%
		Expertise exchange study tours	35	168	51.2%
		Workshops relating to countries' projects	39	19	47.4%
	Total		342	2 792	41.5%
UNCTAD debt management conference			2	820	33.2%

Source: UNCTAD reporting.
Notes:
[1] Workshops in interfacing DMFAS with other financial management information systems
[2] Debt Management Facility (World Bank, 2020), including missions in DMFAS user countries for debt management performance assessment, medium-term debt management strategy and debt management reform plans

Increasing DMFAS debt coverage facilitates debt management

Debt data recorded with the DMFAS software are easier to manage and report transparently to support financial policy and stability. The DMFAS software facilitates the recording of both external and domestic debt. The DMFAS programme uses a 90 per cent threshold to determine whether a country has comprehensive coverage of their government external debt; i.e., if a country has at least 90 per cent of external debt instruments covered in the DMFAS system it is considered comprehensive. The same 90 per cent threshold is set for government domestic debt.

Figure 1 shows that over the last nine years, a consistently high proportion of DMFAS countries had comprehensive data on external debt. In 2020, 52 of the 57 countries using DMFAS had at least 90 per cent of external debt instruments recorded in DMFAS.

Over the last 10 year the number of countries recording domestic debt using DMFAS has increased from 4 to 41

4 → 41

Figure 1 also shows an increasing number of countries using DMFAS to record domestic debt. The number of countries with comprehensive data on domestic debt also increased over the time period, but the figure shows that it takes some time for new DMFAS users to develop a more comprehensive debt database. In 2020, 41 institutions were recording domestic debt in DMFAS. Among these 41 institutions, 28 had at least 90 per cent of domestic debt recorded in DMFAS.

Figure 1. Number of countries recording debt using DMFAS

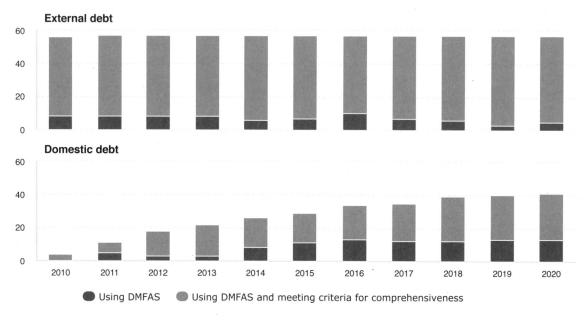

Source: UNCTAD reporting.

DMFAS helps to improve transparency and quality of debt reporting

The DMFAS programme also supports its clients to disseminate debt statistics and to perform debt analysis. The programme does this by offering initial and follow-up capacity development modules. For example, a first module helps countries to develop their first debt statistics bulletin; a second helps them to review and improve the content of the existing publications.

Both the number of DMFAS user countries that publish debt statistics bulletins and that publish debt portfolio reviews on a regular basis has increased during the last seven years (see figure 2). Countries publishing debt statistics have increased from 26 to 36 and countries publishing debt analysis have increased from 12 to 32. In 2020, some countries experienced a setback in publishing a debt bulletins due mainly to the disruptions related to the COVID-19 sanitary crisis.

Figure 2. Number of DMFAS-supported countries publishing debt reports on a regular basis

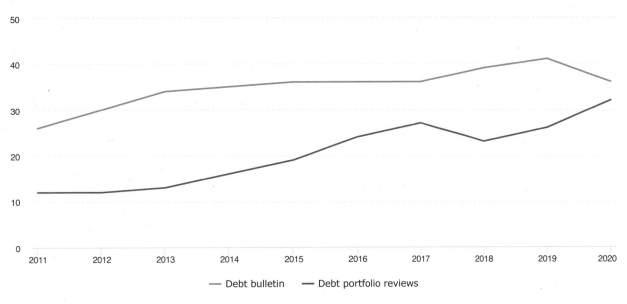

Source: UNCTAD reporting.

More integrated operation risk management with DMFAS

Several countries have asked that the DMFAS debt management operations be integrated with other financial management systems, such as those typically used by treasury departments and budget departments. The latest version of DMFAS software includes this facility, improving the accuracy and timeliness of debt service payments and debt data. As a result, the number of countries where DMFAS is integrated with other financial management information systems has increased from 8 countries in 2006 to 23 countries in 2020 (figure 3).

 Figure 3. Number of countries with interfaces between DMFAS database and other financial management information systems

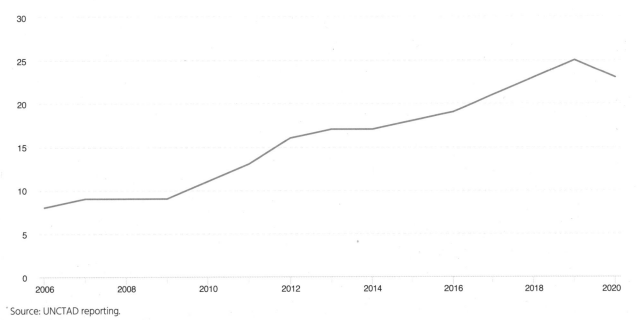

Source: UNCTAD reporting.

References

- IMF (2014). *External Debt Statistics: Guide for Compilers and Users*. IMF. Washington, D.C.
- UNCTAD (2015). DMFAS programme strategic plan 2016 - 2019: Strengthening the foundations for effective debt management. Available at https://unctad.org/divs/gds/dmfas/who/Pages/Our-Strategic-Plan.aspx (accessed 15 May 2019).
- UNCTAD (2016). Nairobi Maafikiano. From decision to action: Moving towards an inclusive and equitable global economic environment for trade and development. TD/519/Add.2. Nairobi. 5 September.
- UNCTAD (2020). Available at http://unctad.org/dmfas (accessed 19 May 2019).
- United Nations (2020). Resolution adopted by the General Assembly on 29 December 2020 on external debt sustainability and development. A/RES/75/205. New York. (accessed 17 May 2021).
- WHO (2020). Q&A on coronaviruses (COVID-19). Available at https://www.who.int/emergencies/diseases/novel-coronavirus-2019/question-and-answers-hub/q-a-detail/q-a-coronaviruses (accessed 11 May 2020).
- World Bank (2020). Available at http://www.worldbank.org/en/topic/debt/brief/debt-management-facility (accessed 11 June 2020).
- World Bank and IMF (2018). Strengthening public debt transparency: The role of the IMF and the World Bank June. Available at http://documents.worldbank.org/curated/en/991171532695036951/Strengthening-public-debt-transparency-the-role-of-the-IMF-and-the-World-Bank-G20-note (accessed 6 June 2019).

UNCTAD Empretec – Inspiring entrepreneurship

UNCTAD Empretec[1] (UNCTAD, 2020) promotes entrepreneurship and enhances the productive capacity and international competitiveness of SMEs in developing countries. The Empretec programme is implemented through its national centres, established in 40 countries. Empretec's core product, the Entrepreneurship training workshop, promotes behavioural changes that helps entrepreneurs put their ideas into action and helps fledgling businesses to grow.

> *One of the best programs I've ever been. It was an eye-opening experience for me because I realized what I have to do more to become successful (or more successful) in my business.*
>
> — Marcus Schmidt, CEO, Siedler Alarm

Empretec enhances entrepreneurial skills and competences

The objective of Empretec training workshops is to develop entrepreneurship. In practice, this means developing a set of specific competencies and practices that can be acquired and applied by entrepreneurs. Training is delivered by 600 local, certified trainers and by a pool of approximately 30 international, master trainers. All trainers are themselves entrepreneurs.

Target beneficiaries include micro, small and medium sized businesses; youth entrepreneurs; women entrepreneurs; and intrapreneurs[2]. The Empretec programme targets SMEs with a track record of good business performance, potential entrepreneurs with promising business ideas, and start-up companies with bankable project proposals. Training should lead to SME growth, linkages with larger enterprises including MNEs, job creation and increased investment. Empretec also supports and promotes entrepreneurship among women and provides tailored mentoring and training. The Women in Business Awards also contribute to realizing these aims.

Empretec trains managers or intrapreneurs to identify business opportunities. It also trains employees to adapt to changes, like downsizing or outsourcing, or those who have lost their job and would like to start their own businesses. Empretec also participates in the Global Entrepreneurship Week (Global Entrepreneurship Network, 2020) with the aim of inspiring young people to embrace innovation, imagination and creativity.

Empretec contributes directly to SDG 4 and its target 4.4 to substantially increase the number of youth and adults who have relevant skills, including technical and vocational skills, for employment, decent jobs and entrepreneurship by 2030. It also supports SDG 8 and its target 8.3 to promote development-oriented policies for productive activities, decent job creation, entrepreneurship, creativity and innovation and in support of micro, small and medium enterprises. In addition, Empretec supports the achievement of the 2030 Agenda more widely, as it contributes indirectly to progress towards SDGs 1 (no poverty), 2 (zero hunger), 5 (gender equality), 10 (reduced inequalities), and 17 (partnerships for the SDGs). See the UNCTAD Toolbox (UNCTAD, 2015) on entrepreneurship development for more details about the link between Empretec and the SDGs.

Entrepreneurs train entrepreneurs in Empretec training activities

Empretec has active training centres in 40 locations around the world. Since its inception in 1988, Empretec has successfully trained over 477 000 people, or *empretecos*, helping them to found or expand businesses and create jobs in the process.

Almost half a million persons trained since 1988
477000

📊 **Figure 1. Cumulative number of empretecos trained**
(Thousands of persons)

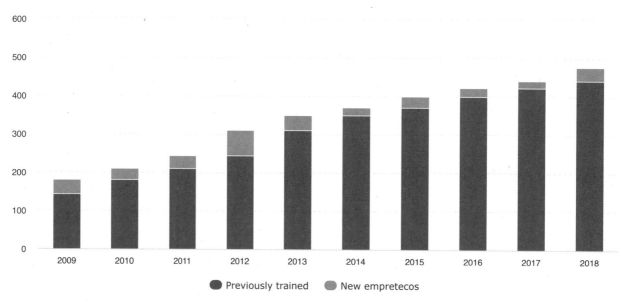

● Previously trained   ● New empretecos

Source: UNCTAD Empretec.

Over 4000 workshops between 2014 and 2018

Since 2014, Empretec has collected activity and outcome statistics on a regular and systematic basis. Between 2014 and 2018, more than 4 000 workshops have been held at which more than 103 000 people were trained.

Table 1. Number of Empretec workshops and persons trained

Region	Centres	Workshops	Number of people trained					
		2014 - 2018	2014	2015	2016	2017	2018	2014 - 2018
Sub-Saharan Africa	17	790	6 144	6 928	5 939	5 182	4 909	29 102
Latin America and the Caribbean	15	3 326	12 299	17 280	14 941	13 828	14 859	73 207
Central Asia	1	12	75	21	96	-	72	264
Western Asia	3	23	365	93	32	-	22	512
South-Eastern Asia	2	8	-	176	-	-	-	176
Europe	2	10	120	-	113	-	-	233
Total	**40**	**4 169**	**19 003**	**24 498**	**21 121**	**19 010**	**19 862**	**103 494**

Source: UNCTAD Empretec.
Note: See appendix 1 for workshops per year and figures per country.

Latin America and the Caribbean and Sub-Saharan Africa accounted for the bulk of this capacity development, accounting for 80 and 19 percent of the workshops, respectively, and 71 and 28 percent of all persons trained, respectively.

 Map 1. Geographical distribution of Empretec training centres

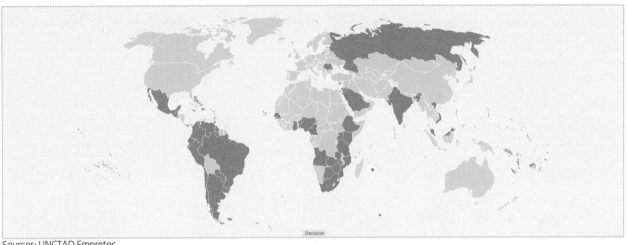

Sources: UNCTAD Empretec.

> VERY useful as it focused on me as a person. It forced me to take a hard and honest look at myself and the way I do things and defined precisely strong and weak points.
> — Stephane Ferraton, Head of Procurement, Swiss Federal Railways in 2016

Empretec's Women in Business Awards focus on women's role in advancing the SDGs

In 2008, Empretec launched the Women in Business Awards for developing countries. The award is granted every two years to women who have participated in Empretec training to become outstanding businesswomen. Table 2 shows that African and Latin American countries account for the majority of entries (47 percent and 44 percent respectively). Despite a modest number of entries, Western Asia, in particular Jordan, has been very successful, garnering four podium positions, including two first places, in 2008 and 2014.

In 2018, civil engineer Uneiza Ali Issufo won the Women in Business Gold Award. She is the founder of ConsMoz Ltd., a construction company based in Nampula, Mozambique. She was awarded this prize for her commitment to quality, sustainability and environmental protection, as well as her pioneering leadership in a traditionally male-led sector. After participating in an Empretec entrepreneurship training workshop in 2017, Ms. Issufo was able to expand her business so that it now employs 800 people and lands large building contracts demanding top quality and green credentials.

Table 2. Women in Business Awards

Region	Number of entries							Number of top 3 rankings
	2008	2010	2012	2014	2016	2018	2008 - 2018	2008 - 2018
Sub-Saharan Africa	14	23	10	15	25	25	112	8
Southern and South-Eastern Asia	0	0	1	0	2	1	4	1
Latin America and the Caribbean	9	18	26	17	21	16	107	5
Western Asia	1	2	3	5	5	4	20	4
Total	**24**	**43**	**40**	**37**	**53**	**46**	**243**	

Source: UNCTAD Empretec.

Empretec is a stepping stone on the way to more business activity

About half of the Empretec centres have followed up on the business activities of empretecos at three and twelve months after the workshops. Participants have been followed up on four measures: sales, number of employees, profitability of the participants' businesses and number of businesses started among the participants.

Participants in Empretec workshops increase their business activity during the year after the workshop by 34 to 38%

Table 3 shows the average percentage increases reported by centres. The follow-up shows that after the workshops, empretecos have increased their business activity on all four indicators. Over the 5-year period from 2013 to 2017, the average increase over three months ranges from 12 per cent for the number of people employed to 25 per cent for the number of new businesses created. The corresponding numbers after twelve months are 34 and 38 per cent.[3]

Table 3. Business activity among empretecos after the Empretec workshops

(Percentage increase from baseline, at follow-up times of 3 and 12 months)

Indicator	3-month follow-up					12-month follow-up				
	2013	2014	2015	2016	2017	2013	2014	2015	2016	2017
Sales	14	14	16	17	21	32	38	31	31	42
People employed	13	11	8	14	15	37	44	28	33	27
Profitability	12	17	14	16	22	29	45	36	32	40
New businesses	10	22	15	44	33	27	37	31	29	63

Source: UNCTAD Empretec.

Notes: Numbers displayed are arithmetic averages of improvements (in percentage) reported by centers at country level. Reports that were not in the form of percentages are excluded from this average. On average the numbers are based on 8 reports (range 5–11). See appendix 2 for figures per country.

Notes

1. Empretec is a Spanish acronym which blends *emprendedores* (entrepreneurs) and *tecnología* (technology). The term was introduced in Argentina in 1988.

2. Intrapreneur refers to a manager within a company who promotes innovative product development and marketing

3. Unfortunately, no control groups are available. Therefore, the growth figures presented here cannot be compared with enterprises in same sectors and size classes that did not participate in Empretec

References

- Global Entrepreneurship Network (2020). Global Entrepreneurship Week. See https://www.genglobal.org/gew (accessed 12 June 2020).

- UNCTAD (2015). UNCTAD Toolbox: Delivering results. UNCTAD/TC/2015/1/iPub. Available at https://unctad.org/en/Pages/TC/TC-Products-in-the-Toolbox.aspx (accessed 7 June 2019).

- UNCTAD (2020). Empretec: Inspiring entrepreneurship. See https://empretec.unctad.org/ (accessed 12 June 2020).

Trade facilitation – making trade easier and faster

Administrative hurdles and cumbersome border procedures can account for 75 per cent of all delays to shipments. The main objective of trade facilitation is to reduce the complexities and costs associated with lengthy border procedures and controls, while maintaining efficient compliance controls. Trade facilitation contributes to the achievement of the 2030 Agenda, in particular to the integration of developing countries to global trade, tackling trade barriers and improving the efficiency of trade by reducing delays and transaction costs.

To facilitate the implementation of the technical and institutional obligations arising from the 2017 WTO TFA, the UNCTAD Trade Facilitation Programme UNCTAD (2020a) improves trade processes and competitiveness of developing countries, including economies in transition, LDCs, LLDCs and SIDS. The programme aims to support trade facilitation reforms and countries' capacity to comply with related international and regional rules and standards, including WTO commitments.

I have learned so much in this programme. Now, I think of trade facilitation in a different way. I understand better all the things that the Sudan can do and how important it is to mainstream trade facilitation in its development policy.

— Mohammed Adam, rapporteur of Sudan NTFC

Supporting national trade facilitation committees

By providing intensive professional training - via the Empowerment Programme for National Trade Facilitation Committees – UNCTAD helps committees fulfil their mandate and implement, in a coordinated manner, trade facilitation reforms, including the provisions of the Agreement on Trade Facilitation, and monitor implementation. UNCTAD also supplies technical assistance, including: tailored training in trade, transit and transport facilitation[1]; advisory services on ratification of the Agreement; and assistance in the creation and sustainable operation of national trade facilitation committees.

The UNCTAD Trade Facilitation Programme assists developing countries with the implementation of trade facilitation measures, such as needs assessments and development of national trade facilitation and project plans. UNCTAD capacity building and advisory services help countries to monitor and evaluate trade facilitation initiatives, establish legal frameworks for trade-related single windows, simplify trade procedures and train national transit coordinators. UNCTAD also supports regional trade facilitation initiatives.

The effectiveness of the programme stems from strong cooperation not only with external partners such as the World Customs Organization and the International Trade Centre, but also with other experts within UNCTAD, working at the crossroads of trade facilitation with customs automation and e-commerce or non-tariff measures.

Trade facilitation – has assisted 56 countries since 2016

Since 2016, UNCTAD has developed capacity in 56 countries around the world to improve their trade facilitation. Of these, 34 countries were in Africa, 10 in Latin America and the Caribbean and 12 in Asia and Oceania. In total, 21 countries were SIDS and 17 LLDCs (see Map 1). 60 per cent of capacity development was done in English, 35 per cent in French, and 5 per cent in Portuguese.

Map 1. Countries receiving UNCTAD trade facilitation support in the empowerment programme (4 categories)

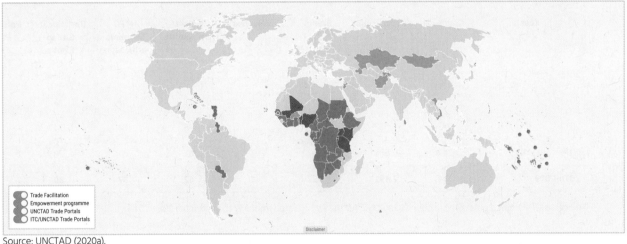

Source: UNCTAD (2020a).

Of those 56 countries, 45 are WTO Members. 89 per cent of them have ratified the WTO trade facilitation agreement and 96 per cent have notified to the WTO Committee on Trade Facilitation their category A, B and C provisions.

The UNCTAD Trade Facilitation Programme builds on the cooperation with other related UNCTAD technical assistance programmes, such as the UNCTAD ASYCUDA , which is used by the Customs administrations of over 90 countries, and UNCTAD Trade Portals. These programmes are key instruments for the implementation of various provisions of the WTO TFA.

UNCTAD Empowerment Programme

The UNCTAD Empowerment Programme (UNCTAD, 2020b), as part of the wider Trade Facilitation programe, provides an intensive professional programme for NTFCs. The main objective is to help them implement trade facilitation reforms in a coordinated manner, including the provisions of the WTO FTA. This programme is undertaken in cooperation with a number of partners, including the ITC, Deutsche Gesellschaft für Internationale Zusammenarbeit, UNECE, UNIDO, World Bank Group, World Customs Organization and the WTO.

Almost 2,500 participants trained since 2016

Since 2016, the Empowerment Programme has trained almost 2,500 people in 34 countries. Of these, 24 countries completed the full empowerment programme and 10 received other support to their NTFCs. 26 countries are African, and eight were from Latin America and the Caribbean (see Map 1). On average female

Since 2016, 34 countries have completed the Empowerment Programme

participation was 42 per cent, but this ranged from as high as 73 per cent in some countries to no female paticipation in one country. 19 per cent of participants were from the private sector and 81 per cent from the public. Members of the NTFCs accounted for 57 per cent of course participants on average. 80 per cent of participants sat the exams, with 91 per cent of those successfully passing. In 2020, a further eight countries in Africa began receiving support.

Table 1. Total capacity development training provided by Empowerment Programme

	Number of					Per cent		
Year	Countries	Participants	Events	Languages	Female participation	NTFC Members participation	Participants Sitting Exams	Participants Passed Exams
2016	3	291	9	1	45	43	96	94
2017	14	1 162	30	3	29	69	71	84
2018	12	402	18	3	45	54	74	96
2019	12	636	35	1	52	61	78	91
2016-2019	**34**	**2 491**	**92**	**3**	**42**	**57**	**80**	**91**

Source: UNCTAD, based on answers received to an UNCTAD survey circulated from July to September 2019.

Empowerment programme supports NTFCs

> *The knowledge shared by the resource experts has encouraged greatly the inter-agency collaboration in Nigeria to enhance trade and reduce time as well as cost of imports and exports.*
>
> — Austin Oko Opiege, Member of Nigeria NTFC

94% of countries apply the knowledge acquired

support their NTFCs.

UNCTAD evaluates the training by collecting feedback from participants. According to this feedback, 94 per cent of respondents reported using the knowledge acquired during training. 87 per cent reported improved knowledge of trade facilitation, and 78 per cent felt they were in a better position to

 Table 2. Feedback on training

(Percentage)

Year	Improved knowledge of trade facilitation	Improved specific knowledge	Taking exams helped	Practical Exercices helped	Participants better able to support NTFC
2016	85	82	66	84	75
2017	79	76	43	72	70
2018	88	85	51	69	78
2019	97	95	63	95	90
2016-2019	**87**	**84**	**56**	**80**	**78**

Source: UNCTAD, based on answers received to an UNCTAD survey circulated from July to September 2019.

All countries make changes after training

All 34 countries reported making changes during and after taking the UNCTAD Empowerment Programme. 10 countries introduced supporting legislation, 20 drafted terms of reference, 20 prepared trade facilitation roadmaps and 26 issued notifications in preparation for the WTO TFA.

Table 3. Number of countries implementing changes

(by type of changes and year)

Year	Countries implementing changes	Types of changes implemented								
		Legislation	ToRs	Project proposal	Roadmap	Knowledge Transfer Strategies	Repository Case	NTFC Workplans	Notifications to WTO TFA	Other
2016	3	1	2	1	1	1	1	2	2	0
2017	14	2	5	4	4	3	9	2	10	5
2018	12	3	6	2	7	3	3	5	5	0
2019	12	4	7	7	8	6	0	7	9	4
2016-2019	34	10	20	14	20	13	13	16	26	9

Source: UNCTAD, based on answers received to an UNCTAD survey circulated from July to September 2019.

The feedback shows that the Empowerment Programme has helped countries prepare for the WTO trade facilitation negotiations and for the Agreement itself. Today, according to data gathered in the UNCTAD Repository for NTFCs (UNCTAD, 2020c), 103 countries have established NTFCs. 29 of these committees have only been established since 2016.

76% of participating countries send notification for 2017 WTO Trade Facilitation Agreement

Figure 1. "Year of establishment and cumulative number of NTFC

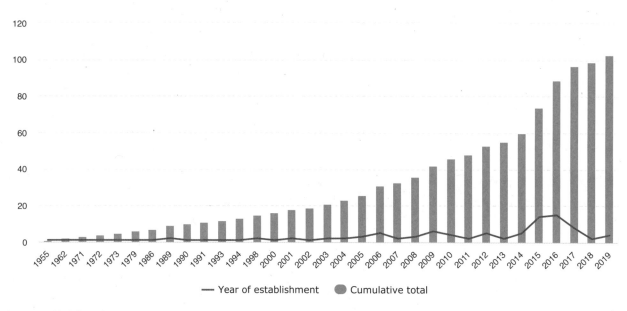

Source: UNCTAD (2020c).

In 2019, UNCTAD launched a series of online courses which recapitulate some of the key lessons of the Empowerment Programme. Since their launch in September 2019, up to March 2020, the online courses had registered 3,500 users, who have benefited from over 1,000 training hours. During 2020, UNCTAD plans to make these courses available additionally in French and Portuguese.

> *The courses show that trade facilitation is much more than just the Trade Facilitation Agreement, in that they also help to put the Agreement into a broader perspective by addressing the intricate interplay of the various provisions with commerce and the wider sustainable development agenda.*
>
> — Ricky Jnbaptiste, Attaché, Mission of the Organisation of Eastern Caribbean States in Geneva

Outcomes

UNCTAD's approach to supporting NTFCs in developing economies, including LDCs, seems to be working. This is reflected in the results of a survey undertaken during the summer of 2019, where countries benefitting from the Empowerment Programme reported being more optimistic about the sustainability of their Committees. On a scale of 0 to 100, LDCs that have been supported by UNCTAD rated the sustainability of their Committees at 63, compared to 50 for those committees that were not assisted by UNCTAD.

Notes

1. For more information, please see UNCTAD transport and trade facilitation newsletter (UNCTAD, 2020d).

References

- UNCTAD (2020a). Trade facilitation. Available at https://unctad.org/TF (accessed 6 May 2020).
- UNCTAD (2020b). Empowerment Programme for national trade facilitation bodies. Available at https://unctad.org/EPTF (accessed 6 May 2020).
- UNCTAD (2020c). Trade Facilitation Committees around the world. Available at https://unctad.org/TFC (accessed 6 May 2020).
- UNCTAD (2020d). Transport and trade facilitation newsletter. Available at http://unctad.org/transportnews (accessed 6 May 2020).
- WTO (2019). WTO trade facilitation agreement. Available at https://www.wto.org/english/tratop_e/tradfa_e/tradfa_e.htm (accessed 6 May 2020).

Adding to the sum of knowledge with research on trade and sustainable development

In July 2017, UNCTAD launched a new research paper series (UNCTAD, 2020). Since that time, 41 research papers have been published, which have been downloaded almost 86,000 times. This chapter provides a brief statistical overview of this series.

> " *Research is to see what everybody else has seen,*
> *and to think what nobody else has thought*
>
> — Albert Szent-Gyorgyi "

The papers cover a wide variety of topics, ranging from Brexit, to digital platforms, to fishery subsidies. For the purposes of this analysis, the research papers have been categorized into seven broad themes (see table 1). This is of course a simplification, as most papers deal with several complex themes simultaneously.

Table 1. Number of research papers published, by broad theme

Year of publication	Broad theme							Total
	Trade	Development / SDGs	Digital	Finance	Competition	Climate change	Industrialisation	
Jan - Mar 2020	2	0	-	-	1	-	-	3
2019	7	2	0	2	-	-	-	11
2018	7	2	1	1	-	1	-	12
July - Dec 2017	8	3	2	1	-	-	1	15
Total	**24**	**7**	**3**	**4**	**1**	**1**	**1**	**41**

Source: UNCTAD calculations based on data from UNCTAD (2020).

Trade related papers accounted for almost 60 per cent of all research papers published. They cover a rich variety of topics including tariffs, non-tariff measures, subsidies, gender-in-trade, global gender indices, nowcasting trade, development status, free trade agreements and value chains. Sustainable development, which included papers dealing with the political economy of SDG measurement, the digital and infrastructural divide, Big Data, enterprise contribution to SDGs and inclusive development, accounted for a further 17 per cent.

Research papers downloaded almost 86 000 times since July 2017

Since the series was launched in July 2017, almost 86,000 papers have been downloaded. Unsurprisingly, trade-related papers account for the bulk of these (70 per cent) – see table 2.

Table 2. Number of downloads by year of publication, year of download

Year	Number of downloads							
	Trade	Development / SDGs	Digital	Finance	Competition	Climate change	Industrialisation	Total
Per year of publication								
Jan - Mar 2020	2 420	-	-	-	853	-	-	3 273
2019	24 752	1 945	-	1 429	-	-	-	28 126
2018	9 559	2 218	2 259	441	-	4 110	-	18 587
July - Dec 2017	23 091	5 900	4 047	701	-	-	2 167	35 906
Total	**59 822**	**10 063**	**6 306**	**2 571**	**853**	**4 110**	**2 167**	**85 892**
Per year of download								
Jan - Mar 2020	14 019	1 117	930	357	853	795	145	18 216
2019	31 698	4 278	3 915	1 525	-	1 669	812	43 897
2018	13 521	3 724	1 461	689	-	1 646	923	21 964
July - Dec 2017	584	944	-	-	-	-	287	1 815
Total	**59 822**	**10 063**	**6 306**	**2 571**	**853**	**4 110**	**2 167**	**85 892**

Source: UNCTAD calculations based on data from UNCTAD (2020).

Table 2 shows that downloads have been steadily increasing, from less than 2,000 in the first year (2017), to almost 44,000 two years later.

The monthly UNCTAD research papers views are illustrated in figure 1. The total number of downloads has steadily increased since 2019, reaching more than 10 thousand in November 2019.

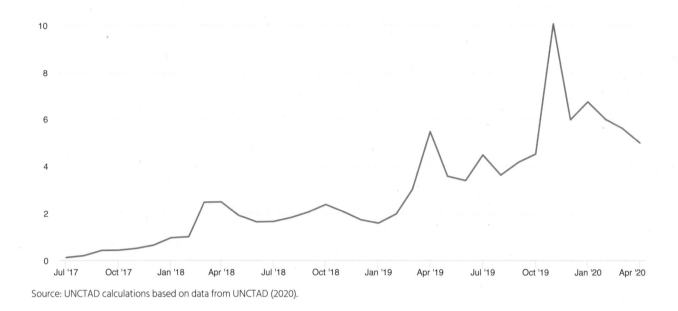

Figure 1. Publication downloads per month

(Thousands)

Source: UNCTAD calculations based on data from UNCTAD (2020).

The three most downloaded research papers are:

16,423 downloads: African Continental Free Trade Area: Challenges and Opportunities of Tariff Reductions (Saygili et al., 2017).

13,776 downloads: Trade and trade diversion effects of United States tariffs on China (Nicita, 2019).

6,114 downloads: Brexit. Implications for Developing Countries (Nicita et al., 2019).

These three papers account for more than 36,000 downloads, or 42 per cent of all UNCTAD research papers downloaded.

 Table 3. Number of research papers by UNCTAD Division

Year of publication	UNCTAD divisions					External	All
	ALDC	DGDS	DIAE	DITC	DTL		
Jan - Mar 2020	-	-	-	3	-	-	**3**
2019	-	6	-	5	-	-	**11**
2018	2	4	1	4	1	-	**12**
July - Dec 2017	5	1	-	5	1	3	**15**
Total	**7**	**11**	**1**	**17**	**2**	**3**	**41**

Source: UNCTAD calculations based on data from UNCTAD (2020).

Table 3 shows the number of research papers by division. In cases where a paper was co-authored by an UNCTAD staff member and an external author, that paper was classified to the division of the UNCTAD staff member. In cases where no UNCTAD staff were authors, papers were classified as 'external'. Given the prominence of trade related papers, it is not surprising that DITC accounted for more than 40 per cent of papers published.

Table 4. Number of research papers by SDG

Year of publication	SDG								All
	1	5	8	9	10	13	14	17	
Jan - Mar 2020	-	-	-	1	2	-	-	3	**6**
2019	-	1	-	1	2	-	3	8	**15**
2018	-	-	1	1	-	1	-	10	**13**
July - Dec 2017	1	-	-	3	2	-	-	12	**18**
Total	**1**	**1**	**1**	**6**	**6**	**1**	**3**	**33**	**52**

Source: UNCTAD calculations based on data from UNCTAD (2020).

The research papers have been coded to SDGs. As with theme classification, this is necessarily a simplification, as several papers deal with more than one SDG. In table 4, some papers are classified to two SDG goals, hence the total of 52 rather than 41. The importance of goals 9, 10 and 17 is evident.

Most UNCTAD research papers focus on SDG 17

It is important to note that research papers are only one of the release channels employed by UNCTAD. A number of flagship reports, publications, policy briefs, conference documents and news articles have also been published on topics relevant for sustainable development.

References

- Nicita A (2019). Trade and trade diversion effects of United States tariffs on China. UNCTAD Research Paper No. 37. UNCTAD/SER.RP/2019/9. (accessed 5 June 2020).

- Nicita A, Saygili M and Koloskova K (2019). Brexit. Implications for Developing Countries. UNCTAD Research Paper No. 31. UNCTAD/SER.RP/2019/3. (accessed 5 June 2020).

- Saygili M, Peters R and Knebel C (2017). African Continental Free Trade Area: Challenges and Opportunities of Tariff Reductions. UNCTAD Research Paper No. 15. UNCTAD/SER.RP/2017/15Rev.1. (accessed 5 June 2020).

- UNCTAD (2020). UNCTAD Research Paper (Series). Available at https://unctad.org/en/Pages/Publications/Research-Paper-Series.aspx (accessed 10 June 2020).

The convening power of UNCTAD

> **SDG indicators**
>
> SDG 17: Strengthen the means of implementation and revitalize the Global Partnership for Sustainable Development
>
> SDG target 17.16: Enhance the global partnership for sustainable development, complemented by multi-stakeholder partnerships that mobilize and share knowledge, expertise, technology and financial resources, to support the achievement of the sustainable development goals in all countries, in particular developing countries.
>
> SDG target 17.17: Encourage and promote effective public, public-private and civil society partnerships, building on the experience and resourcing strategies of partnerships.

The UN brings the world together to advance sustainable development and inclusive trade and economy for all important for a better future for people and the planet, cannot be realized without
increased and effective cooperation of all stakeholders at all levels (Sustainability Knowledge Group, 2020). UNCTAD uses its convening power to bring together governments, businesses, civil society, academia and other international organizations. Together they debate, exchange experiences, identify best practices, and develop global standards on the most pressing issues of the day. Most of these meetings and events take place at UNCTAD headquarters in Geneva, Switzerland.[1]

> *Alone we can do so little; together we can do so much*
>
> — Helen Keller

Meetings include intergovernmental meetings, such as the TDB and its subsidiary bodies, and the Commission on Science and Technology for Development, and fora, such as the Global Commodities Forum and e-Commerce Week. But included are also study visits, seminars, short courses for diplomats and bilateral government visits.

In 2019, UNCTAD hosted 290 meetings (as registered on the INDICO conference management system), up from 219 in 2017. For roughly 60 - 65 per cent of meetings, detailed participant information has been recorded, allowing more detailed analyses to be undertaken (see tables 2, 3 and 4). Of the meetings where no detailed participant information was recorded, more than a third

were internal UNCTAD meetings, including the UNCTAD Research Seminar Series, the UNCTAD Crossing the Line: Research in Motion series, the Secretary General's Town Hall meetings, and so forth. See table 1.[2]

Table 1. Number of meetings registered on INDICO conference management system, 2017-2019

Year	Total number of meetings registered on INDICO	Number of meetings with details	Number of meetings without details	Of which number of meetings without details of which external	Of which number of meetings without details of which internal
2019	290	189	101	60	41
2018	264	157	107	68	39
2017	219	136	83	50	33
Total	**773**	**482**	**291**	**178**	**113**

Source: UNCTAD calculations based on data from UNOG-Indico (2020).
Note: The data do not include meetings related to the World Investment Forum.

More than 12 000 delegates attended UNCTAD meetings in 2019

In 2019, 189 meetings were held for which detailed information is available. More than 12,000 delegates attended, of which almost 40 per cent (5,000) were female. Intergovernmental meetings, such as the TDB, and topics like e-commerce drew the largest numbers of participants, together accounting for more than 40 per cent of all participants. Both total and female participation numbers were up in 2019 compared with previous years. Investment (including the multi-year expert meeting on investment, innovation and entrepreneurship for productive capacity-building and sustainable development) and trade meetings (including the multi-year expert meetings on transport, trade logistics and trade facilitation and on trade, services and development) also attracted high participant numbers (see table 2).

40 % of delegates were female

Table 2. Number of registered meetings and participants, by broad meeting category and sex, 2017 - 2019

Theme	Number of events	Number of participants	Number of female participants	Number of female participants (%)
2019	189	12 277	4 871	40
Academic	50	1 228	725	59
ASYCUDA	18	73	17	23
Commodities	4	370	260	70
CSTD	4	683	65	10
Debt/Finance	14	759	218	29
Development/Climate	14	366	246	67
E-Commerce	7	2 627	993	38
Intergovernmental	12	2 632	896	34
Investment	12	1 163	479	41
Legal/Competition	4	442	157	36
Maritime	2	61	17	28
Other	29	534	268	50
Trade	19	1 339	530	40
2018	157	9 631	3 643	38
Academic	32	807	510	63
ASYCUDA	22	204	42	21
Commodities	6	933	278	30
CSTD	1	103	31	30
Debt/Finance	7	97	36	37
Development/Climate	12	380	108	28
E-Commerce	10	2 510	989	39
Intergovernmental	19	2 123	668	31
Investment	9	600	253	42
Legal/Competition	4	583	220	38
Maritime	4	286	104	36
Other	16	252	116	46
Trade	15	753	288	38
2017	136	9627	3359	35
Academic	25	570	322	57
ASYCUDA	15	58	13	22
Commodities	2	561	170	30
CSTD	6	523	155	30

Theme	Number of events	Number of participants	Number of female participants	Number of female participants (%)
Debt/Finance	9	673	227	34
Development/Climate	8	175	58	33
E-Commerce	8	1 446	577	40
Intergovernmental	17	2 312	714	31
Investment	7	880	323	37
Legal/Competition	4	466	179	38
Maritime	6	307	94	31
Other	20	838	266	32
Trade	9	818	261	32
2017 - 2019	482	31 535	11 873	38

Source: UNCTAD calculations based on data from UNOG-Indico (2020).

Representatives from national governments are the single largest group attending UNCTAD meetings, accounting for between 44 and 52 per cent, depending on the year. Academia, the private sector and non-governmental organizations together account for between 30 and 39 per cent. In 2019, more than 5,400 participants representing national governments attended UNCTAD meetings. This is an underestimate because, as noted in table 1, a further 60 external meetings were registered that year on the INDICO system, for which no participant details are available.

Table 3. Number of participants by broad meeting category, 2017 - 2019

Theme	Government	IGO (Inter Governmental Organizations)	United Nations	Private sector	Academia	NGO (Non Governmental Organizations)	Other	Press / media	Total number of participants
2019	**5 437**	**553**	**583**	**1249**	**2 297**	**1 226**	**897**	**35**	**12 277**
Academic	38	1	12	9	1 095	12	61	-	**1 228**
ASYCUDA	45	3	10	2	-	-	13	-	**73**
Commodities	318	43	34	85	44	103	55	1	**683**
CSTD	134	6	7	3	3	10	1	-	**164**
Debt/Finance	555	30	28	24	37	37	31	-	**742**
Development/Climate	188	68	49	86	68	112	16	2	**589**
E-Commerce	956	106	215	556	210	346	225	13	**2 627**
Intergovernmental	1 881	111	47	91	190	112	198	2	**2 632**
Investment	362	23	34	166	302	159	116	1	**1 163**
Legal/Competition	288	27	2	19	63	25	15	3	**442**
Maritime	19	5	2	13	4	5	13	-	**61**
Other	188	16	34	33	130	78	47	8	**534**
Trade	465	114	109	162	151	227	106	5	**1 339**
2018	**4 121**	**483**	**487**	**935**	**1710**	**965**	**890**	**40**	**9 631**
Academic	4	3	-	3	777	3	17	-	**807**
ASYCUDA	105	6	11	-	77	-	5	-	**204**
Commodities	420	64	37	127	70	99	113	3	**933**
CSTD	60	3	1	7	6	23	3	-	**103**
Debt/Finance	36	6	14	13	14	10	4	-	**97**
Development/Climate	203	37	36	24	26	30	24	-	**380**
E-Commerce	772	104	192	446	211	442	335	8	**2 510**
Intergovernmental	1 528	116	43	88	83	112	148	5	**2 123**
Investment	145	9	19	98	144	54	127	4	**600**
Legal/Competition	351	46	10	33	87	32	21	3	**583**
Maritime	131	22	33	26	27	27	20	-	**286**
Other	45	12	14	14	77	72	2	16	**252**
Trade	321	55	77	56	111	61	71	1	**753**
2017	**5 037**	**523**	**499**	**684**	**1 481**	**817**	**551**	**35**	**9 627**
Academic	-	-	-	-	566	-	4	-	**570**
ASYCUDA	42	3	6	1	3	-	3	-	**58**
Commodities	246	29	42	70	31	91	51	1	**561**

Theme	Government	IGO (Inter Governmental Organizations)	United Nations	Private sector	Academia	NGO (Non Governmental Organizations)	Other	Press / media	Total number of participants
CSTD	345	12	26	28	29	72	11	-	523
Debt/Finance	504	26	16	16	49	16	46	-	673
Development/Climate	83	14	26	8	11	24	9	-	175
E-Commerce	552	55	167	233	196	148	82	13	1 446
Intergovernmental	1 632	151	67	88	101	133	139	1	2 312
Investment	371	55	24	81	172	87	85	5	880
Legal/Competition	262	32	4	8	92	40	25	3	466
Maritime	104	26	24	55	37	48	10	3	307
Other	504	33	45	36	96	76	39	9	838
Trade	392	87	52	60	98	82	47	-	818
2017-2019	14 595	1 559	1 569	2 868	5 488	3 008	2 338	110	31 535

Source: UNCTAD calculations based on data from UNOG-Indico (2020).

One third of participants who recorded their country of origin came from Africa

participants (see table 4).

More than one third of participants did not record which country they represented at the time of registration. Many of these participants represented international organisations, NGOs, academia, or the private sector rather than countries. Of those that represented governments, almost one third came from Africa, with Europe and Asia and Oceania together accounting for half of all

Table 4. Number of participants by geographic region, 2017 - 2019

Theme	Africa	Europe	Latin America and the Caribbean	North America	Asia and Oceania	Not Specified	Total
2019	**2 259**	**1 712**	**1 186**	**103**	**2 238**	**4 779**	**12 277**
Academic	2	116	4	25	137	944	**1228**
ASYCUDA	23	12	-	-	10	28	**73**
Commodities	124	49	76	5	80	36	**370**
CSTD	140	36	47	7	67	386	**683**
Debt/Finance	173	117	68	11	156	234	**759**
Development/Climate	75	21	53	-	50	167	**366**
E-Commerce	639	493	289	21	624	561	**2 627**
Intergovernmental	611	550	437	23	659	352	**2 632**
Investment	122	79	54	4	156	748	**1 163**
Legal/Competition	88	69	32	4	99	150	**442**
Maritime	9	5	2	1	3	41	**61**
Other	73	72	31	-	62	296	**534**
Trade	180	93	93	2	135	836	**1 339**
2018	**2 264**	**1 374**	**883**	**70**	**1 515**	**3 525**	**9 631**
Academic	-	77	-	-	2	728	**807**
ASYCUDA	53	7	1	-	44	99	**204**
Commodities	222	52	70	11	107	458	**920**
CSTD	-	-	-	-	-	22	**22**
Debt/Finance	12	27	10	6	38	102	**195**
Development/Climate	84	29	30	-	59	174	**376**
E-Commerce	633	521	383	27	619	327	**2 510**
Intergovernmental	757	456	216	12	304	378	**2 123**
Investment	76	31	23	1	86	383	**600**
Legal/Competition	151	70	50	5	85	222	**583**
Maritime	54	38	27	1	15	151	**286**
Other	69	20	12	2	30	119	**252**
Trade	153	46	61	5	126	362	**753**
2017	**2 184**	**1 564**	**1 228**	**252**	**1 991**	**2 408**	**9 627**
Academic	0	218	42	123	36	151	**570**
ASYCUDA	29	6	3	1	19	-	**58**
Commodities	182	87	75	10	101	106	**561**

Theme	Africa	Europe	Latin America and the Caribbean	North America	Asia and Oceania	Not Specified	Total
CSTD	66	103	67	26	118	143	**523**
Debt/Finance	167	120	82	3	195	106	**673**
Development/Climate	33	17	21	1	28	75	**175**
E-Commerce	318	205	213	22	351	337	**1 446**
Intergovernmental	678	401	323	38	535	337	**2 312**
Investment	164	133	70	10	141	362	**880**
Legal/Competition	77	78	58	6	102	145	**466**
Maritime	27	23	32	1	27	197	**307**
Other	243	97	121	8	186	183	**838**
Trade	200	76	121	3	152	266	**818**
2017-2019	**6 707**	**4 650**	**3 297**	**425**	**5 744**	**10 712**	**31 535**

Source: UNCTAD calculations based on data from UNOG-Indico (2020).

Reviewing meetings calendar as response to COVID19

Due to COVID-19, all meetings on the UNCTAD premises were put on hold. UNCTAD has been able to react quickly to these novel circumstances, however, already organising and hosting a myriad of online events, consultations and webinars in 2020. The e-Week of online events, for instance, was held from 27 April to 1 May 2020 and attracted more than 2000 registered participants (UNCTAD, 2020a).

Notes

1. More information about the UNCTAD upcoming events and the UNCTAD meetings calendar are available online (UNCTAD, 2020b, 2020c).
2. These statistics only cover meetings and events organized by UNCTAD at its headquarters in Geneva. Many other meetings organized by UNCTAD at the regional or national level, outside Geneva, are not counted. The data also do not include meetings co-organized by UNCTAD outside the Palais and do not include the World Investment Forum.

References

- Indico (2020). Indico. Available at https://getindico.io (accessed 21 May 2020).
- Sustainability Knowledge Group (2020). Available at https://sustainabilityknowledgegroup.com/achieving-the-sdgs-the-power-of-partnerships/ (accessed 15 May 2020).
- UNCTAD (2020a). eWeek of Online Events: Dialogues, Webinars and Meetings. Available at https://unctad.org/en/pages/MeetingDetails.aspx?meetingid=2240 (accessed 21 May 2020).
- UNCTAD (2020b). UNCTAD Calendar. United Nations conference on trade and development. Available at https://unctad.org/en/Pages/calendar.aspx (accessed 15 May 2020).
- UNCTAD (2020c). Upcoming events (2020). United Nations conference on trade and development. Available at https://unctad.org/en/Pages/Meetings/Upcoming.aspx (accessed 15 May 2020).

- UNOG-Indico (2020). Available at indico.un.org (accessed 21 May 2020).

Remoteness

Remoteness

Overcoming the tyranny of distance to achieve sustainable development

Little has been said about the challenges and opportunities associated with remoteness for achieving the 2030 Agenda for Sustainable Development. Remoteness or isolation is an important dimension of vulnerability; one that is not always negative. Isolation or geographic remoteness can create unique, resilient communities with strong traditions and cultures, help preserve rare or fragile ecosystems; and as witnessed over the last 18 months, shield communities from the worst effects of global pandemic.

Building a strong economy may require more innovation in a distant location without natural trade relations with bordering countries and with long distances to markets that offer higher volumes of demand. Remoteness results in higher costs of connecting to global value chains that need to be overcome to ensure competitiveness. Remoteness can also be especially challenging for small economies where domestic demand is insufficient for sustained economic growth, forcing businesses to access far-away destinations to reach larger markets.

Remoteness has many attributes other than just geographical distance. A standard dictionary definition of remoteness is typically comprised of two parts: The first focuses on physical distance (the geographic dimension) and the second on a lack of connection. Due to its multidimensional nature, remoteness can influence all aspects of sustainable development.

The 2030 Agenda (United Nations, 2015) set 17 goals for sustainable development addressing economic, social and environmental development challenges with the principle of leaving no one behind. In view of that principle, it is important to consider the specific challenges and opportunities faced by remote economies, such as small island developing states, some LDCs or LLDCs that must start their pursuit of sustainable development from a more challenging baseline.

The plight of island nations has been an issue of analyses and concern going back to the 1960's. The SIDS, that set of countries recognized as being particularly vulnerable to economic and environmental shocks, was first formally recognized at the Earth Summit (United Nations, 1992), held in Rio de Janeiro, Brazil in 1992. But the international community had recognized that developing island countries were a special category from a developmental perspective long before that.

For instance, Kakazu (2007) discusses the characteristics of island societies, noting that remoteness and smallness are their most distinguishable characteristics. He uses the term 'tyranny of distance' and lists the related challenges: high transport and communication costs; barriers to market access; fragile environments; dis-economies of scale and scope; limited division of labour; segmented market; remoteness or insularity; high-cost economy; over-blown public sector; and a high dependency on

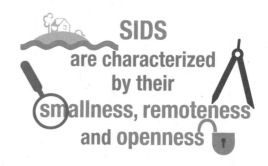

tourism. Kakazu finds that because of their smallness, remoteness and openness, island economies have a distinctive economic structure.

These findings are reflected by the UNCTAD (2021a) "Development and Globalization: Facts and Figures" which provides statistical analysis of the economic, environmental and social situation of SIDS. The report notes that goods production in agriculture and manufacturing has declined in relative terms in many SIDS, while services like tourism, financial intermediation and the public sector have gained prominence.

Among the many challenges faced by SIDS, remoteness remains one the most formidable and deserves a comprehensive in-focus analysis in relation to the SDGs. Greater distance from markets translates into increased costs, including transportation and insurance, weakening the competitiveness of domestic products in international markets and increasing the import bill. It typically means isolation from the main transportation routes or corridors, potentially making supply of resources more costly and unreliable. Additionally, infrastructure projects, such as those enabling connections to energy and communication networks, are more costly to implement and maintain.

Nevertheless, some small island economies have achieved high income levels based on exports, not of goods, but of financial, logistical or tourism services, for instance Singapore and the Bahamas. Indeed, an analysis of the new UNCTAD (2021b) PCI shows that SIDS' productive capacities are highly correlated with human development, and that GDP per capita is highest in SIDS which have succeeded in transforming from agriculture to service activities, not necessarily through industrial transformation. Moreover, in the context where financial flows can move from one side of the planet to the other instantaneously and where a growing share of value added comes from the digital economy and intangibles, physical distance is no longer the impediment it once was. This illustrates how digital connectivity can alleviate at least some of the obstacles brought about by geographic isolation.

Cantu-Bazaldua (2021) presented a review of the ways in which remoteness has been studied in economics, for instance as a factor increasing transaction and information-exchange costs influencing bilateral trade or investment flows or by looking at the role of geographical distance on economic spillovers, such as technological diffusion. Remoteness is also one of the criteria included in the EVI, used to determine inclusion and graduation from the LDC category. According to Briguglio and Galea (2003) the idea for the EVI dates back to 1985, originally to help explain the 'Singapore Paradox', where islands enjoying relatively high GDP per capita could be simultaneously economically vulnerable. In the EVI, remoteness is defined as the weighted average distance from closest world markets. It is calculated as the average distance to the nearest neighbours with a cumulative share of 50 per cent of world trade (exports and imports of goods and services). In addition, the indicator is adjusted for landlockedness (CDP, 2015).

Remoteness relates to more than just geographical distance from markets resulting in higher transportation costs. It also involves integration into transport networks, as well as political and cultural linkages. Thanks to the greater importance of the digital economy, access to and performance of digital networks is gaining greater importance. This chapter presents the main dimensions of remoteness and proposes indicators for measuring them in the context of the sustainable development of SIDS.

In the outcome document of the most recent global conference on SIDS, signatory countries called on the United Nations, its specialized agencies and relevant intergovernmental organizations to "elaborate appropriate indices for assessing the progress made in the sustainable development of small island developing States that better reflect their vulnerability and guide them to adopt more informed policies and strategies for building and sustaining long-term resilience", as well as requesting "the tracking of progress and the development of vulnerability-resilience country profiles" (UN-OHRLLS, 2014). The indicators proposed herein represent a contribution to this direction.

This chapter studies remoteness as geographical distance adjusted for connectivity. All things being equal, a greater distance imposes additional costs and increases the isolation from markets and people. However, better connectivity could considerably reduce the distance premium. An economy can be distant from others yet well connected (Australia, for instance). While a country cannot control its physical location, it can influence its connectivity through targeted investment in infrastructure and through greater participation in cultural and political networks.

Remoteness has multiple dimensions

From a policy perspective, the broader analysis of remoteness introduces a more complete monitoring of sustainable progress, fully taking into consideration one of the most salient challenges faced by SIDS. More importantly, although location and geographical distance cannot be changed, the expanded definition of remoteness considers factors that can be improved through targeted investment and appropriate policies. This can serve as guidance when analysing the approaches taken by some small island economies to reach a high national income level in spite of their geographic remoteness.

Distance could be measured with respect to main populated areas, markets or sources of financing, for instance. Connectivity could refer to transport routes, socio-cultural linkages or digital networks, among others. Cantu-Bazaldua (2021) provides a discussion of dimensions of remoteness (see figure 1) and proposes a set of indicators for measuring them.

Figure 1. Dimensions of remoteness

1. *Geographical distance from markets.* This traditional dimension of remoteness indicates geographical proximity to other territories and separation from economic centres. It will be measured using three variables: distance to nearest neighbour, distance to economic centres, and distance to trading partners.
2. *Distance from financing sources.* While distance is not an obstacle for financial flows, financial activity tends to cluster around centres, where most business and investment decisions are made. Countries far from these centres risk falling off the radar. The indicators include distance to business centres, distance from sources of FDI, and distance from ODA donors.
3. *Distance from cultural and political centres.* A frequently neglected aspect of remoteness is the potential isolation from the centres of cultural and political power. These are the countries with a great deal of influence in defining international rules, shaping global discourse and setting cultural trends. This dimension will be assessed as the distance to the main centres of global soft power[1] and the countries with the strongest global presence, as measured through international indicators available in the literature.
4. *Transport connectivity.* Well-developed transport links could ease the burden of distance, facilitating the inflow and outflow of products and people. Maritime, air and land connectivity are measured in this dimension.
5. *Social and political connectivity.* It is important to consider also the cultural or social connections of a country with the rest of the world. This dimension is studied through indicators on the number of immigrants in the country and the stock of nationals living abroad, foreign (tertiary) students registered in the national education system and nationals studying (tertiary education) abroad, foreign diplomatic representations in the country, and membership in economic, trade, defence or other alliances.
6. *Digital connectivity.* For digital economy to mitigate disadvantages of geographic remoteness, ICT infrastructure needs to be well developed with widespread access to these tools among businesses and individuals. This dimension will be assessed through three indicators: Internet access of the population; international bandwidth per Internet user, as a proxy of the available Internet infrastructure; and the latency rate, a measure of network performance.

Source: UNCTAD deliberations based on Cantu-Bazaldua (2021).

Cantu-Bazaldua (2021) includes complete information on the variables considered, including their definition, data sources, and details on imputation methods. His paper also includes summary statistics for all the variables. The variables considered vary considerably in terms of data ranges and units of measurement and are thus transformed to a 0-100 scale through a min-max transformation to facilitate comparison. The variables will be presented for all SIDS, as well as aggregates for relevant comparison groups.[2] The visualizations use lighter colours to indicate a higher relative remoteness. Unless otherwise indicated, data refer to 2019.

SIDS are situated far from their main markets

SIDS are situated in remote locations as measured by distance to their nearest (non-SIDS) neighbour (figure 2, column 1). While the global (weighted) average is a distance of only eight km to the nearest neighbour, an average citizen from a SIDS has to travel 371km to the closest non-SIDS country. Moreover, the distance ranges from zero for those SIDS sharing a border with another country, to 3 264km required to cover the distance from the

A SIDS citizen has to travel 371km to the closest non-SIDS

Marshall Islands to its nearest non-SIDS neighbour (Indonesia). Tuvalu, Nauru and Samoa also register a high remoteness according to this variable.

Figure 2. Distance from markets, SIDS and selected country groups, 2019

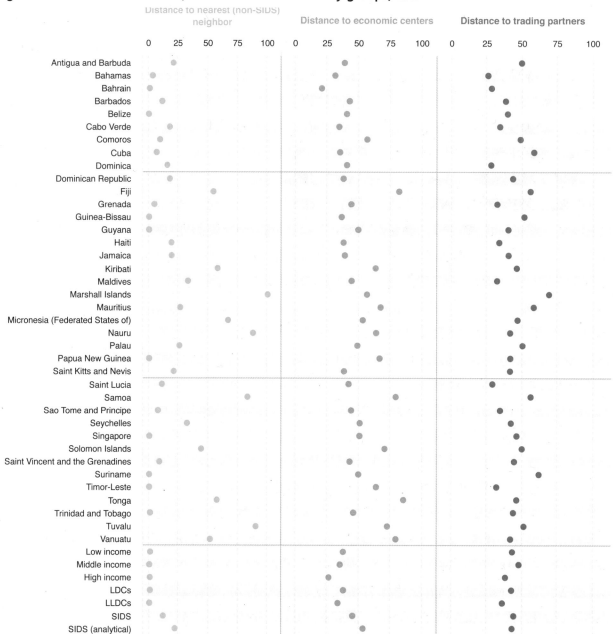

Source: Cantu-Bazaldua (2021) based on UNCTAD (2021a), UNSD (2021), UN Population Division (2021), CEPII and R package cshapes.
Notes: Country groups are calculated as averages using population as weights. All variables presented as indices with zero indicate the world minimum and 100 the world maximum.

It is also important to consider the distance to the largest countries to appreciate the economic opportunities for trade, investment, cross-border interactions and spillovers. SIDS are located far away from the main economic centres (figure 2, column 2), as measured by the average distance to countries weighted by their GDP. Different SIDS regions are situated in relative proximity to some large economic centres (e.g. Caribbean islands) but far from others. On average, SIDS are more remote than other country groups, such as LDCs or LLDCs, and especially when compared to all middle and high-income countries. According to this indicator, the most remote SIDS is Tonga, with an average (weighted) distance of 12 175km, followed by Fiji, Vanuatu and Samoa. However, the top 5 most remote countries according to this variable are not SIDS, but are mostly located in Oceania and South America, including New Zealand, Australia, Chile, Argentina and Uruguay, in that order; Tonga is ranked sixth.

SIDS are not necessarily more remote than other country groups when distance to trading partners (figure 2, column 3), weighted by their bilateral trade (exports plus imports of goods) has been taken into account. In fact, the average distance for all groups is remarkably similar, suggesting that countries tend to specialize in products and services tailored to nearby markets. However, for SIDS, there is a relatively high dispersion, ranging from the Bahamas (3 806km) to the Marshall Islands (8 864km), with Suriname, Cuba and Mauritius also registering high trade-weighted average distances. While the Marshall Islands is the SIDS economy most distant from its trading partners, it is only twelfth in the world rankings. The top 5 most distant countries using this variable are Chile, Brazil, Peru, New Zealand and Argentina, in that order.

SIDS are more distant from financing sources than others

The three distance variables from financing sources are correlated as the countries with the largest companies are also the main sources of other types of financing (in this case, private foreign investment and development assistance). Across all three dimensions, SIDS are on average more distant from financing sources than other country groups. High-income countries and LLDCs tend to be closer in proximity to origins of financial flows.

In terms of distance from main business centres (figure 3, column 1), measured by the revenues of the largest 500 firms, Tonga is the most isolated SIDS, followed by Fiji, Mauritius, Vanuatu and Samoa. However, from a more global perspective, the extremes are located in South America (Uruguay, Argentina, Chile, Paraguay, Brazil, Plurinational State of Bolivia), Oceania (New Zealand and Australia) and Southern Africa (Lesotho, South Africa).

Figure 3. Distance from financing sources, SIDS and selected country groups, 2019

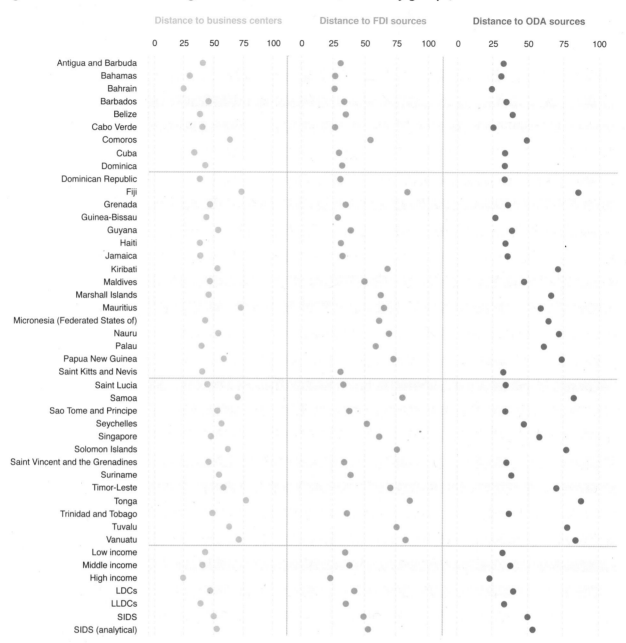

Source: Cantu-Bazaldua (2021) based on UNCTAD (2021a), Fortune, OECD (2021), UN Population Division (2021) and CEPII.

Notes: Country groups are calculated as averages using population as weights. All variables presented as indices with zero indicate the world minimum and 100 the world maximum.

The five SIDS with the greatest distance from FDI sources (figure 3, column 2) are Tonga, Fiji, Vanuatu, Samoa and Solomon Islands. In terms of distance to ODA donors (figure 3, column 3), the first four SIDS are also the most remote, with Tuvalu taking fifth place. According to both metrics, New Zealand and Australia are the most remote countries in the world, followed closely by the SIDS mentioned here.

Among SIDS, Fiji, Samoa and Tonga are farthest away from financing sources

SIDS remain distant from cultural and political centres

SIDS are also located far away from soft power centres (figure 4, column 1), as measured by the Global Soft Power Index published by Brand Finance (2020). This group's average is significantly above those of all other comparison groups. The most remote country according to this indicator is New Zealand, but six SIDS are ranked in the top 10: Tonga, Samoa, Fiji, Vanuatu, Tuvalu and Solomon Islands.

SIDS are also situated at a greater distance from centres of global presence (figure 4, column 2) than most countries, although less so than in the case of soft power centres. Here too, the most remote countries in the world are New Zealand and Australia, and in addition the top 10 includes a mix of SIDS, such as Tonga, Fiji, Vanuatu, Samoa and Tuvalu, and some South American nations, such as Chile, Argentina and Uruguay.

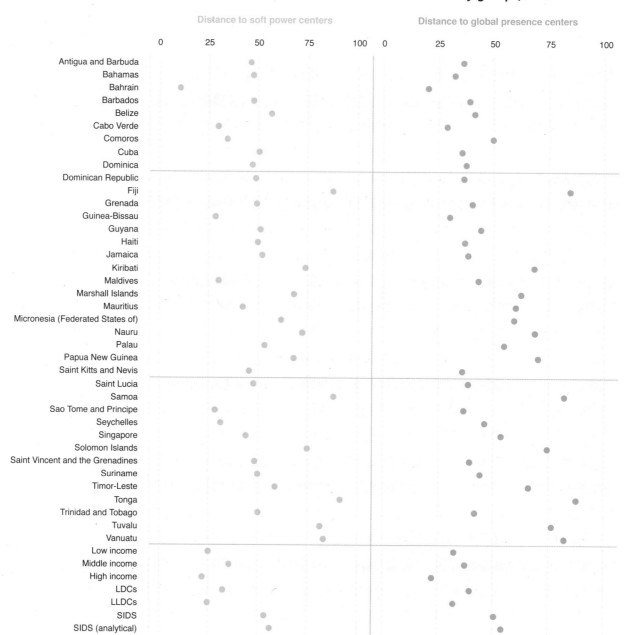

Source: Cantu-Bazaldua (2021) based on data from Brand Finance, Elcano Royal Institute, UN Population Division (2021) and CEPII.
Notes: Country groups are calculated as averages using population as weights. All variables presented as indices with zero indicate the world minimum and 100 the world maximum.

SIDS are well connected by air – less so by sea

For island economies, land connectivity is (mostly[3]) non-existent so other means of transport gain a greater relevance. For maritime connectivity (figure 5, column 1), Singapore is a clear outlier within SIDS, with a score almost three times higher than the second ranked small island economy, the Dominican Republic. In fact, Singapore is ranked second globally, after the most connected country in maritime networks (China) and just above the third placed country (Republic of Korea). Maritime connectivity is estimated through the liner shipping connectivity index, which indicates a country's level of integration into global liner shipping networks.

In addition to Singapore and Dominican Republic, mentioned above, only three more SIDS exceed the average connectivity for middle income countries: Jamaica, Mauritius and Bahamas. On average, SIDS are not very well integrated into shipping connections. For countries with a high dependence on the sea, this low maritime connectivity could further aggravate the challenges of geographical remoteness (see UNCTAD, 2021a).

Some SIDS are among the countries best connected by air in the world, but many have challenges with maritime connectivity

For air connectivity, as measured by the number of international flights per year relative to population (figure 5, column 2), some SIDS with a high reliance on tourism are among the best connected in the world: Antigua and Barbuda, Saint Kitts and Nevis, Bahamas, Dominica, Nauru, Barbados and Palau. In addition to these SIDS, most of the top ranked countries are either micro-States (Luxembourg) or other island economies (Iceland, Malta, Cyprus). On average, SIDS are comparatively well connected by air transportation, with international flights per capita at a level comparable with high-income countries. However, not all SIDS are as well integrated. Papua New Guinea, Haiti and Guinea-Bissau are among the lowest ranked economies in this variable.

Most European micro-States (landlocked, with extensive land borders relative to their area and excellent roadways) are the best ranked considering land connectivity, constructed from the length of land borders, relative to total area, weighted by road infrastructure.[4] Unsurprisingly given their lack of land borders, SIDS mostly scored zero, with a few exceptions, but nevertheless low scores (Timor-Leste, Belize, Dominican Republic and SIDS that are not islands or that share an island with another country).

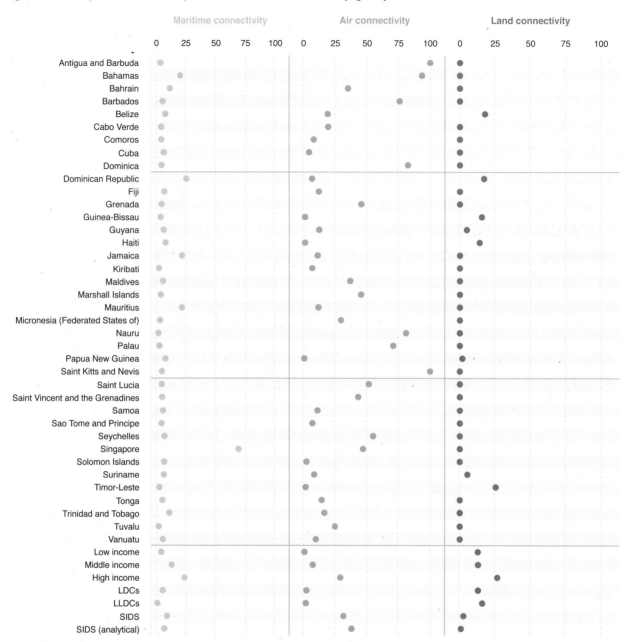

Source: Cantu-Bazaldua (2021) based on UNCTAD (2021a), ICAO (2021), CIA (2021) and UN Population Division (2021).
Notes: Country groups are calculated as averages using population as weights. All variables presented as indices with zero indicate the world minimum and 100 the world maximum.

SIDS are relatively well connected socially

Contrary to centrally located countries, working with neighbours over common border issues or tackling regional challenges, SIDS could lack opportunities to join alliances or shared initiatives, movement of persons and ideas. This dimension of remoteness is broader and more difficult to measure than the others. A full account would involve monitoring all spaces that allow exchanges between individuals, societies and governments. Given data limitations, this dimension is estimated using the seven indicators included in figures 6 and 7. These include immigration and emigration, cross-border exchange of students, diplomatic representations and participation in defence and trade agreements. While cultural and political links clearly extend beyond the areas measured by these variables, they are difficult to conceptualize and measure, especially through internationally comparable indicators with worldwide coverage.[5] Cross-national trust can be important for connectivity and cultural spillovers, and is sometimes used as an indicator of cultural ties (see Delhey and Newton, 2005).

Migrants take with them ideas, traditions, practices and businesses. They build networks and bridges between their communities of origin and destination. For this reason, it is important to consider rates of both immigration and outward migration. Foreign immigrants constitute a sizable share of the population in several high-income SIDS, such as Bahrain, Singapore, and Antigua and Barbuda. However, other SIDS feature some of the lowest immigration rates in the world: in Cuba, Haiti, Papua New Guinea, Solomon Islands, Timor-Leste and Jamaica, immigrants constitute less than one per cent of the population. Overall, the average immigration ratio in SIDS is higher than in low and middle-income countries, although still at about one third of the levels observed in high-income countries.

A similar story is told by emigration (figure 6, column 2). One SIDS, Saint Kitts and Nevis, has the largest emigration rate in the world, with 2.4 nationals living abroad for each person living in the country. Other countries with high outward migration are Dominica, Suriname, Tonga, Grenada, Guyana and Samoa. Other SIDS, such as Maldives or Solomon Islands, exhibit a very low ratio in this variable. Nonetheless, with an overall emigration rate of 33.6 per cent, SIDS are significantly above the world average in this aspect.[6]

SIDS are significantly above the world average emigration rate with 33.6%

An interesting group of migrants, for which detailed statistics are available, are students that move to another country to pursue a tertiary education. The inbound mobility rate, measured as the percentage of students from abroad enrolled in a tertiary education program at a local university (figure 6, column 3), is very high in Grenada and Saint Kitts and Nevis, where 85 and 73 per cent of tertiary students are foreigners. Although these are clear extremes, the SIDS average remains well above the average for low and middle-income countries. In terms of outbound mobility rate (figure 6, column 4), SIDS are on par with high-income countries, although far from the high student mobility rates observed in some cases.

Figure 6. Social and political connectivity (part 1), SIDS and selected country groups, 2019

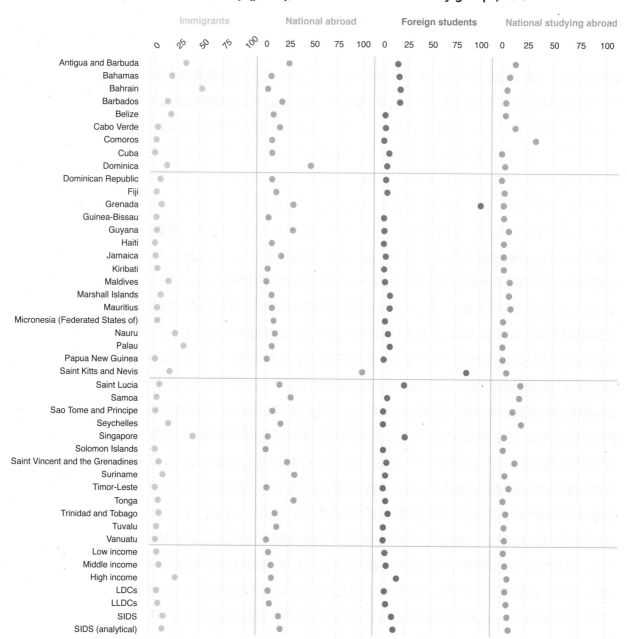

Source: Cantu-Bazaldua (2021) based on data from UNESCO Institute for Statistics (2021) and UN Population Division (2021).
Notes: Country groups are calculated as averages using population as weights. All variables presented as indices with zero indicate the world minimum and 100 the world maximum.

Many SIDS are less well connected politically

The number of foreign nations with at least one diplomatic representation (embassy, consulate or permanent mission) in a SIDS (figure 7, column 1) ranges from 50 in Singapore to two in Antigua and Barbuda, Dominica, Nauru, Saint Kitts and Nevis, Saint Vincent and the Grenadines, and Tuvalu. Based on the Global Diplomacy Index (Lowy Institute, 2019), it is evident that as a group, SIDS have one of the lowest numbers of diplomatic representations, below low-income countries and other groups such as LDCs and LLDCs. The results vary from zero in Yemen (no diplomatic missions at all) to 61 in Switzerland and the United States of America, meaning that all 61 origin countries featured in the dataset are represented in the country.

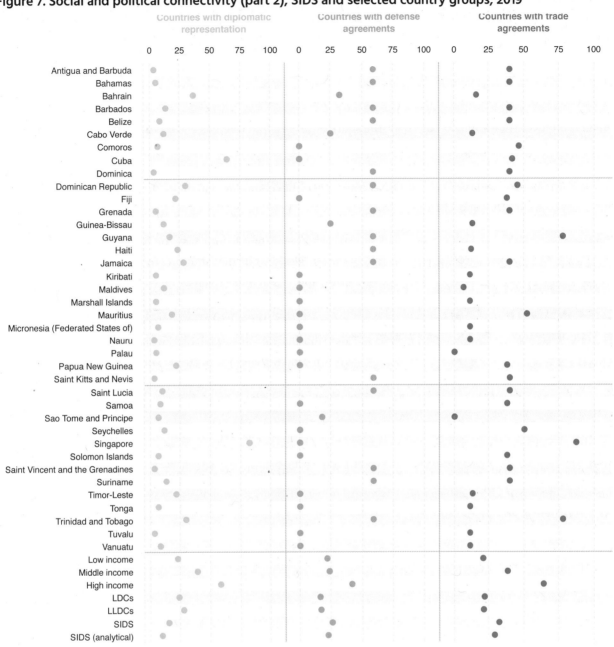

Figure 7. Social and political connectivity (part 2), SIDS and selected country groups, 2019

Source: Cantu-Bazaldua (2021) based on data from Gibler (2013), WTO and UN Population Division (2021).
Notes: Country groups are calculated as averages using population as weights. All variables presented as indices with zero indicate the world minimum and 100 the world maximum.

Inter-country linkages can also be analysed through agreements, pacts and other alliances. Defence agreements, some of the oldest international pacts in existence, are one manifestation of this. By using the somewhat outdated database from Gibler (2013), which only includes data up to 2012, the most connected nations are the United States of America and Canada, having some type of defence agreement in force with 56 and 51 nations, respectively. Conversely, 45 countries have no such alliance in force. According to this variable, the average SIDS has defence agreements with 15 countries (figure 7, column 2), above the world average but still limited compared to other cases, particularly high-income countries.

A similar situation is observed when trade agreements are examined. According to the WTO (2021) database, Egypt has the highest number of active bilateral or plurilateral trade pacts in force. They have active trade agreements with 105 countries, closely followed by members of the European Union, who have a common international trade policy involving trade agreements with 98 countries. On the other hand, a handful of nations have no active agreements covering trade, including two SIDS (Palau and Sao Tome and Principle). The average SIDS has a trade agreement with 34 partners, less than the average for middle and high-income countries (40 and 67, respectively).

Digital connectivity of SIDS varies while some of them reach the world top

The first indicator of digital connectivity, the share of population that has access to the Internet (figure 8, column 1), shows that SIDS are well connected, although with a great deal of variability. Indeed, this variable ranges from 99.7 per cent in Bahrain, the highest digital connectivity in the world, to only 3.9 per cent in Guinea-Bissau, the country with the fifth lowest Internet access. On average, SIDS have similar outcomes than middle-income countries and better scores than LDCs and LLDCs.

Bahrain had the highest digital connectivity in the world in 2019

International bandwidth per Internet user (figure 8, column 2) shows a skewed distribution for SIDS, with a few countries (Singapore, Bahamas, Saint Vincent and the Grenadines, and Saint Kitts and Nevis) among the best performers in the world, while many other SIDS' score is very close to zero. This mirrors the world distribution of this variable, which serves as a proxy for the Internet infrastructure in place. On average, SIDS have a relatively good attainment in this variable, outperforming the average for low- and middle-income economies, although still behind the high-income group.

The average SIDS performs as well as the average middle-income country and LLDC in the latency rate (figure 8, column 3), based on all tests conducted in each country in 2019. SIDS perform significantly better than low-income countries or LDCs. This average hides a large variance, with one SIDS at the bottom of the world rank (Tuvalu, with a median latency of 1 821 milliseconds), whereas other SIDS have some of the best Internet connections worldwide, like the Bahamas or Singapore.

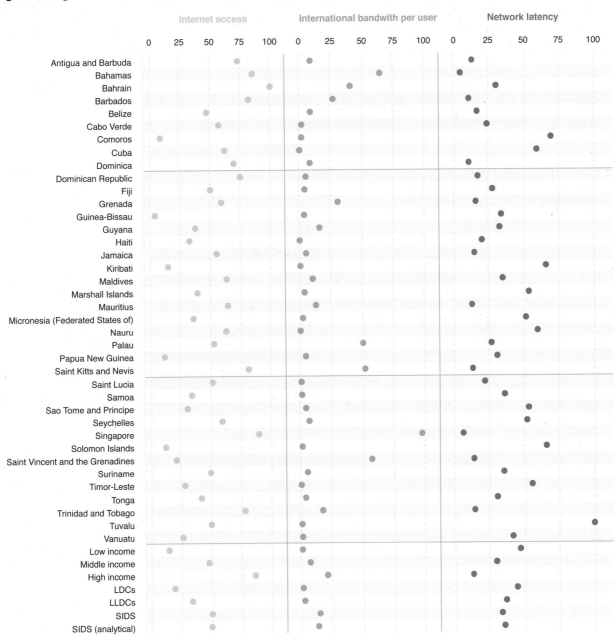

Figure 8. Digital connectivity, SIDS and selected country groups, 2019

	Internet access	International bandwith per user	Network latency

Source: Cantu-Bazaldua (2021) based on data from ITU, Measurement Lab and UN Population Division (2021).
Notes: Country groups are calculated as averages using population as weights. All variables presented as indices with zero indicate the world minimum and 100 the world maximum.

An overall remoteness index – top 15 featuring mostly SIDS

The previous analysis presented 21 variables that can provide a comprehensive assessment of remoteness across six dimensions. This shows that traditional measures of geographical distance to markets are not sufficient to give a complete panorama of the challenges of distance. Moreover, a large number of connectivity factors could mitigate or accentuate remoteness, and they should be taken into account. This section presents the steps for

The remoteness index analyses 21 variables across six dimensions

calculating a remoteness index and the results for SIDS and relevant benchmarks. The methodology is discussed in more detail by Cantu-Bazaldua (2021).

For some of the variables presented in the above analysis, a higher score indicates greater remoteness, whereas for others the opposite was the case. To overcome this problem, all variables were transformed so that a higher value corresponds to greater remoteness. The index for each dimension was calculated through a simple average of the variables included, and the results were adjusted to a 0-100 scale through a min-max transformation. This way the most remote country takes a value of 100 and the most proximate country a value of zero. The overall remoteness index was calculated as a simple average of the aggregate indicators for all six dimensions.

9 in 10
most remote countries
are SIDS

According to the overall remoteness indicator (figure 9), the most remote SIDS is Tuvalu, closely followed by Tonga and Vanuatu. Samoa and the Solomon Islands complete the top 5. The top 10 is composed of nine Pacific SIDS, which are remote on all or most dimensions. New Zealand is the only country that makes top 10 and is not SIDS.

Figure 9. Remoteness index for the 30 most remote countries globally, 2019

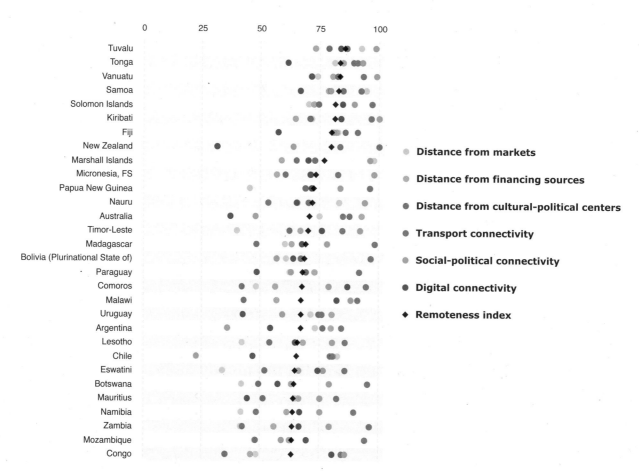

Source: Cantu-Bazaldua (2021).
Notes: For all dimensions a higher score indicates higher remoteness. The coloured circles represent the six dimensions of remoteness and the diamond shape indicates the overall index. This chart is ordered from the most remote to the least remote country, in terms of the overall index.

For some SIDS, the overall index is improved by positive scores in one or a few dimensions of remoteness. For example, while Timor-Leste and Papua New Guinea score high in most dimensions, their overall index score is reduced by their geographical location, as they are relatively close to their main markets and trading partners. A similar situation is observed in Nauru, although in this case it is the relatively high transport connectivity, mostly based on air transport, which lowers the overall remoteness score. Mauritius' score is significantly improved by its well-developed digital connectivity.

Figure 9 also shows some SIDS that are more proximate across most dimensions, but whose score is penalized by a poor result in one dimension. For Suriname, Cuba, Guyana, and Trinidad and Tobago, the area lagging behind is transport connectivity. For the Maldives and Palau, it is their social and political isolation.

The least remote SIDS are at the bottom of the figure starting with the Bahamas which compensates for a relatively low social and political connectivity with shorter average distances to markets and an excellent digital infrastructure. Following closely are Singapore, Bahrain and some of the high-income SIDS in the Caribbean, such as Saint Kitts and Nevis, Antigua and Barbuda, and Barbados.

Comparing SIDS' scores to the world distribution, they are indeed among the most remote economies in the world, particularly Pacific SIDS. All top-15 most remote countries are Pacific SIDS except New Zealand (8th), Australia (13th) and Madagascar (15th).[7] The most remote SIDS outside the Pacific is Comoros, ranked 18th in the world. For scores for all countries see Cantu-Bazaldua (2021).

Figure 10 presents the aggregate results for SIDS with several benchmarks. A first highlight of this graph is the strict ordering of each of the six dimensions of remoteness according to income level. This indicates a clear link between remoteness and economic performance, as well as a clustering effect. SIDS' a score in the remoteness index is comparable to low-income economies.

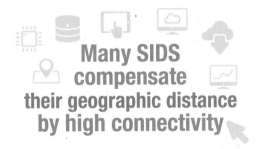

Many SIDS compensate their geographic distance by high connectivity

Another striking result is that SIDS are not worse off than LDCs or LLDCs in terms of remoteness. While they are located at a greater distance from markets, financing sources and cultural centres, they partially compensate for this disadvantage through better connectivity, especially in terms of ICT and digital technologies. This draws attention to the importance of connectivity and considering all aspects of remoteness beyond just geographical distance when studying the development of SIDS.

As shown in the country-level results (figure 9), the SIDS' average hides some important differences between countries. SIDS in the Pacific are distinctly more remote, with a higher score in most dimensions, particularly transport and socio-political connectivity. SIDS in the Atlantic and Indian Ocean are the least remote, thanks in part to their improved digital and transport connectivity.

Figure 10. Remoteness index for selected country groups, 2019

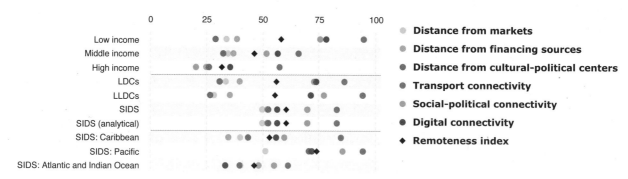

Source: Cantu-Bazaldua (2021).
Notes: Country groups are calculated as averages using total population as weights. For all dimensions, a higher score indicates a higher remoteness.

The figures presented in this chapter also include an aggregate for analytical SIDS (see UNCTAD, 2021a). This analytical group is more homogeneous and reflects more closely the remoteness challenge faced by SIDS across the six dimensions.

Does remoteness hamper sustainable development?

To study the relationship of remoteness to the economic, social and environmental pillars of sustainable development, we compare the remoteness index with some composite indicators broadly representing these themes. The 231 SDG indicators designed to measure the 17 goals and their respective 169 targets are rather narrow in scope when looked at individually, and comprehensive data coverage is not available. Therefore, six indicators are selected to evaluate their interaction with the remoteness index and dimensions of sustainable development. These include GDP per capita, PCI, Gini index, GII, HDI and EVI.

Data for SIDS show that GDP per capita is negatively correlated with remoteness ($\varrho = -0.61$) (see figure 11). The more remote the country, the lower their GDP per capita. Singapore had the highest GDP per capita in 2020, and the lowest overall remoteness score, together with the Bahamas and Saint Kitts and Nevis. The negative correlation between GDP per capita and remoteness is even higher ($\varrho = -0.66$) among the rest of the SIDS excluding Singapore. When looking at poor connectivity only (dimensions 4-6 of the overall index on transport, socio-political and digital connectivity), the negative correlation with GDP per capita is notably higher ($\varrho = -0.79$).

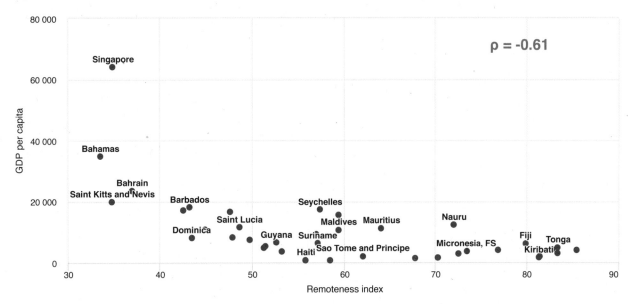

Source: UNCTAD calculations based on Cantu-Bazaldua (2021) and UNCTADStat (UNCTAD, 2021c).
Note: Data available for all 38 countries.

We also look at the new UNCTAD PCI as another proxy indicator of the economic pillar (figure 12). It provides a more comprehensive measure than GDP per capita as it assesses productive capacities from the perspective of eight categories: natural capital, human capital, energy, institutions, private sector, structural change, transport and ICT (UNCTAD, 2021b). Again, generally small island economies with the lowest remoteness score, have the highest PCI (ϱ = -0.49). The negative correlation of poor connectivity

(dimensions 4-6) and PCI is higher (ϱ = -0.75), underlining the importance of mitigating geographic remoteness for achieving sustainable economic development, for instance by investing in transport and digital connectivity.

Figure 12. Remoteness and productive capacity in SIDS

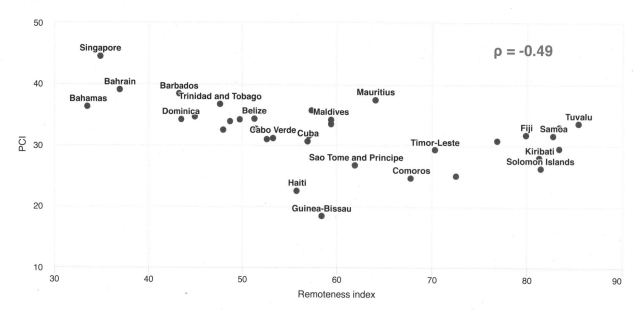

Source: UNCTAD calculations based on Cantu-Bazaldua (2021) and UNCTADStat (UNCTAD, 2021c).
Note: Data available for 34 countries.

Overall remoteness is negatively correlated with income inequality (ϱ = -0.45) in SIDS, as measured by the Gini index (figure 13). Geographic remoteness i.e., distance (dimensions 1-3 on distance from markets, financial and cultural-political centres) is more strongly negatively correlated with income inequality (ϱ = -0.51) than poor connectivity (ϱ = -0.21). People living in the most geographically remote SIDS experience lower income inequality. Remote locations may offer less opportunities for achieving high income levels, especially small rural communities. It should be noted, however, that the Gini index is not available for the eight least remote SIDS, including Bahamas, Saint Kitts and Nevis, Singapore, Bahrain, Antigua and Barbuda, Barbados, Dominica and Grenada.

Figure 13. Remoteness and income inequality in SIDS

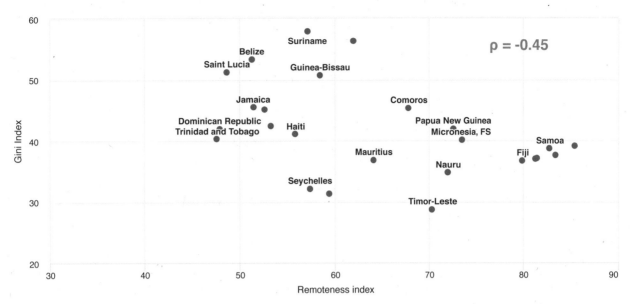

Source: UNCTAD calculations based on Cantu-Bazaldua (2021) and World Bank (2021).
Note: Data available for 26 countries.

SIDS with
high connectivity
also succeed in
human development
and
gender equality

For SIDS that have GII data, gender inequality has a relatively high positive correlation ($\varrho = 0.68$) with poor connectivity (dimensions 4-6), but not with geographic remoteness ($\varrho = 0.13$). The overall remoteness index is positively correlated with gender inequality ($\varrho = 0.46$) (figure 14). In general, SIDS with higher transport, social, political and digital connectivity provide a more gender equal environment, but geographic distance does not mean increased gender inequality. GII data are available for 19 SIDS only. Data gaps are somewhat more common for the most remote SIDS.

Figure 14. Remoteness and gender inequality in SIDS

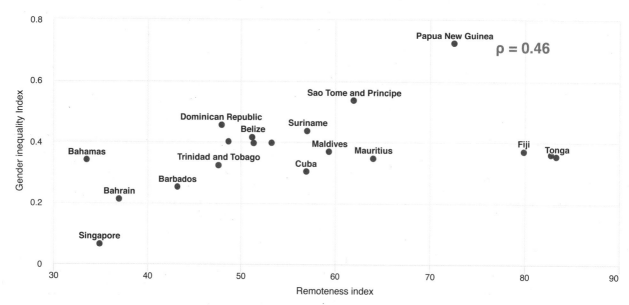

Source: UNCTAD calculations based on Cantu-Bazaldua (2021) and UNDP (2020).
Note: Data available for 19 countries.

The overall remoteness index correlates negatively with the HDI (ϱ = -0.57) (figure 15). The negative correlation of human development and poor connectivity (dimensions 4-6 of remoteness) is significantly higher, -0.76, with little correlation with geographic remoteness only (dimensions 1-3), -0.22. Small island economies with good transport, social, political and digital connectivity have achieved higher human development.

Figure 15. Remoteness and human development in SIDS

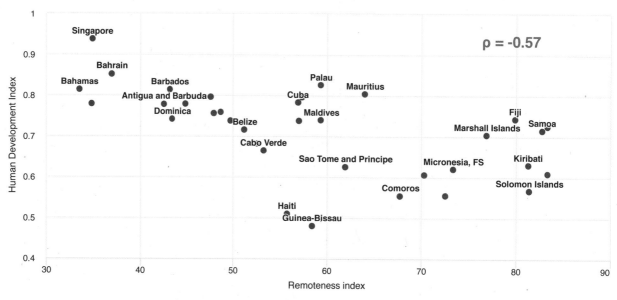

Source: UNCTAD calculations based on Cantu-Bazaldua (2021) and UNDP (2020).
Note: Data available for 36 countries.

Due to their geography, SIDS face a unique and varied mix of environmental concerns, ranging from increased exposure to storms and floods, to the loss of their actual land. SIDS account for three of the top five most environmentally vulnerable countries according to the EVI in 2020. Kiribati, Marshall Islands and Tuvalu are the most vulnerable countries globally according to the EVI. These small island economies are also among the most remote countries in the world. Overall remoteness is positively correlated with economic and environmental vulnerability ($\varrho = 0.58$).

Remoteness and vulnerability go hand in hand

📊 **Figure 16. Remoteness and economic and environmental vulnerability in SIDS**

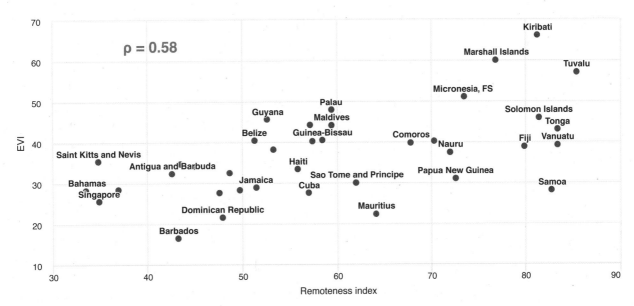

Source: UNCTAD calculations based on Cantu-Bazaldua (2021) and UNDESA (2020).
Note: Data available for all 38 countries.

Geographic remoteness adds an extra barrier but can be mitigated

The analyses presented here show that remoteness has a negative impact on the economic, social and environmental aspects of sustainable development and places additional demands on countries. Figure 17 summarizes the correlations of overall remoteness, geographic remoteness and limited connectivity across the themes covered by the indicators analysed in figures 11 to 16. The analyses show that geographic distance correlates most positively with environmental vulnerability and most negatively with income inequality. They also show that the correlations with geographic distance are weaker than for limited connectivity, and distant location can, thus, be mitigated by improving transport, social, political and digital connectivity. Limited connectivity has the strongest negative correlation with GDP per capita, human development and productive capacity, and a strong positive correlation with gender inequality and vulnerability in SIDS.

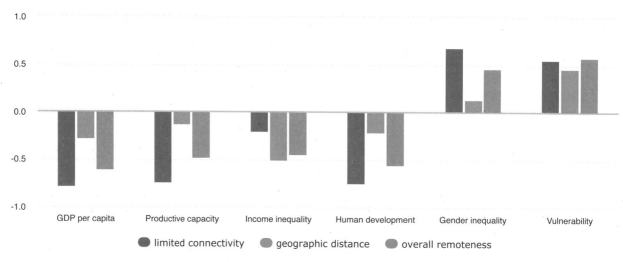

Figure 17. The correlations of overall remoteness, geographic distance and limited connectivity with selected sustainable development themes in SIDS

● limited connectivity ● geographic distance ● overall remoteness

Source: UNCTAD calculations based on Cantu-Bazaldua (2021), UNCTADStat (UNCTAD, 2021c), World Bank (2021), UNDP (2020) and UNDESA (2020).

There are examples of highly geographically remote countries outside of SIDS that have also managed to mitigate the impacts of geographic isolation. Across all geographical indicators (the first three dimensions), New Zealand is the most remote country in the world, sometimes by a large margin. However, it partially makes up for this disadvantage through a well-developed connectivity infrastructure, especially ICT. A similar situation can be observed in Australia. Uruguay, for instance, compensates for its location with excellent digital and transport connections, whereas Chile has well developed social and political networks, including one of the world's highest number of defence and trade pacts. The remoteness ranks for these four selected countries are shown in table 1, where top ranks (i.e., high relative remoteness) in the first three dimensions are offset by good performance in the connectivity dimensions, therefore improving the overall remoteness score.

Table 1. Ranks in remoteness index by dimension, selected countries

Dimension	New Zealand	Australia	Uruguay	Chile
Distance from markets	1	9	14	7
Distance from financing sources	1	2	7	5
Distance from cultural and political centres	1	3	10	7
Transport connectivity	90	80	118	100
Social and political connectivity	81	130	92	165
Digital connectivity	175	151	132	108
Overall remoteness	**8**	**13**	**20**	**23**

Source: Cantu-Bazaldua (2021).

These four cases strengthen the message that geographic remoteness is not an insurmountable obstacle. While geographical distance does entail higher transportation costs and hinders participation in global decision-making, this can be offset by targeted investments in transport and ICT connectivity, as well as an active participation in cultural and political networks. SIDS have already done important progress in this front and, on average, according to the index, they are not more remote in digital connectivity than other groups of countries, such as LDCs or LLDCs.

Remoteness is a gap that needs to be bridged to progress towards SDGs (see figure 18). It brings challenges, many of which can be mitigated by investing in transport and digital connectivity and cultural and political networks. But those investments naturally require sufficient resources and finances. It seems that highly remote countries do not start their journey towards the 2030 Agenda on equal footing, and this should be taken into consideration in global development assistance and finance.

Remoteness gap needs to be bridged to progress towards SDGs

 Figure 18. Remoteness as a factor in sustainable development

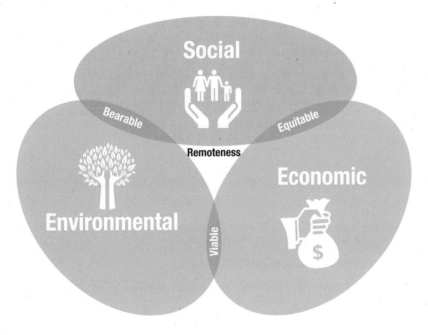

Source: UNCTAD deliberations.

The broader study of remoteness presented herein also highlights the heterogeneity within SIDS. While most SIDS located in the Pacific are objectively remote in all dimensions, SIDS in the Caribbean or in the Atlantic and Indian Oceans are no more remote than the average middle-income country. This illustrates the importance of having detailed, disaggregated statistics for SIDS that reflect the most pressing challenges they face and highlights the usefulness of regrouping SIDS for analytical purposes, reflecting discussions in UNCTAD (2021d) and MacFeely et al (2021).

A remoteness index, along the lines presented here, could be used as a measure to evaluate the challenges faced by SIDS due to their isolated location. The index reflects the importance of geography, but also of attenuating factors stemming from targeted policies for improving connectivity. Moreover, it reflects key aspects of remoteness, including the limited options for transport connectivity with no land borders for most SIDS, but also lack of access to maritime transport for most LLDCs. As suggested by Cantu-Bazaldua (2021), the index could be used as a broad indicator to measure economic vulnerabilities arising from remoteness and determining objective inclusion and graduation criteria for SIDS, LDCs, LLDCs and other groups of countries.

Notes

1. An idea originally developed in Nye (2005), "soft power" refers to the ability to influence the behavior of others to get the desired outcomes through attraction and co-option rather than coercion (or "hard power"). According to the author, it relies on three pillars: political values, culture and foreign policy.

2. Note that country aggregates are calculated as a weighted average of the corresponding variables, using population as weight.

3. Some islands, however, have a better land connectivity, e.g., in the case of shared islands, mainland islands and connected islands (MacFeely et al., 2021).

4. This indicator is only a proxy for land connections and does not consider important factors affecting cross-border transportation, including geographical features (mountainous or fluvial borders), border-crossing infrastructure, customs and border-crossing administrative efficiency, or other obstacles.

5. For instance, an interesting indicator would be the share of the world population that share the same language. A shared language facilitates exchange and transmission of ideas, and gives access to larger knowledge pool and more media sources, therefore reducing isolation. Although there are specialized databases for this variable (for instance, CEPII or Ethnologue), they present important data gaps, particularly for some SIDS.

6. Some cases could be affected by practices where countries grant citizenship by investment. This could have an ambiguous relationship with social connectivity, but the available data do not allow a more detailed disaggregation.

7. On the other hand, the 30 least remote countries in the world are all located in Europe. The five less remote countries are Luxembourg, Belgium, the Netherlands, Cyprus and the United Kingdom.

References

- Brand Finance (2020). Global Soft Power Index 2020. The World's Largest Brand Value Database. Available at https://brandirectory.com/globalsoftpower/ (accessed 5 June 2021).

- Briguglio L and Galea W (2003). Updating the economic vulnerability index.

- Cantu-Bazaldua F (2021). Remote but well connected? Neighboring but isolated? The measurement of remoteness in the context of SIDS. Available at https://unctad.org/publications.

- CDP (2015). Measuring Remoteness for the Identification of LDCs. Available at https://www.un.org/development/desa/dpad/wp-content/uploads/sites/45/remoteness.pdf (accessed 5 June 2021).

- Delhey J and Newton K (2005). Predicting Cross-National Levels of Social Trust: Global Pattern or Nordic Exceptionalism? *European Sociological Review*. 21(4):311–327.

- Doshi P (2011). The elusive definition of pandemic influenza. Bulletin of the World Health Organisation. *WHO Bulletin*. 89(7):532–538.

- Gibler D (2013). Formal Alliances 4.1. Available at https://correlatesofwar.org/data-sets/formal-alliances (accessed 5 June 2021).

- Kakazu H (2007). Islands' Characteristics and Sustainability. SPF Seminar on Self-supporting Economy in Micronesia. Micronesia.

- Lowy Institute (2019). The 2019 Lowy Institute Global Diplomacy Index. Available at https://www.lowyinstitute.org/publications/2019-lowy-institute-global-diplomacy-index (accessed 5 June 2021).

- MacFeely S, Hoffmeister O, Barnat N, Hopp D and Peltola A (2021). Constructing a criteria-based classification for Small Island Developing States: an investigation. Available at https://unctad.org/webflyer/constructing-criteria-based-classification-small-island-developing-states-investigation (accessed 11 May 2021).

- Nye Jr (2005). *Soft Power: The Means to Success in World Politics*. PublicAffairs Books.

- OECD (2021). DAC glossary of key terms and concepts. Available at http://www.oecd.org/dac/dac-glossary.htm (accessed 20 April 2021).

- UN DESA (2020). United Nations Committee for Development Policy Secretariat. Triennial review dataset 2000 - 2018. Available at https://www.un.org/development/desa/dpad/least-developed-country-category/ldc-data-retrieval.html (accessed 1 November 2020).

- UNCTAD, ed. (2006). *The Least Developed Countries Report 2006: Developing Productive Capacities*. United Nations. New York and Geneva.

- UNCTAD (2016). *World Investment Report 2016: Investor Nationality: Policy Challenges*. United Nations publication. Sales No. E.16.II.D.4. Geneva.

- UNCTAD (2021a). Development and globalization: Facts and figures 2021. Small island developing States. Available at https://stats.unctad.org (accessed 14 June 2021).

- UNCTAD (2021b). Productive Capacities Index. Available at https://unctad.org/topic/least-developed-countries/productive-capacities-index (accessed 5 June 2021).

- UNCTAD (2021c). UNCTADStat. Available at https://unctadstat.unctad.org/EN/Index.html (accessed 21 April 2021).

- UNCTAD (2021d). UNCTAD Development and Globalization: Facts and Figures 2021: Small Island Developing States. Available at https://unctad.org/statistics (accessed 10 June 2021).

- UNDP (2020). Human Development Report 2020. The next frontier. Human development and the Anthropocene. Human Development Reports. New York. (accessed 9 February 2021).

- UNESCO Institute for Statistics (2020). Glossary. Available at http://uis.unesco.org/en/glossary (accessed 15 March 2021).

- United Nations (1992). Earth Summit. UN Conference on Environment and Development. Rio de Janeiro. Available at https://web.archive.org/web/20180330231819/http://www.un.org/geninfo/bp/enviro.html (accessed 16 June 2021).

- United Nations (2015). Transforming our world: the 2030 Agenda for Sustainable Development. A/RES/70/1. New York. 21 October.

- UN-OHRLLS (2014). SIDS Accelerated Modalities of Action (S.A.M.O.A.) Pathway. (accessed 25 November 2020).

- World Bank (2021). World Development Indicators. Available at http://data.worldbank.org/data-catalog/world-development-indicators (accessed 20 April 2021).

- WTO (2021). Regional Trade Agreements Database. Available at http://rtais.wto.org/UI/PublicMaintainRTAHome.aspx (accessed 15 May 2021).